To Create a New World?

PETER LANG
New York • Washington, D.C./Baltimore • Boston • Bern
Frankfurt am Main • Berlin • Brussels • Vienna • Canterbury

John Allphin Moore, Jr.
and Jerry Pubantz

To Create a New World?

American Presidents
and the United Nations

PETER LANG
New York • Washington, D.C./Baltimore • Boston • Bern
Frankfurt am Main • Berlin • Brussels • Vienna • Canterbury

Library of Congress Cataloging-in-Publication Data

Moore, John Allphin.
To create a new world?: American presidents
and the United Nations / John Allphin Moore, Jr. and Jerry Pubantz.
p. cm.
Includes bibliographical references and index.
1. United States—Foreign relations—1945–1989. 2. United States—Foreign
relations—1989–. 3. United Nations—History. 4. Presidents—United States—
History—20th century. I. Pubantz, Jerry. II. Title.
E840.M586   327.73—dc21   98-53628
ISBN 0-8204-3935-5

Die Deutsche Bibliothek-CIP-Einheitsaufnahme

Moore, John Allphin:
To create a new world?: American presidents
and the United Nations / John Allphin Moore, Jr. and Jerry Pubantz.
–New York; Washington, D.C./Baltimore; Boston; Bern;
Frankfurt am Main; Berlin; Brussels; Vienna; Canterbury: Lang.
ISBN 0-8204-3935-5

Cover design by Nona Reuter

The paper in this book meets the guidelines for permanence and durability
of the Committee on Production Guidelines for Book Longevity
of the Council of Library Resources.

Printed in the United States of America

For Joanna, Lisa, David, and Jeffrey Pubantz
and
to the memory of Sean Hager, Maggy Morcos, and Drew Fuller

Table of Contents

Preface

The idea for this book germinated at a day-long symposium in February 1995, on the occasion of the fiftieth anniversary of the Yalta Conference. Each of us presented a paper at the meeting, and collaboration continued as we attended other conferences over the ensuing years, becoming intrigued by the critical personal role American presidents have played in the historic development of the United Nations. The worldview of our presidents, who themselves have emerged from the democratic processes of American life, has shaped not only this country's foreign policies but also global institutions and politics in incalculable ways. The existence of the United Nations, its historical development, its successes, and its failures are very much consequences of the decisions made by the individuals who have occupied the Oval Office since 1945. This book attempts to capture the important contribution each president has made to UN history, and to assess the motivations that have driven presidential policy.

In 1997, at a conference on the Bush presidency held at Hofstra University, we met with a young editor from Peter Lang Publishing, Owen Lancer. He offered us a contract and began his steady and skilled encouragement and guidance of the project. Along with Owen's able involvement, Lang provided us as well the efficient and affable help of Karla Austin in the production of the book. A good copyeditor brings humility to any author. In our case Susan Gamer brought simplicity and elegance to our work. We thank her for that.

Over several years we have benefited in ways too numerous to recount from acquaintance with gifted colleagues who have encouraged our work on this project. First among them are the faculty advisers who attend with us the National Model United Nations, held annually in New York City at the United Nations. This largest student-administered conference in the United States brings together students and faculty members from around the nation and from foreign countries who have an abiding interest and faith in the worth of the United Nations. It was here, long ago, that the two of us first met. We also have appreciated the assistance of Cindy Combs at the University of North Carolina in Charlotte, who has given us the opportunity on several occasions to put our work before our peers at the International Studies Association–South for critical review. We also want to thank Kenneth Thompson at the

University of Virginia's Miller Center for allowing us to test some of our ideas in a public forum before some of that community's most revered scholars. Ambassador William vanden Heuvel, president of the Eleanor and Franklin Roosevelt Foundation, was also helpful in providing encouragement and information for our work.

The library staffs at California Polytechnic University, Pomona, and at Salem College have provided us invaluable aid; a generous Research, Scholarship, and Creative Activity grant from California Polytechnic University furnished a spring term free of any other obligations so that it could be used for concentrated research and writing. At Salem the grant of a summer sabbatical award by the Faculty Affairs Committee made possible the final drafting of the text. Many colleagues have proved helpful, including, at California Polytechnic University, Gayle Savarese, Stephen Englehart, Mahmood Ibrahim, Tara Sethia, and Anthony Brundage; and at Salem College, the always supportive academic dean Eileen Wilson-Oyelaran, and the ever-resourceful reference librarian Susan Taylor. At Salem, Fran Swajkoski's secretarial assistance was invaluable.

Three good friends—John Murphy, Errol Clauss, and Shirley Hanson—have each read large portions of this manuscript, which together total most of it, and their unsparing criticism has made the book much better than it would otherwise have been. Professors Murphy and Clauss have also provided invaluable bibliographic assistance, sharing the intellectual wealth of years of their own scholarly research, for which we are deeply indebted to them.

The gratitude customarily accorded spouses in this section of books carries an added significance here. Not only have our wives, Linda and Gloria—each with her own busy career—tolerated our obsession with this labor of love, but, in the course of the labor, the four of us have forged a friendship between families and across a wide country, from California to North Carolina. Thus a lasting benefit of our scholarship extends beyond the pages of the book.

Finally, a very special acknowledgment must be accorded to John Stephen Moore, whose computer savvy and long hours, not to mention remarkable good humor, have without question been the indispensable factors in the final execution of this work.

It is of course needless to say that despite all this beneficent help and encouragement, and notwithstanding the enjoyment of the endeavor, if there are mistakes of commission or omission in the following pages, the fault lies with the authors alone.

John Allphin Moore, Jr.
    Pomona, California
Jerry Pubantz
    Winston-Salem, North Carolina
—*January 1999*

Frequently Used Citations

Public Papers of the Presidents of the United States (Washington, D.C.: U.S. Government Printing Office).

PPP, followed by annual *date* and page number.

Yearbook of the United Nations (New York: United Nations, Office of Public Information).

YUN, followed by annual *date* and page number.

Introduction

January 22, 1917   There must be, not a balance of power, but a community of power; not organized rivalries, but an organized common peace...I am proposing...that the nations should with one accord adopt the doctrine of President Monroe as the doctrine of the world: that no nation should seek to extend its polity over any other nation or people...that all nations henceforth avoid entangling alliances which would draw them into competitions of power...These are American principles, American policies. We could stand for no others. And they are also the principles and policies of forward looking men and women everywhere, of every modern nation, of every enlightened community. They are the principles of mankind and must prevail.

—*Woodrow Wilson*

January 23, 1997   History was made this morning in the White House. America's UN Ambassador Madeleine Albright was sworn in as the nation's first female secretary of state. Minutes later she and President Clinton welcomed to the Oval Office the newly-elected United Nations Secretary-General Kofi Annan. It was Mr. Clinton's first meeting of his second term with a foreign leader. For the secretary-general it was fittingly his first official visit with a head of state. Without Mr. Clinton's opposition to the secretary-general's predecessor and his subsequent support of Mr. Annan's candidacy, this meeting would not be happening.

From the moment that President Woodrow Wilson proposed a League of Nations during World War I through the 1945 Yalta Conference, the Persian Gulf War of 1991, and the United States' proposals of 1997 to increase the number of permanent members on the United Nations' Security Council, American presidents have been at the forefront in twentieth-century developments to create and maintain a universal and workable world political association. Mr. Annan's pilgrimage to the White House graphically displayed the success Clinton and his predecessors have had over the last eighty years in establishing and shepherding a vision of a new world and an international organization to sustain that vision on the basis of American principles.

This book will describe and analyze the origins and history of the United Nations by emphasizing the relationship each American president has had with the organization. Thus, the book takes an

American perspective. The authors believe that a crucial factor in grasping the course of United Nations history has been the particular role played by American presidents. Although it is arguable that over time presidents have either ignored the United Nations or engaged it only when it could act as a pliable tool of U.S. national interests, the United Nations has been a persistent factor in foreign policy. In part this is because of the close connection the United States has had with the initiation and financing of the organization; in part it is because the United Nations offers the most public forum for all the nations in the world to react to policies pursued by the United States; and most importantly it is because the United Nations has become the recognized locus for attempted resolution of the most intractable world problems, in the Middle East, Africa, Central America and the Caribbean, southern and Southeast Asia, and elsewhere.

The quotation that begins this introduction suggests an additional coupling of presidents and the United Nations. Chief executives are inclined to pronounce the distinctive and superior nature of the American political system. This avowal seems to be a required incantation in American politics and reflects a theory that many students of the United States call "American exceptionalism." In the pages that follow we will suggest that Woodrow Wilson joined the idea of America's exceptionalism to the twentieth-century U.S. foreign policy of "internationalism." By arguing for U.S. leadership in a new world organization (the League of Nations), Wilson appeared to be promising that the organization's composition and activities would reflect American principles. Certainly many Americans expect no less of the United Nations, the heir to Wilson's dream. However, since the United Nations is virtually worldwide in membership, its rhetoric has sometimes sounded distant from what we think of as universal (but also American) standards. Thus, presidents must deal with a United Nations born of American initiative, actively involved in virtually all major world issues, but sometimes perplexing, even exasperating, to the very constituents that sustain the president and expect the world to conform to American principles.

This book will also discuss the alternative approaches to foreign policy challenges sometimes characterized in the academy as "realist" and "idealist." We will describe these positions in more detail in Chapter 1 and in the ensuing chapters covering each president. For the moment we should note that *realism* refers to looking at the world as it really is and pursuing policies that clearly promote the country's national interests. *Idealism* refers to looking at the world as we would like it to be and pursuing policies that we hope will effect this desire. Idealism emphasizes the use of moral and legal principles in the conduct of international affairs. Wilson is often considered the prototypical idealist because he proclaimed that the First World War was fought "to make the world safe for democracy," rather than for the specific gains of the victorious nations, and because he extolled the League of Nations to bolster more ideal relations among nations. Theodore Roosevelt and later Richard Nixon and Henry Kissinger are often considered realists because they saw the world in terms of competitive more than cooperative nations and they sought to advance specific national interests rather than transcendent abstract ideals. We will apply the realist and idealist models to individual presidents as we investigate their administrations' approach to the United Nations.

Presidents must respond to more than the United Nations and realist and idealist aims. The United States is a constitutional federal republic. This means that even in foreign affairs, a president does not act in a vacuum. The U.S. Constitution itself delimits presidential action; Congress represents a considerable restraint; and, on occasion, even Supreme Court decisions may check a president. Electoral politics, internal state politics, and the condition of the economy, as well as the larger public disposition provide an environment that factors into presidential decision-making regarding international affairs and the United Nations. And rarely is there a clear and preponderant public opinion about foreign matters and UN actions. Environmentalists, women's rights and human rights activists, exporters of American goods and investment, various ethnic groups, recently arrived immigrants, religious organizations, talk show hosts, editorial writers, and academics in universities and think tanks all may weigh in on foreign policy matters that particularly interest them. Television and radio, the Internet, newspapers, and congressional mailboxes all are filled with the passionate foreign policy exhortations of many different interest groups.

Additionally, there is a complex bureaucracy responsible for developing foreign policy and conducting the nation's diplomacy. The president directs this bureaucracy with varying—but normally limited—input from Congress. Congress, of course, declares war, appropriates money, and discusses foreign affairs, but the president (or his designated agent) is the only person who can communicate officially for the United States with other nations or with the United Nations. In performing the job of chief diplomat for the country, the president is aided by the Department of State with its secretary of state and diplomatic and consular officials throughout the world, including the U.S. ambassador to the United Nations, who now has cabinet rank. Since the end of World War II the Department of State has increasingly shared its role of making and conducting policy with other agencies, including the Department of Defense and the Central Intelligence Agency. The National Security Council, created by congressional act in 1947, coordinates all of the foreign policy agencies under a presidential adviser for national security.

Finally, the attitude of foreign powers and foreign leaders, frequently expressed in UN debates, affects presidential actions. The United Nations itself is neither the unified power many critics fear nor the totally inept organization others disdain. It is useful to remember that the United Nations is neither a unitary government, where sovereignty rests with a central authority, nor a federal government, where dual sovereignty is shared between individual nation states and a central government (as in the United States today). Rather, the United Nations is a *confederacy* in which sovereignty remains with each individual member, much as sovereignty rested with each individual state under America's Articles of Confederation. In addition, the permanent members of the Security Council, including the United States, may veto any substantive matter. Thus, the United Nations can work only when there is substantial and wide agreement among equally sovereign nations and, usually, among all the permanent members of the Security Council. Not even majority voting can ensure UN performance. Skilled diplomacy, not majority rule, activates the United Nations.

As we examine each president's relationship with the United Nations, we must bear in mind numerous factors that influence presidential policy, including the Wilsonian legacy, the tradition of American exceptionalism, the contrasting diplomatic approaches of realism and idealism, the many constraints on the Executive Office, the fact of the Constitution and the separation of powers and checks and balances, and the historic international challenges facing the United States from World War II into the new century.

We begin that analysis in Chapter 1 with a look at the tradition of American "exceptionalism" and the origins of the United Nations.

1

To Create a New World?
American "Exceptionalism" and the Origins of the United Nations

> We have it in our power to begin the world over again.
>
> —*Thomas Paine*
> *Common Sense, 1776*

> America does not go abroad in search of monsters to destroy. She is the well-wisher to the freedom and independence of all. She is the champion only of her own.
>
> —*John Quincy Adams*
> *July Fourth Address, 1821*

1989 brought the end of the Berlin Wall, the Warsaw Pact, and the cold war, and presaged even more unanticipated drama. As these breathtaking events entered America's consciousness, the nation rejoiced in the apparent, and long prophesied, triumph of American ideals worldwide. The quick victory over Iraq in early 1991 added relish to the victory feast, causing an unusually popular President Bush to proclaim a "New World Order," by which he, and his listeners, meant a world more nearly conforming to the political and economic norms we associate with American-led western society: rule of law, democratic elections, market economics, and the advancement of individual rights, all within the context of a world of cooperating sovereign nations. The United Nations, many Americans began to say, could now be the energizing institution of that new world, just as its founders had intended, and just as it had only now, against the aggressor Saddam Hussein, proved it could be. With the cold war over, the West triumphant, and market economics intruding everywhere, there was a possibility, it seemed suddenly, of a serendipitous truce between the rival American foreign policy views of, on the one hand, a distant, cool, realistic appraisal of the outside world ("realism"), and on the other, a commitment to making the world over, preferably in the image of some idealistic vision of what *we* had become ("idealism"). The truce was possible because for Americans the real world now appeared to conform to our idealized version. As President Bush, surveying the worldwide rush to free markets, free speech, and free elections, proclaimed in his inaugural address: "We know what works: Freedom works. We know what's right: Freedom's right."[1]

If this heady assessment now seems premature, it was not just because of the quickly ensuing unpleasantness in Somalia, Bosnia, Chechnya, Cambodia, and elsewhere, as important as these events undoubtedly were, but also because of the inescapable consequences of an enduring warp and woof in the American disposition regarding our place in the world. We began as a nation announcing our "exceptionalism" and determined to maintain our independence and to avoid entanglements that might compromise our unique status. Thus, the seventeenth-century Puritan leader John Winthrop called on the new world to be a "City on a Hill," a model for the old world; George Washington warned us to avoid entanglements and determinedly gather our certain strength; and John Quincy Adams, conceivably our greatest secretary of state, built diplomacy on the principles of unilateral action promoting clear national interests. America was exceptional not because it could master the world through involvement and intrusion, but because we could provide the archetype of a novel and enlightened system of civic society, emphasizing liberty, equality, and economic and class mobility. If the rest of the world was wise, it would follow that example. Otherwise, others could stew in their own juice. That's the warp.

But there was the woof as well, intricately woven into America's fabric from the beginning. For if we have it in our power to "begin the world over again," how do we not only start but continue in a world that is imperfect, yet certain to encroach on us? While Thomas Paine doubtless intended the words that open this chapter to be directed only to America and not to foreign adventure, think for a moment about his assertion juxtaposed with John Quincy Adams' remarks, also at the head of this chapter. Adams was in the main broadcasting resistance to an urge at large in the land to offer some kind of direct assistance or solace to revolutionary movements in South America and Greece. Revolution was well under way in Latin America, seeking to remove Spanish colonial control from the new world. In the spring before Adams' July Fourth address of 1821, Greeks had begun rebelling against their

---

[1]   January 20, 1989; all presidential inaugural addresses are in the Bartleby Library Archive, Columbia University, available on the World Wide Web at *www.columbia.edu/acis/bartleby/inaugural/index.html*

overlord, the Ottoman Empire. In each instance the revolutionaries used liberal rhetoric very familiar to Americans, and, along with many others, Henry Clay, a potential national political rival of Adams, had publicly manifested an interest in providing tangible support to the rebels. The South Americans and the Greeks (the originators, after all, of democracy) were, it seemed, in a life and death struggle to gain their deserved independence from imperial oppressors. Adams wished them well and said we could not and should not do a thing about it.[2]

Now, fast forward to our own time, and consider the heart-wrenching scenes that can be summoned up in an instant in unfortunate places like Somalia, Bosnia, or wherever CNN mini-cameras can penetrate.[3] It is not surprising that many Americans at any given moment experience two simultaneous if converse sentiments: to stay clear of foreign troubles while at the same time longing to intervene in order to bring relief. The long history of American resistance to becoming involved in European squabbles while nonetheless sending forth to the world reform-minded missionaries (and later eager Peace Corps volunteers) gives evidence of this admirable incongruity. Only with the crisis of World War II did the world, under the guidance of Franklin Roosevelt, institute the Wilson-inspired United Nations, which even now, half a century into its history, remains for Americans problematic. Thus, the scholarly debate about "realists" and "idealists," explicated below, actually derives from discordant sentiments in the very texture of the American historical experience. We must say more later about this polarity, and particularly its connection with the accordion-like attitude Americans have for half a century evinced toward the United Nations.

Dismissing the United Nations

But, first, we need note that there are those who have never shared the recurrent euphoria about the United Nations. Many of the influential

---

[2] William Earle Weeks, *John Quincy Adams and American Global Empire* (Lexington: University of Kentucky Press, 1992), 21; Ernest R. May, *The Making of the Monroe Doctrine* (Cambridge, Mass.: Harvard University Press, 1975), 8–11, 183; Allan Nevins (ed.), *The Diary of John Quincy Adams* (New York: Scribner, 1951), 300.

[3] Much has been written about the media's impact on foreign policy. See, for example, Andres Natsios, *From Massacres to Genocide: The Media, Public Policy and Humanitarian Crises* (Washington, D.C.: Brookings, 1997).

commentaries of these times ignore, disparage, or find irrelevant to global matters anything related to the organization. Celebrated writers relegate the United Nations to the periphery as they analyze, sometimes with the broadest of strokes, the problems and paradigms we are asked to consider for the post–cold war world. Former secretary of state Henry Kissinger's widely read *Diplomacy* contains the common, dismissive assessment that the United Nations has been simply ineffective in every important crisis since its inception, failing "to fulfill the underlying premise of collective security."[4]

The political philosopher Francis Fukuyama has agreed that the United Nations has not been a success, but for reasons quite different from those announced by Kissinger and by other realists, who see the world fragmented into discrete, competing, dissimilar political entities. Fukuyama's controversial essay "The End of History" appeared in 1989 at the very moment of the cold war's collapse. Later expanded into a book, the thesis forwarded the notion of a final apotheosis of particular "liberal" ideas dating from the eighteenth century's high Enlightenment period. Drawing on the philosopher G.W.F. Hegel, Fukuyama argued that there was now, at the conclusion of the twentieth century, an end of the process of dialectical conflict between and among equally powerful and persuasive sets of ideas. Liberalism (that is, a fusion of political liberty, individual rights, the rule of law, the primacy of science, and market economics) had, over time, defeated monarchy, romantic fascism, and Marxism-Leninism. Looking around the world, Fukuyama saw these vanquished ideologies as having no committed supporters. The "liberal idea," cosmopolitan and hegemonic, was in the ascendancy; it had no competitor. The United Nations' problem was that such an organization could work only if all its members were "liberal democracies"; and since the United Nations had been from the beginning open to any state, democratic or not, possessing definable sovereignty, it too was an idea of the past.[5]

---

[4] Henry Kissinger, *Diplomacy* (New York: Simon and Schuster, 1994), 249–250. There are, of course, exceptions to the rule; see, for example, John Ikenberry, "The Myth of Post–Cold War Chaos," *Foreign Affairs* (May/June 1996), 79–91.

[5] Francis Fukuyama, *The End of History and the Last Man* (New York: Macmillan, 1992), 281–282.

Fukuyama's assertions attracted much criticism, and thus began an intellectual search for the most suitable explanation of the post–cold war world. Realists struck hard at the Hegelian idealism proclaimed by Fukuyama. Professor Samuel P. Huntington provided the hardest blow, starting with his stunning essay "The Clash of Civilizations?" published in the journal *Foreign Affairs* in the summer of 1993. Huntington, who also refined his views in a subsequent book, challenged the notion of a universal liberalism dominating the world. Instead he proffered a more disquieting suggestion, that the post–cold war world would henceforth be plagued by serious clashes between and among deeply different "civilizations" and cultures. Western civilization was but one of some seven or eight distinct civilizations, each with its own unique cluster of political and social ideas, standards of behavior, and above all religion. Huntington saw in the former Yugoslavia, in Chinese-American tensions, in Chechnya, in the Islamic-Pakistan/Hindu-India standoff, in the rise of the "Islamic Resurgence," and in much more, the certain and perilous collision of incompatible and suspicious civilizations. He urged a serious effort to "renew" the West, and an end to soft optimism, including any expectation that a flawed United Nations could somehow gloss over such differences.[6]

While most commentators came down somewhere between Fukuyama and Huntington (usually criticizing both), there was a school of thought that concentrated specifically on U.S. foreign policy. Professor Walter A. McDougall's short but well-received book, *Promised Land, Crusader State*, combined a historical survey of America's place in the world with a critique reminiscent of George F. Kennan's influential (and "realist") *American Diplomacy*, first published in 1951. Kennan had argued that the problem of twentieth-century American foreign policy had been its overemphasis on moral and legal principles, in contrast to more important considerations of national interest.[7] McDougall updated Kennan with a sweeping examination of America's unfortunate shift from the "unilateral" policies of the founding generation to the unwise "multilateral" policies characteristic of the Wilson-influenced twentieth

---

[6]　Samuel P. Huntington, *The Clash of Civilizations and the Remaking of World Order* (New York: Simon and Schuster, 1996); note the index entry "United Nations, failures of," 365.

[7]　George F. Kennan, *American Diplomacy, 1900–1950* (Chicago: University of Chicago Press, 1951).

century. The League of Nations and the United Nations, "utopian" in conception, were both doomed to failure. "Today," asserted McDougall, "as Kissinger observes, the dream of a Wilsonian order has even less chance of success."[8]

In the most disturbing, if trendy, proposition that has been contributed to the post–cold war debate, both realists and idealists take some heat. Among others, Professor Paul Kennedy and the journalist Robert Kaplan have argued that the plight of the world may just be hopeless, unlikely to experience the requisite reform, given the limitations of current political regimes, whatever their theoretical stance. Kennedy's *Preparing for the Twenty-First Century* is a dreary recital of unmanageable worldwide demographic explosion, rampant environmental despoliation, risky biotechnological advances, malnutrition, uncured diseases, ethnic strife, and more.[9] Kaplan's travel journal, *The Ends of the Earth,* acknowledging Professor Kennedy's groundbreaking work, adds more misery to our picture of the world. Traveling in remote spots in Africa, the Middle East, South Asia, and Southeast Asia, Kaplan finds a nether world in perilous disintegration, plagued by overpopulation, lack of education, disease, environmental disasters, rampant crime and corruption, anarchy, and civic collapse. For Kaplan, the situation is without hope: "*We are not in control*" he concludes (his emphasis). Moreover, "As societies grow more populous and complex, the idea that a global elite like the UN can engineer reality from above is…absurd."[10]

The United Nations at Half Century

Undoubtedly, as we proceed to face the new century more voices will be raised to find wanting any claim that human society collectively and through international organizations can reasonably address world problems and make the situation a bit better. Thus, dismissing the United Nations as irrelevant will continue to be in vogue.

---

[8] Walter A. McDougall, *Promised Land, Crusader State: The American Encounter with the World Since 1776* (Boston: Houghton Mifflin, 1997), 213.

[9] Paul Kennedy, *Preparing for the Twenty-First Century* (New York: Random House, 1993).

[10] Robert D. Kaplan, *The Ends of the Earth; A Journey to the Frontiers of Anarchy* (New York: Random House, 1996), 436.

Yet it is the task of the historian to contextualize before making judgments; and to set into context the past half century's major world happenings requires more than a passing reference to the United Nations—and, importantly, more than a nod to the connection between the United Nations and specific American presidents and comprehensible presidential foreign policy. Apart from the oft-remarked activities of UN agencies in bringing about social and health reforms, consider, just for example, the following: (1) Israel came into being via a UN resolution, initiating the modern Middle East quandary; the UN has been the central institution in defining, in international legal terms, the nature of the Middle East problem. From the establishment of Israel through the crisis of 1956, to UN Resolutions 242 and 338 through the Camp David Accords to the handshake at the White House in 1993, the internationally recognized legal basis of any possible resolution of this seemingly intractable dilemma rests in a long-term connection with the United Nations. As is also true of the following examples, American presidents have been at the forefront in this. (2) The remarkable developments in South Africa and Namibia over the last decade of the twentieth century, resulting in the elimination of apartheid and the establishment of democratic government in South Africa and full independence of Namibia, were conditional upon UN resolutions. (3) The 1993 elections in troubled Cambodia took place under the legal rubric of UN resolutions and with UN administration. (4) The ongoing negotiations to settle the Cyprus problem are based in UN resolutions. (5) By the mid-1990s the UN, by passing resolutions and establishing observer groups to provide necessary supervision, guided the end of civil wars and ultimate general elections in three beleaguered Central America countries: Nicaragua, El Salvador, and Guatemala. (6) The restoration of the democratically elected government of Haiti and the placement of peace forces in that country (by the summer of 1997) occurred under the auspices of UN resolutions. (7) The Dayton Accords of 1995 were U.S.-led NATO impositions to implement the UN's insistence on ending the brutal fighting in the former Yugoslavia. (8) The UN Declaration of Human Rights is the basis of constant (if controversial) interstate diplomacy crafting an evolving body of international law regarding human rights. The Human Rights tribunals at The Hague (to try alleged war criminals from the Balkan civil war) and in Arusha, Tanzania (to do the same for those accused of human rights violations in the Rwanda massacres), are results of these efforts.

(9) The Persian Gulf War in 1991, which removed Iraqi forces from Kuwait, was based on UN Security Council resolutions (particularly 678); thus this war was a genuine "collective security" operation designed to uphold the sovereignty of a UN member.[11]

Significant to understanding all these UN-related events is the relationship each had with various American presidents. That is, in all the cases mentioned above, American presidents have demonstrated a keen interest or, more often than not, taken a direct leadership role. None of these activities could have taken place without approval and support of presidents. The customary scholarly approach to UN studies is to point out that the organization works when the great powers all concur on an action, and that, thus, the United Nations essentially "reacts" to traditional great power politics, which continues to be the most important factor in international affairs.[12] While there is merit to this proposition, an additional factor—maybe the most crucial factor—in the course of UN history has been the particular role of American presidents.

There is no reason to engage in clamorous debate with hardened opponents, from pure idealists to crafty realists,[13] to sense a troubling confusion: America desires to see the spaceship earth on a trajectory toward liberal democracy while at the same time avoiding unwise, hopeless, and potentially expensive U.S. involvements overseas. The following study will underscore the role of presidents in the evolution of the United Nations by charting that wavering history of, on the one hand, an idealistic vision of world affairs often associated with Woodrow Wilson and his followers, and, on the other hand, a realistic vision of the world, as frequently associated with Richard Nixon and Henry Kissinger, among others.

Woodrow Wilson and American Idealism

It was, indeed, President Woodrow Wilson who wedded American "exceptionalism" to a nascent internationalism, and in a way that commanded a new level of support in American public opinion. We

---

[11] A quick and efficient way to chart these developments is through the UN website at *www.un.org*.

[12] John G. Stoessinger, *The United Nations and the Superpowers*, 4th ed. (New York: Random House, 1977).

[13] See the debate between Senator Jesse Helms and several UN supporters in *Foreign Affairs* (September/October 1996 and November/December 1996).

could say that since Wilson, internationalism in U.S. foreign policy has reflected one of three variants: realism, idealism, or a peculiar amalgam of the two. Each is compelled by public opinion to reflect the "exceptionalism" Americans believe is theirs. For the sake of clarification, let us postulate the following definitions.

The *realist* has believed that the United States must act in the world to protect its national interests, that its values and prescriptions for the good society will mean little if its power and influence are diminished. Presidents Theodore Roosevelt and Richard Nixon are often cited as examples of internationalists who have pursued the realist course, believing that conscious efforts to impose our values or to expect other states to act according to American democratic and legal procedures are escapist folly.[14] Realism emphasizes geopolitical analysis and power arrangements in the international community.

The *idealist* often has been a crusader,[15] believing that America has a special responsibility to promote universal values, individual liberties, and democracy. The idealist seeks a *moral* world order based on self-evident human virtues. The United States must be the driving force in the creation of the ideal, for only in a world built on law, cooperation, and democracy can America find true peace and prosperity. It is in this spirit that the United States has fought wars "to make the world safe for democracy." Often the idealist (or *moralist*) tradition denigrates the value of force and traditional diplomacy as meaningful instruments of foreign policy. Rather, the idealist would substitute the procedures of liberal politics, that is, democratic institutions, judicial proceedings, self-rule, debate, and votes. The idealist also believes in the power of "world public opinion." The voices of humanity are supposedly more powerful than the forces of nation-states and their leaders. By rallying popular sentiment to the ideals of moralist policy, it should be possible to maintain peace and global stability.[16]

Realists, then, try to look at the world as it really is and calculate policy with that reality in mind. Idealists tend to look at the world the way they want it to be and develop policies to effect that vision. Realists

---

[14] Kissinger, *Diplomacy*, 18.

[15] John G. Stoessinger, *Crusaders and Pragmatists: Movers of Modern American Foreign Policy* (New York: Norton, 1979), xv–xvi.

[16] See Akira Iriye, *The Cambridge History of American Foreign Relations*, III (New York: Cambridge University Press, 1993), 68.

may thus overlook the historic role played by idealists in history. After all, the American and French revolutionaries, the abolitionists, and some socialists (all "idealists") may have "caused" history to evolve as it did. On the other hand, idealists, by being "unrealistic," may find themselves actually promoting policies that lack the very morality that originally guided them. The Robespierre-led French revolutionaries, committed to a "Republic of Virtue," used the feared guillotine to force morality on recalcitrant citizens; Lenin honed state terrorism to create a "New Soviet Man;" and Mao Zedung's "Cultural Revolution" of the 1960s, intended to elevate Chinese society to a condition of pure equality, left chiefly a legacy of indignation and dread.

Of course reality does exist. And within the real world, power usually must be exerted in order to effect a nation's goals. Also, in the real world we can perceive human beings as having a capacity for both good and bad behavior. While realists might be more inclined to consider "natural" human beings as prone to do bad unless constrained or guided, idealists tend to emphasize that humans are, by nature, mostly good. The question that thus arises is whether it is possible to construct institutions, including international institutions, that are likely to restrain the badness of human nature while taking advantage of the goodness. In this light, one attraction of idealism is that it seeks an outline of human relations professedly built on considerations beyond self-interest, or even national interest, assuming not that power and thus rights belong to a limited circle, but that rights, and thus power, belong to all human beings.[17] This notion historically has had strong appeal among Americans. It has affected our perceptions of world events and thus strongly influenced our foreign policy.

*   *   *

No president has had a greater impact on the direction and tenor of American foreign policy in the twentieth century than Woodrow Wilson. His contribution to America's perception of its place in the world rivals George Washington's. Both presidents had an underlying faith in the uniqueness of the United States, whose principles and values they believed had universal application. The difference between the two lay

---

[17] See John H. Herz, *Political Realism and Political Idealism; A Study in Theories and Realities* (Chicago: University of Chicago Press, 1951), 29–39.

in how that uniqueness should express itself. Washington and the other founders certainly believed that the United States would be active in the world (they were not in the strictest sense *isolationists*[18]), but they sought to sustain the uniqueness of America by maintaining independence from the encumbrances and entanglements of international politics; by acting in the world unilaterally, not in conjunction with a host of allies; and by pursuing above all the national interest, not the dictates of overarching abstract principles. Wilson, in contrast, argued for an active internationalism, for joining and leading multilateral organizations (chiefly the League of Nations), and for committing the United States to help make the world over in light of universal values. Washingtonian unilateralism (sometimes called "isolationism," but not by Washington or his followers) dominated American foreign policy throughout nearly the entire nineteenth century. The Wilsonian tradition has held sway for most of the period since World War I.

Wilson's hold on the American mind was no doubt the more powerful because he merged the doctrine of American exceptionalism with his view of America's responsibilities to the world. If from the beginning we have thought of our society as virtuous and consequently a proper model for all humankind, Wilson, in the midst of the brutal Great War, began to attract adherents to the notion that we must take a fundamental leadership role in order to effect appropriate change in the world. The consequence, Wilson assumed, should have been the recognition around the globe of the universal truths of liberty, equality, the rule of law, democratic processes, and market economics. Lyndon Johnson's 1965 Inaugural Address, Wilsonian in tone, said what previous generations had probably felt, that the American experiment "was meant one day to inspire the hopes of all mankind....[It] called on us to help show the way for the liberation of man, and that is our goal....For we are a nation of believers....We believe that every man must someday be free."[19]

---

[18] McDougall, *Promised Land, Crusader State*, 39–40; John Allphin Moore, Jr., "Empire, Republicanism, and Reason: Foreign Affairs as Viewed by the Founders of the Constitution," *History Teacher* (May 1993), 297–315.

[19] Quoted in Dean Acheson, *Present at the Creation; My Years at the State Department* (New York: Norton, 1969), 741. The full address is available in the Bartleby Library Archive, Columbia University, and can be found on the World Wide Web. See footnote 1 above.

Wilson determined to convince us that only an international system infused with certain values could bring peace. The "old" diplomacy of power politics must be replaced with the politics of the "new" world. As Henry Kissinger has noted, there is an optimistic sense in American culture that the "rest of mankind [can] attain peace and prosperity by abandoning traditional diplomacy and adopting America's reverence for international law and democracy."[20]

We will thus accord to Wilson the title of classic moralist in foreign policy. One month after the United States entered World War I he met with the British foreign minister, Lord Balfour. Balfour informed Wilson about the various secret agreements reached among the Allies concerning the planned dismemberment of the Ottoman Empire. The president was shocked by plans to carve up the region into new colonial zones of influence. In his view morality and good sense dictated a need for ethnic self-determination. Wilson's Fourteen Points, presented to Congress eight months after his meeting with Balfour, made clear his outrage at the realpolitik of the European powers and his commitment to a higher idealism.

As early as August 1914 Wilson had discussed with his closest adviser, Colonel Edward House, the merits of an association of states to avoid conflicts such as the war just then under way. From the beginning the president wedded America's interest in peace, national independence, and law with the idea of an international organization to ensure these things.[21] The best evidence suggests that Wilson had gotten the idea for the League from the British foreign secretary, Sir Edward Grey. Wilson was also deeply influenced by British intellectuals like Norman Angell, author of *The Great Illusion*, who actually made suggestions to Wilson prior to his May 1916 speech proposing the League.[22] Wilson told his advisers during the transatlantic trip to the Paris peace conference that under his plan "no nation would be permitted to be an outlaw free to work out its evil designs against a neighbor or the world."[23] The League of Nations would embody the American faith in democratic and moral politics as the guarantor of a just

---

[20] Kissinger, *Diplomacy*, 18.

[21] Charles Seymour (ed.), *The Intimate Papers of Colonel House*, IV (London: Ernest Benn, 1928), 3.

[22] Patrick Glynn, *Closing Pandora's Box* (New York: Basic Books, 1992), 47.

[23] Ibid., 292.

international order. The League would also ensure, in Wilson's view, reform, not revolution, in the international system. In 1917, the victory in Russia of the other great advocate of self-determination, Lenin, by violent means, further strengthened Wilson's resolve to have a League.[24]

At Paris Wilson found in the British prime minister, David Lloyd George, and the French premier, Georges Clemenceau, two leaders more interested in the traditional resources of power politics and national interests than in his idealistic vision of a better world. The forsaking of empire and the sacrifice of the advantages of victory were not part of their diplomatic repertoire. In order to achieve his beloved League, the president had to make significant concessions on other aspects of his peace plan, including a provision requiring Germany to pay reparations, a clause specifying Germany's guilt in initiating the war, and a compromise of the commitment to self-determination resulting in the mandate system.

The irony (or tragedy), of course, was that the U.S. Senate never ratified the Versailles Treaty. Having disdained the participation of senators in the peace negotiations, President Wilson was the first to learn that "Wilsonianism," while speaking to deep sentiments in the American psyche, succeeds only when broad political support is coupled with an overwhelming sense in public opinion that America's national interests are also served by the moral impulse. The United States could see no need to remain involved in the interstate affairs of Europe. The League system went on without U.S. participation, much less U.S. leadership, and ultimately foundered on the rocks of economic depression, nationalist revanchism, ideological politics, and a new round of aggression and international violence. The Wilsonian effort to create a workable organization to maintain the peace would have to await another war and another president. Perhaps Wilson's plans were flawed; perhaps they were too early; perhaps they were too novel for his time.

Traditional Arrangements of International Politics

Empire

Wilson and his admirers were bucking resilient historical practice. For most of history public order had been maintained by hierarchical imperial administrations whose dominance was punctuated by periodic

---

[24] See N. Gordon Levin, *Woodrow Wilson and World Politics; America's Response to War and World Politics* (New York: Oxford University Press, 1968).

uprisings and dissolution, too often resulting in violence. The great periods of Chinese history are normally considered to be those times when powerful consolidating empires brought widespread peace, some prosperity, Confucianist (or, later, Maoist) standards of conduct, artistic grandeur, and systematic rule to a society that nonetheless intermittently plunged into chaotic and disruptive warlordism. The Roman Empire is the prototypical administrative unit of the western legacy. Rome brought stability, peace (the *Pax Romana*), law, infrastructure, a common language, and eventually Christianity to the known western world. Byzantium was the imperial reflection of Rome in much of eastern Europe, and it lasted longer and left an impressive legacy of Slavic orthodox culture neither nationalist nor liberal in configuration. The Ottoman Empire imposed an organizing and flexible bureaucracy on a wide swath of land with an extremely diverse population. And great Russian empires, whether Romanov or Bolshevik, brought to heel the squabbling medley of ethnic groups covering its large landmass. As a rule, when the imperial power was challenged the consequence was unfortunate and often unwanted disruption (the nineteenth-century Taiping rebellion in China provides an example). Empire, whether imposed willingly and brutally or reluctantly and benignly, seemed the common solution to international disorder. In fact, as late as the turn of the last century, international diplomacy was something typically conducted among empires (Romanovs in Eurasia, Manchus in China, Ottomans in the Middle East, Hapsburgs in south-central Europe, Hohenzollerns in Germany and east-central Europe, and the British and French worldwide).

Nation-States

What could be called the "postempire" era of political organization is more familiar to us. The notion of "national sovereignty" based on "nationality" gave a "nation-state" the ultimate authority over populations within discernible boundaries. The nation-state, usually thought to have surfaced in Europe in about the fifteenth and sixteenth centuries, heralded what some scholars have called "international anarchy." There being no commanding sovereign authority above the nation, international order depended on the good faith of its individual sovereign members, just as order in a governmentless society (anarchy) would depend on the goodwill of each individual person. In the West this phenomenon led to the development of modern international relations and international law. Scholars and practitioners such as Hugo Grotius (1583–1645) and Emmerich de Vattel (1714–1767) tried to codify rules of international behavior, on the understanding that each sovereign state would need to determine whether or not to abide by them. Of course, just as would be the case with the "state of nature" theories of the seventeenth and eighteenth centuries, the state of nature in international matters suggested an underlying possibility of conflict. And, in fact, although early theorists—Vattel among them—supported the notion of national sovereignty, much as liberals support the notion of individual rights, we must remember that the ultimate end of absolute liberty, whether local or international, is anarchy. In the international sphere, an initial resolution of this conundrum was the theory of "balance of power." In essence this meant that if any one nation were to gain such overwhelming power as to represent a danger to others, a group of the others would join together purposely to restrain—that is, balance—the powerful entity. In such wise, through balance engineered by sovereign states, order could be maintained in the international community. In addition to the theory of balance of power, early theorists posited notions of what we would later call international human rights law. The earliest approaches to this issue derived from concern about the condition of civilians during the brutal religious wars, particularly the Thirty Years' War (1618–1648). Thus Grotius and Vattel, and their readers in Europe and the Americas, sought ways to codify into an embryonic international law accepted practices against what we have come to call "war crimes." It is in this way that an international system of sorts developed as the nation-state became the accepted norm of political organization. While there was certainly truth in describing this system as "international anarchy," there came to be discernible patterns of accepted diplomatic practice and wartime procedures.[25]

Following World War I, new nation-states surfaced in central Europe. In 1947 India and Pakistan became independent of Great Britain, while various states emerged out of the former Ottoman Empire and the mandates administered there by Britain and France; and by the 1960s many new states in what we call the "developing world" gained independence from former colonial rulers. As of 1998 the United Nations

---

[25] Arthur Nussbaum, *A Concise History of the Law of Nations* (New York: Macmillan, 1954).

had a membership of 185 sovereign nations. The nation-state had become the accepted mode of political organization.

The Concert of Europe

The American and French revolutions brought to world politics the idea of universal principles applicable at all times and to all peoples. The idea that human beings (*all* human beings) were *by their nature* free and equal both inspired and disturbed existing politics. The French Revolution, taking a deviating course of its own,[26] culminated in a very long world war and the age of Napoleon. While it may have been a traditionally forged "balance of power" alliance that finally brought the little general down, the finally victorious allies determined at the Vienna Conference of 1814–1815 to restructure Europe and its diplomatic practices in a way that would avoid another descent into violence such as they had just witnessed. The major leaders at Vienna—Viscount Castlereagh of England, Alexander I of Russia, Talleyrand of France, Frederick William III of Prussia, and, most important, Prince von Metternich of Austria's Hapsburg Empire—crafted a complex solution to build a peaceful Europe. The principles agreed to included a new and transformed balance of power, complemented by territorial compromise among all the former belligerents, monarchical legitimacy and restoration (including in France), and an agreement to meet in the future to consult on what to do should disruptive crises arise in Europe. In addition, three of the allies—Russia, Prussia, and Austria—instituted a less formal arrangement, dubbed the "Holy Alliance," to promote genial relations among Christian monarchs and to resist any future revolutionary radicalism.[27] Understandably, the Vienna program has been seen by historians as a "conservative" solution to the challenge of international disorder. In fact, no major protracted war broke out in Europe for almost a century after the Vienna conference. For some realist scholars Vienna remains one of the most attractive models of

---

[26] Stephen F. Englehart and John Allphin Moore, Jr., eds., *Three Beginnings: Revolution, Rights and the Liberal State: Comparative Perspectives on the English, American, and French Revolutions* (New York: Peter Lang, 1994).

[27] See Paul W. Schroeder, *The Transformation of European Politics, 1763–1848* (Oxford: Clarendon, 1994).

international relations. Henry Kissinger wrote approvingly of the conference in his well-known Ph.D dissertation.[28]

The Twentieth-Century Crisis

Crescendoing crises challenged the Concert of Europe right up to its ultimate collapse in the Great War of 1914–1918. We have reviewed above Wilson's role at the Paris peace conference, where the president joined statesmen more attuned to the older diplomacy to hammer out a new version of international order. Wilson, as we know, brought with him the principled positions he had earlier articulated in his Fourteen Points, plus an outline for a new worldwide organization committed to collective security and to the elimination of war. When the peacemakers arrived in the Paris suburb of Versailles to sign the completed agreement, there were, as we have seen above, several compromises that troubled Wilson's most resolute supporters. But it is safe to say that the Wilsonian principles of "self-determination" and "internationalism," though from a certain perspective ominously antipodal, had been clearly presented to the world's peoples. Yet problems remained. Wilson, who had been welcomed to Europe as a savior, became by the conclusion of the treaty the target of unhappy nationalist frustrations abroad as well as partisan resistance at home. As might have been expected with initial expectations so high, almost no one was exactly sanguine about the new national boundaries; and in the United States, anxiety about Wilson's compromises and the apparent grubby politics of the peace conference joined a weariness against foreign crusades. Although there remained enduring support for the League, by the time the president collapsed with a stroke during a railroad campaign across the United States to promote the new organization, his grand plans were on the brink of defeat in his own country. His illness accompanied his disappointment as the Senate rejected the Versailles Treaty.

The Versailles settlement may have been doomed to failure despite the American snub. The statesmen at Paris had before them a disintegrating world. Most of the major organizing empires of the previous century were gone. The Manchu dynasty in China had collapsed in 1911, replaced by a weak republican government; a confusing and devastating civil war followed which some would say

---

[28] Henry Kissinger, *A World Restored: Europe After Napoleon* (New York: Grosset and Dunlap, 1964).

continued on through 1949. In Russia, Romanov rule ended with finality when the Bolsheviks brought their brutal revolution and ultimate civil war; in the humiliating treaty of Brest-Litovsk, forced on Lenin by the Germans in early 1918, Russia lost control of a vast east European empire. The Hohenzollerns and Hapsburgs, defeated in war, saw their rule in central and southeast Europe likewise ended; in its place sprang up a myriad of ethnic entities that now demanded sovereign national independence. And the defeated Ottoman Empire completely dissolved, leaving a further political vacuum in the volatile Middle East. From a certain perspective, world leaders have since 1918 been trying to restore order out of the chaos left by World War I.

*   *   *

In the interwar period the United States did not "retreat into sullen and selfish isolationism," as a disappointed Wilson charged. What the United States did not do in the whole period between the wars was join the League of Nations. By the early 1920s the Warren Harding administration, under the guidance of Secretary of State Charles Evans Hughes, called the Washington Conference, which brought together the major powers of the world to negotiate three important agreements: one calling for naval disarmament, another for stability in east Asia, and a third elevating to the status of international law the American "open door" policy in China. By the middle of the 1920s the United States had joined with several other nations in signing the Kellogg-Briand Pact to outlaw war as a national policy. The United States, refraining from committing itself to collective security arrangements and avoiding involvement in intra-European politics, nonetheless, by approving these "multilateral" treaties, engaged in world affairs more actively than it had in the nineteenth century. But during the 1930s, troubled by the Great Depression at home and the collapse of international order abroad, Congress demonstrated tenacious resistance to Franklin Roosevelt's subtle attempts to draw the nation into closer collaboration with countries resisting aggression.

By the early 1940s the League was no more, World War II raged, and many Americans shifted to their more idealistic mode, as angst and guilt set in over our perceived error in rejecting the League. By 1945 at Yalta, FDR, well aware of Wilson's failings, had skillfully crafted a new plan for an international organization, had attracted support for a new postwar international initiative from both major political parties, and had successfully drawn Winston Churchill and Joseph Stalin into his plans for a United Nations, an organization whose name derived from the designation FDR gave to the Allied forces coming together in early 1942 to battle fascism. The path Roosevelt chose began with the Atlantic Charter of 1941, where he and Prime Minister Churchill agreed to eight guiding principles for the aftermath of the war, including full collaboration among all nations. Twenty-six nations signed the Declaration of the United Nations in January of 1942, accepting the principles of the Atlantic Charter and pledging victory in the war. As we will describe in Chapter 2, at Moscow in 1943 China, Britain, the Soviet Union, and the United States agreed to set up an international organization at the conclusion of the war, and the "Big Three"—the Soviet Union, Britain, and the United States—began serious talks on the creation of the new organization in 1944 at Dumbarton Oaks near Washington, D.C. The Yalta Conference of February 1945 witnessed the resolution of some of the more important features of voting and representation in the new organization, and the first fifty members signed the charter at San Francisco in 1945.

The challenges confronting the president as he forwarded the new plan at the conclusion of the war were many: (1) to assuage Russian suspicions of any western-bred international organization, (2) to persuade his own country not to retreat from leadership in the postwar period, (3) to convince the rest of the world that the United States would not fall back into a constricted "isolationism," and (4) to work with the British to complete the Wilsonian plan to dismantle existing empires, including the United Kingdom's.

Although the League of Nations was a model for the United Nations, in important respects the new organization was different from its predecessor. The League had been ensconced in the full Treaty of Versailles; thus to reject the League the Senate of necessity had to reject the entire peace agreement. The United Nations, conversely, was purposely separated from the peace treaties that ended World War II; Roosevelt, informed by Wilson's lack of success, determined on a separate process of ratification. The League Covenant had been a traditional agreement among governments, called in the Covenant "The High Contracting Parties." The preamble of the later Charter begins, "We the *peoples* of the United Nations." The League required unanimous votes in both the Assembly and the Council, but decision-making in the

United Nations is quite a bit more flexible. Parties to a dispute before the League were prohibited from voting because of the obvious conflict of interest. In the United Nations, in a concession to the realities of power politics, member states had no such limitations. When coupled with the veto, this meant a permanent member of the Security Council could block UN action.

From the beginning the United States and particularly U.S. presidents wielded considerable influence on the United Nations. The pattern began with FDR, who devised the name. The language of the preamble also reveals an American presence. The preamble was composed by the poet and Harvard professor Archibald MacLeish, who was a friend of the president, librarian of Congress, and at the time undersecretary of state. Its language is strikingly reminiscent of the eighteenth-century documents founding the United States, combined with the more recent rhetoric of the New Deal. The organization of the United Nations, which initially was something of a mystery to Stalin, rings familiar to Americans: for example, there are executive (the Secretariat), legislative (the General Assembly), and judicial (the International Court of Justice) branches, and the charter emphasizes the "Good Neighbor" policy (Article 39) and the principles of America's Open Door policy (equal trade and "territorial and administrative integrity" of sovereign states—Article 2). The original ratifications are deposited in the United States, and the organization had its headquarters in New York City, on a site donated by the Rockefeller family.

All the above notwithstanding, as we have earlier noted, the United Nations rarely takes front stage in the continual discussions of America's role in the world. In the aftermath of the cold war what we should remember is not that the United Nations is irrelevant but that it is simply not alone at a pinnacle above all other institutions that connect the world. The Roosevelt and Truman administrations' purposeful crafting of an international order after the devastating world war has proved enduring and mature. Today, the North Atlantic Treaty Organization (NATO) seeks to expand its membership; the General Agreement on Tariffs and Trade (GATT) has become the World Trade Organization (WTO); the World Bank and the International Monetary Fund (IMF) have extended their activities; regional groupings from the North American Free Trade Association (NAFTA) to the Association of Southeast Asian Nations (ASEAN), to the Asian Pacific Economic Cooperation organization (APEC) to the European Union (EU) link sovereign states into ever-widening and more closely knit international units. And the United Nations, unlike any comparable multistate organization in history, has remained with us for an unprecedented half a century, expanding its membership to virtual universality.

It is almost trite to say that something called "globalization," which began long ago, has accelerated in our own time, conforming to a conscious American policy of 1945 to attract the world into a cooperative international diplomacy. Woodrow Wilson offered a vision that combined internationalism with self-determination. Today the world and individual nations are characterized by both integrating and fragmenting pressures, all at the same time. Along with alarming evidence of ethnic tension, national rivalries, religious fanaticism, ancient prejudices, and powerful grievances, we also have centripetal forces such as the World Wide Web, extensive travel, CNN International, unprecedented mixing of peoples, and a substantive, developing, credible set of international norms, agreed to at least rhetorically by most nations.

Of course the human experiment *is* problematic. Indeed, in broad terms we may expect the human species to disappear someday, as many others have disappeared in the course of Earth's existence. Whether we are on the verge of unmitigated disaster or not remains questionable. Whether we are capable of grasping with sharp discernment the challenges to our existence, and dealing with them sensibly, while providing a life just a little bit better for just a few more of our fellows, remains open to debate. Invariably romantic optimists and pessimistic Cassandras will continue to inform us, each with their own set of data. So, at the *fin-de-millenium*, it could be the worst of times (as the scholars Kennedy and Kaplan have insisted); or it could be the best of times (as President Bush thought in 1991). Unfortunately, neither the president nor the United Nations has the leisure to cogitate on this Dickensian brain-teaser. Both are too busy dealing with one another and with attendant challenges.

2

The Founders

You know, I dream dreams but am, at the same time, an intensely practical person.

—*Franklin Delano Roosevelt*
Private letter to Jan Christiaan Smuts, November 24, 1942

FDR and the UN

President Franklin Roosevelt, the practical dreamer, must be ascribed the title "architect" of the United Nations, even if he did not live long enough to become its primary builder. Out of the ruins of World War II FDR and his advisers crafted a new world organization which they hoped would keep the peace as Wilson's League of Nations had not been able to do. They sought to institutionalize the wartime cooperation of the great powers for years to come.

It was Roosevelt who cajoled the hard-bitten realist and defender of the British Empire Winston Churchill into accepting an institution committed to the self-determination of colonial peoples around the world. It was Roosevelt who pressured, bargained, and compromised with the ever-suspicious Soviet leader Joseph Stalin to bring about a universal collective security system dominated, at least initially, by the United States. Most important, it was FDR who worked assiduously to ensure congressional and public support for the idea of a universal organization, thus avoiding the tragic failure experienced by Wilson in the debate over the Versailles Treaty and America's membership in the League. Beginning in 1942 and culminating with the Yalta Conference in 1945, Roosevelt honed his own ideas about how a new world order might be built and maintained, undertook the diplomatic effort to bring those ideas to fruition, and succeeded in convincing his countrymen and his country's allies of the merits of his prescription. By the time of his death in 1945 Franklin Roosevelt had made the United Nations the heart of America's postwar strategy. While it would be left to President Truman to implement that strategy, Roosevelt came to the end of his life believing that the world's best hope for a lasting peace resided in the great powers' cooperation in the new organization.

That Roosevelt should leave the United Nations as his legacy is itself somewhat surprising. A member of Woodrow Wilson's administration and then the Democratic Party's vice-presidential nominee in 1920, he nonetheless had been a late convert to the idea of the League of Nations. In his campaign speeches he spoke of it only as a "practical necessity." His postmortem on that organization had been that its virtues were dissipated by the need for unanimity among its members and by the decision of the United States not to participate. Out of office in 1923, Roosevelt submitted to the *Saturday Evening Post* his own "Plan to Preserve World Peace," which eliminated any unanimity requirement for League decisions. Wilson's vision, in FDR's view, was utopian and lacked practicality. While Roosevelt was an internationalist, he saw himself more in the tradition of Theodore Roosevelt, the geopolitician, than in that of Wilson, the idealist.

For Franklin Roosevelt, politics was always a struggle between ideals and practical realities. The ideals were permanent; realities had to be surmounted or accommodated. In 1947 his widow, Eleanor, had occasion to reread twenty-year-old newspaper columns Franklin had written for the Macon, Georgia *Daily Telegraph* and the *Standard* of Beacon, New York. She was "struck" by the fact that FDR's interests "had remained through the years attached to many of the same things, no matter how many new things were added."[1] In a May 2, 1925 column he wrote, "Every American wants to see this country play the part of the man and lead in the advancement of civilization as a whole, and in the lessening, not only of the horrors of war, but of the chances of war itself."[2] He proposed to his New York readers that America "ought to begin right away to do a great deal more than we are doing now to cooperate with other nations in the peaceful working out of more methods for settling international disputes in their earlier stages....We have lost our leadership of the moral forces of mankind and have contributed nothing officially to the settlement of international problems."[3] The moral leadership of the United States emerged in Roosevelt's foreign policy during the war years and became an

---

[1]   Donald Scott Carmichael (ed.), *FDR, Columnist: The Uncollected Columns of Franklin D. Roosevelt* (Chicago: Pelegrini and Cudahy, 1947), introduction.

[2]   Ibid., 65

[3]   Ibid.

increasingly important element of his efforts to mobilize cooperation among the great powers after the war.

There is much debate about just how "Wilsonian" Franklin Roosevelt was. Henry Kissinger calls him one of the three great idealists (along with Wilson and Reagan) to occupy the White House in this century.[4] Patrick Glynn describes him as "airy" and in a "Wilsonian reverie" at the wartime conferences.[5] Yet some historians of the period, such as John Lamberton Harper, Georg Schild, and Warren Cohen, see little evidence of idealism at work in Roosevelt's thinking. At best, they find a politician who thought it expedient domestically to propose idealist solutions to the war and its aftermath. Cohen says that FDR "committed himself to the United Nations Organization, to an international organization, primarily to soothe public opinion and the Wilsonians around him."[6] Somewhere between the two extremes are biographers like Warren Kimball, who see little enthusiasm on the president's part for grand designs, but who believe that FDR shared Wilson's faith in American moral superiority and America's need for a lasting and just peace. At best, Kimball argues, the president preferred the "city on the hill/an example-for-all-to-follow approach."[7]

Certainly Franklin Roosevelt came to his idealism late. His earliest wartime statements and conversations about the postwar period suggest a fairly hardheaded realist who saw a few great powers essentially dictating policy for the rest of the globe. His actions in the late 1930s also reflect a savvy domestic politician who was not about to lead the nation into war for anything less than the defense of vital national interests. Even in his August 1941 meeting with Churchill aboard the *USS Augusta* off the coast of Newfoundland, which produced the Atlantic Charter, FDR specifically rejected the prime minister's proposed creation of an

---

[4] Kissinger, *Diplomacy*, 427.

[5] Patrick Glynn, *Closing Pandora's Box*, 92.

[6] Warren I. Cohen, *The Cambridge History of American Foreign Relations*, IV (New York: Cambridge University Press, 1993), 7–8. See also John Lamberton Harper, *American Visions of Europe* (Cambridge, England: Cambridge University Press, 1994), 95–107; and Georg Schild, *Bretton Woods and Dumbarton Oaks: American Economic and Political Postwar Planning in the Summer of 1944* (New York: St. Martin's, 1995), 31.

[7] Warren F. Kimball, *The Juggler: Franklin Roosevelt as Wartime Statesman* (Princeton: Princeton University Press, 1991), 186.

"effective international organization." The Charter, like Woodrow Wilson's "Fourteen Points," laid out the highest hopes for a future peaceful world; but when it came to the reincarnation of Wilson's League of Nations, all FDR would agree to was "the establishment of a wider and permanent system of general security."[8] He confided to Churchill that he could not conceive of another League with a hundred signatories, all needing to be satisfied. The president was far more interested in using this summit to promote nondiscriminatory trade practices and to assure himself that the British government had signed no secret agreements with the Soviets concerning territorial rearrangements in Europe.

Three weeks after Pearl Harbor the United States and its new allies signed the "Declaration of United Nations"[9] outlining their war aims. Roosevelt personally decided on the order of signatories, listing them on the basis of power differentials,[10] altering the original draft—which had placed the Soviet Union and China among the lesser states in global influence and had promoted the British empire and its dominions. He then held a signing ceremony for the representatives of the United States, Great Britain, China, and the USSR, followed the next day by the signatures of the twenty-two lesser states at war with the Axis powers. The event reflected Roosevelt's belief that the great powers would determine the outcome of the war and the subsequent preservation of peace.

Undersecretary of State Sumner Welles first publicly broached the idea of a general "association of nations" to keep the peace after the war. FDR assured Welles that when "the moment became ripe," the United States would pursue policies to create the world envisioned in the Atlantic Charter.[11] Initially, however, the president saw the postwar peace as best preserved by the might, not the moral righteousness, of the

---

[8]   Robert C. Hilderbrand, *Dumbarton Oaks: The Origins of the United Nations and the Search for Postwar Security* (Chapel Hill: University of North Carolina Press, 1990), 13.

[9]   The term "United Nations" was Roosevelt's creation. He first tried it out on Winston Churchill during Churchill's visit to the White House at New Year's 1942.

[10]   Robert E. Sherwood, *Roosevelt and Hopkins: An Intimate History* (New York: Harper, 1948), 453.

[11]   Townsend Hoopes and Douglas Brinkley, *FDR and the Creation of the U.N.* (New Haven: Yale University Press, 1997), 35.

great powers. He envisioned a four-nation (United States, Great Britain, China, Soviet Union) balance-of-power system. The United States would be the ultimate balancer, largely between the British and the Soviets.

As early as 1942 Roosevelt spoke of "Four Policemen" who would be the guarantors of peace. They would oversee the dismemberment of colonial empires (an idea highly unpopular with Churchill) and the disarmament of other states. He shared his idea for the first time with Soviet leaders when he met with Foreign Minister Molotov in May. By November the president was suggesting that the "Four Policemen" would conduct inspections to verify that all other nations had disarmed themselves, quarantining and even bombing violators.[12] The following month he directed the military to draw up plans for an international police force to sustain this proposal.

In April 1943 President Roosevelt floated his proposal in an interview with the *Saturday Evening Post*.[13] The public reaction was not particularly positive. FDR's secretary of state, Cordell Hull, himself a strong Wilsonian internationalist, advised the president that the public was not much interested in balance-of-power schemes but would rather see a broad international organization with strong American participation.

There were intrinsic practical problems with the "Four Policemen" concept. It was not at all clear how disarmament could be imposed on states other than the enemy nations of World War II. Additionally, one could expect small states to balk at the condominium of the great powers. Latin America would be a problem for the United States. The dismantling of empire would not be palatable to the British. Furthermore, it would be difficult to discern and disentangle conflicting national interests among the great powers, particularly between Britain and the USSR in Europe. France would also want a place at the table. Finally, China clearly had internal problems that would limit its ability to be a major force for order in Asia after the war.

The president's view began to change or, rather, expand in the spring of 1943, largely because of the efforts of Secretary of State Cordell Hull and Undersecretary Sumner Welles. Hull, who had hoped to

---

[12] Elliott Roosevelt (ed.), *F.D.R.: His Personal Letters, 1928–1945*, II (New York: Duell, Sloan, and Pearce, 1950), 1366–1367.

[13] Forrest Davis, "Roosevelt World Blueprint," *Saturday Evening Post* (April 10, 1943), 20–21,109–111.

succeed Roosevelt as president in 1940 only to see the commencement of war in Europe lead the president to run for a third term, had begun thinking about the postwar period and America's role in it even before the attack on Pearl Harbor. In his New Year's Day address in 1940 Hull asserted, "If peace should come, we shall be confronted, in our own best interest, with the vital need of throwing the weight of our country's moral and material influence in the direction of creating a stable and enduring world order under law."[14] Hull was far more open than Roosevelt to the possibilities of an international organization maintaining the peace in the future.

Even more enthusiastic than Hull about the possibilities inherent in a reincarnated League of Nations was the "devoted Wilsonian"[15] Sumner Welles. A longtime friend of the president, Welles used his access to the White House on many occasions to circumvent Hull's leadership of the State Department, advising the president to push the process of creating a workable postwar organization as quickly as the political system would allow. Since Hull, who was in his seventies and in poor health when America entered the war, was often away from the State Department for long periods, Welles was able to use his position as acting secretary to promote his own ideas.

Personal and professional relations between Hull and Welles were never very good. Hull may have shared his deputy's basic commitment to a new international body, but he was a cautious veteran of Congress, and he believed any public effort to create an organization would have to await success in the war effort. Hull often differed with Welles on fundamental elements concerning the proposed body. He also resented Welles' influence with the president, which he thought Welles was using inappropriately to undermine his own position as secretary of state. Yet Hull could not fire Welles, given Welles' friendship with the president and given his acknowledged energy and administrative skills. Instead, this unlikely partnership went forward from the outbreak of war in Europe to August 1943, creating—with much tension—the outline of what would be the new United Nations.

The American development of a plan for a new international organization, and its diplomatic efforts to bring the organization into being, occurred in three distinct phases. From 1940 to June of 1944,

---

[14] Quoted in Schild, *Bretton Woods*, 50.

[15] The characterization is Hoopes and Brinkley's, *FDR*, 49.

Hull's State Department dominated the process, as various committees worked to lay out a proposal that would be acceptable to Roosevelt and then to Stalin and Churchill. The summer of 1944 witnessed the second period in the UN's creation with the convening of the Dumbarton Oaks Conference, at which many of the organizational details were resolved by the Allies. The important issues not settled at Dumbarton Oaks would have to await negotiation at the highest level during the Yalta Conference in February 1945. Roosevelt's meeting with Churchill and Stalin at Yalta would mark the third and most critical stage in the great powers' acceptance of another attempt at peace through international organization. It would also reflect an extraordinary movement by the president away from his earlier geopolitical thinking and toward a Wilsonian plan for the postwar world. The credit for that movement, in addition to FDR's own thinking about the problems of the postwar era, must be given to his advisers at the State Department.

Secretary Hull established several State Department committees in December 1939 to explore likely postwar issues that the United States would have to address. Out of the work of those committees emerged the first outlines of what a new global organization might look like and do. In January 1940, the department's efforts were centralized in an Advisory Committee on Problems of Foreign Relations chaired by Welles. Additionally, a research unit was set up under Leo Pasvolsky. While the early efforts produced little that could be conveyed to the president for his endorsement, Welles and Pasvolsky, who was Hull's close adviser, became the prime movers in the department's growing commitment to a new kind of League.[16]

Shortly after Pearl Harbor and America's entrance into the war, Welles set up a new Department Planning Group, which in February 1942 recommended the creation of a "United Nations Authority," consisting of the twenty-six Allied nations. The planning group expected that the Authority's Provisional Armistice Administration would serve as the major organ of the body during the war, with the responsibility of preparing for obvious postwar challenges. There would also be a Security Commission consisting of the United States, the United Kingdom, China, and the Soviet Union. This was a clear effort to

---

[16] For a detailed description of the various State Department committees and reports related to the creation of the United Nations, see Hoopes and Brinkley, *FDR*, 34–68; see also Schild, *Bretton Woods*, 50–70.

incorporate Roosevelt's idea of the "Four Policemen" into Welles' more general organization. The Security Commission would have the authority to use military force to maintain the peace. We can see in this proposal the beginnings of a bifurcation in the new organization by the recognition of the unique role of the great powers among the other states that would also be members of the Authority. This effort to fulfill FDR's vision of postwar security requirements laid the basis for the eventual creation of the UN Security Council, assigned with enforcing the peace.

Neither Secretary Hull nor President Roosevelt was much interested in pushing America's allies or Congress to create a new organization that would probably be seen as a revived and equally flawed League of Nations. Thus, Welles' specific proposals were shelved. However, Hull was not opposed to further exploration and was personally supportive of a new, strengthened structure proposed at a more propitious moment. Various State Department committees and individuals continued to look at the possibility of creating such a world body. While the president continued to proselytize for the "Four Policemen" as peacekeepers, Hull was moving slowly in another direction.

The secretary of state first mentioned to President Roosevelt in July 1942 the need for some postwar agency that could enforce the rule of law and pacific settlement in disputes. The secretary then set up a technical committee to draft plans for an international organization. This committee, largely under Pasvolsky's leadership, worked tirelessly until the end of the war to develop the proposals that would ultimately be the basis for the Dumbarton Oaks Program and for the UN Charter itself. At the behest of the committee, first Secretary Hull and then his successor Edward Stettinius would carry those plans and recommendations to the president.[17] In March 1943 a draft constitution for an international organization was forwarded to Roosevelt. The proposed Charter created a general conference, a secretariat, agencies for technical services, and most importantly an executive committee consisting of the "Four Policemen" and a council made up of the four powers plus seven other representatives of regional organizations. The need for regional representation was occasioned in part by Prime Minister Churchill's known interest in the creation of regional bodies rather than a universal

---

[17] Hilderbrand, *Dumbarton Oaks*, 6–16; Thomas M. Campbell, *Masquerade Peace: America's UN Policy, 1944–1945* (Tallahassee: Florida State University, 1974), 1-86.

international organization. He was worried about the diminution of British influence in Europe and in its imperial dominions, and he argued that states would be more likely to take the necessary steps to keep the peace if they were focused on disputes in their own region. Hull and the State Department feared any postwar arrangement that depended exclusively on regional bodies that would exclude American leadership on a global scale and would encourage neoisolationism at home.

In a series of meetings during the spring and summer of 1943, Franklin Roosevelt informally gave his blessing to the effort to obtain British and Soviet assent to a new international organization. At least "in principle" he was willing to encourage Welles and Hull to pursue the matter along the lines of the draft charter. The war effort was now going the way of the Allies, and concerns about maintaining cooperation among the great powers after the war were of growing importance to the president. Including his "Four Policemen" in a universal body seemed far preferable to either the British regional strategy, which was formally proposed by London in July, or the apparent Soviet desire for military security through the creation of spheres of influence. On the basis of the president's support, Hull set up the Informal Political Agenda Group in the State Department to draft an American charter proposal. The first serious effort by the administration to convince America's two major allies of the merits of such an organization came at the Moscow Conference of Foreign Ministers in October.

Cordell Hull traveled to the conference hopeful that he could convince the Soviets that cooperation in a global international organization would serve their interests after the war. Stalin, however, was primarily concerned with winning the war. Only after the Americans and the British had agreed to open a second front in 1944 were the Soviets willing to consider the idea of a "general international" organization. Foreign Minister Molotov also insisted on language that would allow wide latitude for Soviet military operations in Eastern Europe without subjecting them to Great Power or multilateral vetoes. Hull made the necessary concessions to achieve a Four Power Declaration supporting the American initiative.[18] Following the conference Hull became a constant advocate for the continuing cooperation of the great powers through the new organization as the key

---

[18] Ruth B. Russell, *A History of the United Nations Charter: The Role of the United States, 1940–1945* (Washington, D.C.: Brookings, 1958), 118.

to peace in the postwar era. His efforts in Moscow were so welcome back home that the Senate quickly passed the Connally Amendment by a resounding vote of 85 to 5, calling for an international organization at the end of the war. Generally, public sentiment was now overwhelmingly supportive of a new institutional structure to maintain the peace. Even many Republicans, including the party's standard-bearer in 1940, Wendell Willkie, were criticizing the administration for not moving fast enough to put an organization in place by the end of hostilities. Ever in tune with shifting public opinion, the president had strong reason to push ahead with the State Department's proposals.

Returning to a hero's welcome, Cordell Hull assured a Joint Session of Congress, "There will no longer be a need for spheres of influence, for alliances, for balance of power, or any other of the special arrangements through which, in the unhappy past, the nations strove to safeguard their security or to promote their interests."[19] For both foreign and domestic reasons the Moscow Conference marked the emergence of the UN as the central goal of the Roosevelt administration's postwar policy.

* * *

After the Moscow Conference, the president became much more directly involved in the planning for the new international organization and in the negotiation of its details. This was essential if the United Nations was to see the light of day, since its creation was inextricably interwoven with other substantial foreign policy issues that only the president could decide. Most important was the future disposition of Eastern Europe once it was liberated from German occupation. Having suffered massive loss of life and destruction from two wars with Germany, the Soviet regime intended to ensure its future defense with the creation of a buffer zone. Central to the Moscow deliberations was the future of Poland in particular. Hull wanted the Soviets to recognize the government-in-exile in London, but Stalin would have none of it. Stalin, in the tradition of national interest politics, was already planning a Russian monopoly of influence over future Polish affairs. Criticized at home for making no progress on this front, Hull told Congress that the Moscow meeting was not "intended to bring about the solution of all the problems that are before us." Roosevelt, for his part, halfheartedly

---

[19] Quoted in Schild, *Bretton Woods*, 41.

confided to Hull that he would appeal to Stalin on the basis of "high morality" concerning Poland.[20] In fact, he intended to accede to Soviet security interests in the Baltic states and eastern Poland as part of the price of hoped-for Soviet participation in a global organization.

By the time the Teheran Conference convened in November 1943, Roosevelt's thinking about postwar arrangements had evolved to the point of combining Wilsonian organizational solutions with a hoped-for long-lasting friendship among the Great Powers. In Roosevelt's view there were no overwhelming conflicts of national interest between the Soviet Union and the United States. There was, moreover, a common interest in maintaining the peace. Thus, it was essential that the Soviet Union participate as a full partner in the proposed United Nations.

At Teheran FDR outlined to Stalin privately his proposal for a worldwide assembly with an executive committee and a four-nation enforcement body. Stalin, concerned about possible limitations on Soviet actions, asked whether the executive committee could make decisions binding on the member states. Roosevelt assured him it could not. This was a fateful commitment on the part of the president. Stalin and his emissaries would return to it many times over the next two years as they tried to limit proposals that would give the body some control over the Great Powers. In particular, Stalin would insist on an absolute veto for the Soviet Union. Stalin, in effect, exacted a fundamental revision from the earlier League of Nations which had not allowed states to vote on disputes in which they were involved. After initially suggesting at Teheran that he preferred the regional approach, which the British had been promoting, Stalin informed the president that he had no objection to the American plan. The president believed he now had the basis and strategy for achieving long-term U.S.-Soviet cooperation.

Following his return from the meeting with Soviet and British leaders, Roosevelt received from Secretary Hull a "Plan for the Establishment of an International Organization for the Maintenance of International Peace and Security." The president approved it on February 3, 1944. Over two years FDR had not come to a "reluctant acceptance" of a United Nations Organization, as John Lamberton Harper argues,[21] but rather had shifted his internationalist outlook from purely geopolitical perspectives toward the idealist tradition of

---

[20] Campbell, *Masquerade Peace*, 157.

[21] Harper, *American Visions*, 107.

Woodrow Wilson. To be sure, he believed that concrete postwar national interests demanded close cooperation among the great powers, and that no geopolitical problems would be resolved without it. In his view, only with the active involvement of the Soviet Union could the United Nations be successful. However, he also believed that the new organization could embody and promote traditional American values such as self-determination, democracy, and a rising standard of living for the world's population. Additionally, like Wilson before him, the president had little tolerance for continuing political spheres of influence or colonial domination. On his way to his meeting with Churchill in Casablanca in January 1943, FDR had paid a particularly upsetting stopover visit to Gambia, a British colony. The poverty and squalor outraged him. In place of the old mandate system of the League, the American government would now push for full self-determination. The future United Nations, through its Trusteeship Council, would provide the mechanism.

It was in this atmosphere that President Roosevelt broached the idea of another meeting to Marshall Stalin on July 17, 1944. Much had happened since Teheran. Soviet armies had tightened their grip on Eastern Europe as they liberated areas from German control. Moscow had refused to recognize the Polish government in London and had given full support to the Lublin Committee, consisting of Polish communists and puppets of Stalin. In the west France had been liberated the month before. The Third Reich was in its last days, and postwar Europe needed to be constructed. Roosevelt also wanted Stalin to declare war on Japan.

Winston Churchill urged a meeting as soon as possible. For the realist Churchill, the critical issues to be settled were the treatment of defeated Germany, relations with France, the Great Powers' policy toward the Balkans, the Polish Question—which he said "ought not be left to moulder"—and the future role of any international organization.[22] Churchill, like Stalin, saw the questions of power, territory, and future influence in Europe as far more important than building institutional frameworks for democratic diplomacy.

---

[22] *Foreign Relations of the United States, The Conferences at Malta and Yalta, 1945* (Washington, D.C.: Government Printing Office, 1955), 17. Hereafter cited as *FRUS.*

Building such an edifice was terribly important to Roosevelt and the advisers around him. He believed he could finesse the other issues by securing the cooperation of "Uncle Joe." If the three powers could maintain their cooperation, all was possible. Disquieting events during the summer of 1944 could not shake him from his course. In Poland, Soviet forces stood by while Germans decimated Polish revolutionaries in the Warsaw uprising. Many in the U.S. government thought Stalin's inaction clearly showed his true attitude toward the Poles and called for a much harder policy from Washington.[23] This was not the president's reaction. Even as he reviewed the advice he had received from trusted confidants like William Bullitt, who was deeply suspicious of Stalin's motives,[24] his policy seemed to be, "Win Stalin's confidence."

It was not until December 23 that the three leaders agreed on Yalta in the Crimea as the site for their talks. The long delay allowed Stalin to tighten his hold on Poland and the rest of Eastern Europe. The five months between Roosevelt's suggestion of a meeting and the decision on a site also witnessed the conclusion of two significant events: the successful completion of the Bretton Woods agreement on the creation of a liberal trade regime for the postwar world, and the deliberations at the Dumbarton Oaks Conference, which resolved many of the issues surrounding the proposed United Nations. It also saw a break in western unity with the surprise visit of Winston Churchill to Moscow in October to discuss territorial influence in Europe at war's end. In particular, Churchill sought an agreement with Stalin to recognize each nation's sphere of influence in the Balkans. The prime minister's trip set off alarm bells in Washington. FDR was highly critical, fearing that "secret treaties" rather than "collective security" might gain the upper hand. The president now had a new incentive to bring the efforts to create the United Nations to a successful conclusion.

The Dumbarton Oaks Conference in the Georgetown neighborhood of Washington was the most important event in the development of the president's thinking about the role and operation of the proposed United Nations leading up to his Yalta summit with Stalin. The U.S. government

---

[23] George Kennan, *Memoirs, 1925–1950* (Boston: Little, Brown, 1967), 210–211.

[24] Letter from Bullitt to the president, January 29, 1943, in *For the President, Personal and Secret*, edited by Orville H. Bullitt (Boston: Houghton Mifflin, 1972), 78.

invited Russia, Britain, and China to convene in two separate sessions beginning on August 21 to thrash out the technical aspects of the new international organization. They met for five weeks, and the items still being contested were left for the three wartime leaders—Roosevelt, Stalin, and Churchill—to resolve. By meeting in Washington, the administration could maintain reasonable control over the deliberations and the president could receive daily updates and materially influence the proceedings. The basis of the discussions was a set of tentative proposals developed by Hull, Edward Stettinius (Sumner Welles' replacement in August 1943), Pasvolsky, and the advisory committee in the Department of State, and submitted one day after Roosevelt had contacted Marshall Stalin about the possibility of another three-power meeting.

Two issues arose at Dumbarton Oaks, which threatened to scuttle any possibility for a new organization capable of fulfilling Wilsonian dreams. While most of the American proposal was adopted with little revision, Undersecretary of State Stettinius on August 25 recommended that parties to a dispute before the Security Council not be allowed to vote on the matter, even if a party happened to be one of the permanent members. He argued that, while unanimity among the great powers was essential to the success of the new organization, if one of the powers could veto discussion of, much less action on, a dispute, the United Nations would be as moribund as the League of Nations. To the extent that the State Department and the president were thinking in realist terms, they were focused on how to correct the inherent weaknesses that had doomed the last effort at collective security. FDR regularly referred to the mistakes made in 1919. Stettinius, Hull, and the president believed that public opinion in the United States would reject an organization that appeared unlikely to work because it suffered from the League's deficiencies.

The Soviet delegate, Andrei Gromyko, announced that his government could not accept Stettinius' proposal and that all issues before the Security Council should be subject to the unanimous agreement of the permanent members. The Soviets believed this was the clear meaning of FDR's assurances to Stalin at Teheran, and that the American suggestion was an attempt to change the organization fundamentally. The Soviets feared being outvoted in what was likely to be an American-dominated organization. This would certainly be on Stalin's mind as he contemplated the UN's reaction to his intended domination of a "buffer zone" in Eastern Europe. More surprising than the Russian rejection of the voting procedure proposed by the United States was Gromyko's additional demand that the sixteen Union Republics of the USSR each be admitted as original members of the United Nations, in effect giving Stalin sixteen votes in the General Assembly. Such a blatant grab for power could not be accepted by U.S. leaders. Neither public opinion nor the Senate would approve American participation on those terms. The Security Council's voting procedure and the matter of the Soviet's voting strength in the General Assembly stood in the way of a final agreement at Dumbarton Oaks.

Two episodes in the effort to resolve the issue of the veto are instructive about the shifting mind-set of the president in his dealings with Moscow. The first occurred on September 8, while the Dumbarton Oaks Conference was still under way. FDR invited Gromyko to the White House for a little presidential persuasion. Accompanied by Stettinius, Gromyko met the president in his bedroom. Roosevelt told Gromyko that the American position was based on this country's time-honored tradition of "fair play." He contended that the issue of whether a permanent member should be allowed to vote on a dispute in which it was involved was analogous to husbands and wives in America who sometimes have to go to court to resolve their differences. While each partner was allowed to present his or her side of the issue, neither was permitted a voice in determining the decision of the court.[25] The Soviet delegate must have found the president's nonchalance in assuming that American jurisprudential traditions should be applied in international affairs, without concern for the calculus of power, an unusual way to conduct diplomacy. Of course, it did not seem unusual to FDR, who regarded the universal application of American democratic processes simply as the logic of history. The pragmatist president was retreating into idealist arguments.

This did not seem unusual to Stettinius either. Stettinius also approached negotiations with the Russians as if the issue at hand were to be won in an American courtroom. In an effort to break the stalemate, he suggested to President Roosevelt that the administration "compromise" by limiting the requirement that a party to a dispute abstain from voting to only the questions of discussing the issue and recommending methods of pacific settlement. The unanimity rule for permanent members would

---

[25] Campbell, *Masquerade Peace*, 47.

still apply to decisions about enforcement where a breach of the peace had been determined. Applying good American domestic legalist thinking, he told the president:

> This proposal should be acceptable to this country, since no party to a dispute would sit as judge in its own case so long as judicial or quasi-judicial procedures are involved, but would participate fully in procedures involving political rather than judicial determination. It should be acceptable to Soviet Russia because it meets her desire that no action be taken against her without her consent.[26]

The president authorized the transmittal of the revised American position to the Soviet government by way of the U.S. Ambassador in Moscow, Averell Harriman. In his cable to Harriman, Stettinius was encouraging: "We have great confidence in your ability to convince Marshall Stalin of the reasonableness of our views."[27] The disputes between the United States and the Soviet Union were disputes of reason, not power; of judicial determination, not the balance of forces. The president cabled Stalin:

> I am convinced that such procedures [for the pacific settlement of disputes] will be effective only if the Great Powers exercise moral leadership by demonstrating their fidelity to the principles of justice [by not voting on disputes in which they are involved]....I firmly believe that willingness on the part of the permanent members not to claim for themselves a special position in this respect would greatly enhance their moral prestige and would strengthen their own position as the principal guardians of the future peace.[28]

Unfortunately, Stalin—and for that matter Churchill—was operating by different rules. The Soviet leader summarily rejected the proposal. Ambassador Harriman could see the difference in approach clearly from Moscow. He reported back to Stettinius that while the United States was

---

[26] *FRUS*, 51.

[27] Ibid., 60.

[28] Ibid., 59.

seeking a general framework and procedures for maintaining the peace, the Soviets had specific territorial and political objectives in mind.

The deep involvement of the administration in both the Bretton Woods and the Dumbarton Oaks negotiations in the summer and fall of 1944 focused Roosevelt on the importance of achieving a general international organization to maintain the peace. It is not that Roosevelt did not have a realist's appreciation of what the British and Soviets were up to. He understood the likely consequences of Soviet "liberation" and the British desire to maintain influence in the Mediterranean area. He also knew there was no way of dislodging the Russians without a confrontation. The only viable American response to European machinations was an idealist one. Confrontation and new unilateral military and political responsibilities for a war-weary people were not politically acceptable options for FDR on the eve of peace.

* * *

America's UN initiative *was* America's response to the national interest politics of Marshall Stalin. Like Wilson before him, Franklin Roosevelt placed his hopes in a long-term American-style democratic institution that would be capable of rising above mundane international politics and in so doing would garner public support for U.S. involvement in the world, as well as keep old-world diplomacy from reasserting itself. It was also essential in FDR's thinking to ensure the USSR's participation in the new international organization. If Stalin did not join, it was likely that the Soviet and British governments would retreat into building spheres of influence and America might seek its security in a repeat of the failed "isolationist" policies of the 1920s. The president was determined to achieve Stalin's cooperation in this undertaking. He was willing to make the arduous trip to the Crimea in February 1945 to get that cooperation. Yalta was to be Franklin Roosevelt's Versailles.

There were questions left unresolved at the Dumbarton Oaks Conference, which only the leaders could settle. The most important was the voting procedure in the Security Council. Could the permanent members veto discussion or action? Could a supermajority override a permanent member's negative vote? Additionally, Stalin, as we noted above, wanted all of the USSR's Union Republics admitted. What arrangements should be made for drafting the Charter and the Statute of the International Court of Justice? Stettinius counseled the president, "It would appear that some of these matters had best be settled by your own direct action in such manner as you yourself determine."[29]

Yalta

It was already a victory for Stalin that the three aging leaders were meeting at the Livadia Palace in Yalta. For Roosevelt, particularly, the trip to the shore of the Black Sea was grueling. He broke his journey by first meeting with Churchill on the island of Malta. The two leaders attempted to create a common front on the important issues before meeting with Stalin. Now ill—he was in fact in the last two months of his life—the president saw as his primary task the achievement of lasting cooperation with Russia and the creation of the United Nations.[30] Poland and other European adjustments were secondary and, in his mind, largely dependent on long-term harmony among the great powers.

While the president was in transit, Secretary Stettinius provided him with a briefing book of points to be pursued at Yalta. It is instructive that the first goal was to be a Soviet-British agreement on the voting procedure of the Security Council along the lines of the United States proposal. It was left to item number five to find a "solution to the Polish problem" by "the establishment of an interim government which would be broadly representative of the Polish people and acceptable to all the major allies."[31]

In his assessment of the Yalta Conference, John Stoessinger concludes, "In retrospect it is difficult to see how Roosevelt could have done much better."[32] Indeed, he got a commitment out of Stalin to "broaden" the Lublin government in Poland and to permit "free" elections based on open suffrage and a secret ballot. At the last plenary session of the conference, Stalin made it clear that Poland was a question of "life and death" for Russia. Unless the United States was willing to take on a new adversary immediately after the defeat of Nazi Germany, Senator Vandenburg's question upon hearing the results of Yalta

---

[29] Ibid.

[30] For a good discussion of Roosevelt's thinking about the United Nations during his last months, see Jim Bishop, *FDR's Last Year, April 1944 to April 1945* (New York: Morrow, 1974), 32.

[31] Ibid., 43

[32] John G. Stoessinger. *Crusaders and Pragmatists*, 51.

regarding Poland, and surmising that they meant Soviet control, remained the deciding one: "What can we do about it?"[33] Stalin, once Polish and military issues were out of the way, agreed to accept the American formulation on voting in the Security Council. This last item was far more important than European questions in the eyes of Roosevelt and his advisers.

On the matter of all the Soviet Republics being seated as charter members of the United Nations, Roosevelt won a concession. It was Molotov who raised the issue. He said the Soviet Union would be satisfied with the admission of "three or at least two" republics (specifically Ukraine and Byelorussia). This would be the quid pro quo for Soviet acceptance of the U.S. proposal on voting procedure in the Security Council. While his advisers opposed the bargain, Roosevelt accepted it. He needed Soviet help for the continuing war in Asia, and he did not believe that Stalin would go any lower in his offer. Moreover, the United States conceivably benefited even more in terms of original membership in the new organization by a provision at Yalta allowing all nations at war with Germany by March 1, 1945, to be charter members. This resulted in the membership of several pro-west Latin American countries.[34] Ultimately, FDR thought the agreements made at Yalta would be kept only if the Allies' unity could be maintained and if the new organization succeeded. Like Wilson at Versailles, he put much of his hope in the future of the new "League" and world public opinion.

Yalta, in fact, had been something of a triumph for American policy, not least because of the begetting of the United Nations. The United States got Stalin's promise to enter the war against the Japanese and to recognize the pro-American government of Chiang Kai-shek in China, and the Soviet leader kept both promises. A pro-west China and France joined the Soviet Union, the United States, and Britain as permanent members on the Security Council; elections were promised in Eastern Europe; and three western nations—the United States, England, and France—were granted occupation zones in Germany, along with the

---

[33] Russell, *History*, 544.

[34] Ironically, in the aftermath of the breakup of the Soviet Union in 1991, there are now as many votes from the former USSR as Stalin at first requested, and the United States finds this not only acceptable but reflective in the best sense of representation for independent sovereignties. Russia, of course, retains permanent membership on the Security Council. Here, Yalta seemed to work out in FDR's favor.

Soviet Union. But, probably most important, when the USSR entered the American-sponsored United Nations it agreed to join an international organization that had the clear mark of an American enterprise.

Beyond the questions of specific borders in 1945, self-determination, provisional governments, and individual and immediate national interests, the president had tried to encourage a world order that would not suffer from the sins and inadequacies that had produced two cataclysms in thirty years. In so doing he hoped to use U.S. leadership to create a framework for the final victory of American values and democratic principles in world affairs. Coupled with what Roosevelt thought was a new level of friendship and understanding among the three powers, the creation of the United Nations and the compromise on Eastern Europe augured a new era. Sitting in the well of the House of Representatives, Roosevelt reported to the legislators upon his return:

> [Yalta] spells the end of the system of unilateral action and exclusive alliances and spheres of influence and balances of power and all the other expedients which have been tried for centuries—and have failed. We propose to substitute for all of these a universal organization...of peace-loving nations.[35]

The president spent the last two months of his life making plans for his address to the San Francisco organizing conference scheduled for April 25, preparing the delegates to the conference, and fending off objections to the newly leaked agreements made at Yalta. While reports of concessions at Yalta were disturbing to many commentators and politicians, the enthusiasm for the new organization remained. The administration had a stake in reinforcing favorable public opinion and encouraged the most positive endorsements imaginable. In effect, there was a concerted effort to sell the American people on the view that the United Nations marked a wholly new form of peaceful international relations in the history of world politics. The now-retired secretary of state, Cordell Hull, called the organization "the fulfillment of humanity's

---

[35] Russell, *History*, 547; see also Patrick Glynn, *Pandora's Box*, 92.

highest aspirations and the very survival of our civilization."[36] No cautionary notes were sounded about the continuing challenges to a peaceful world. Even disturbing news of Soviet occupation in Eastern Europe was couched in the expressed expectation that the new United Nations held out the likely possibility of resolving any differences among the Great Powers cooperatively. Hyperbole both before and after the San Francisco conference suggested that this was, as the House Foreign Relations Committee Chairman Sol Bloom put it, a "turning point in the history of civilization."[37]

As late as the ninth of April, Franklin Roosevelt was telling the State Department that there would be time upon his return from Warm Springs, Georgia, to make final decisions about the trusteeship of non-self-governing territories under the United Nations and other outstanding issues before the conference convened in two weeks. Three days later the architect of Representative Bloom's "turning point" died. Final decisions and the formal birth and development of the United Nations would have to be guided by his successor.

Truman and the UN

> I have but one ambition as President of the United States, and that is to see peace in the world, and a working, efficient United Nations to keep the peace in the world. [Having accomplished that I would be] willing to…pass on happily.
>
> —*President Harry Truman*[38]

The act of creation is the combination of two intertwined but nevertheless distinct activities: conception and implementation. And, at least in politics, it appears that the German philosopher Hegel was right: the idea generally precedes the thing itself. In almost dialectical form the history of the United Nations is the story of an American idea brought to reality. Initiated by Woodrow Wilson, the idea was carried forward by

---

[36] Thomas Franck, *Nation Against Nation: What Happened to the U.N. Dream and What the U.S. Can Do About It* (New York: Oxford University Press, 1985), 9. For a discussion of the 1945 generation's perspective on the United Nations, see Kenneth W. Thompson, *Political Realism and the Crisis of World Politics* (Princeton: Princeton University Press, 1960), 68.

[37] Franck, *Nation*, 9.

[38] "Remarks to the Women's Patriotic Conference on National Defense," January 26, 1950, *PPP, 1950*, 129–130.

Franklin Roosevelt, who fulfilled the final stage of conception, leaving the implementation of the decisions made at Dumbarton Oaks and Yalta to his successor. Truman began that process within minutes of becoming president.

Truman was having drinks with Speaker of the House Sam Rayburn and other old political friends on Capitol Hill around 5 P.M. on Thursday, April 12, when he was told of a telephone call from the White House. Returning the call, he was summoned immediately to the president's mansion. Upon his arrival Mrs. Roosevelt informed Truman that the president had died. Less than two and a half hours later he took the oath of office. His first policy decision, within minutes of the ceremony, was to confirm that the San Francisco Conference to organize the United Nations would go ahead as planned on April 25.

Few presidents have entered office with as many foreign policy challenges immediately on their plate as Truman had. The Second World War was in its last weeks, but critical decisions needed to be made about the occupation of Germany and postwar relations with the Soviet Union. Stalin was moving to consolidate his position in Poland, rejecting any role for the London-based Polish exile government. In the Pacific the United States was moving closer to the critical decision to invade Japan. To support that effort, Truman urgently needed a Soviet commitment to declare war on Japan. The San Francisco Conference would be making detailed and specific decisions about the new UN Charter that would affect how the UN worked for years to come. Additionally, there were problems of which the new president was still unaware. For example, following his first meeting with the cabinet, War Secretary Stimson stayed behind to apprise the president of a new explosive "of almost unbelievable destructive power."[39]

President Truman thought it important to provide continuity in American foreign policy following Roosevelt's death. Since during his brief vice-presidency he had been entirely excluded from the formulation of that policy, he had few alternatives to depending on the advice of Roosevelt's foreign policy team and reaffirming the previous administration's commitments. This did not mean, however, that Truman moved forward on UN matters only out of loyalty to the dead

---

[39] Harry S Truman, *Memoirs, I, Year of Decisions* (Garden City, N.Y.: Doubleday, 1955), 10.

president. He was a strong supporter of the UN, seeing in it a second opportunity for America to guarantee world peace well into the future.

The generational event in Harry Truman's life had been World War I. In his reading of history the United States had not made the right decisions in 1919 to ensure that there would not be another global war. He had supported the League of Nations and U.S. participation. Like Roosevelt, he was an internationalist who believed American interwar foreign policy and its forfeiture of leadership in the League had contributed to the rise of dictatorships and the renewed conflagration in 1939.

As Americans turned to consideration of the postwar world, *Senator* Truman had argued strongly for not repeating "the blunders of the past." David McCullough, Truman's biographer, tells us that the senator was the "guiding spirit" behind the B2H2 Senate Resolution in the summer of 1943, calling for the creation of a new international organization.[40] Named for its public sponsors, Joseph H. Ball (R-Minnesota), Harold Burton (R-Ohio), Carl Hatch (D-New Mexico), and Lister Hill (D-Alabama), the proposal called for the organization to be established even before the war ended.[41] Supporters endorsed giving the body a world police force to enforce the peace. Truman spent much of that summer traveling in the Midwest and speaking on the merits of internationalism. The Senate withdrew the resolution only after Cordell Hull counseled patience, fearing that any effort then to create the organization might undermine the war effort and raise contentious issues among the "Big Three." The failure to enact the legislation, however, did not dampen Truman's support for a new and stronger institution than the League of Nations.

Arising at 5 A.M. on Saturday, April 14, Truman prepared to go to Union Station to meet the train carrying Roosevelt's body back to the nation's capital. It is instructive that, before leaving, the president reviewed the latest memorandum from Secretary of State Stettinius on the San Francisco Conference. Knowing that he would meet the U.S. delegation members on Tuesday, he needed to decide, among other things, whether an invitation should be extended to the Ukraine and Belorussia, the two "extra" Soviet votes agreed to by Roosevelt,

---

[40] David McCullough, *Truman* (New York: Simon and Schuster, 1992), 287.

[41] For a discussion of the B2H2 Resolution see Hoopes and Brinkley, *FDR*, 65–67.

Churchill, and Stalin in February. Truman spent much of the next several weeks focusing on the Conference and the issues yet to be resolved. His goal was to achieve a world organization that could "prevent another world war...that would pass the U.S. Senate and that would not arouse such opposition as confronted Woodrow Wilson."[42] Fortunately, a masterful FDR already had generated bipartisan and public support for the new United Nations. Thus, Truman could concentrate on the substantive issues at hand. He decided that the commitments made at Yalta must be honored and, therefore, that the United States would support three votes in the General Assembly for the Soviet Union.

The San Francisco Conference proved to be a wide-open affair with broad negotiation not only among the great powers over issues not handled at Dumbarton Oaks or the Yalta meeting, but also between the designated permanent members of the Security Council and the smaller states. The most contentious issue was the proposed veto power of the Security Council's permanent members. Almost immediately upon the opening of the meeting, the Soviet delegation restated its demand for an absolute veto over all matters before the Council. This would include even the discussion of disputes and all procedural matters. Stettinius and Truman understood that an acceptance of this position would doom the Charter in the U.S. Senate and would probably mean the stillbirth of the United Nations. Since Dumbarton Oaks the United States had urged a compromise that would allow an absolute veto of all enforcement actions but would prohibit the veto of Security Council debate on conflicts brought to its attention, even if those conflicts involved the permanent members. Roosevelt and Stettinius thought they had obtained Stalin's commitment to this at Yalta. Truman now interpreted the USSR's proposal as a retreat from Yalta and an important part of a new, threatening postwar Soviet foreign policy. Wartime cooperation seemed to be at an end.

The day Roosevelt's remains returned to Washington, Truman, in addition to meeting his ceremonial duties, conferred with the late president's old friend and adviser Harry Hopkins. Although desperately ill, Hopkins briefed Truman on everything he knew about "Russia and Poland and the United Nations."[43] The president asked him to undertake a personal mission to Moscow in order to see if there were some

---

[42] Truman, *Memoirs*, I, 46.

[43] Ibid., 31.

possibility of resolving the outstanding issues between the two powers. High on his list was the matter of the veto. In his meeting with Hopkins on June 6, Stalin feigned surprise at the position his delegation had taken in San Francisco and immediately directed that the American proposal be accepted. Truman had succeeded in bringing to conclusion the Charter issue that had vexed negotiations since the Teheran Conference.

Another item that the great powers had not been able to resolve prior to the Conference was the question of the UN's role in newly liberated territories, both those that had been controlled by the enemy states and those that were part of former colonial empires. Roosevelt had found Churchill particularly adamant in opposing any structure or measure that might endanger the British Empire. He was not about to have Britain's colonial policy "put in the dock and examined by everybody."[44] So, too, the French government opposed efforts that might limit its freedom of action in Indochina and Africa. Conversely, smaller states from the African continent, South America, and Asia encouraged U.S. endorsement of "independence" for non-self-governing territories.

The State Department's draft charter of 1943 had proposed transferring to the new organization the rights and powers of the League of Nations under its mandate system. In December FDR had approved the addition of an "agency for trusteeship responsibilities" reporting to the General Assembly. However, faced with repeated British objections, Roosevelt was unwilling to press the matter with his allies even as he encouraged his advisers to find a formula that would lead to full independence for colonial possessions. By the summer of 1944 the American UN initiative included a "Trusteeship Council" made up of equal representation from administering and nonadministering states.

The American army and navy also had objections to any system that might mean the United States would have to place strategic possessions under UN control. As important Pacific islands were liberated from Japanese administration, the military opposition to the State Department's recommendations became more strenuous. Secretary of War Stimson made several personal entreaties to Roosevelt on the issue. While the president rejected military proposals to take direct control of Japanese islands, he thought it prudent to exclude the topic of trusteeship from the Dumbarton Oaks conversations. He urged the State Department and the military to work out their differences, keeping in

---

[44] Russell, *History*, 541.

mind his general commitment to include *all* territories in any future UN
system. In his view, not to do so would be a violation of the Atlantic
Charter.

Roosevelt wanted to discuss these matters at Yalta, but Churchill
objected. In their preliminary meeting on Malta the two leaders
compromised by agreeing that the trusteeship issue would be resolved at
San Francisco. The prime minister extracted a further promise that no
specific territories would be discussed. This preliminary commitment,
however, did not keep him from "exploding" during the Yalta meeting
when the foreign ministers recommended that the UN Charter deal with
trusteeship. While Roosevelt was able to raise the matter privately with
Stalin, including the possible creation of a trusteeship over Korea, he was
forced by both Allied and American military criticisms to postpone the
matter once again.

Harry Truman believed deeply in Woodrow Wilson's philosophy of
"self-determination." Democracy, human rights, and independence were
inextricably intertwined. They were all part of the American tradition
both at home and abroad. Colonialism was "hateful to Americans,"
because "we, as a people, have always accepted and encouraged the
undeniable right of a people to determine its own political destiny."[45] In
his view, "there can be no 'ifs' attached to this right, unless [the United
States were] to backslide on our political creed."[46] The president was
willing to use the "procedure and method" of the United Nations to
meet the increasing demands for national freedom, which were loud and
clear at the end of the war.

The president saw the matter of decolonization as an element of a
general international "Bill of Rights." Far more than Roosevelt, Truman
expressed a desire to see the freedoms and structure of American life
writ large on a global scale. In early May, the four powers introduced
amendments to the Dumbarton Oaks Plan, including an American
proposal for a UN Declaration on Human Rights and the establishment
of a Human Rights Commission. Truman worked to convince Churchill
that the old "power politics" had to give way to a new "frame of mind."
And when Charles de Gaulle's government in Paris moved to reestablish
control in Syria, even as the San Francisco Conference was meeting,

---

[45] Truman, *Memoirs*, I, 237.

[46] Ibid.

Truman sided with the Arab states and small states that objected to French actions.

In the two months after Yalta, the State Department and the War Department worked through an Interdepartmental Committee on Dependent Areas to reconcile their deep differences. Unable to settle on a compromise position, the sides presented the alternatives to Roosevelt in early March. At a cabinet meeting on the ninth, the president decided that trusteeship in the Pacific would mean that "sovereignty would be vested in all of the United Nations,"[47] but the United States would seek authorization to administer the strategic islands in the region. He approved dividing designated trusteeship areas into "strategic" and "nonstrategic" territories, and limiting the role of the Trusteeship Council in those defined as strategic. On April 3 the administration revealed that at Yalta the parties had agreed to a trusteeship system as part of the new general international organization. Roosevelt scheduled a meeting for April 19 to finalize details of the American proposal. His death on the twelfth, and Truman's immediate decision to go ahead with the San Francisco Conference, meant that the new president would have to decide quickly on decolonization issues. Truman's personal inclination and the work completed to that point led him to endorse the distinction between strategic and nonstrategic territories in the proposed Charter, and to push forward with the Trusteeship Council's recommendation.

Onset of the Cold War

Complicating final resolution of issues at San Francisco was the atmosphere of tension developing in U.S.-Soviet relations during the spring of 1945. Even Roosevelt, who predicated so much on cooperation between the two powers, had expressed consternation at Stalin's actions in Eastern Europe. The Polish Question in particular undermined the spirit of goodwill evident at Yalta.

Less than two weeks after becoming president, Truman met with his advisers and made clear his intention to be tough with the Russians over Poland.[48] Stalin was reneging on the inclusion in the new government of Poles not part of the Lublin group. The American ambassador to the

---

[47] Russell, *History*, 582.

[48] Lloyd C. Gardner, *Architects of Illusion* (Chicago: Quadrangle, 1970), 60–61.

USSR, Averell Harriman, warned of a "barbarian invasion of Europe" if the United States did not stand up to the Soviets. The Russian system—involving secret police and the extinction of personal freedoms—was quickly overrunning Eastern European peoples. Harriman, meeting with the president on April 20, argued that Stalin was pursuing two policies, the subjugation of neighboring buffer states and continued cooperation with Britain and the United States. The Soviet dictator believed that one need not conflict with the other. The president said he would tell the Soviet foreign minister "in words of one syllable" that Poland would have to be settled along Yalta's terms or there would be no possibility of getting the UN Charter through the U.S. Senate.[49] Truman intended to link Soviet behavior in Poland with the level of U.S. cooperation on other issues.

On the same day that Foreign Minister Molotov arrived in Washington en route to San Francisco, Moscow recognized the Lublin government in Poland and signed a mutual assistance agreement with it. On April 23, Molotov met President Truman at the White House. With few pleasantries, the president immediately raised the matter of Poland and America's intention to withhold recognition of any government not the product of free elections. As the foreign minister began to explain the national security interests of the Soviet regime in Poland, Truman cut him off, saying that he did not want to hear any Soviet propaganda.[50] Truman made clear that the good relations of the war years could continue only if the Soviet Union understood that cooperation "was a two-way street." Abruptly dismissing the foreign minister, the president struck a new adversarial tone with the Soviets that they had not experienced during the Roosevelt years. A letter the following day from Stalin, reiterating Soviet interests in Poland, proved to be, in Truman's own words, "one of the most revealing and disquieting messages"[51] he received in the early days of his presidency. A new era of confrontation was at hand.

The new tension in Soviet-American relations did not mean to Harry Truman that the United Nations was moribund or that there were not important elements of international affairs that could best be solved through UN action. Rather, it created a conflicted and vacillating policy

---

[49] McCullough, *Truman*, 373.

[50] Ibid., 375–376.

[51] Truman, *Memoirs*, I, 86.

toward the institution. Throughout his term he never gave up on the prospects for the United Nations as a vehicle for preserving the peace. Particularly during his first year and a half in the White House, Truman launched several initiatives to encourage international cooperation.[52] Significantly, Truman decided that the United Nations could be the institutional structure for managing the new problem of the atom bomb.

The detonation of America's new weapon over Hiroshima in August 1945 ushered in the nuclear age, with all of its dangers for global peace and security. Politicians, scientists, commentators, and the general public expressed deep concern about the implications of nuclear power, and many pressed for international controls before an arms race could drive the world into another war. The United States had developed the atom bomb in secret. Only the British had participated in limited ways in its creation. The success of the Manhattan Project had made the United States the only nuclear power in the world and had given it a position of strategic superiority which many believed could be used to bring about a peaceful postwar order.

Sometimes the close and coincidental proximity of events in international affairs has the most profound impact on the course of nations' actions. The conclusion of the San Francisco Conference in June 1945, Truman's subsequent submission of the Charter to the Senate, the dramatic public attention given to the new United Nations during that summer, and the incineration of Hiroshima almost immediately after these matters produced strong public pressures to find ways to put atomic energy under UN auspices and international control. Within the U.S. government there was also strong sentiment to transfer the American nuclear monopoly to some international structure.

The first issue to present itself was whether the "science" of the bomb should be shared. Many people believed it could not be kept a permanent "American secret." The scientists who had worked on its development lobbied the White House for international cooperation in the further investigation of the atom. Within the administration's Secretary of War Henry Stimson argued for sharing what we knew with our wartime allies. In a crucial cabinet meeting on September 18, Stimson

---

[52] Gardner, *Architects*, 77–81. An early example occurred during the Potsdam summit in July 1945. The president put forward a proposal to internationalize the major waterways of central and east Europe. Stalin's outright rejection of the idea led Truman to the extraordinary conclusion that the Soviets were planning world conquest.

made an impassioned appeal for collaboration with the Soviets on atomic matters. It was unrealistic to assume that Stalin's government would not undertake the necessary research and ultimately produce an atomic device. Furthermore, the Soviets would be deeply suspicious of American intentions if they saw the United States developing atomic power either alone or only in cooperation with the British.[53] To keep the research data from the Soviets was bound, in Stimson's view, to produce a deadly and costly arms race.[54]

Stimson had several supporters among the president's entourage. Undersecretary of State Dean Acheson strongly endorsed some form of international cooperation. Even the Joint Chiefs of Staff, fearing the need to rearm in spite of a declining military budget, initially supported the idea.[55] As Acheson put it, "The advantage of being ahead in [an arms] race is nothing compared with not having the race."[56] The natural reflex to keep the bomb America's weapon in a time of growing U.S.-Soviet tensions had to be seen as an unrealistic expectation. If the United States wanted Soviet cooperation on other issues and at the United Nations, then nuclear partnership was critical.

The September cabinet meeting was acrimonious and resolved little in terms of long-term U.S. policy. Strongly opposed to Stimson's proposal was James F. Byrnes, Truman's new secretary of state. Byrnes, a former senator from South Carolina, reflected the congressional opinion that the Soviets could not be trusted. Without a fail-safe international inspection system, it would be foolhardy to turn over American scientific

---

[53] Stalin interpreted the attack on Hiroshima as "blackmail" directed at the Soviet Union. He saw in it a threat of a new war and the critical need to develop a Soviet nuclear capability. See Vladislav Zubok and Constantine Pleshakov, *Inside the Kremlin's Cold War: From Stalin to Khrushchev* (Cambridge, Mass.: Harvard University Press, 1996), 42.

[54] The president had already decided not to share American "know-how" on building a bomb. The issue for the administration concerned the sharing of basic scientific information. Truman intended to keep even London in the dark on the specific engineering details for the bomb's construction. There is some evidence that the president believed no nation had the capability to replicate American genius and construct a bomb for many years to come.

[55] Gerard H. Clarfield and William M. Wiecek, *Nuclear America* (New York: Harper and Row, 1984), 89–90.

[56] Quoted in David S. McLellan, *Dean Acheson The State Department Years* (New York: Dodd, Mead, 1976), 63.

information or—worse—atomic materials to international control. Byrnes also thought that the American atomic advantage could be used to make the Soviets more amenable on other matters dividing the two powers. The American threat might make Stalin more accommodating, for example, on Eastern Europe.

In the fall of 1945, in an address to Congress, Truman suggested that "the release of atomic energy constitutes a new force too revolutionary to consider in the framework of old ideas."[57] "The hope of civilization" depended on "a satisfactory arrangement for the control of this discovery."[58] A new framework, however, eluded his administration. When Stimson had first described to the president the nature of the Manhattan Project and the expected power of the bomb, Truman immediately appreciated the historic significance of the new weapon. Nonetheless, the pressure of wartime decisions, including Truman's authorization to use the bomb against Japan, meant that he gave little consideration to the future control of atomic energy until Stimson's impassioned plea. Events in October and November, however, forced Truman to move forward with a plan for international control.

In October, Secretary of State Byrnes returned from a meeting of foreign ministers disheartened by his inability to use America's new superiority to leverage the USSR diplomatically on a wide range of contentious issues. Instead, the American nuclear monopoly seemed to harden Soviet attitudes. Stalin was unwilling to appear concessionary in the face of apparent nuclear blackmail. In the same month there was also growing pressure from the British government to obtain American technical information on atomic energy. London believed it had a right to this information as a result of commitments made by President Roosevelt to cooperate with Great Britain and Canada in the development of nuclear power. Prime Minister Clement Atlee traveled to Washington to press his demand. As a result, he, Truman, and the Canadian prime minister, Mackenzie King, agreed on November 10 that control of atomic energy should eventually be under the auspices of the United Nations.

Byrnes put Acheson in charge of a committee to draft a proposal for the international control of atomic energy. The Undersecretary

---

[57] Quoted in Paul Boyer, *By the Bomb's Early Light* (New York: Pantheon, 1985), 134–135.

[58] McLellan, *Acheson*, 63.

immediately convened a working group of experts and politically savvy individuals who drafted what became known as the Acheson-Lilienthal Proposal.[59] The Committee's plan was surprisingly innovative. Recognizing the difficulties of constructing a meaningful inspection system, the plan envisaged an Atomic Development Authority (ADA) which would own and control all uranium mines, fissionable materials, and processing facilities around the world. Only "denatured" materials unsuitable for weapons would be distributed by the ADA to national governments. Inspection would be kept to a minimum. Any effort by a government to interrupt ADA activities or seize the authority's assets within the state's borders would signal other nations of an impending threat. Countermeasures could then be taken. Realizing that Congress would not approve the relinquishment of the American nuclear monopoly until there was assurance that the system was fully functional, Acheson and David Lilienthal proposed phasing the plan in. The United States would not turn over its weapons until all states had submitted their facilities and resources to the authority.

Secretary Byrnes, even as Acheson's committee was completing its work, persuaded the president to appoint a fellow South Carolinian, Bernard Baruch, as the U.S. representative to the inaugural meeting of the United Nations Atomic Energy Commission (UNAEC) in June. Baruch, a respected "elder statesman" and financier, had numerous friends on Capitol Hill. While Truman thought him the ultimate "egotist," he felt Baruch's prestige might make proposed international control of America's atomic power palatable. Indeed, his appointment was greeted with enthusiasm.[60]

---

[59] The plan, officially titled *Report on the International Control of Atomic Energy*, was approved by the president in March 1946. David Lilienthal, the former head of the Tennessee Valley Authority, was often credited with the most innovative elements of the committee's recommendations. However, some argue that J. Robert Oppenheimer was the more important author. See Clarfield and Wiecek, *Nuclear America*, 92. For Acheson's own perspective on the work of the committee, see Dean Acheson, *Creation*, 149–156.

[60] Acheson, however, was so disturbed by Baruch's appointment, thinking him totally uninformed and a man of little substance, that he resigned from the State Department. In his memoirs, Acheson reflects "My own experience led me to believe that [Baruch's] reputation was without foundation in fact and entirely self-propagated." Acheson, *Creation*, 154.

Truman quickly found the Baruch appointment problematic. The expectation was that he would present the Acheson-Lilienthal Proposal with little change to the UNAEC. Unfortunately Mr. Baruch insisted on gathering his own advisers and making significant alterations to the proposal. He threatened to quit his post, an action politically damaging to the president, if he were not given extensive leeway in the preparation of the final report. Truman acquiesced. The result was a proposal that found much domestic favor but one which was dead on arrival at the United Nations.

The Baruch Plan incorporated Acheson's Atomic Development Authority, but it rejected the innovative idea of the Authority owning all atomic resources. Instead, Baruch saw the ADA as a super-inspection organization, independent of all other bodies in the United Nations, with the responsibility of monitoring all national facilities. Furthermore, it could impose sanctions and fines on offending nations. The veto would be denied to the Permanent Members in decisions made by the UN body. Finally, the United States would be allowed to continue its research and development until the full system was in place and operating. While the original Acheson-Lilienthal Plan depended on individual foreign policies to respond to offending behavior by states rejecting international control, Baruch's alternative envisioned an international atomic police to punish violators.

There was nothing in the Baruch Plan that would entice the Soviets to participate. "Penalties and no veto" was a formula that could be interpreted in Moscow only as an attempt by the United States to maintain its monopoly and to use the American-dominated United Nations to restrict Soviet defense efforts.[61] It was rejected out of hand. The Soviet delegate, Andrei Gromyko, proposed a moratorium on atomic development prior to any plan for internationalization. This would, of course, freeze the American program and allow the Soviets, with no inspection program in place, to catch up. The Soviets also insisted that the proposed Atomic Authority be subject to the Security Council and, thus, to the USSR's veto power. The Baruch Plan died in the

---

[61] Boyer, *Early Light*, 54–56; Clarfield and Wiecek, *Nuclear America*, 96–97. From 1945 to 1950 Stalin saw little possibility of challenging the American majority in the United Nations. The task was to ensure that American initiatives did not restrict the Soviet Union's freedom of action. See Ernst B. Haas, *Why We Still Need the United Nations: The Collective Management of International Conflict, 1945–1984* (Berkeley: University of California Press, 1986), 45.

growing acrimony of the summer of 1946. The UNAEC recommended a plan similar to the American proposal in December by a vote of 10 to 0, with the USSR and Poland abstaining, but nothing more came of Baruch's efforts.

The administration's instinct to use the United Nations to avoid an arms race, while well-intentioned, was badly managed and ultimately ran head-on into the developing cold war. Truman turned his attentions to ensuring civilian control of atomic energy in the United States and to supporting further military applications of nuclear power. The failure to achieve international control of atomic weapons meant that each superpower would have to proceed with the creation of sufficient strategic forces for its defense. The Truman administration approved the development of the hydrogen bomb in January 1950, and the creation of a "second-strike capability" that could ensure deterrence of a Soviet attack. Most important, in April of that year the president approved NSC-68, a blueprint to proceed with the procurement of a strategic triad of weapons systems: intercontinental ballistic missiles, sea-launched missiles and manned bombers for purposes of nuclear deterrence. This was necessary, NSC-68 argued, because "the Soviet Union, unlike previous aspirants to hegemony, is animated by a new fanatic faith, antithetical to our own, and seeks to impose its absolute authority over the rest of the world."[62]

It may be that no workable plan for international control of atomic energy was possible. In February 1946 Stalin addressed an "election" rally in Moscow, speaking out for the first time since the war's conclusion about the "threats" to the socialist motherland. Finding capitalism and communism incompatible, the generalissimo returned to an old ideological theme about the inevitability of war between the two camps and the need to rearm the Soviet Union. Speaking at the Bolshoi Theater Stalin asserted that his country would have to ensure its security unilaterally.[63] His speech marked the formal beginning of a long confrontation with the United States. In response to the Kremlin's hard line, the American chargé d'affaires to the USSR, George Kennan, submitted his famous "Long Telegram" to the State Department, outlining a grim evaluation of Soviet intentions and policy initiatives. Acheson and others concluded that the Soviets were steering foreign

---

[62] Clarfield and Wiecek, *Nuclear America*, 137.

[63] Zubok and Pleshakov, *Stalin to Khrushchev*, 35.

policy on an "ominous course" and were interested in nothing less than world conquest.

Still, Truman's first recourse in dealing with the international crises of 1945 and 1946 was to enlist the United Nations in the effort to turn back Soviet challenges. The first such episode involved Soviet troops in Iran. The USSR had occupied northern Iran during the war, with the Allies' blessing. The occupation allowed the flow of Lend-Lease materials to Russia and kept German armies out of the area. Stalin had promised to withdraw his forces six months after the end of hostilities. By the winter of 1945–1946, however, Soviet forces had not withdrawn and were supporting local Azeris seeking secession from Iran. Stalin argued that he needed to keep forces in the area to protect the Baku oil fields, but his assertions fell on deaf ears in Teheran and Washington. Through this action and his actions in Iran, Stalin was increasingly putting pressure on Turkey to allow joint control of the Dardanelles and to cede several strategic areas to the USSR.

At the inaugural session of the Security Council in January 1946, the United States demanded the immediate withdrawal of Soviet forces from Iran. This was followed, in March, by a two-pronged strategy. The administration dispatched an American warship to the eastern Mediterranean, not only to signal Moscow about Washington's seriousness, but also to strengthen Turkey against Soviet demands. Meantime, Washington worked through the United Nations to put diplomatic pressure on the Soviets. Security Council debate began in late March on a U.S.-supported Iranian proposal to order the USSR's troops out. On March 29 a proposal passed the Council, in large part because the Soviet delegate, Andrei Gromyko, walked out over the issue. The measure sought "to ascertain Soviet intentions."[64] Two months of negotiations ensued before western pressure moved Stalin to withdraw his forces. Part of that decision was predicated on Secretary Byrnes' promise to drop the matter at the UN. Nonetheless, the administration read the results as a victory for the world body, Byrnes arguing that they were "proof of the strength and effectiveness of the United Nations."[65]

* * *

---

[64] See Acheson, *Creation*, 198; see also Franck, *Nation*, 26.

[65] Franck, *Nation*, 26.

If Iran was a warning sign about the potential expansionist threat posed by the Soviets, the case of Turkey and the Dardanelles, soon to be followed by the confrontation in Greece, were far more "ominous" portents in U.S.-USSR relations. They demonstrated, for the first time, the limits to which the United Nations could be used in the furtherance of American foreign policy. They mark a critical juncture in Truman's "learning curve" about the institution and its role in the postwar effort to maintain the peace and avoid another worldwide conflagration.

What Truman discovered, particularly in the Greek crisis, was that from the moment of their inception, institutions have two lives: their *teleological life*, that is, their existence and promotion as a way of human operation toward some final goal for which they were originally created; and their *practical life*, the day-to-day existence in which the members defend their self-interest and quite often pursue disparate ends. This certainly was, and continues to be, true of the United Nations. The *practical* necessities of power also make clear that no international institution can provide a comprehensive answer to every problem U.S. foreign policy must confront. President Truman was the first American chief executive to face this combination. While Roosevelt believed the United Nations might be a place for long-term international consensus built on American values, Truman increasingly found it a place of votes and confrontation, an institution whose origins were the dictates of moral purpose but whose workings were those of national interest. While he told the San Francisco Conference in June 1945 that international peace depended upon the defense of law and on each state's meeting its "obligations" to the world community, his policies in the Turkish and Greek episodes demonstrated that his own evolving calculus of peace was a unique mix of idealist commitment to the grandest goals of the organization and a realistic assessment of how U.S. power would have to be used unilaterally to check Soviet ambition and force.

By 1946 the focal point of American-Soviet confrontation was in southeast Europe. As the Iranian crisis receded it was replaced by Soviet demands for bases on Turkish territory and a revision of the Soviet-Turkish border. Further to the west the communist government of Tito (Josip Broz) in Yugoslavia asserted a claim to Trieste, punctuated by the downing of an unarmed American transport plane on August 19. The outrage in the United States was palpable. The administration also faced growing communist insurgency in Greece. The regime, to that time sustained by Great Britain, was near economic collapse. One could envisage all of the Balkans and eastern Mediterranean falling under Soviet influence, changing the balance of forces in Europe irretrievably.

Yugoslavia and Iran were peripheral to Greece and Turkey in American strategic thinking. On the same date, the USSR demanded that Turkey allow it to assist in the defense of the Dardanelle Straits, and it also launched an effort in the United Nations to see the communist-dominated Greek National Liberation Front (EAM) replace the official Greek government. Stalin had provided extensive support to communist forces involved in the complicated politics of postwar Greece. A national coalition government had taken office following the war but had been unable to mend the fractures in Greek political life; nor had it surmounted the overwhelming economic problems confronting the country. Additionally, the government had made territorial claims of its own on surrounding states and suffered from corruption and weak leadership. Nonetheless, the collapse of the regime would certainly mean the accession of the communists and new influence for Moscow.

General George Marshall, who succeeded James F. Byrnes as secretary of state in January 1947, was particularly concerned about Greece. He directed Dean Acheson to draft recommendations for immediate economic and military aid to Athens. This became even more urgent when the British decided to end their support of the regime. On Monday and Tuesday, February 24–25, 1947, in a meeting with the president and congressional leaders, Marshall and Acheson outlined the gravity of the situation and the stakes for American national security. In Acheson's view the world had arrived at a point unparalleled "since ancient times." Only two great powers remained in the world, and they were locked in a death struggle. The president made the critical decisions to do whatever was necessary to sustain the Greek government and, from his point of view, Greek national independence. He also prepared to address Congress and the people on the essential danger communism and Soviet expansionism posed for the United States.

The *Truman Doctrine* enunciated by the president to a joint session of Congress on March 12, 1947, proposed a unilateral commitment by the United States "to support free people who are resisting attempted subjugation by armed minorities or by outside pressures." His focus was on Greece and Turkey, but his message was directed at the general world situation. The United Nations was not in a position to extend the help needed because of the divide between the United States and the Soviet

Union.[66] In actuality Truman had given little thought to how the United Nations might address this crisis. At most, the president would assert that the actions he was recommending were meant to give effect "to the principles of the Charter of the United Nations." By March 1947 Truman was in cold war mode; gone was the universalist preoccupation with the United Nations as the chief vehicle of U.S. foreign policy. He asked Congress for $400 million to assist Greece and Turkey. In addition to funds, he asked Congress to authorize the dispatch of civilian and military personnel to both countries. If Congress concurred—and by late May it did concur—the effort to aid the governments in Ankara and Athens would establish a model for future U.S. assistance in the decades-long battle with the communist threat. In that battle the United Nations played a secondary, though often useful, role in the determination and execution of U.S. policy.

In the late 1940s Harry Truman could not have sold the long-term containment of Soviet power to the American people on the grounds of crass power politics. When the president announced the Truman Doctrine, nearly 66 percent of the public disapproved of America's going it alone. More than half thought the United Nations could and should find a solution to the Greek problem.[67] Truman's implicit assertion that communism and Soviet policies were a mortal danger to the values of all people was meant to strike a chord with idealist sentiment at home. But for many the Second World War had been fought for higher ends; too much blood had been spilled in the name of principle to give up on collective security as embodied in the United Nations. Only in the call for a defense of freedom and law could the president find sufficient suasion with American public opinion to garner the support he needed to achieve congressional approval of his policies.

Implicit in President Truman's policy was the assertion that a peaceful world was still possible and could be achieved through U.S. leadership in the world, but now through confrontation, not cooperation, with Stalin's Russia. Truman stood Yalta on its head. The American

---

[66] For a general summary and review of Truman's address, see Robert J. Donovan, *Conflict and Crisis: The Presidency of Harry S Truman, 1945–1948* (New York: Norton, 1977), 283–285; John T. Bernhard, *United Nations Reform: An Analysis* (UCLA, unpublished doctoral dissertation, 1950), 56–69; Acheson, *Creation*, 222–223.

[67] Haas, *United Nations*, 36.

people took up the contest with Soviet power and sustained it for fifty years because Truman and succeeding administrations framed it as a struggle between good and evil, a fight between freedom and enslavement, a showdown between American exceptionalism and Soviet aggression. The faith in the universality of American principles sustained popular support for U.S. foreign policy in the cold war just as it had produced the spirit of Yalta in 1945. Idealism was put at the service of national security, and, ultimately, it worked.

That same faith also sustained Harry Truman. While events in the eastern Mediterranean may have diminished his proclivity to follow a UN-based multilateral strategy in response to every crisis, they also encouraged him to see American foreign policy initiatives in moralist terms. He told Congress in 1949: "We are following a foreign policy which is the outward expression of the democratic faith we profess. We are doing what we can to encourage free states and free peoples throughout the world,…and to strengthen democratic nations against aggression."[68] Policy became increasingly a moral crusade in which the United Nations served, depending on the nature of the Soviet challenge, as the embodiment of U.S. aspirations, the first actor, a bit player, or something to be ignored yet defended through unilateral American action. Truman was in a learning process.

To the extent that the United Nations became a diplomatic instrument for American confrontation with Stalin's Russia, it was due to a brain trust consisting of the president's closest advisers. Truman's "wise men" saw the Soviet Union as a nation with great-power interests inimical to western security and values. Ambassador Averell Harriman was not alone in his estimation of Soviet intentions. He was joined by State Department officials and policy advisers such as George Kennan, Dean Acheson, Loy Henderson, Charles Bohlen, John J. McCloy, Robert Lovett, and others[69] who all shared an abiding suspicion of Soviet policies. With each succeeding crisis they advised the president to get tough with the Soviets and to relegate the United Nations to a

---

[68] Annual Message to the Congress on the State of the Union, January 5, 1949, *PPP, 1949*, 6.

[69] For a detailed presentation of their views and their motives, see Walter Isaacson and Evan Thomas, *The Wise Men: Six Friends and the World They Made* (New York: Simon and Schuster, 1986).

supporting role in American foreign relations. For them the idealism embodied in the United Nations was a flight into fantasy.

Dean Acheson, Truman's last secretary of state, thought the Charter of the United Nations "impracticable." He wrote years afterward that the Charter's "presentation to the American people as holy writ and with the evangelical enthusiasm of a major advertising campaign seemed to me to raise popular hopes which could only lead to bitter disappointment."[70] In most non-Wilsonian terms, Acheson argued that the United Nations should have the "modest role" of a "modest aid to diplomacy." Acheson, like Henry Kissinger in a later administration, rejected the moralist perspective in foreign policy. He was an internationalist quite willing to support, for example, the Keynesian Bretton Woods liberal economic trade system because it was in U.S. interests, but unwilling to see the new world order as an extension of American life. Moralism was a "grand fallacy" that was bound to fail in the international arena. The assumption that what is reasonable and right could be determined in UN votes, or that liberal democratic procedures could be applied to international affairs was a dangerous diversion from the real interests of the United States. In Acheson's view diplomacy was an instrument of power, not morality.

President Truman was more complex than Acheson and other realists in the administration regarding the purposes of the United Nations and America's role in it. He understood the need to protect self-interest and "to work out with cool detachment a practical adjustment of our troubles with other nations as they may arise."[71] Clearly, he believed that the Soviet Union posed a mortal threat to the United States and its allies, that the USSR was obstructing U.S. interests in the United Nations, and that only the strongest show of allied unity and American power was likely to maintain a world balance favorable to the United States. Realists were heartened by presidential speeches such as one in 1948 at a Saint Patrick's Day dinner in New York City, in which Truman recognized that "the people of the United States have learned that peace will not come in response to soft words and vague promises."[72] There was, however, another side to Truman that is often obscured by the

---

[70] Acheson, *Creation*, 741.

[71] The President's Address to the American Legion, October 18, 1948, *PPP, 1948*, 816.

[72] *PPP, 1948*, 189.

American-Soviet confrontation. The president, ever the historian, saw and regularly spoke of the United Nations as a worthy successor to the League of Nations, embodying the best hope for future world peace.

As we noted earlier, Truman agonized deeply over what he believed to be the isolationist turn the country had taken following World War I. On the campaign trail in 1948 he told a crowd gathered at Boys Town in Nebraska that the nation in 1920 had shirked its "God-intended" leadership, allowing catastrophe to ensue.[73] Repeatedly during his 1948 whistle-stop tour the first item in his stump speech was the American commitment to make the United Nations a viable instrument for a peaceful world. His message to the folks in York, Pennsylvania, that June seems today a classic example of fanciful Wilsonianism. That an American audience would find it politically appealing seems to mark a truly different era than our own. He told them:

> We are trying manfully to maintain that situation in the world which will make the United Nations the means of attaining peace and of settling differences between nations without going to war. That is my one ambition. That is what I have been working for ever since I have been President.[74]

Rhetoric spoken often enough becomes reality. Truman's rhetoric was strewn with moralist goals for the United Nations, far beyond anything envisioned by his predecessor. The president understood the pitfalls of a universal international organization, but he also believed that in "a world without such machinery we would be forever doomed to the fear of destruction."[75] Having read "carefully all of Woodrow Wilson's writings on the League of Nations," Truman saw the current effort as part of a vision long held by humankind, dating back to the seventeenth century. The United Nations represented the "idea of universal morality."[76] He expressed the hope that the UN Charter "would become

---

[73] Ibid., 292.

[74] Ibid., 363.

[75] Truman, *Memoirs*, I, 271.

[76] *PPP, 1950*, 683.

the Constitution of the world, just as the Constitution of the United States is the Constitution of the 48 states."[77]

Under the "Constitution," the American methods of resolving disputes could be transposed to the world setting. Even the World Court, in Truman's view, should be given compulsory jurisdiction. The United Nations would be "a place," according to the president, "where the troubles of the world can be argued and settled in a court, just as we argued the differences between Arkansas and Missouri when they were fighting over the Arkansas river. They don't go out and shoot each other; they go into court....That is what we are trying to get the world to do but it takes time....It is the only way in the world we can have peace."[78] The only outstanding issue in this Americanization of world politics was time. The president believed it might take eighty years—much as it had taken eight decades, from 1787 to the end of the Civil War, for the Constitution to establish a single body politic—for the UN Charter to make over world affairs.[79]

The times, however, now required American leadership in the effort to "contain" communism. Unless Soviet expansionism was thwarted, the United Nations could not survive, much less achieve its founders' purposes. With each decision to use American power, Truman described it not only as an effort to blunt Stalin's avarice but also as an essential step to preserve the United Nations. The president saw the institution in proprietary terms. When the United States acted, it was to the UN's benefit; thus, power politics was being put to the purpose of ensuring the ultimate success of the United Nations.

Events in Greece brought Truman and his advisers to one mind: the Soviet Union sought nothing less than the global defeat of the United States and the principles it espoused. Iran, Turkey, the blockade of Berlin, and the solidification of communist regimes in Eastern Europe were all part of a single Moscow strategy to overwhelm the West. The administration's response—the creation of the North Atlantic Treaty Organization and other worldwide military alliances, the Berlin airlift, the provision of aid to beleaguered allies, and the overwhelming decision to achieve a nuclear deterrent capability—rested on a geopolitical internationalism not seen in Washington since Theodore

---

[77] *PPP, 1948,* 363.

[78] Ibid., 342.

[79] Ibid.

Roosevelt occupied the White House. Truman made little use of UN mechanisms[80] in the implementation of these policies; the UN served as no more than a venue for Soviet-American recriminations. At bedrock, however, Truman believed his policies served the highest aspirations of Wilsonianism and its living manifestation, the United Nations. His thesis would find its greatest test on the Korean peninsula.

Korea

> "Dean...we've got to stop the sons-of-bitches no matter what!"
>
> —*President Truman's comment to Secretary of State Acheson upon learning of the North Korean invasion of South Korea*

Saturday, June 24, 1950, had been a long day for President Truman. It had begun in Washington, then taken him to Baltimore. Before leaving for Independence, Missouri, the president had dedicated the new Baltimore-Washington Airport. It was now past 9 P.M. at Harry and Bess Truman's two-story frame house, and the president was taking a call from his secretary of state, Dean Acheson. The news was not good. North Korean forces had invaded the south, with the likely goal of overrunning the Republic of Korea (ROK) and reuniting the peninsula under the communist leader Kim Il Sung. The assault across the 38th parallel was a clear case of aggression under the UN Charter and yet another apparently Soviet-inspired challenge to American power. Appeasement would produce two losers—the United States and the United Nations—not to mention world peace. Truman decided immediately to stand and fight.

While Acheson talked with the president, Assistant Secretary of State for UN Affairs, John D. Hickerson telephoned Secretary-General Trygve Lie. Over the lonely objection of George Kennan,[81] Truman's team instinctively decided to engage the United Nations in any response the United States might take. The overwhelming American dominance in the

---

[80] An exception to this was the Berlin crisis. The administration's representative, Philip Jessup, conducted quiet diplomacy with the Soviet ambassador, Jacob Malik, in an effort to resolve the issue. See Franck, *Nation*, 31–32.

[81] Kennan thought the decision to take the matter to the United Nations a case of "fuzzy-minded idealism." See Glenn D. Paige, *The Korean Decision* (New York: Free Press, 1968), 337.

world body meant that the administration would receive broad support for action against the North Korean forces. The fortuitous absence of the Soviet delegate from the Security Council also meant that there would be no veto of UN action. The Soviets had walked out of the Council in January to protest the organization's unwillingness to seat the delegate of the new communist government in Beijing as China's official representative. The Nationalist Chinese on Taiwan continued to cast China's vote and strongly supported U.S. retaliation.

The "problem" of Korea was not a new one. The United States had put the Korean matter on the UN agenda in November 1947. It had been lingering in world affairs since the close of the Second World War. In 1945 the Allies had agreed to the establishment of a provisional democratic government, and the subsequent meeting at Potsdam had reaffirmed that decision.[82] However, in the closing days of the Pacific conflict, by common consent, Soviet forces occupied the peninsula north of the 38th parallel, while U.S. troops occupied the southern portion. As the dividing line hardened, Truman recommended a four-power trusteeship of Korea, but nothing came of the proposal. By late 1947 no progress had been made on reunifying the two halves of the ancient Korean nation.

At American urging the UN General Assembly established the Temporary Commission on Korea (UNCTOK) and scheduled nationwide elections for the spring of 1948, but only the Seoul regime in the south allowed them to go forward. Nevertheless, the United Nations certified the election results and recognized Seoul as the new government of all Korea on August 15, 1948. The United States recognized the Republic of Korea on December 12.

The Korean peninsula was not a central part of U.S. defense planning after the war. Military advisers excluded it from the defense "perimeter" they thought essential to U.S. interests in Asia. Even following the successful communist revolution in China there was no significant move to bolster the ROK against possible subversion or overthrow. The primary strategy if the Soviets or Chinese moved on Korea was to fall back to Japan and secure the American position at that

---

[82] In a meeting with Anthony Eden in 1943, President Roosevelt suggested a trusteeship for the peninsula with several great powers participating. He mused that it might take twenty to thirty years before Koreans would be ready for independence. Carl Berger, *The Korea Knot* (Philadelphia: University of Pennsylvania Press, 1964), 36–41.

point. Consequently, if the president now acted to repel the surprise invasion it would have to be on political grounds or global strategic considerations, not immediate military ones.

In his first meetings with his advisers Truman made it clear that Korea was the "Greece of the east." There was no doubt that Kim Il Sung's forces were surrogates for the Soviet Union, and, thus, had to be turned back or the worldwide balance of forces would tilt in favor of the USSR. The president also made clear his intention to undertake all retaliatory steps in the name of the United Nations. Following one senior-level meeting, he told Assistant Secretary Hickerson that the United Nations "was our idea, and in this first big test we just can't let them down."[83] The United States would be "working for" the United Nations in Korea. The fate that befell the League of Nations must not be repeated with the new world body.

The United Nations was to be kept informed of efforts to stop the North Koreans, and authorization should be sought for U.S. actions. Nonetheless, Truman proceeded to make a series of unilateral decisions—ordering resupply of the South Koreans, directing General Douglas MacArthur in Japan to provide immediate assistance, and counseling the Nationalist Chinese to remain out of the conflict—without any UN consultation. It was as if the United States and the United Nations had become one in Truman's mind. Later administrations would have to worry whether the United Nations would support U.S. actions in world crises. The lopsided U.S. majority in the world body made that concern unnecessary for President Truman. Even if the Soviets could block the Security Council's endorsement, Truman intended to act alone. In that eventuality he could argue that he was sustaining the principles of the UN Charter in the face of Russian obstructionism.

On many occasions the United States has used the United Nations for the collective legitimation of its intended policies.[84] On various occasions during the cold war, presidents from Eisenhower to Bush sought Security Council or General Assembly ratification of American actions. The Truman administration established the pattern in Korea. On

---

[83] McCullough, *Truman*, 779.

[84] For a lengthy discussion of the factors that have enhanced the perceived utility of the United Nations to U.S. policy actions, see Margaret P. Karns and Karen A. Mingst, *The United States and Multilateral Institutions: Patterns of Changing Instrumentality and Influence* (Boston: Unwin Hyman, 1990), 7–24.

the evening of June 27, the Security Council determined that there had been a "breach of the peace." For the first time in history the UN mandated action under the Charter's Chapter VII. It called on all states "to furnish such assistance to the Republic of Korea as may be necessary to repel the armed attack and to restore international peace and security in the area." The Security Council called upon members to "render every assistance to the United Nations in the execution of this resolution."[85] The secretary-general subsequently proposed a genuine joint command, but this was ignored in Washington. Instead, the administration obtained permission from the Council to appoint the commander of UN forces and to act immediately on behalf of the ROK. Truman appointed Douglas MacArthur.

Truman publicly argued that this was a UN "police action." Nevertheless, it was very much a "solo"[86] American performance. In addition to appointing MacArthur, the president ordered military forces into the battle to blunt the overwhelming assault. Secretary Acheson later admitted that many of the U.S. decisions and actions in support of pertinent UN resolutions were "in fact ordered, and possibly taken, prior to the resolution."[87] Truman directed MacArthur to launch air attacks against bases, fuel storage sites, and ammunition dumps in North Korea without UN authorization. His administration also negotiated the troop participation agreements with other countries. Twenty-two nations offered troops. Fifteen finally joined the United States "under" the UN flag. Other than with Soviet, Polish, and Nationalist Chinese officials, the State Department recorded no direct consultations between president Truman and foreign governments. There were offers of facilities and supplies from Canada, the Netherlands, New Zealand, and Australia. Truman accepted all of these offers, saying, "We may need them."[88] Following the brilliant invasion by American forces at Inchon, Truman, without consulting the United Nations, decided to push across the 38th parallel and complete the reunification of Korea. His decision was based in part on MacArthur's assessment that there was little chance that communist China would enter the war. The president downplayed the

---

[85] Robert J. Donovan, *Tumultuous Years* (New York: Norton, 1982), 196. See also *YUN, 1950*, 222–224.

[86] Secretary-General Trygve Lie's description. Franck, *Nation*, 37.

[87] Acheson, *Creation*, 408.

[88] Donovan, *Years*, 212.

decision, however, for fear of embarrassing the United Nations, which had not yet authorized the action.[89]

By the time UN forces crossed the dividing line between north and south, the Soviets had ended their boycott of the Security Council. This meant that it would now be impossible to obtain the Council's endorsement of efforts to unite the two Koreas. Stalin could use the veto to block U.S. initiatives. The administration's response to the changed circumstance was ingenious, to say the least. The United States pushed through the General Assembly the "Uniting for Peace" Resolution, which allowed the members to "discuss" threats to the peace and "recommend" UN action or response from individual states when the Security Council was deadlocked over an issue. Clearly not a procedure outlined in the Charter, the resolution provided diplomatic cover and legitimation for U.S. actions. The "Uniting for Peace" Resolution, devised by the Truman administration, would be used six years later by President Eisenhower during the Suez Canal crisis.

Glenn Paige writes, "Crisis tends to evoke a *dominant goal-means value complex* that persists as an explicit or implicit guide to subsequent responses."[90] He notes that in Korea the United States saw the preservation of world peace as the goal and the utilization of the UN collective security system as the means. Coming together with this goal in the cold hills of Korea was the American interest in stopping the Soviet threat to the free world. The purely American strategy outlined in NSC-68 now merged with the UN effort to maintain world peace through collective security. In Washington the administration prepared to ask Congress for a massive increase in defense spending, ballooning expenditures well beyond Truman's carefully crafted balanced-budget proposals. The fight over Korea was part of a larger struggle between freedom and dictatorship, good and evil.[91] In New York, Pusan, and Seoul the means to be used in that struggle was American leadership of

---

[89] John Toland, *In Mortal Combat: Korea, 1950–1953* (New York: Morrow, 1991), 235.

[90] Paige, *Decision*, 296.

[91] Truman noted in his diary on June 30 that he expected the Russians to take advantage of events in Korea to try to lay claim to the Black Sea and the Persian Gulf, which "Moscow has wanted since Ivan the Terrible." *Off the Record: The Private Papers of Harry S Truman*, edited by Robert H. Ferrell (New York: Harper and Row, 1980), 185.

the United Nations, so all-encompassing that U.S. unilateral action could be defined by Truman as UN action. The president no longer distinguished between the success of the United Nations as an "end" to be served and the idealist goals of the Truman Doctrine laid out in 1947.

The "American" character of the war in Korea became particularly evident as the fortunes of battle turned against MacArthur and the allied troops. The general's expectation that Mao Zedong's China would not enter the war proved wrong. With the United Nations on the verge of final victory, Chinese "volunteers" poured across the border in late October 1950 to reinforce the North Korean army. Steadily UN forces were pushed back to the 38th parallel and beyond. The Chinese intervention challenged all of the previous expectations in the White House about the likely course of the war. Truman, as usual, put it succinctly: "This is the worst situation we have had yet. We'll just have to meet it as we have met all of the rest."[92]

The Chinese attack changed everything. Public support, which had already begun to erode, now nearly collapsed. Republican Senator Robert Taft and other opponents increased their criticism of the administration's handling of the war. At the United Nations, new worries became public. Among our allies there was growing sentiment for a political settlement. Pressure to find a route out of the war heightened dramatically after a news conference on November 30 during which Truman seemed to suggest, in response to a reporter's question, that atomic weapons might be used in Korea. When asked if the use of the atomic bomb in Korea would require prior UN authorization, the president said it would not. This was a decision the military commander in the field could make.

Opposition to the possible American use of the bomb was immediate and worldwide. Responding to distress in the House of Commons, British Prime Minister Clement Atlee made a sudden trip to Washington to "confer" with Truman. The fear of a wider war gripped many national capitals, particularly in Asia. Significant criticism was leveled at Washington for its unilateral decision-making without UN involvement. Truman made it clear that the United States intended to stay and continue the fight in Korea whether others remained or not. Atlee, for his part, sought a cease-fire, particularly with China, and a negotiated

---

[92] Donovan, *Years*, 306.

settlement.[93] He was supported at the United Nations by the Indian government and several other delegations, which put forward a formal cease-fire proposal. In the end the White House took the calculated risk of supporting the resolution in the hope that the Chinese would reject it. Fortunately for Truman, they did. By January 1951 American allies were once again supportive, albeit cautiously, of U.S. policy. Nonetheless, a critical moment in our Korean policy had passed. The administration was now set on a course that would result in a determination to seek an armistice with a division of forces at the antebellum dividing line, the 38th parallel. UN policy was changing because an American president was changing his objectives.

By March 1951 the military situation had stabilized, owing to General Matthew Ridgeway's effective leadership of the Eighth Army. No longer retreating before Chinese forces, UN troops reclaimed land in the south and moved toward the 38th parallel. Washington needed to decide whether it still sought its broader goal of Korean reunification or simply the restoration of the circumstances that had existed before the North Korean invasion. In the end the second course seemed more reasonable. Acheson put it clearly:

> Despite some illusions to the contrary, United Nations and United States war aims had not included the unification of Korea by armed force against all comers, and Chinese intervention had now removed this as a practical possibility. The aim was to repulse the aggression and to bring about such a condition of stability that the large UN army could be withdrawn by stages and a line held against the North Koreans by a rearmed and competent Korean Army. The ultimate political aim—a Korea united by peaceful means—though clearly remote, should be retained.[94]

On March 21 the president approved a cease-fire draft proposal to be considered by governments with troops in Korea. Gaining their approval, the administration was ready to move forward to bring the war to a diplomatic conclusion. Only one major actor appeared to want a

---

[93] Acheson, *Creation*, 481–485; McCullough, *Truman*, 826.

[94] Acheson, *Creation*, 517.

different outcome—the UN commander in Korea, America's "Caesar," Douglas MacArthur.

Relations between Truman and his general had never been good, but MacArthur had been the obvious choice to head the military effort when the war began. His extraordinary victory at Inchon, coupled with a superb public relations operation, had made MacArthur more popular than the president, and apparently unassailable. MacArthur's public statements on military strategy and on foreign policy issues had irked the president throughout the war. They had led to a meeting between the two on the Pacific island of Wake. As the administration now moved to find a political settlement of the conflict, General MacArthur once again injected himself into the public maelstrom. In addition to his pronouncements on what should be done in Asia, MacArthur wrote to Joseph W. Martin, the Republican leader in the House of Representatives, rejecting the administration's policy in the region and calling for the use of Nationalist Chinese forces in Korea. This action was directly disobedient of orders given by Truman to have all senior military officials clear their public statements with their superiors in Washington. The president decided to remove the UN commander and replace him with General Ridgeway. Preceding that decision, there was much consultation in the offices and hallways of the White House, the Pentagon, and the State Department. No one consulted the United Nations, its secretary-general, or its membership. This was solely an American decision by a commander-in-chief faced with rank insubordination. For the administration the constitutional arrangement of civilian control of the military and the president's prerogatives were the only issues; this was not a UN decision.

Ridgeway made steady progress toward clearing the south of Chinese and North Korean troops. Crossing the 38th parallel at various points during late April 1951, the advancing troops gave the administration a final opportunity to decide whether to attempt the reunification of the peninsula yet again or to reach an armistice. In spite of a UN vote on May 18 to support a U.S.-led embargo of both mainland China and North Korea, the administration knew there was little international support for a continuation of the war. Truman decided to float the American cease-fire proposal in quiet diplomatic back channels. Interestingly, he and his advisers "unanimously" believed that pursuing a peace settlement "through the public procedures of the United Nations…would be fatal."[95]

The United Nations might be the postwar embodiment of the search for world peace, but the administration had learned that there were limits to its ability to resolve conflicts through public diplomacy. The cold war diminished the value of the processes laid out in the UN Charter for making resolutions. The use of the veto by the Soviet Union paralyzed action by the Security Council; and while the General Assembly's "Uniting for Peace" Resolution had provided a stratagem for endorsing U.S. efforts in Korea, that body was caught up in the ideological polemics of the time. Superpower confrontations were distorting expected UN procedures At the same time, the UN could be a venue for the quiet diplomacy of superpowers intent on finding a way out of a crisis. In the case of Korea the administration decided to approach the Soviet's UN Ambassador, Jacob Malik, through the skilled interlocutor George Kennan.

Kennan broached Washington's proposal to end the fighting by the establishment of an armistice line in the vicinity of the 38th parallel. He conveyed to Malik America's desire to avoid an expansion of the conflict that might lead to a direct U.S.-Soviet confrontation. Malik had had the same kind of conversation in 1948 with Philip Jessup when the United States tried to defuse the Berlin blockade. He knew his task was to carry the proposal to Moscow, which he did. Within a brief period Stalin was signaling agreement. By mid-July the two sides had begun armistice talks. The fighting had ended. The United States had fought a war on behalf of the United Nations, earning neither complete victory nor defeat.

* * *

Surprisingly, the Korean War did not appreciably change Harry Truman's view of the United Nations. He had fought the war in its name. It had provided the legitimation the United States needed to pursue its global containment of Soviet ambitions, in this case in Asia. Soviet opposition and complaints from other UN members did not seem to alter Truman's general confidence in the organization, both as an ally of American foreign policy and as the "last best hope" for humankind in

---

[95] Ibid., 531.

the search for world peace. America's ability to command a majority in the UN against the much smaller Soviet bloc reinforced Truman's sense that the United Nations could serve America's exceptionalist goals for a world built on peace and democratic principles.

Truman did learn that an American president can manipulate the United Nations, that it can be in a number of ways an effective instrument of U.S. foreign policy. Roosevelt did not live to see the new organization in that light. At best he hoped that the "Four Policemen," working in harmony, might use the United Nations to disarm threatening states and to act decisively against governments which endangered the peace. The architect's design, however, proved reasonably efficient for Truman's efforts to restrain Soviet ambitions. With the Truman Doctrine in 1947, the president outlined a unique American responsibility in the world community; with the Korean War, he demonstrated on the one hand how the United Nations might be used to carry out that responsibility, and on the other how America's role in the world was one and the same with the teleological purposes of the United Nations.

Dean Acheson may have been soured by the events of the Truman years when it came to believing that the United Nations could be much more than a modest aid to diplomacy. But President Truman never lost faith in the institution bequeathed to him by FDR. His actions reflected a desire to build upon, not change or set aside, the structure Roosevelt had conceptualized. In the process, the institution did change. It expanded its role in decolonization, arms control, and restoring the peace. It found a way, at least momentarily, around the veto through the "Uniting for Peace" Resolution. It served as a setting for critical diplomacy leading to the resolution of hot spots such as Iran and Berlin. With all its imperfections, the United Nations demonstrated a resilience that did not exist in the old League of Nations.

Truman drew optimism from all this. Just a few months before the Korean War broke out, he told Congress, "We believe that [the UN] can ultimately provide the framework of international law and morality without which mankind cannot survive."[96] In that speech he equated "international law and morality" with "the spirit in which this great Republic was founded," including a foreign policy that throws its weight

---

[96] Annual Message to the Congress on the State of the Union, January 4, 1950, *PPP, 1950*, 4.

"on the side of greater freedom and a better life for all peoples." The war itself did not diminish his enthusiasm. In his last state of the union message, he defined what he thought was the "overriding question of our time—could there be built in the world a durable structure of security, a lasting peace for all the nations, or would we drift, as after World War I, toward another terrible disaster—a disaster which this time might be the holocaust of atomic war?"[97] In answering his own question, he argued, "Our starting point...has been and remains the United Nations." Having decided not to run for another term as president, he was asked by Charles Gallagher, a citizen of Lynn, Massachusetts, what was the greatest contribution a citizen could make to his country under current conditions. The president responded, "I think the average person ought to inform himself fully as to just exactly what the United Nations stands for, what it means to world peace." After a moment's reflection, he added, "also become a local politician."[98] That was Harry Truman, the dreamer and the builder.

---

[97] Annual Message to the Congress on the State of the Union, January 7, 1953, *PPP, 1953*, 1117.

[98] *PPP, 1952*, 273.

3

The Cold Warriors

The Soviets are the real enemy and all else must be viewed against the background of that truth.
—President Eisenhower to Prime Minister Churchill
November 27, 1956

The developing Soviet-American confrontation of the late 1940s ended the hope that the United Nations could work as its founders envisioned. The world body became an arena for skirmishes in that confrontation, a place where even allies challenged U.S. actions, and only once in a while was it a setting in which quiet diplomacy might facilitate a resolution of particularly serious differences between the USSR and the United States. Beginning with the president's declaration of the Truman Doctrine in 1947 American foreign policy steadily shifted to a new road, one committed to U.S. leadership of the "free" world in the effort to halt Soviet-inspired communist expansion around the globe. The United Nations served as an instrument of American foreign policy but increasingly was seen as a minimal actor, secondary to a system of military alliances, unilateral initiatives, and strategic defense spending.

The Truman years were interesting because they marked the transition from the earlier idealized hope that universal collective security could greatly lessen the prospects of another war, to a recognition of a unique American responsibility for world peace and stability in the face of a determined enemy. In Korea, as we described in Chapter 2, the American goal of stopping Soviet expansion merged with the means of utilizing the United Nations to achieve that end. Truman could do this, however, only because the Soviets were boycotting the Security Council when the war broke out, and because the United States commanded an overwhelming majority in the General Assembly. Even under those circumstances, though, the war was conducted as an American affair, with an American commander, largely American troops, American funding, and presidential decision-making in the Oval Office. When the Soviets returned to their seats in the Security Council, the United States had to resort to a revision of UN procedures with the passage of the "Uniting for Peace" Resolution to ensure UN legitimacy for United States' actions on the Korean peninsula.

The American effort in Korea was far more a reflection of Truman's doctrine of U.S. assistance to halt Soviet aggression than it was of Roosevelt's "four policemen" keeping world peace. It is true that President Truman left office arguing that Korea had been the United Nations' first great test and that it had acquitted itself well. He could still believe that Korea demonstrated the potential worth of the world organization. Few political leaders, however, shared his conclusion on the meaning of the war. By January 1953 the cold war was evident to all, and to most American internationalists the responsibility of fighting that war, even on behalf of the principles embodied in the UN Charter, fell to the United States. For the next generation American presidents, their administrations, and the public they led depended less and less on the United Nations to keep the peace, pursued policies that were often criticized by UN majorities, and turned to the United Nations only when it was thought that the body might provide some advantage in the contest with Moscow. Dwight Eisenhower was the first in a succession of these cold war presidents who perceived a diminished role for the United Nations in the central issues of the international struggle.

If the central question for Harry Truman had been, "Can there be built in the world a durable structure for peace and security?"[1] President Eisenhower asked, "Can the Soviets be stopped short of war?" The different nature of the questions dramatically affected each president's construction of American foreign policy. More often than not, for Truman the starting point in the resolution of international challenges was the United Nations; for Eisenhower, it was U.S. initiative. While the new president pledged in his first inaugural address to make the United Nations "not merely an eloquent symbol but an effective force" for peace, his emphasis was on the "responsibility" that "destiny" had placed on the United States for leadership of the free world.[2]

Eisenhower held no animosity toward the United Nations. He had strongly endorsed its creation at the time of the San Francisco Conference, later evaluating that meeting as "hope's high point."[3] As an

---

[1] Inaugural address of Harry S Truman, January 20, 1949.

[2] Inaugural address, January 20, 1953. See Robert L. Branyan and Lawrence H. Larsen, *The Eisenhower Administration, 1953–1961: A Documentary History* (New York: Random House, 1971), 29.

[3] Dwight D. Eisenhower, *Mandate for Change, 1953–1956* (Garden City, N.Y.: Doubleday, 1963), 137.

internationalist, Eisenhower saw the institution as part of the American commitment to permanent participation in world affairs after the war. Given his service as supreme commander of the Allied forces during World War II and later as the first supreme commander of NATO, Eisenhower put a high premium on international cooperation among allied states to keep the peace. Experience, however, had proved the limitations of the United Nations in a world increasingly subjected to the east-west struggle. "The implacable purpose of the men in the Kremlin to achieve Communist domination of the world"[4] had largely destroyed the UN's ability to serve as a vehicle for constructing peace for the next generation.

Eisenhower approached the United Nations as he did most things, as a pragmatic internationalist seeking to get things accomplished. Other than his deep-seated feelings about "that damnable philosophy" of communism,[5] and his strong belief that the United States must remain heavily involved in world affairs, the president had no grand worldview in which the world organization fit neatly. There is nothing in the Eisenhower record like the explicit statements of Harry Truman on the United Nations as an international political system in the making. Instead, there is a mild Wilsonian and liberal rhetoric of support for the institution, which seems not to have affected daily decision-making in the Oval Office.[6]

A sense of duty, not aspiration, brought Eisenhower to the White House. The national turn inward worried Eisenhower, who feared a repetition of the interwar years. In one of the coincidences of history, Eisenhower personally marked his entrance into public life with his

---

[4] Eisenhower's view, Ibid.

[5] This description of communism Eisenhower made in the privacy of his own diary. See H. W. Brands, Jr., *Cold Warriors: Eisenhower's Generation and American Foreign Policy* (New York: Columbia University Press, 1988), 196–197.

[6] For evaluations of Eisenhower's outlook on world affairs and his approach to foreign policy decision-making, see Caroline Pruden, *Conditional Partners: Eisenhower, the United Nations, and the Search for a Permanent Peace* (Baton Rouge: Louisiana State University Press, 1998), 27; Brands, *Warriors,* xi; Kenneth W. Thompson, "The Strengths and Weaknesses of Eisenhower's Leadership," in Richard A. Melanson and David Mayers, eds., *Reevaluating Eisenhower: American Foreign Policy in the 1950s* (Urbana: University of Illinois Press, 1987), 28; Stephen Ambrose, *Eisenhower, the President,* Vol. 2 (New York: Simon and Schuster, 1984), 43–44.

matriculation at West Point Military Academy and his participation in 1913 as a cadet corporal in the first inaugural parade of Woodrow Wilson. He shared Wilson's belief that America must be permanently a part of world affairs. The two world wars and the unhappy turn of events between 1919 and 1939 further convinced him of Wilson's wisdom. It was in that context that Eisenhower believed President Wilson would have taken pride, as the general himself had, in the creation of the United Nations, the "lineal descendant" of the League of Nations. It was against the possibility of the United States repeating its mistakes of the 1920s and 1930s that Eisenhower fought to win the White House.

A new menace, as great as Hitler's Germany, now threatened American survival—namely Soviet communism. For the president it was nothing less than a life-and-death matter. Believing that the confrontation with Moscow was "the struggle of the ages,"[7] Eisenhower argued that only the unity of free nations led by the United States could provide a "hope for survival." In that conceptualization there was only a limited role for a world organization built on universal collective security and characterized by the regular use of the Soviet veto. Invoking the collective self-defense provisions of the Charter's Article 51, the administration pursued a series of military alliances as the most effective means of preserving the principles embodied in the UN founding.

The President, His Foreign Policy Team, and the UN

The first weeks of 1953 proved to be extraordinarily challenging for the new president. An expected armistice proved elusive in Korea, where continued fighting produced ongoing American causalities. Having promised to "go to Korea," and having met the letter of that promise with a visit to the war zone as president-elect, Eisenhower was under pressure domestically and from the allies to conclude the United Nations' effort successfully and quickly. In Europe the solidification of the iron curtain with a huge Soviet army threatening a divided Germany put a premium on American defense of the western democracies. Yet the president had promised to cut the ballooning federal deficit, and hoped to do so by putting the brakes on military spending. Contributing to military costs was the emerging strategic arms race with the Russians. Faced with a Soviet conventional military advantage, the administration

---

[7] News conference of December 2, 1953, *PPP, 1953*, 801–802.

had to decide whether to go forward with developing atomic and hydrogen weapons in order to maintain effective deterrence. In domestic politics the country was going through the wrenching experience of *McCarthyism*. Joseph McCarthy, the Republican junior senator from Wisconsin, was leading a crusade to "unmask" communists and eliminate them from sensitive government positions. He was provoking near-hysteria over the effects of supposed communist subversion in the American government. In particular, he had trained his sights on the State Department, the Defense Department, and the United Nations as "nests" of communist activity. If Eisenhower, a Republican, was going to be able to work with a Congress controlled by his own party, and also maintain his constitutional independence in foreign policy, he needed to find a way to deal with the powerful senator. Then, in March, Joseph Stalin died. No one could be sure what a change in Kremlin leadership portended.

To meet the challenge of the times, the president surrounded himself with like-minded advisers. His secretary of state was the highly experienced John Foster Dulles, the nephew of Woodrow Wilson's secretary of state, Robert Lansing. Dulles' first diplomatic assignment had been to the Hague Conference of 1907. He was one of the earliest advocates of a postwar universal organization. During World War II he chaired the Federation Council of Protestant Churches' Commission to Study the Bases of a Just and Durable Peace, which recommended in March 1943 the creation of a world government, complete with a parliament, a court, and regulatory agencies. The commission's proposals contemplated international control of all military forces and authority over many aspects of global interactions such as world trade.[8] Dulles brought a strong religious and ethical orientation to foreign affairs, which often gave him a doctrinaire and absolutist perspective on the merits of international organization and on the behavior of nation-states in international politics. [9]

---

[8] Hoopes and Brinkley, *FDR and the UN*, 56. For a full discussion of Dulles, see Pruden, *Partners*, 28–32.

[9] Dulles was not, however, rigid on all issues and in all circumstances. Particularly on disarmament issues the secretary initiated a number of proposals meant to ease the Cold War stalemate between the two sides. See Gerard C. Smith, *Disarming Diplomat* (Lanham, Md.: Madison, 1996), 35–48.

Serving as an adviser to the U.S. delegation to the San Francisco Conference in 1945, John Foster Dulles retained a Wilsonian idealism for the functionalist possibilities of the new organization. The UN Charter provided an opportunity to encourage the development of a global community, which would be responsive to the human search for international peace and prosperity. Unfortunately, the cold war that emerged following San Francisco dampened Dulles' hopes. By the time of his appointment as secretary of state he had even less expectation than Eisenhower did that the United Nations might keep the peace.[10]

Eisenhower appointed the former senator Henry Cabot Lodge as America's permanent representative to the United Nations, simultaneously raising the position to cabinet rank. Ostensibly, the cabinet-level designation demonstrated the importance Eisenhower gave the United Nations in U.S. foreign policy; but, probably more importantly, it was meant to assure Lodge of access to the president and an important role in decision-making. Lodge had encouraged General Eisenhower to get into the presidential race, and when his "candidate" remained unconvinced, Lodge led the "draft Eisenhower" effort in the Republican primaries. Strongly internationalist, Lodge believed that the UN post should be used to counter Soviet propaganda and to improve American ties to the growing nonaligned bloc of new nations in Africa and Asia. With his extraordinary speaking skills and quick intellect, Lodge became one of the most visible and credible members of the Eisenhower inner circle. Often circumventing Dulles, Ambassador Lodge went directly to the president with proposals to increase American leadership in the United Nations, particularly in regard to aid and development issues.

At the White House the president depended heavily on two advisers when it came to UN issues: Charles Douglas ("C.D.") Jackson, a former executive at *Time* magazine, whom he appointed his special assistant for

---

[10] In general, presidents seem to hold out more hope for the UN's effectiveness than their secretaries of state do. The only significant exception to this seems to be President Nixon, who shared Secretary of State Henry Kissinger's distaste for the United Nations. It may be that the political need and desire to find publicly acceptable solutions to difficult foreign challenges lead presidents to look to the United Nations more often than their chief foreign policy advisers are likely to do. Secretaries of state, after all, are toiling in the pragmatic and realist vineyards of diplomatic negotiations, and are not focused as directly on the voters and on immediate public opinion demands.

psychological warfare; and Harold Stassen, a former governor of Minnesota and presidential aspirant, whom Eisenhower appointed to several posts during his presidency, including as special assistant for disarmament matters. Both approached negotiations with the USSR and activities in the United Nations from a cold war perspective. Each advised the president to seize opportunities in the propaganda battle with the Russians. The UN General Assembly, with its pro-American voting majority, could be counted on for anticommunist resolutions. Their advice to the president reinforced Ambassador Lodge's efforts to use the organization as a publicity platform from which the administration could reach the world's media. Lodge's strategy was to answer every Soviet allegation immediately, thus taking the public relations initiative away from the Kremlin.[11]

If the United Nations was to be used in the struggle with the Soviet Union, or even to be preserved as a beacon of hope for better times, it was critical that public support for the organization be maintained. Under the withering attack of Senator McCarthy and other important Republican leaders, such as senators William F. Knowland and Robert Taft, the United Nations for the first time began to lose its luster in American public opinion. McCarthy, beginning in 1949 with the trial of Alger Hiss, focused attention not only on U.S. diplomats at UN headquarters in New York City, but more importantly on Americans serving in the UN's Secretariat. He charged that the UN establishment had become a haven for spies and saboteurs. Moreover, there was fear among isolationists that the world organization might violate U.S. sovereignty by intruding in its domestic affairs. Senator John W. Bricker introduced a constitutional amendment, which found broad support, limiting the authority of treaties to override existing federal and state laws without specific congressional authorization. Aimed directly at restricting the potential effect of UN resolutions and conventions, the Bricker Amendment seemed sure of passage in the first days of the Eisenhower administration, an outcome the president opposed.

Eisenhower, Dulles, and Lodge believed that only by assuring the Congress and the people that the administration was vigilant about communist infiltration of the United Nations, and about undue UN influence on U.S. domestic affairs, could the president hope to use the organization as an element of his foreign policy strategy. The first

---

[11] Brands, *Warriors*, 167.

casualty was American endorsement of the UN Human Rights covenants. Fearful of giving Bricker Amendment supporters an issue, Eisenhower decided to foreclose any contention that the Covenants might give the United Nations authority to change American laws.

The more serious challenge of McCarthyism was met with a new loyalty and security check program developed by Lodge and pressed on the world body in New York.[12] Secretary-General Trygve Lie had already felt the pressure of the American government on the "communist issue" during the last months of the Truman administration. He had repeatedly asked Washington for materials on Secretariat employees who were American nationals. It was his policy to dismiss any U.S. employee who was a member of the American Communist Party, given its designation as a "subversive" organization in the UN's host country.[13] By the summer of 1952 the State Department was providing the secretary-general with discreet evaluations of American employees, often judging them "questionable" and urging their termination.

Trygve Lie later wrote, "I was dismayed and horrified as I saw the American concern for security go far beyond the reasonable precautions against subversion that any government should take."[14] Whatever his dismay and reservations, however, Lie implicitly endorsed the American hunt for communists by dismissing several employees who had come under attack. Eighteen American members of the Secretariat exercised their Fifth Amendment constitutional right against self-incrimination by refusing to testify before the Senate's Internal Security Subcommittee in October 1952. The secretary-general fired them on the ground that their action was a violation of Article 1.4 of the staff regulations, which required Secretariat members to act in a manner "befitting their status as international civil servants."[15] Lie did not believe the United Nations or its secretary-general should "fight the battle which is properly to be left to the American liberal tradition," and so he made the concessions he

---

[12] The administration made much of its intention to focus on "security" rather than "loyalty" in its various programs to root out personnel in the bureaucracy who might be "risks" to national security. However, as things worked out at the United Nations, there was little effort to define the difference.

[13] Trygve Lie, *In the Cause of Peace* (New York: Macmillan, 1954), 388.

[14] Ibid., 391.

[15] Quoted Ibid., 396.

considered necessary to appease political and popular opinion in the United States.

Within two weeks of Eisenhower's inauguration the administration pressured Lie to allow the Federal Bureau of Investigation to fingerprint and question all American employees of the United Nations. That process went on until November 1953, when the new secretary-general, Dag Hammarskjöld, ordered the FBI to end it. In the interim, the administration, wishing to demonstrate to conservative congressional republicans Eisenhower's and Dulles' commitment to removing possible communist sympathizers, established the International Organizations Employees Loyalty Board to investigate all U.S. employees at the United Nations. Information gathered was then forwarded to Hammarskjöld with the expectation that the secretary-general would terminate any security risks. Over 4,000 cases were reviewed by the board,[16] including an investigation of the much-respected Ralph Bunche. His particular file was personally reviewed by the president and the secretary of state. In addition to searching out possible American subversives, the administration also limited the movement of foreign diplomats who might conduct spying activities while in the United States. The administration prohibited movement of eastern bloc representatives more than twenty-five miles beyond New York.

It was an extraordinary display of American influence in the United Nations that a national government could intrude on the internal independence and integrity of the Secretariat. There was nothing in the Charter that gave any member of the body the authority to impose its domestic loyalty programs on UN personnel, who were legally identified as "international" civil servants. That neither Lie nor Hammarskjöld felt he could ignore U.S. demands was clear evidence of the overwhelming political and financial importance the United States had in the life of the world organization.

All this, however, was but prologue. Closing the gap between isolationist and internationalist congressional Republicans and blunting McCarthyite criticism were preliminary steps in developing a general cold war foreign policy. Particularly upon receiving the news of Stalin's death in March 1953, Eisenhower thought it important to articulate a grand design for American foreign policy, which would give the country and the world a hope for permanent peace. Less than a week after the

---

[16] Pruden, *Partners*, 52.

Russian leader's death, the president convened the National Security Council (NSC) to discuss possible American initiatives to thaw the cold war. Eisenhower rejected the idea of a summit with the new Kremlin leadership, but he put under active consideration the possibility of a meeting of the western powers. More important, he told the NSC he wanted to deliver a speech that would capture world interest in the search for peace. Written largely by C.D. Jackson and Walt Rostow,[17] the speech was first intended to be given to the American people or to the General Assembly. Another possibility was to deliver it to the Pan American Union. Whatever the setting, the president decided to define early in his term his approach to American-Soviet relations and world affairs.

Often presidential statements are viewed as politically motivated appeals to public opinion, rarely expressing the true intent of their authors. At worst, they are seen as Machiavellian in that their purpose is to deceive, manipulate, or attract the public. For the presidents who make them, however, these pronouncements regularly provide a framework for understanding and explaining future events and actions. Presidents, precisely because their political fortunes depend on public support, create the parameters for future policies by the commitments they "make to the voters." Thus, what they say tends to carry a sense of importance to themselves that many of their listeners may miss. Eisenhower often referred to past speeches he had made, some of them seven years in the past, as the authority for his policy decisions. The nature of public life in America forces our political leaders to "think out loud." Thus, to maintain internal consistency they must at least rationalize later statements and actions in terms of their past pronouncements. Roosevelt spoke of "four policemen" keeping the peace, and Truman described the UN Charter as a "constitution" for the world. Presidents after Eisenhower also created conceptual paradigms out of the words and phrases they employed in public. These mileposts provide the symbols and ideas through which presidents make sense of the outside world.

---

[17] For a description of the various drafts written for Eisenhower's approval see W. W. Rostow, *Europe After Stalin* (Austin: University of Texas Press, 1982). Eisenhower considered presidential addresses very important. Not only did they make clear a particular president's policies; they also had the ability to motivate national populations and their leaders to action. The speech Eisenhower contemplated making was meant to be of that genre.

The "Eisenhower Model"

On April 16, 1953, the president addressed the American Society of Newspaper Editors, delivering what became known as his "Chance for Peace" speech. In it he outlined the essential ingredients of his thinking about contemporary international affairs and America's foreign policy. Implicit in his argument was a design for American use of the United Nations in the cold war era. The "Eisenhower model" for employing the world organization as an element in the overall U.S. strategic defense of the "free" world served as the basic template for U.S.-UN relations not only during his tenure, but also during that of his immediate successors, presidents Kennedy and Johnson.

Eisenhower argued that the period since 1945 had seen the hopes for peace "waver, grow dim, and almost die."[18] The sense of common purpose that permeated the creation of the United Nations had "lasted an instant and perished." In its place there had been eight years of "fear and force" during which the free world had been driven to create a military behemoth to block the aggressive aspirations of Soviet leaders. Eisenhower could see only two possible outcomes emerging from this scenario: at worst, atomic war; at best, "a life of perpetual fear and tension, a burden of arms draining the wealth and the labor of all peoples."[19] The only opportunity to change the course of events, in his view, resided with the leadership in Moscow. Concrete signs of goodwill were needed from the Soviets before sufficient trust could be established between east and west to allow for progress on the issues separating the two sides. Deeds, not words, were required of the new Soviet leadership. Specifically, Eisenhower indicated that he would take as evidence of Russian seriousness helpful Soviet efforts to achieve an armistice in Korea, the signing of an Austrian treaty (which had not been concluded since the war ended), progress on the reunification of Germany, repatriation of prisoners of war still being held in the USSR, and an end to communist attacks on French forces in Indochina.[20] Instead of recrimination, the president outlined a litmus test of Soviet

---

[18] Address "The Chance for Peace" delivered before the American Society of Newspaper Editors, April 16, 1953, *PPP, 1953,* 179.

[19] Ibid., 182. These options led Eisenhower to the assessment that either future was "not a life at all, in any true sense."

[20] Ibid., 184.

trustworthiness in the effort to jointly solidify peace for the next generation.

The president then proposed to the newspaper editors that if a new era in Soviet responsibility was forthcoming, the two superpowers could move forward on the most pressing issue of world affairs, the reduction of armaments. The threat of the nuclear arms race and the potential for use of modern weapons of mass destruction profoundly worried Eisenhower throughout his presidency. The arms race was also proving to be extraordinarily expensive to an administration that sought a "new look" in defense policy, emphasizing decreased spending in order to close the budget deficit left by the previous administration. Yet economy achieved in conventional military areas forced the government to depend even more heavily on the nuclear arsenal as the first line of deterrence against Soviet aggression. Secretary Dulles would later define this dependence as a policy of "massive retaliation." However, the threat to respond to Soviet military challenges with an all-out nuclear attack on the Russian homeland only raised the fears of an atomic Armageddon. The problem for the administration was finding a way to defend American national interests without pushing the arms race to a point of confrontation and disaster. The solution, according to Eisenhower, was to achieve a change in Soviet behavior that would allow some movement toward disarmament, at least of the most horrific weapons.

The reduction of arms should be accomplished "under the United Nations" and was to include a "practical system of inspection." Calling it the "next great work," Eisenhower proposed that arms limitation should include the bilateral reduction of forces, the prohibition of certain types of weapons, and a percentage limitation on total production dedicated to military purposes. By moving in this direction the USSR and the United States, working through the United Nations, could remove humanity from the "cross of iron" on which it found itself. Equally important, slowing the arms race would free up resources for more important tasks. "Every gun that is made, every warship launched, every rocket fired signifies in the final sense, a theft from those who hunger and are not fed, those who are cold and are not clothed."[21]

As the third piece of his general view of world affairs, Eisenhower proposed that money saved through arms reduction should be put to the task of meeting human needs in the poorest parts of the globe. He

---

[21] Ibid.

suggested the establishment of a UN fund from the military savings for aid, reconstruction, and development in the new states emerging from colonialism. The fund would finance roads, schools, hospitals, housing, and food and health programs. He concluded that through these actions the world could "make of the United Nations an institution that can effectively guard the peace and security of all peoples."[22]

In the president's speech was the essence of the "Eisenhower model" for dealing with the Soviet threat and incorporating the United Nations in the general design of American foreign policy. It had three parts. First, the confrontation with the Soviet Union infected everything, and must be dealt with directly by the United States. Eisenhower had forsaken the possibility of collective security with the other superpower. What was needed now was a change in attitude and policy in the Kremlin. There was no fundamental role for the United Nations in the settlement of strategic issues between the superpowers. Yet those issues must be the central concern of American cold war policy. Second, if trust could be established between Washington and Moscow, disarmament might be pursued under the aegis of the UN. The United Nations could not serve as the prime actor in arms control—the issues were too critical to the very survival of the nuclear powers. However, its institutions and structure might provide the venue, and legitimacy, for Soviet-American disarmament agreements. Finally, the United States looked to the United Nations as the central institution for the effective distribution of the expected savings from disarmament. The president highlighted the unique economic crisis in the so-called "third world," and he urged UN leadership in solving that problem, using American and Russian funds.

The approach outlined in his "Chance for Peace" speech remained Eisenhower's model for U.S. policy toward the United Nations throughout his presidency. He returned to it on several occasions.[23] One of those was the eve of his reelection in 1956. Speaking philosophically about the vision Americans held of their country's role in the world, the president told an audience in Philadelphia's Convention Hall that the United States was locked in a struggle with communism, a struggle in which Americans would never condone Soviet aggression. He reiterated

---

[22] Ibid., 187.

[23] See his Address at the Tenth Anniversary Meeting of the United Nations, San Francisco, California, *PPP, 1955*, 609. See also Eisenhower's television address to the American people, April 5, 1954.

his administration's commitment to use the United Nations as a "world forum" to denounce the USSR's policy of international subversion. He went on to condemn the arms race, saying, "Humanity must now cease preying upon itself." America wished "to lift—from the backs of men and all nations—their terrible burden of armaments." Completing his three-part approach, Eisenhower expressed "special concern for the fate and future of those 700 million people—in eighteen nations—who have won full independence since World War II."[24] He noted the vast economic need in those states and the hope that the world community could respond.

This approach of (1) seeing strategic relations with the Soviet Union as largely outside the purview of the United Nations, (2) considering disarmament to be under the auspices of the UN, but only tangentially involving it, and (3) emphasizing an American commitment to UN-directed economic and social programs in the underdeveloped world served as the framework for two decades of U.S. policy. While Eisenhower's successors brought different nuances to each aspect of his approach, they did not challenge the basic formula. The model's strength lay in the fact that it kept alive for some future date the hope of a United Nations which met the highest aspirations of its founding generation while recognizing, first, that the cold war had eliminated any possibility of achieving superpower cooperation, and second, that the United States in those circumstances had to defend its national interests both in the United Nations and outside it.

Implicit in the Eisenhower Model were a number of "rules"[25] for U.S. policy in the United Nations. First, the more important and strategic the issue, the more likely it was that the United Nations could not solve it. Given the veto power of the Soviets, the United States needed to rely on bilateral negotiations, allied support, or unilateral action when its fundamental interests were concerned. Despite Roosevelt's hope that cooperation would continue between the two sides, thus making the United Nations the center of global coordination among the great

---

[24] Address in Convention Hall, Philadelphia, Pennsylvania, November 1, 1956, *PPP, 1956*, 1072–1073.

[25] For a detailed discussion of some of the "rules," see Stanley Hoffmann, "Ethics and Rules of the Game Between the Superpowers," in Louis Henkin, (ed.), *Right v. Might: International Law and the Use of Force* (New York: Council on Foreign Relations, 1991), 71–93.

powers, in the depths of the cold war, the issues separating Moscow and Washington were so grave that only direct negotiation could be risked by either side. Future crises over Berlin, arms control and disarmament, Vietnam, Cuba, and the Middle East were reserved in American foreign policy for settlement or confrontation directly between the superpowers.

Second, the United Nations, at best, might serve as a venue for negotiation when direct confrontation loomed. However, it was more likely that behind-the-scenes contact with the Kremlin would produce better results.

Third, the United Nations worked best as an arena for promoting the nation's position on issues. Thus, the General Assembly, with its plenary membership, increasingly became a more important body than the Security Council. The Assembly provided a platform for propaganda and visionary statements.

Fourth, "peripheral" issues could be left to the world body. These might include secondary or minor disarmament proposals, as well as third world development. During the cold war, when strategic interests seemed remote, the United States was far more willing to allow multilateral solutions, sometimes with little U.S. leadership, to carry the day. The moment, however, any of those issues took on heightened meaning in the Soviet-American contest, the United Nations could no longer be allowed to dispose of them through its normal parliamentary procedures. Often they became matters to be resolved by private diplomacy, the outcomes being ratified later by UN action.

Superpower Confrontation and the United Nations, 1953–1969

Korea was the pressing international concern for the new administration in 1953. It should be remembered that President Truman had achieved a commitment from UN allies to a cease-fire proposal. Cease-fire negotiations began in the summer of 1951 at Kaesong, and then resumed in the fall at the neutral site of Panmunjom. Hopes for peace were high, but fighting continued to rage while the talks went on. An armistice eluded Truman to the end of his term. He left office with the war in a bloodletting stalemate, which ominously included soldiers from communist China. Conducting the war as a UN "police action," Truman had treated the effort as essentially an American undertaking. Eisenhower intended to keep it that way and to bring it to an end on American terms.

Just three weeks after taking office, President Eisenhower met with his National Security Council to discuss strategy in Korea. He raised the possibility of using nuclear weapons to bring the conflict to a conclusion.[26] He thought it wise to convey to the enemy that failure to move toward a settlement would lead to a wider war. He also thought it important to keep deliberations and decisions about Korea secret, not divulging them to either the United Nations or close allies. Not even Secretary-General Hammarskjöld was to be briefed. In the words of one contemporary commentator, the United Nations was "left watching from the sidelines."[27] Through diplomatic channels in Asian capitals, however, the administration "discreetly" let it be known that use of nuclear weapons was under serious consideration.[28] The hope was that this threat would reach the Chinese and North Korean authorities through friendly governments. At Panmunjom the United States intended to direct the armistice negotiations without interference from either the Secretariat or allies, despite growing calls from Britain and other allies for a greater voice in the talks.[29]

The president's threat to escalate the war apparently reinforced a growing sentiment in Moscow and Beijing to seek a settlement. There were increasing signs of flexibility by communist representatives at the negotiating table. Given the territorial stalemate, the most important issue standing in the way of an armistice was the repatriation of prisoners of war. Many of the North Korean prisoners were unwilling to return to the north, and President Syngman Rhee of South Korea opposed their forcible transfer. Under mounting diplomatic pressure the Eisenhower administration lent its support to an Indian resolution in the General Assembly, which established a neutral commission to oversee repatriation.[30] The compromise allowed the immediate return of POWs

---

[26] McGeorge Bundy, *Danger and Survival* (New York: Random House, 1988), 241.

[27] Richard N. Swift, "International Peace and Security," *1954 Annual Review of United Nations Affairs*, edited by Clyde Eagelton, Waldo Chamberlin, and Richard N. Swift (New York: Oceana, 1955), 15. Hereafter cited as *Annual Review, 1954.*

[28] Eisenhower, *Mandate*, 181.

[29] William Stueck, *The Korean War: An International History* (Princeton: Princeton University Press, 1995), 320–321.

[30] Ibid., 298–299; Pruden, *Partners*, 88. See also *YUN, 1952*, 201–202.

wanting to go home, and a process for persuading the others to do so as well. The final disposition of remaining prisoners was left to a future international conference. The resolution of the POW issue in the late spring, helped by a Soviet peace initiative following Stalin's death, made movement toward an armistice swift, an agreement being reached on July 27, 1953. Only a last-minute maneuver by South Korea's president threatened to scuttle the negotiations. On June 18 he released more than 27,000 prisoners of war, prompting the communists to walk out of the talks. It took a stern rebuke from President Eisenhower, and the mission of the president's personal emissary, not a UN delegation or the secretary-general, to rein in President Rhee and get the negotiations back on track. Eisenhower, in the end, achieved an armistice in what had become an American-communist confrontation with only a nodding glance to the United Nations' supposed authority. The armistice agreement called for an international conference to resolve the matter of Korean unification, which was duly endorsed by the General Assembly. The United States, however, intended such a conference to be tightly controlled and to include only the parties to the conflict. When it finally met in 1954, the conference also took up the matter of the French-communist conflict in Indochina, which we discuss below.

Both of President Eisenhower's terms were characterized by the kind of secondhand recognition of the United Nations seen in the Korean conflict. If the organization could be supportive of U.S. efforts to blunt Soviet and communist Chinese expansionism, then the administration was willing to use it. The first consideration, however, was given to unilateral or allied responses to apparent provocations. That approach reflected not only Eisenhower's and Dulles' thinking but also the attitudes of conservative Republicans in Congress. In fact, the president's strategy was more moderate than some on Capitol Hill thought wise; they favored an end to U.S. financing of the UN, and even American withdrawal.

Two flashpoints in the cold war to which Eisenhower applied the same strategy were Indochina and Guatemala. In Indochina, the French Fourth Republic sought to reimpose its old colonial control after the Second World War. In so doing, it became bogged down in a war with Vietnamese nationalist and communist forces dedicated to liberation. It was a war which the French government could not afford and which it was steadily losing. It was the "communist" character of the forces arrayed against France that attracted Eisenhower's attention. While the

United States was opposed to the continuing colonialism of its European allies, the threat of a communist victory overrode other considerations. Any thought of turning the matter over to the United Nations was also rejected because of French concern that it might bring about UN resolutions condemning all French colonial policies.

The administration initially bankrolled the French effort, covering about 75 percent of the war costs.[31] At the same time it urged Paris to make clear its intent to grant independence in the near future—something France had no intention of doing. In the spring of 1954, however, the situation became perilous. Vietminh forces had surrounded the bulk of French defenders at Dienbienphu. Eisenhower and his advisers understood that if Dienbienphu fell, all French pretensions to maintaining control in the region would disappear. The French government asked for massive American assistance to stave off defeat.

Eisenhower's advisers told him it would take at minimum extensive bombing, possibly including tactical nuclear weapons, and at maximum a large U.S. ground force to turn the tide. He believed that neither option would be reasonable unless several preconditions were met. First, there must be "a legal right under international law,"[32] represented by a request from the French with support from local governments in the region. Second, there would have to be "a favorable climate of Free World opinion," which in Eisenhower's view could happen only if the United Nations or the Associated States of the French Union in Indochina asked for American intervention. Finally, there would have to be "favorable action by Congress," which could be forthcoming only if American public opinion strongly supported action. Anything short of these conditions was likely to tar American military intervention as "a brutal example of imperialism."[33] None of these prerequisites was present in the environment of 1954. In the wake of Korea there was no support for another Asian war, nor was the world community likely to endorse continuing French control. Thus, the administration had to allow a French defeat.

---

[31] Ambrose, *Eisenhower*, 175. The administration also provided several bombers and the personnel to operate them.

[32] Eisenhower, *Mandate*, 340.

[33] Ibid.

However, defeat for France could not become a victory for communist forces. Such an outcome could lead to "falling dominoes" throughout south and Southeast Asia. The president believed the French were going to have to cede the fight to an international coalition led by the United States. He did not consider seriously the possibility of a UN effort in the region. He wrote to Winston Churchill, "I suppose that the United Nations should somewhere be recognized, but I am not confident that, given the Soviet veto, it could act with needed speed and vigor."[34] In place of a UN force, the president proposed a regional coalition similar to NATO, which could bring together nations with a vital concern in stopping communist expansion. The Philippines, Thailand, Australia, Laos, Cambodia, Vietnam, and New Zealand were Eisenhower's prime candidates for membership.[35] America would not go it alone, nor would it turn over the matter to the United Nations. Instead, the administration launched a diplomatic effort, which culminated in September 1954 in the signing of the Southeast Asia Collective Defense Treaty and the formation of a new military regional alliance, SEATO.

Prior to the creation of a new alliance, however, the Eisenhower-Dulles team had to navigate the shoals and eddies of a Geneva conference on "Far Eastern questions," which began in April 1954. Proposed by the Soviet Union during a foreign ministers' meeting in Berlin, the conference was supported by the United States' allies as a possible way out of the Korean and Indochinese difficulties. Circumventing the United Nations machinery, the United States, Great Britain, the Soviet Union, France, and the People's Republic of China met on April 26, as Dienbienphu succumbed to communist forces. In July, all of the parties with the exception of the United States signed a "Final Declaration" and armistice agreement covering Indochina, extricating France from the area. While the United States did not sign the final documents, it declared that it would not try to undermine them. Rather, the administration now went to work constructing its new coalition to defend the region against communism, unfettered by the possible charge of supporting colonialism.

---

[34] *The Churchill-Eisenhower Correspondence, 1953–1955*, edited by Peter G. Boyle (Chapel Hill: University of North Carolina Press, 1990), 137.

[35] David L. Anderson, *Trapped by Success* (New York: Columbia University Press, 1991), 33–35.

The president often said that he thought the principle of collective security was the best way of providing peace and defense in the postwar era. He also willingly admitted that the United Nations was the living symbol of universal collective security. Unfortunately, the Soviet veto made impossible the success of the system. "Under the present conditions," he argued, the best collective security substitute was a series of military alliances. No one at the White House or on Capitol Hill wanted to repeat the Korean experience with another UN war in Asia or elsewhere. Expanding on the Truman strategy that had led to NATO, and giving a global meaning to George Kennan's proposed "containment" of the Soviet Union, the administration developed regional military alliances with forty-two states by 1956. Citing Article 51, which allowed for collective self-defense, Eisenhower argued that these alliances represented "the best and most effective means of preserving world order within the framework of the United Nations Charter."[36] They were, in fact, an alternative to the UN system.

Where a coalition of partners could not be assembled to confront the communist challenge, Eisenhower was ready to act unilaterally. This he did in Guatemala in 1954. Four years earlier Colonel Jacobo Arbenz Guzman had been elected president of Guatemala. His domestic policies of broad economic and social reform had attracted the attention of administration officials. His nationalization of large portions of the United Fruit Company's holdings raised concerns about the introduction of socialist and communist practices. Dr. Milton Eisenhower, following a visit to the region, reported to his brother that the Arbenz government was becoming a channel for communist influence in Central America. There is little doubt that both the president and Secretary of State Dulles believed Arbenz was an extension of Soviet intrigue into the Western Hemisphere.

When the Swedish ship *Alfhem* docked in Guatemala on May 15, 1954, carrying weapons for Arbenz's expanding armed forces, Dulles called the action a violation of the Monroe Doctrine. The president decided to employ the Central Intelligence Agency (CIA) to subvert the regime, largely by funneling weapons to anti-Arbenz rebels. Led by Castillo Armas, the rebels carried out cross-border raids from Honduras and Nicaragua in June. "Operation Pbsuccess,"[37] as it was dubbed by the

---

[36] Statement by the President, June 7, 1956, *PPP, 1956,* 556.

[37] Ambrose, *Eisenhower,* 192–195.

administration, even used American pilots to bomb fuel depots and to strafe several cities in the country. On the 19th Guatemala City itself was machine-gunned by attacking planes. Foreshadowing President Kennedy's quarantine of Cuba during the 1962 Missile Crisis, Eisenhower imposed a naval blockade to end any possibility of Soviet military shipments to Arbenz.

All these actions were taken in lieu of putting the matter before the United Nations or the Organization of American States (OAS). They were also pursued in the face of growing protests from America's allies. London and Paris strongly objected to a naval blockade during peacetime and initially encouraged a Guatemalan appeal to the Security Council. Eisenhower was incensed by European criticism that his actions were in direct violation of the United States' obligations under the Charter. He told advisers to pass the word that he expected support in return for American endorsement of French and British actions in Indochina and the Middle East.

President Arbenz requested a meeting of the UN Security Council to take up Guatemala's complaint against its neighbors and the United States. Guatemala cited Articles 34 and 35,[38] which allowed states to bring up disputes or situations that might lead to "international frictions"; and Article 39, which gave the Council the authority to discuss threats to the peace. Secretary-General Hammarskjöld supported the Guatemalan request, arguing that the Council had jurisdiction in the first instance and should take up the matter. This was important because the U.S. permanent representative, Henry Cabot Lodge, argued that the issue was wholly an internal matter for the Guatemalan people, and that the first body which should consider the complaint was the OAS. The question of putting Guatemala on the agenda came to a vote on June 25. By placing inordinate pressure on its allies the United States managed to defeat a Soviet resolution to that effect. Within a week the Arbenz government collapsed and was replaced with a friendly military dictatorship. Eisenhower had ignored the United Nations in this "fight with international communism," and he took great pride in having defended the Western Hemisphere. It was not the first time the president had forsaken UN procedures for dealing with apparent communist

---

[38] *Annual Review*, 1954, 25.

threats to U.S. interests and world peace,[39] but it was the most flagrant. In Korea, for example, the facade of a joint UN effort was always maintained, and authorizing resolutions were secured. In the Guatemalan case, the United Nations proved to be an irritant complicating U.S. foreign policy.

If America's two most important allies, Great Britain and France, wanted the United States to bring the United Nations into the Guatemalan affair, they decidedly did not wish the UN to be involved in the Middle East or North Africa, where their colonial and imperial interests were deeply engaged. This attitude created a dilemma for Eisenhower, who needed European support for NATO and yet believed that the day of empire had passed. Furthermore, it had been U.S. policy to support UN efforts to establish peace in the region nearly since the organization's founding. If the United Nations could manage the immense transitional forces under way in the area, then a direct American commitment could be avoided.

The focal point of world attention from the beginning was Palestine, and then rather quickly the politics of the Arab frontline states surrounding the new state of Israel. The British government announced in 1947 its intention to withdraw from its old League of Nations mandate responsibilities in Palestine and to turn the problems of the area over to the fledgling United Nations. The central problem was the conflict between two peoples for one land, the struggle between the indigenous Palestinian Arabs and the Zionist Jews who had been settling in the region since the late nineteenth century. Waves of Jewish immigrants poured into Palestine in the first decades of the twentieth century and were further encouraged by a British policy statement in 1917 (the Balfour Declaration) committing the United Kingdom to the eventual creation of a Zionist state in the mandate. The UN solution was the partition of Palestine into Jewish and Arab states with Jerusalem under international administration. The UN Special Commission on Palestine (UNSCOP) was created to bring about the desired result. President

---

[39] A year earlier, in Iran, Eisenhower and Dulles had already demonstrated a willingness to act without concern for UN involvement. In 1953 a CIA operation was undertaken to topple the "communist" prime minister Mohammed Mossadegh, and to secure power for the young shah, Reza Pahlavi. In this case, however, there was strong support from the British, who wanted to maintain their influence over Iranian oil policy. Also, the shah's government had no need or wish to bring the matter to the UN's attention.

Truman endorsed partition and worked hard to persuade several delegations at the United Nations to vote for the resolution.[40] As tensions led to open warfare in the spring of 1948, Truman remained steadfast in his commitment to a new Jewish state; his government became the first to recognize the new nation on May 14. The United States, however, depended on the machinery of the United Nations to work out the problems among the parties in the area.

Israel immediately found itself at war with its Arab neighbors, all of whom rejected the UN partition plan as theft. By the time the fighting ended, Israeli forces were in control of nearly all of Palestine, with the exceptions of East Jerusalem, the West Bank of the Jordan, parts of the Golan Heights, and the Gaza Strip. Huge flows of Palestinian refugees were created by the war, leading to the establishment of refugee camps in surrounding Arab states. UN relief agencies provided basic assistance, but it was the Arab coalition that felt the political brunt of the Palestinians' plight. Anti-Israeli policies became a staple of Arab foreign policy.

The uneasy peace following the 1948 war lasted until 1956. By the time Eisenhower entered office, the regional opposition to Israel was largely spearheaded by Egypt and its nationalist leader, Gamal Abdel Nasser. He had come to power in 1952 with a group of army officers who had staged a coup in the name of national independence and Egyptian modernization. Nasser was not a communist, but he was highly critical of Western powers, which, in his view, had imposed imperialist domination on his country and the region in general. Much of his domestic support came from his antagonistic stand against powers such as France and Britain, which had controlled Egypt for more than one hundred years.

The most egregious symbol of European imperialism in Egypt was the Suez Canal, built by Napoleon III and still controlled by the British. Unable to obtain American assistance for significant development

---

[40] McCullough, *Truman*, 602. See *YUN, 1947–1948*, 247-257, see also the proposed map for a partitioned Palestine between pages 236 and 237.

projects,[41] Nasser first threatened, then nationalized the Suez Canal in order to secure the income from operating the waterway. Nasser's declaration on July 26, 1956 nationalizing the Canal, sent shock waves throughout the capitals of the United Kingdom, France, and Israel. Prime Minister Anthony Eden immediately convened his cabinet to discuss measures to reverse Nasser's action. Both Britain and France saw the seizure of the canal as a mortal threat to their presence not only in the Middle East but also in Asia. Egyptian control of the canal could also be a death grip on the Israeli economy, given the amount of shipping that passed through it on its way to the port of Eilat on the Gulf of Aqaba.

Nasser's action put the Eisenhower administration in a difficult position. Neither the president nor Secretary Dulles wished to oppose the basic right of sovereignty asserted by the Egyptians. The effort to develop good ties with the emerging states of Africa and Asia would be damaged by appearing to side with the old imperialist policies in the region. On the other hand, the belief that Nasser was acting on behalf of Soviet interests in the Middle East, the possible threat to Israel, and the need to maintain allied unity in Europe all counseled some solution which would keep international control over the canal. Furthermore, turning to the United Nations did not seem a viable route toward resolving the crisis. The British, in particular, were opposed to bringing the matter to New York. The increased membership from the underdeveloped world would be unlikely to support the British position. At the least, the delay for UN consideration would allow Nasser to strengthen his position in the Canal Zone and in diplomatic circles. While Harry Truman assuredly would have sought a UN resolution, Eisenhower and Dulles sought some other avenue to conclude the growing crisis.

The United States proposed an international conference of the involved parties. It also warned London and Paris against using force to

---

[41] In particular, Nasser sought American aid to build the High Dam at Aswân on the Nile. Secretary of State Dulles, offended by the antiwestern tilt of the regime, persuaded Eisenhower to deny the request. Nasser turned to the Soviet Union for assistance, which Chairman Nikita Khrushchev was more than willing to give. Cooperation with the eastern bloc expanded in 1954 and 1955, including a sale of military hardware to the Egyptians by way of Czechoslovakia. These actions further raised suspicions in Washington about Nasser's trustworthiness, and concern that Soviet expansion in the region would threaten American interests.

wrest control from the Egyptians. In this two-step approach it hoped to contain the crisis while finding a solution. Only as a last resort would Eisenhower consider asking the United Nations to act.[42] The key for the president was finding a formula to keep the canal open to the ships of all nations. In late August the London Conference convened, with Egypt boycotting the meeting. Shepherded by Dulles, the conference promulgated an "Eighteen-Nation Proposal" for an international management organization to run the canal while recognizing Egyptian sovereignty. When Nasser rejected the proposal, Dulles organized a second London meeting in September. Out of it came the idea of a voluntary "Users' Association" to manage the canal. In many ways the administration was playing for time and trying to find a solution that neither employed force nor submerged the issue in UN politics.

Despite Dulles' best efforts the British and French governments brought the issue to the Security Council on September 23. Their submission was largely disingenuous; they were hoping only to demonstrate that they had tried every peaceful avenue before using force. The Egyptians responded with a request of their own that the Council take up the "threat to the peace" posed by London and Paris. The allies' decision to go to the United Nations was made without informing the White House.[43] Eisenhower understood it as a pretext for military action. Nevertheless, now that the matter was before the Council the president advised the allies to find a diplomatic compromise. Hammarskjöld, who had been rebuffed by the administration in past weeks when he pressed for UN consideration, now tried to develop a broadly acceptable resolution. The Security Council for its part met regularly on the issue well into October.[44] In private, Hammarskjöld was able to reach consensus on six principles meant to govern future negotiations. They included a recognition of Egypt's sovereignty over the Canal, the country's right to use income from canal operations, a role for a Users' Association in the waterway's operation, free and open

---

[42] Dwight David Eisenhower, *Waging Peace* (New York: Doubleday, 1965), 35–40.

[43] Ibid., 52.

[44] For a full discussion of the diplomatic efforts at the United Nations see Sydney D. Bailey, *Four Arab-Israeli Wars and the Peace Process* (London: Macmillan, 1990), 126–131.

access for all shipping, and the use of arbitration to resolve differences.[45] Eisenhower believed the secretary-general's diplomacy had paid off. In a national television broadcast the president asked Americans for a "great prayer of thanksgiving" because "a very great crisis [has been put] behind us."[46] Hammarskjöld's principles, however, did not convince Britain or France that Nasser could be trusted or that they would continue to have a major influence over canal operations. Clear signs were emerging of British, French, and Israeli preparations for war. Dulles warned all parties that military intervention would be the worst of all options.

On October 24 the three governments signed a secret document that laid out plans for the war. According to the agreement, Israel was committed to attack Egypt on October 29. The British and the French would then call upon both parties to put in place a cease-fire and withdraw at least ten miles from the canal. If this was rejected by Egypt, then the European military forces would attack Egypt, occupying the canal. On the appointed date Israel launched Operation Kadesh, setting in motion the agreed steps that led to the seizure of the canal.

Eisenhower was incensed by this turn of events. He ordered an immediate appeal to the Security Council. He also cabled Anthony Eden in London, expressing his concerns. His highest priority was ensuring that there would be no allied intervention which might expand the conflict. If Britain and France acted, Egypt might request Soviet help. If that happened, he wrote, "the Mid East [sic] fat would really be in the fire."[47] At the United Nations, the United States proposed a cease-fire resolution but was met with a recitation of the British ultimatums to the parties to withdraw from the canal. The United Kingdom cast its first veto in the history of the United Nations by voting against the American draft.

On October 31 Britain and France made good on their commitment to Israel and occupied the canal zone. The second Middle East war was under way owing to what Dulles called the "grave error" of America's allies. Using the "Uniting for Peace" Resolution, first conceived by the

---

[45] William R. Kintner, "The United Nations Record of Handling Major Disputes," in *The United States and the United Nations*, edited by Franz B. Gross (Norman: University of Oklahoma Press, 1964), 99.

[46] "The People Ask the President," October 12, 1956, *PPP, 1956*, 903.

[47] Eisenhower, *Waging Peace*, 679.

Truman administration as a way to get around a Soviet veto on Korean operations, Yugoslavia and the USSR now called for an emergency session of the General Assembly. The administration voted for the motion, joining all other Council members with the exception of Britain and France.

Secretary Dulles attended the General Assembly meeting on November 1. He accused the Israelis of violating the 1949 Armistice Agreements, and he called for an end to hostilities, the withdrawal of foreign forces, and the peaceful operation of the canal.[48] He submitted a draft resolution along these lines, which quickly passed.[49] Passing resolutions, however, could not get America's allies out of the canal or Israel out of the Sinai. Thus the administration was pleased by a Canadian proposal to replace foreign forces along the canal with a UN force. On the fourth, the Assembly approved Resolution 998 (ES-1) calling upon the secretary-general to submit within forty-eight hours a plan "for the setting up, with the consent of the nations concerned, of an emergency international United Nations force (later known as UNEF) to secure and supervise the cessation of hostilities." It was decided that none of the permanent five should provide personnel for the new operation. The intent of the operation was to place a neutral force between the combatants and to monitor the cease-fire. No plan was contemplated for active military movements by UNEF against any of the parties. Since the troops would be on Egyptian soil, it was understood that they could take up positions only upon the invitation of the host country. The need to move quickly with the implacement of UNEF was made clear when the USSR suddenly proposed on November 5 that it, the United States, and other members of the United Nations give military assistance to Egypt if no cease-fire was reached within twelve hours. The Eisenhower administration's worst fears seemed to be coming true: the Soviets might act unilaterally in the Middle East. Thus was born on November 5, 1956, the United Nations' first peacekeeping operation.[50] Subsequent resolutions placed the force under the secretary-general's authority and provided for the financing of the project. The basic outline of all future UN peacekeeping efforts during the cold war was established in the arrangement made for UNEF. The UN effort,

---

[48] Pruden, *Partners*, 241.

[49] GA Resolution 997, November 2, 1956, *YUN, 1956*, 35.

[50] Resolutions 998 and 1000, Ibid., 36–37.

combined with pressure from the United States, led to a British and French announcement on December 3 that they would withdraw, and a similar Israeli announcement on March 1, 1957.

The Suez crisis entangled two American concerns: its relations with the new states of the "third world" and the overarching threat of Soviet expansionism. The crisis also demonstrated how, in the nuclear age, a conflict in an area not perceived to be central to U.S. interests might lead to a more general war involving the most deadly weapons in the superpowers' arsenals. This possibility of a Soviet-American confrontation over the Middle East grew daily in Eisenhower's evaluation of events in Egypt. In the fall of 1956 it appeared that Soviet communism was on the march, extending its influence and its grip over large sections of the globe. The British-French-Israeli action had, in Eisenhower's view, given the Kremlin an opening—an opening that it quickly took—to extend its hold on Egypt and the Arab world. How to deal with the Soviet challenge was of paramount concern. In that regard the United Nations was not likely to give much relief.

The Suez crisis came in the midst of what Eisenhower later called his "twenty busy days,"[51] which included not only his re-election in 1956 but also the Suez matter and unrest in the satellite nations of Eastern Europe. Taken together, the international events during those three weeks merged together for Eisenhower into a general view that the Soviets were making a new effort to consolidate their postwar gains and to extend their influence in the continuing contest with the free world. As the White House grappled with the Egyptian imbroglio, news came on October 20 of popular unrest in Poland. The election of an anti-Stalinist, Wladyslaw Gomulka, to the position of First Secretary in the ruling Polish party seemed to augur a new day for the Polish people. Soon there were demonstrations against Soviet involvement in the Polish government. Within two days the unrest had spread south to Hungary, where a reform government was put in place under Imre Nagy. Events were moving so quickly in Eastern Europe that it took nearly all of the president's time to consult with advisers on what the United States might do to encourage the democratic movement. On just one day, October 22, Eisenhower held twenty-three meetings concerning the possible collapse of the Soviet bloc.[52] Then, on October 24, just as British,

---

[51] Eisenhower, *Waging Peace*, 54.

[52] Ibid., 63.

French and Israeli leaders were signing documents agreeing to go to war in the Suez, Soviet troops moved into Budapest to quell growing Hungarian protests. Not only were the Hungarians demanding reform at home, but many were calling for American and Western defense of a new noncommunist Hungary. While the administration had no intention of military intervention, it certainly wanted to applaud the Hungarian and Polish efforts and condemn Soviet leaders for limiting the sovereignty and freedom of its neighbors.

By the end of the week the Russians announced that they would withdraw their troops from Hungary with the restoration of order. In the meantime the Nagy government indicated that it intended to withdraw from the Warsaw Pact and seek its own independent road in international affairs. After what must have been tense deliberations in the Kremlin, however, the Soviet government reversed course on November 2 and sent 200,000 personnel and 4,000 tanks into Hungary to topple the regime. The Eisenhower administration saw a clear link between events in Hungary and Suez. With the West deeply involved in the crisis with Nasser, the Soviets decided that they could act with impunity in Eastern Europe. They were right. Unless America's allies and the world community were willing to join the United States in the effort to drive the Red Army from Hungary, Eisenhower was not going to start World War III over the issue. He directed that the matter be taken to the Security Council, where the United States offered a resolution of condemnation but little else. The United Nations served in this case as a substitute for substantive action, and as an arena for earning propaganda points against America's superpower rival.

Ambassador Lodge and his Security Council colleagues found themselves holding alternating meetings on Suez and Hungary during the last week of October and the first days of November. It was as if the United Nations had become the center of world politics. The reality, however, was that events were being directed from Moscow, Washington, London, Budapest, Cairo, Tel Aviv, and Paris. The Council served more as a site for recrimination than as a body resolving crises. Dag Hammarskjöld expressed consternation that the great powers were unwilling to bring matters to the United Nations or to seek collective solutions. In the end the United Nations was used only in the aftermath of the Suez crisis to provide a face-saving exit for British, French, and Israeli forces. The establishment of a peacekeeping effort along the canal would have great implications for the future, but at the time its purposes and prospects seemed limited.

At the White House the events in the Middle East and Eastern Europe were seen as part of the larger U.S.-Soviet confrontation. The world had avoided a larger conflict, but the divide between the two powers was now greater than ever. The discrediting of British and French policy in the eastern Mediterranean meant that the United States would now have to guard against the spread of communist influence by way of the Arab states. In particular, Eisenhower and Dulles now saw Egypt's Nasser and his growing reputation in the Arab world as a vehicle for the Kremlin's intrusion into the region. After consultation with congressional leaders, Eisenhower decided to stake out an American commitment to defend the area from Soviet adventurism. On January 5, 1957, the president presented to a joint session of Congress the "Eisenhower Doctrine." The United States would provide military aid to any country in the Middle East requesting help against aggression sponsored by international communism. The president promised to act unilaterally and with dispatch if the Soviet Union or one of its regional cronies attacked a regional ally. Like the Truman Doctrine before it, Eisenhower's plan included no appeal to the United Nations and no effort at collective security.

Fear of Nasser's influence in the Middle East came to a head two years after the Suez events. The Egyptian president persuaded Syria to merge with Egypt in a new pan-Arab state known as the United Arab Republic (UAR). In many speeches, he envisioned the UAR expanding to include several of the smaller Arab kingdoms in the region. One government that felt particularly threatened by Nasser's policies and popularity was the Lebanese administration of Camille Chamoun. Lebanon's historical ties to Syria, coupled with the delicate ethnic and religious balance in Lebanon, contributed to fears that the UAR might try to undermine the nation's independence. Chamoun, a Maronite Christian president in a majority Muslim state, contacted Eisenhower in early 1958 about possible assistance under the Eisenhower Doctrine. The president assured him of help if Lebanon was threatened from beyond its borders. In April, possibly because he now thought he had support from Washington, Chamoun let it be known that he intended to serve a second term as president, in violation of the Lebanese constitution. Broad public protest and street riots ensued. Chamoun quickly retreated from his plan to serve another term. There was suspicion in Washington that the disturbances were not solely negative indigenous responses to Chamoun's political moves but were being orchestrated by communists and Nasser's operatives. The Lebanese president took the same position and brought the matter to the Security Council in late May. A UN observer group was dispatched to Lebanon, and Hammarskjöld himself traveled to Beirut to assess the situation.

Circumstances took a dramatic turn on July 14, when a particularly bloody coup in Baghdad overthrew the pro-Western Iraqi government and slaughtered the royal family. The military officers who came to power representing the Ba'athist Party seemed to be closely aligned with Nasser. It appeared from the Oval Office that all of the conservative regimes in the region might soon fall to the UAR and Soviet control.[53] Israel and oil, the key American interests in the Middle East, were now dramatically threatened. The president accused the UAR of seeking to overthrow Chamoun's government by infiltrating "arms, ammunition, and money."[54] Calling Lebanon a victim of "indirect aggression," Eisenhower decided to respond by sending 14,000 U.S. Marines to stabilize the situation until the world community through the United Nations could organize a force to take the Americans' place. Eisenhower had no wish to get bogged down in an internecine Lebanese struggle and hoped the United Nations might provide a way out. In August President Chamoun was succeeded by Faud Chebab, and domestic Lebanese politics seemed to return to normal. Rather quickly, U.S. forces were withdrawn.

In November 1957 Eisenhower wrote to a friend that "crisis has now become 'normalcy.'"[55] Lebanon, the following year, was one more example of the type of disturbances with which the White House was dealing on a regular basis. In Eisenhower's view, all of them were tainted by the Soviet factor. During his last two years in office the communist "threat" was ever present. In Indochina America's commitment to halting the falling dominoes led the administration to enlarge its economic and military assistance to the South Vietnamese government. In Europe Eisenhower had to stand firm against Nikita Khrushchev's

---

[53] Statement by the President on the Lebanese Government's Appeal for United States Forces, July 15, 1958, *PPP, 1958*, 549.

[54] Special Message to Congress on the Sending of United States Forces to Lebanon, July 15, 1958, Ibid., 551.

[55] Rostow, *Europe*, 73.

threat to sign a separate peace with East Germany, which would put a stranglehold on West Berlin. In Asia the conclusion of war in Korea brought no American retreat. Regular threats by Mao Zedong's communist regime in Beijing against the Republic of China on Formosa required an American guarantee to defend the islands of Quemoy and Matsu. Then, in 1960, just when it appeared that a mild thaw in Soviet-American relations might be occurring, U.S. spy planes (a U-2 surveillance plane piloted by Francis Gary Powers and an RB-47 lost over the Arctic) were shot down over Soviet territory, sending the cold war into a deep freeze. In all these episodes the United Nations played a minor role. Condemnatory resolutions might be passed, but that was about it. Each side used the organization for bombastic speeches about the perfidy of its opponent, and nonaligned nations decried the inability of the organization to meet their needs or temper the contest between Moscow and Washington.

Cold War Tensions and UN Institutions

The cold war perverted the structure and purposes of the United Nations. The confrontation between the United States and the Soviet Union made its way directly into the structure and operations of the UN during the Eisenhower years.

Because the United Nations as a form of *parliamentary diplomacy* worked by votes and semilegislative procedures, it was critical for both superpowers to seek majority support for their resolutions and initiatives. This was not difficult for the United States from 1945 to 1955, when the overwhelming majority of the membership was closely associated with the Western camp. For the USSR it was important to seek the admission of new states from the third world to redress the imbalance. Most significantly, it was critical to the Soviets to seat the representatives of the People's Republic of China in place of the delegation from Chiang Kai-shek's regime, which had been run off the Chinese mainland in 1949.[56]

The admission of communist China was a "hot button" issue in American politics. Mao's introduction of troops in the Korean War, coupled with the anticommunist mood of the United States, produced

---

[56] It must be remembered that the USSR had boycotted the Security Council for a good part of 1950 over this issue. One consequence was to let the United States obtain Council support for intervention in Korea.

overwhelming opposition to the seating of a Beijing delegation in New York. If the mainland Chinese took China's seat in the Security Council, it would also mean another certain veto of Western proposals in that body. On Capitol Hill several influential lawmakers threatened retaliation against the United Nations if China was admitted. Fearing that an armistice in Korea would lead the allied powers to push for communist Chinese representation, the Senate Appropriations Committee on May 28, 1953, reported out a bill barring financial contributions to the United Nations in that eventuality. Eisenhower, while opposed to Mao's government taking the Chinese seat, thought that efforts to retaliate against the United Nations were misguided. Such efforts, like the Bricker Amendment, undermined his independence to conduct foreign policy. He told congressional leaders in a meeting at the White House that the United States might even have to accept a loss on this issue. In his words, "If we [are] to have a workable world organization, every nation must expect to undergo defeats in the UN from time to time."[57] Concluding with a non sequitur, the president pointed out, "The United Nations is essential because global war is now unthinkable."[58] Whenever Republican senators or representatives suggested financial withdrawal from the United Nations, Eisenhower made it clear they were going too far in their efforts to punish the organization.

To fend off Congress, the administration sought to maintain a General Assembly majority in opposition to seating the Beijing government. When that no longer seemed achievable, it was willing to use all parliamentary procedures available toward this end. This remained the American strategy, pursued successfully until the presidency of Richard Nixon in the early 1970s. Eisenhower appreciated that public winds were blowing strongly against admission of communist China. He wrote to Churchill that the American people saw the replacement of the Nationalist regime with a mainland delegation as "unfair, unjust, and immoral."[59] Henry Cabot Lodge led the fight in the United Nations. The first tactic was to "postpone" the question of representation on the UN agenda, keeping the Nationalist delegation in place without a direct vote. When America's allies would no longer go

---

[57] Eisenhower, *Mandate*, 215.

[58] Ibid., 214.

[59] Boyle, *Correspondence*, 156.

along with this approach, Lodge insisted that the issue should be "substantive" rather than "procedural." This ensured that it would take a two-thirds majority to unseat Formosa. Then, Lodge regularly catalogued the international misbehavior of Beijing, in Korea and elsewhere. As long as the United States had the votes in the Assembly, and could pressure its closest allies to at least acquiesce in its demands, the Sino-Soviet bloc had little chance of gaining another veto in the Security Council.

Lodge understood, however, that the national liberation movement in the underdeveloped world would inevitably change UN membership, and thus end the American voting hegemony. Admission of the newly independent states, however—like everything else in the United Nations—was caught up in the contest between the United States and the USSR. On Inauguration Day in 1953 there were fifty-six members of the United Nations. Eisenhower was not interested in seeing Eastern puppet regimes added to the General Assembly. The administration argued that they did not meet the standards of the Charter's Article 4, which required new members to be "peace-loving" and sufficiently independent to carry out their UN obligations. For their part, the Kremlin's leaders were not willing to admit new states proposed by the West unless Warsaw Pact nations were given membership status. There was also serious controversy over particular applicants such as Outer Mongolia, South Vietnam, and the two Koreas. A deadlock ensued in which either the Soviet representative vetoed American-endorsed candidate states or seven Security Council votes could not be mustered for Russian-sponsored governments.

The permanent five had been under pressure from the first secretary-general, Trygve Lie, and his successor, Dag Hammarskjöld, to make the UN truly universal by adding the new members. The newly liberated states themselves conducted public diplomacy toward that end. Meeting at Bandung, Indonesia, in April 1955, twenty-five African and Asian nations launched what became known as the "nonaligned movement." They called upon a divided world to pursue the path of "pancha shila," that is, "peaceful coexistence." This movement quickly found leaders in India, Yugoslavia, and Egypt. For the Eisenhower administration, which endorsed rapid decolonization and sought better bilateral ties with the states of the third world, the desire to meet the nonaligned governments' demands for UN participation was controlling. The logjam was broken in December 1955 when both sides agreed to admit sixteen nations, four from the Soviet bloc and the rest from Africa, Asia, and the Arab world.[60] For the first time since Indonesia's admission in 1950, the General Assembly had enlarged its membership. The expansion meant, however, that the United States could now count on only forty votes in the General Assembly,[61] less than the two-thirds majority needed to initiate dramatic policy initiatives. While Eisenhower had gained some goodwill in the underdeveloped world, he now found the United Nations less useful in the global contest.

The first wave of new members was quickly followed by other successful applicants, so that by the time Eisenhower left office African and Asian nations were approaching a majority of seats in the General Assembly, and they would achieve that majority in 1963. The enlargement meant new voices, new points of view, and new policy emphases in the United Nations. The problems of the less developed countries—poverty, political instability, north-south trade, and multilateral aid—all moved to the fore. The task for the president and his successors was to defend American interests in the changed institution, and to keep the new issues from becoming intertwined with the cold war confrontation. Their efforts were complicated by decreasing public support due to the loss of American control within the organization.

Eisenhower's dexterity in this regard was tested in central Africa in 1960. The Belgian Congo, located in the heart of sub-Saharan Africa, achieved independence on June 30 under the leadership of President Joseph Kasavubu and Prime Minister Patrice Lumumba. Within a few days, however, hopes for stability were destroyed when soldiers in the national army revolted against remaining Belgian officers; the southern province of Katanga, led by Moise Tshombe, seceded; and Belgium rushed troops to the country to protect its economic interests in the region.

Kasavubu and Lumumba appealed to Eisenhower for help against Belgian "aggression." Lumumba made a hurried trip to Washington but was unable to convince administration officials that the United States should intervene.[62] Secretary-General Hammarskjöld expressed his distress that the Congolese were bypassing the United Nations. Secretary

---

[60] *Annual Review*, 1955–1956, 24–27.

[61] Brands, *Warriors*, 167.

[62] Some members of the administration considered Lumumba mentally unbalanced. Ambrose, *Eisenhower*, 586.

of State Christian Herter, who had succeeded Dulles following the latter's death from cancer, promised Hammarskjöld that the United States would involve itself in the Congo affair only through the United Nations. Consequently, Eisenhower urged the new nation to take its concerns to the UN. The president was trying to balance several American objectives. During the cold war the United States supported self-determination in the old colonial empires. It also sought to sustain the territorial integrity of new states, and to minimize internal violence. Also, in this case Eisenhower did not want to worsen relations with a needed European ally, Belgium. The United Nations provided a reasonable vehicle for achieving all of these ends. Most important, the American government wanted to keep the process of self-determination from becoming a catalyst for spreading the superpower confrontation to new regions of the globe.[63] This became a serious possibility when Lumumba, rebuffed by the United States, turned to Moscow for support.

Exercising Article 99 of the UN Charter, Secretary-General Hammarskjöld convened the Security Council to consider action in the Congo. The Council called on Belgian troops to withdraw and opposed the secession of Katanga province. The members established a UN force, which ultimately included 20,000 personnel from thirty nations and cost the UN $168 million. Hammarskjöld obtained authority to replace Belgian troops and to support the central government. In the first weeks of the operation, when Belgian forces delayed their withdrawal and the civil war seemed to be expanding, Lumumba's appeal to Nikita Khrushchev and the Soviet leadership received an affirmative response. Khrushchev airlifted weapons and technical advisers to the Congo and called for the UN to leave the country.

By September the White House perceived events in the Congo as another part of the cold war struggle, with UN forces representing Western interests and the Lumumba government quickly becoming a Soviet surrogate for communist influence. Eisenhower called the Russian actions a violation of the "principles" so far applied in the conflict, and a demonstration of the USSR's "political designs on Africa."[64] The

---

[63] For a full discussion of American criteria used to determine support for self-determination during the cold war, see Morton H. Halperin and David J. Scheffer, with Patricia L. Small, *Self-Determination in the New World Order* (Washington, D.C.: Carnegie Endowment for International Peace, 1992), 11–12.

[64] President's News Conference of September 7, 1960, *PPP, 1960,* 679.

administration undertook direct efforts to remove Lumumba from power, trying among other things to assassinate him. In the end U.S. officials persuaded Kasavubu to dismiss Lumumba, who ignored his dismissal as illegal. In the midst of the chaos, Congolese General Joseph Mobutu seized power, forcing the prime minister to seek UN protection. Hammarskjöld and the United Nations found themselves direct participants in the destruction and reconstitution of a state.

What President Eisenhower did not do was intervene directly. He discussed the possibility of putting Marines into Katanga province but was dissuaded by the argument that such an act would be perceived as a defense of imperialism. Instead, the administration lent its full support to Hammarskjöld's efforts, with the consequence that the secretary-general gained a degree of autonomy and authority which no predecessor had had.[65] At one point, under his leadership, UN forces put Lumumba under arrest and threw the full weight of the military behind the central government. Lumumba was then turned over to a Kasavubu government backed by Mobutu. In turn, Kasavubu, late in 1960, transferred the former prime minister to Katangan rebels, who promptly executed him. In the eyes of many third world nations, the United Nations, and by extension the United States, now shared complicity in the death of the Congo's first government leader. In Eisenhower's view, the whole effort had become a "sorry mess."

While many members may well have expected an operation similar to inserting UN forces into the Suez Canal in 1956, Hammarskjöld qualitatively enlarged the peacekeeping mission by ending its neutrality in the conflict. His actions were particularly disturbing to the Soviets, given the Kremlin's support of Lumumba. Khrushchev viewed Hammarskjöld in the same light as Stalin had seen Trygve Lie—a secretary-general who had lost his independence and who was little more than a tool of American foreign policy. In the closing weeks of Eisenhower's presidency, Khrushchev argued that Hammarskjöld should be replaced with a three-person secretariat. This "troika proposal," as it was called, made the case that while there might well be "neutral" nations, there could not be "neutral" people. Therefore, the position of secretary-general should be filled by one person representing

---

[65] R. J. Barry Jones, "The United Nations and the International Political System," *The United Nations and the New World Order*, edited by Demitris Bourantonis and Jarrod Weiner (New York: St. Martin's, 1995), 35.

Western powers, one person from the socialist bloc, and one person from the non-aligned states. This was a proposal requiring constitutional revision of the Charter, which meant that it had no chance of success. Yet Khrushchev pursued it, even threatening to veto any successor to Hammarskjöld at the end of his term unless the troika was accepted. The Soviets also refused to pay any special assessment for the Congo operation, joining France and a few other states in challenging Hammarskjöld's policy. The following spring the Kennedy administration would have to ask Congress for $100 million in bond issues to keep the United Nations afloat. The troika idea, coupled with the USSR's nonpayment of its assessments, demonstrated the depths the cold war had reached, even threatening the future viability of the United Nations itself.

JFK and the UN

I believe, Mr. Chairman, that you should recognize that free peoples in all parts of the world do not accept the claim of historical inevitability for the Communist Revolution. What your government believes is its own business; what it does is the world's business.

—*President Kennedy to Nikita Khrushchev*
April 18, 1961

The Congo, the troika, Berlin, Vietnam, Formosa—all were part of the foreign policy agenda on a very cold January 20, 1961, as a new president took up the cold war struggle left to him by Truman and Eisenhower. The previous year had only added to the angst felt in world capitals and hometowns. Hopes had risen the previous spring because of a "Big Four" summit planned for Paris in May. Expectations were quickly dashed, however, by the shooting down of an American spy plane over the Soviet Union—which led, on the opening day of the summit, to Khrushchev's demand that Eisenhower apologize for the overflight. When the president refused, the meeting adjourned permanently. In Indochina, communist forces ratcheted up the attacks on the American-supported regime in South Vietnam and fomented revolution in Laos. In the Western Hemisphere, the new Cuban government under Fidel Castro, originally thought an improvement on the dictatorship of General Batista, declared its allegiance to communism, leading to a break in relations with the United States. The pristine white landscape left by a snowstorm in the District of Columbia the night before the inauguration stood in deep contrast to the apparently darkening shadows of potential war between the world's superpowers. President Kennedy took notice of these dangers in a stirring inaugural address, which called the nation to "defend any friend, [and] oppose any foe to assure the survival...of liberty."[66] He reminded the world that the "torch has been passed" to a new generation of Americans "tempered by war, [and] disciplined by a hard and bitter peace." To the United Nations he gave a new vote of confidence, "to prevent it from becoming merely a forum for invective—to strengthen its shield of the new and the weak—and to enlarge the area in which its writ may run."

For all the high drama, however, little changed in American policy toward the United Nations with the arrival of the Kennedy-Johnson administration. The country probably expected more than it got in this regard. The new president was the youngest ever elected, succeeding the oldest occupant (at the time) of the Oval Office. The inauguration marked a change in ruling parties, advisers, and apparent outlook on the world. Yet, for all of the promise of the "New Frontier," the Eisenhower model held firm, with changes only in nuance, not substance. Just as Eisenhower had done in his "Chance for Peace" speech, Kennedy early in his term laid down a litmus test for Soviet responsibility, which included a cease-fire and settlement in Laos, cooperation with the United Nations in the Congo, and the "speedy conclusion" of a nuclear test-ban treaty.[67] The last item was of particular interest to the president, because he, like Eisenhower, believed that some easing of the Soviet-American confrontation might make progress possible on the most disconcerting aspect of the post-1945 era, the arms race between the superpowers.

Sixteen years before the 1961 inauguration, Adlai Stevenson had gathered reporters attending the San Francisco Organizing Conference for the United Nations in a small room of the American delegation's hotel to brief them on each day's deliberations. In a twist of historical irony, among the reporters was a young "stringer" for the Chicago *Herald-American*. John Kennedy had returned from the war a hero, but without a clear idea of where he was headed in his life and career. As a

---

[66] Inaugural address of John F. Kennedy, January 20, 1961.

[67] *PPP, 1961,* 287.

last-minute decision he accepted an offer, arranged by his father,[68] to cover the proceedings in San Francisco and to write a series of reflections from the point of view of the returning veteran. Kennedy's and Stevenson's lives would intersect many times after 1945. In 1956, Kennedy sought to be Stevenson's vice-presidential partner on the Democratic ticket; in 1960, Stevenson sought to take the nomination away from Kennedy; and finally, Stevenson served as President Kennedy's ambassador to the United Nations. Both men had high hopes for the UN in 1945; but far more than Kennedy, Stevenson—a true Wilsonian—saw the United Nations as a plateau in the effort to achieve world peace through the rule of law and democratic practice. Kennedy was more sanguine. He wrote to a wartime buddy with whom he had served on a PT boat in the Pacific, "When I think of how much this war has cost us,…when I think of all those gallant acts that I have seen or anyone has seen who has been to war—it would be a very easy thing to feel disappointed and betrayed…by the timidity and selfishness of the nations" at the Conference. Kennedy's effort to measure the events around him in terms of the world war that had just been concluded reflected his historical orientation to world affairs. Tempering Stevenson's moralism, Kennedy was more interested in the geopolitical implications of diplomacy and the costs and consequences of national foreign policies.

President Kennedy was not enamored of the near religious anticommunism of Dwight Eisenhower and John Foster Dulles. Kennedy's friend, adviser, and biographer Arthur Schlesinger, Jr., contends that the president approached the confrontation with the Soviet Union in "national rather than ideological terms."[69] His confidant Theodore Sorensen noted shortly after the president's death that JFK did not differ much from his predecessor in his judgment about the threat the Russians posed, but his emphasis was far more on "the factual, the rational, and the realistic."[70] Kennedy imposed a realist outlook on Eisenhower's "men in the Kremlin." Soviet leaders were as concerned about the security, interests, and influence of their country as was the

---

[68] Nigel Hamilton, *J.F.K.: Reckless Youth* (New York: Random House, 1992), 687.

[69] Arthur M. Schlesinger, Jr., *A Thousand Days* (Boston: Houghton Mifflin, 1965), 279.

[70] Theodore C. Sorensen, *Kennedy* (New York: Harper and Row, 1965), 510.

government in Washington. Ideology might provide a public rationale for Soviet actions, but it did not explain those actions. Clearly the USSR had international goals, which might well include expansion and which were surely inimical to the interests of the United States; but its leaders were not irrational "true believers" with whom the West could not reach some modicum of understanding.

One of the transforming effects of the Cold War was to push realist concerns about American survival and security to the fore. In 1919 and 1945 Woodrow Wilson and Franklin Roosevelt could think about making a world more in tune with American ideals. Enemies had been vanquished, the United States had emerged from each world war largely unscathed, and no immediate opponent presented itself to challenge American preeminence. By the 1950s the United States no longer had the luxury of international choices without clear possible negative consequences. Eisenhower may have seen the new threat from Moscow as a moral evil that had to be thwarted wherever it presented itself; but he also understood that, in the nuclear age, crusades undertaken unilaterally, with allies, or through the United Nations could bring costs far disproportional to the ends sought. Thus, for all of the rhetoric about godless communism, the Eisenhower years witnessed the steady emergence of a cautious realist foreign policy. The new realism fit Kennedy's outlook well.[71] He intended not only to confront but also to negotiate with Soviet leaders, to conduct negotiations on the presupposition that Moscow, like Washington, had national interests to defend. He assumed that Nikita Khrushchev, like himself, might find many of those interests defensible as much by accommodation as by confrontation.

In a famous speech at American University in 1963, President Kennedy noted, "World peace...does not require that each man love his neighbor...only that they live together in mutual tolerance."[72] He spoke to his audience about a "practical and...attainable peace," not the universal peace "which some fantasies and fanatics dream." The achievement of a *modus vivendi* with the Soviet Union depended not on "some grand or magical formula" but on a "series of concrete actions

---

[71] Sorensen reports that President Kennedy's favorite word when considering policy options was "miscalculation." Ibid., 513.

[72] *PPP, 1963,* 461.

and effective agreements."[73] Assessing the cold war, he acknowledged, "We must deal with the world as it is, not as it might have been had the history of the last 18 years been different."[74] In his address the president made only passing reference to the United Nations, expressing the hope that it might someday become a genuine world security system. Woodrow Wilson may have sought a world safe for democracy, but Kennedy told the commencement gathering that he wanted a world "safe for diversity."

However the relationship with the USSR was to be managed, Kennedy saw little substitute for direct American engagement of the adversary. Superpower diplomacy must be largely bilateral, with little communal or intermediary involvement. This left only a limited role for America's allies, much less for the United Nations. During his first year in office the president held his only summit with Nikita Khrushchev. Meeting in Vienna, the two leaders reviewed all of the important issues between the two countries. Kennedy was particularly interested in making progress on Laos, Berlin, and a nuclear test ban. Only on the final item did he conceive a role for actors other than the United States and the Soviet Union, hoping to include other European nuclear powers in any agreement. On the contentious issues of divided Germany and growing conflict in Southeast Asia, however, there could only be a duopoly of decision-making.

Declining American attention added to the United Nations' woes, in 1961 which were already mounting under the financial crunch of the Congo operation, the USSR's refusal to pay its budget assessment, and the Soviet effort to impose a "troika" secretariat. Another body blow hit the organization on September 18, when Dag Hammarskjöld died in a plane crash in the Congo. Soviet leaders took the occasion to indicate that they would not even endorse an acting secretary-general in Hammarskjöld's place if the "troika proposal" was not accepted. Kennedy addressed the General Assembly under these withering conditions on September 25. He made clear his commitment to maintain the organization and to oppose the Soviet plan. The president, however, did not speak of the United Nations in Wilsonian terms. Rather, he emphasized the practical merits to diplomacy that the UN provided. He pointed out that the United Nations was at its best in the defense of the

---

[73] Ibid.

[74] Ibid., 462–463.

weak, of those states that could not defend their own interests.[75] The great powers had the wherewithal to pursue their interests and to command a worldwide audience. The new nations of Africa and Asia, however, needed the United Nations, and particularly the General Assembly, as a platform for their views and as an institution capable of tempering the unilateral actions of powerful states. The acceptance of troika would silence the Secretariat as the spokesman for the General Assembly and would impose anarchy and confusion, or paralysis. He went on to talk about the role the United Nations could play in disarmament negotiations, peacekeeping, and development. Finally, he felt duty-bound to "report" to the Assembly "on two threats to the peace which are not on your crowded agenda"[76]—South Vietnam and Berlin—and to make the case for American actions in both settings.

Under the articles of the UN Charter, members are obligated to bring to the attention of the Security Council "threats to the peace," so that the UN collective security system might respond effectively. Kennedy had no intention, however, of putting either Berlin or Vietnam before the United Nations. The matter of Berlin and divided Germany was to be kept solely within the purview of the occupying powers. Khrushchev's recurring threats to sign a peace treaty with the German Democratic Republic, ostensibly cutting off western access to West Berlin, were seen as direct challenges to Western interests in divided Europe. Kennedy responded to Khrushchev's initiatives by indicating that the United States and its allies would stay in Berlin no matter what arrangement the USSR imposed on East Germany. Even when the East German government suddenly put up the Berlin Wall on August 13, 1961, to keep its citizens from fleeing to the West, Kennedy's recourse was not to the United Nations. At best he used the UN for back-channel negotiations with the Soviets and with European allies. Far more important, he sent 1,500 American military personnel to Berlin via the Autobahn, past East German checkpoints, to test Soviet intentions. In June 1963 the president himself went to Berlin to demonstrate American resolve to defend the western parts of the city.

The American role in Vietnam, as discussed earlier in this chapter, grew out of lukewarm U.S. support for French policies in Indochina, and then developed as part of the Eisenhower and Dulles containment

---

[75] *PPP, 1961,* 619.

[76] Ibid., 624

strategy directed at world communism. Eisenhower had hoped to forge a collective Southeast Asian response to apparent Soviet and Chinese efforts to topple regimes friendly to the West. This became particularly important after the 1954 Geneva Conference, which divided Vietnam at the 17th parallel, leaving a communist government to the north led by Ho Chi Minh, and the south under President Diem. SEATO, however, did not prove very effective in coordinating a regional defense of South Vietnam. Instead, fearing what he had described as a "domino" effect in the region, President Eisenhower was willing to go it alone in expanding American assistance to the Saigon regime. Eisenhower also thought it important to defend other neutral regimes, such as Laos, from overthrow by the communists, fearing a loss of American prestige and power in the struggle with Moscow. President Kennedy concurred. Within two months of his inauguration, Kennedy was presented with contingency plans for the introduction of American troops into Laos to save the government from imminent collapse. Yet, to introduce American personnel would create an open-ended commitment in Laos and would raise the potential cost to American influence around the world if the Laotian government fell. Kennedy opted for negotiations with all the parties involved, including the Chinese, hoping to achieve a guarantee of Laotian neutrality. His call for negotiations was supported by a credible show of military preparations, convincing the Pathet Lao and Hanoi that the alternative to neutrality was a massive American intervention. Beginning in 1961, a fifteen-month negotiation process began in Geneva. A final document was signed in July 1962 by fourteen nations, including North Vietnam, mainland China, and the United States. All this was conducted and achieved without any serious UN involvement.

Laos and Vietnam had become "strategic" interests to the United States by the time Kennedy came to the White House; therefore, issues regarding them were not likely to be brought to the United Nations for resolution. For Vietnam, however—unlike Laos—the president disregarded advice to find a neutrality arrangement. His undersecretary of state, Chester Bowles, and the chief U.S. negotiator at the Geneva conference, Averell Harriman, proposed expanding the talks in Switzerland to include all regional powers, the Soviet Union, and China in order to achieve neutrality for all of Indochina.[77] Kennedy considered the idea of a negotiated settlement and then rejected it as premature. The

---

[77] Chester Bowles, *Promises to Keep* (New York: Harper and Row, 1971), 409.

defense of Vietnam was an "alliance commitment" growing out of the Eisenhower administration's promises in 1954. Kennedy expanded the military assistance program to Saigon and augmented the adviser force by one hundred. In so doing he violated the Geneva Accord's prohibition against any side introducing personnel other than replacements for forces already there. To avoid international criticism he directed that neither the United Kingdom (co-chair of the Geneva conference) nor the International Control Commission (established to monitor the Accords) be informed of his action. Kennedy also pressed the Diem government to carry out significant domestic reforms to ensure popular support. He would not, however, commit American combat troops to the effort. Like Eisenhower at the time of Dienbienphu, the president made clear to his advisers that troops could be introduced into the war only if that step was supported by allies in the region and by the vast majority of the Vietnamese population.[78] It would be well after the Kennedy years had passed into American history before policy-makers would look seriously at the possibility of multilateral diplomacy at the United Nations or in some other setting to bring the war to an end. The administration was interested in victory,[79] not a UN-brokered compromise. The consequence was that the U.S. government never seriously brought its most tragic cold war initiative to the councils of the world organization which it had created for exactly such conflicts. Denying the Soviet Union a public relations victory, and possibly a strategic victory, was too important to consider such an option.

Probably no single event better illustrated Kennedy's unwillingness to trust strategic interests to United Nations deliberations than the Cuban Missile Crisis of 1962. Coming at the end of the tensest four years of the cold war,[80] a period marked by increasing hostility between Washington and Havana, the Cuban crisis seemed to bring collective security to its ultimate refutation. The United Nations had been created to ensure that the world would never again experience a global holocaust like the Second World War. Yet almost no use was made of the UN during a crisis that Kennedy later estimated had put the possibility of a nuclear exchange at one out of four.

---

[78] Sorensen, *Kennedy*, 654.

[79] Stanley Karnow, *Vietnam: A History* (New York: Viking, 1983), 293.

[80] Jerry Pubantz, "Non-Proliferation Treaty of 1968," *Modern Encyclopedia of Russian and Soviet History*, Vol. 25, 46–51. Hereafter cited as *MERSH*.

The problem of Fidel Castro had been bequeathed by the previous administration. Eisenhower's hostility toward the Cuban regime had led to his approval of CIA plans to overthrow Castro. Using the same strategy as the one Eisenhower employed in Guatemala, John Foster Dulles and his brother, Allen Dulles, the director of the Central Intelligence Agency, proposed U.S. support for an insurgency effort by Cuban exiles. An invasion of Cuba by opponents of the government would be secretly financed and encouraged by Washington. Plans for the operation were completed in the last days of the Republican administration. The CIA briefed Kennedy during his first weeks in office. The president did little to review the components of the plan critically, and he gave the go-ahead, reserving the right to terminate it at any point and making clear he did not intend to allow direct military action by U.S. forces. The operation was a complete failure. On April 17 Cuban nationals went ashore at the Bay of Pigs; by April 19 the invasion had been defeated by Castro's forces. The president was forced to admit American complicity and his responsibility for the debacle.

Castro quickly appealed his case to the United Nations. World public opinion broadly condemned the invasion, and several resolutions to that effect were circulated. America's UN ambassador, Adlai Stevenson, found his credibility severely undermined by the fact that he had been given the false CIA cover story and had unwittingly conveyed it to foreign delegations in New York.[81] At the White House there was a bunker mentality—advisers even suggested imposing economic sanctions on any country that voted to condemn U.S. involvement in the affair.[82] In the end, activity at the United Nations devolved into lengthy cold war recriminations. The following July Nikita Khrushchev forged an alliance with Cuba, and Castro shortly thereafter declared himself a communist. The basis had been laid for further confrontation between Moscow and Washington over Cuba.

Decades after the events surrounding the 1962 crisis there is still much debate about Khrushchev's motivation in putting missiles capable of threatening the Western Hemisphere in Cuba. Certainly Kremlin leaders and Castro believed rumors that still further American efforts to overthrow the Havana regime were likely. Thus, Khrushchev's decision may have been a form of insurance against a repetition of the Bay of

---

[81] Schlesinger, *Thousand Days*, 254–255.

[82] Bowles, *Promises*, 331.

Pigs. It is also true that Khrushchev came away from the 1961 Vienna Summit believing that the new president was an indecisive adversary. It may also be that the Soviet leader simply miscalculated Washington's response would have to the Kremlin's action. From the Soviet perspective, putting missiles in Cuba was no different than the American policy of putting equivalent weapons in Turkey. Whatever the factors that led to Khrushchev's decision, by the fall of 1962 offensive missiles and their launchpad facilities had been secretly moved to Cuba, and they were about to become operational when the Kennedy administration discovered them in October.

The president believed, in classic realist terms, that the placement of missiles in Cuba altered the strategic balance. He convened a highly secret group of advisers (ExComm) to assess the threat and the options available to remove the missiles. He confessed to his advisers, "It's a goddamn mystery to me"[83] why the Soviets had decided on such a provocation. He conjectured that it might well be an effort by the Kremlin to create a crisis in one part of the world in order to gain some freedom of action in another. He remembered the dual crisis of the Suez Canal and Hungary that Eisenhower had faced in October 1956. In this case the real prize for the Russians appeared to be Berlin. On September 28, Khrushchev had written to the president about perceived American provocations toward Cuba and seemed to link matters in the Caribbean with issues in divided Germany.[84] At ExComm's first meeting, Kennedy's secretary of state, Dean Rusk, suggested that the Cubans were being set up by the Kremlin and would be sacrificed in order to get a favorable deal on Berlin.

Rusk, who had been assistant secretary for UN Affairs in the Truman administration, expressed no interest in taking the matter to the United Nations, and only slightly more in taking it to the Organization of American States. At best, he proposed communicating with Castro through "his representative at the UN" or, preferably, through the Canadian ambassador in Havana.[85] In the early stages of the crisis Kennedy and his advisers demonstrated no confidence in the United Nations to achieve a withdrawal. It was, in fact, important to act in secret

---

[83] Ernest R. May and Philip D. Zelikow, *The Kennedy Tapes: Inside the White House During the Cuban Missile Crisis* (Cambridge, Mass.: Belknap, 1997), 107.

[84] Ibid., 38.

[85] Ibid., 54.

so that the Soviets did not bring the matter to the United Nations before the United States acted. At one point the president even indicated that he wanted to "frighten" UN delegations through ambiguity[86] about possible U.S. retaliation, thus making more likely the future achievement of an Assembly resolution favorable to American interests.

Only United States Ambassador Stevenson among those in the inner circle made the case for UN diplomacy. Briefed by Kennedy personally, Stevenson counseled negotiations before any military action. The president, however, feared public criticism, believing any action that seemed to delay removal of the missiles or allow the Soviets the appearance of even a partial victory was likely to raise the cry of "Munich" or "Yalta" in its most pejorative sense. The president also rejected the ambassador's advice because, as he told the nation on October 22, "this urgent transformation of Cuba into an important strategic base…[constitutes] an explicit threat to the peace and security of all the Americas."[87] Where strategic interests were directly involved, the president had no intention of leaving America's fate to the fortunes of parliamentary diplomacy.

ExComm eventually developed and evaluated six policy options. Of those, three—doing nothing, negotiating secretly with Fidel Castro, and appealing to the Security Council—were rejected quickly as ineffective.[88] The remaining options involved the use of force. Kennedy limited his choices to air strikes, an invasion, and a blockade. Air strikes, however, could not be guaranteed to remove all of the missiles. Just as important, he and his advisers feared that a surprise air attack would be "inappropriate," particularly for the United States: a "moral" nation could not repeat the Pearl Harbor outrage. During a heated ExComm meeting, Robert Kennedy angrily told Dean Acheson, "My brother is not going to be the Tojo of the 1960s."[89] RFK advised, "For one hundred and seventy-five years [the United States] had not been [the type] of country"

---

[86] Ibid., 209.

[87] For a discussion, see Cohen, *Cambridge History*, 121; Jerry Pubantz, "U-2 Incident," *MERSH*, Vol. 40, 136.

[88] Patrick Glynn, *Pandora's Box*, 50–51.

[89] Ibid., 190.

that started wars; "a sneak attack is not in our traditions."[90] The president concluded that the only option "compatible with American principles" was a blockade. Realist presidents, of course, can make use of the United Nations despite its moralist American origins. It can serve as a platform for propaganda, a venue for negotiation and persuasion, and, most importantly, a structure for legitimation, placing a stamp of global authority on unilateral American actions.[91] Once having taken decisive measures to quarantine Cuba, President Kennedy immediately looked for ways to incorporate the United Nations into his efforts to avoid war with the Soviet Union while achieving the removal of the missiles. The United States went on the offensive in the Security Council, accusing the Soviet Union of creating a threat to peace. Stevenson presented photographic evidence of the missile sites and demanded of Valerian Zorin, the Soviet ambassador, an explanation for the installations, threatening to wait until "hell freezes over" for an answer. While Stevenson's performance was good theater, his real contribution was made behind the scenes. Working privately with Acting Secretary-General U Thant, the American ambassador explored ways in which Thant might serve as an intermediary. The United States proposed that the United Nations provide observation teams to oversee any missile withdrawal. Kennedy also let Stevenson suggest to the secretary-general that if it became necessary to trade installations in Turkey for those in Cuba, it should be U Thant who "spontaneously" proposed it. Thus, the trade would not appear to be an American concession to the Russians.

Khrushchev suggested using the secretary-general as the principal "intermediary" to resolve the dispute. The substantive negotiation of the crisis was conducted through correspondence between the two leaders and secret back-channel contacts. It was also orchestrated on the high seas, where Kennedy allowed the first Soviet ship encountering the quarantine line to pass, but prepared to stop other ships in transit. The

---

[90] Isaacson and Thomas, *The Wise Men*, 625. Even when realism required unilateral action, American foreign policy was restrained by its own exceptionalist self-image. While submitting the crisis to the United Nations, an institution supposedly constructed on law and liberal doctrine, was unacceptable, moralist inhibitions still limited U.S. choices.

[91] For a discussion of realist uses of the United Nations, see Abraham Yeselson and Anthony Gaglione, "U.S. Foreign Policy and the United Nations," in Joseph R. Harbert and Seymour Maxwell Finger, eds., *U.S. Policy in International Institutions* (Boulder, Colo.: Westview, 1978), 179–182.

confrontation concluded on November 26, when the Kremlin ordered the ships to reverse course and Khrushchev agreed to withdraw the missiles. Subsequently, Kennedy indicated that the United States would not invade Cuba and would remove its missiles from Turkey. The crisis had been concluded with little UN involvement. Even in the aftermath of the confrontation the administration demonstrated caution in employing the United Nations, reneging on its earlier suggestion to use UN observation teams to monitor the removal of the missiles. Kennedy decided to depend on CIA surveillance flights for this purpose.

The Cuban crisis marked the nadir of U.S.-Soviet relations in the cold war. The ultimate confrontation that both sides thought they could avoid while pursuing brinkmanship around the world had nearly happened. Reality from time to time jolts the long-held perceptions of foreign policy which have driven a country's decision-making for a lengthy period. The events in the Caribbean had that cathartic effect on Moscow and Washington. Afterward, both sides looked for ways to lessen the tension between them. A "hot line" that allowed direct communication between the Kremlin and the White House was established. As 1963 began, both Khrushchev and Kennedy spoke about the necessity of what the former called "peaceful coexistence." A step-by-step retreat from the precipice seemed to be under way. Most important, both sides quietly moved toward some accommodation on the arms race by intensifying the effort to get a nuclear test ban in place. We will describe those negotiations later in this chapter; it is enough to say at this point that Kennedy's and Khrushchev's efforts at minimal *détente* culminated in the Partial Test Ban Treaty in August 1963. That agreement was foreshadowed in the president's commencement speech of American University, discussed earlier. There was a reasonable prospect, as Kennedy looked forward to his reelection campaign (set to begin in the fall), that the first requirement of the Eisenhower model—responsible Soviet global behavior—was now within reach, and thus that the two superpowers might move forward on disarmament. If that could happen, then the saved resources of the diminished arms race could be turned to development in the third world, areas of the globe Kennedy worried would be a breeding ground of war if the overwhelming human problems were not addressed. In the arenas of disarmament and development the United Nations surely could play a broader role than it had played in the contest with Moscow. One might have expected that within a year Khrushchev and Kennedy could be employing the United

Nations in very effective ways. Unfortunately, Kennedy would not live beyond November, and Khrushchev was out of power by October 1964, accused by his successors of "harebrained schemes."

Lyndon Johnson and the UN

> The United States of America wants to see the Cold War end; we want to see it end once and for all.
>
> —*President Johnson at the United Nations*
> *December 17, 1963*

It was past 11 P.M. on Friday, November 22, 1963 before *President* Lyndon Johnson collapsed on his bed in the Washington suburbs. The day had been surreal beginning with the first campaign event of the 1964 election season. He, President Kennedy, and Mrs. Kennedy had started the morning with a rally in front of the Texas Hotel in Fort Worth, then a breakfast with the Fort Worth Chamber of Commerce, followed by the Dallas motorcade, and the horrible events at Dealy Plaza. At 3:40 P.M. Washington time, aboard Air Force One, Johnson took the oath of office with Lady Bird and the slain president's widow at his side. Upon his arrival in the nation's capital, he addressed the American people and began making arrangements for the transition. As he lay on his bed, he talked to aides gathered around about his plans for his administration. He talked about new programs in education, civil rights legislation, conservation efforts, and domestic affairs in general. Foreign policy was little mentioned, Vietnam not at all.[92] This was a man of the New Deal, a leader of Congress who saw all things in domestic political terms. Like Truman, LBJ now found himself thrust into the office of the presidency. Truman's first act had been to confirm the United States would go ahead with the San Francisco Conference to organize the United Nations. Johnson's first thoughts were of ending want at home.

The thaw in the post-Cuba cold war provided an opportunity for the president. He himself noted, "It was almost as if the world had provided a breathing space within which I could concentrate on domestic affairs."[93] It would be only a few months before the growing war in

---

[92] Karnow, *Vietnam*, 322. Jack Valenti, who was with Johnson that evening, said Vietnam was of such little apparent significance to those gathered, including the president, that "it wasn't worth discussing."

[93] Doris Kearns, *Lyndon Johnson and the American Dream* (New York: Signet, 1976), 201.

Vietnam changed the circumstances, but LBJ began with a hiatus. During that period he addressed the United Nations General Assembly, reaffirming his predecessor's commitment to a "world safe for diversity." He made a special point of expressing his personal desire to leave the tensions of the previous years behind, hoping that the Soviet leaders would pay particular attention.[94] He highlighted the need for arms reductions and a nonproliferation treaty between the United States and the Soviet Union. It was a speech of continuity, with little clue to how Lyndon Johnson intended to approach the United Nations and its role in the world.

The historian Doris Kearns has written that President Johnson inherited not only an office but also a worldview.[95] He came to Washington from the hill country of Texas as part of FDR's sweep of American national politics. His preoccupations were those of a local politician seeking to lift his constituents out of the Depression's worst evils. Thus, his efforts on Capitol Hill were in support of the liberal agenda put forward by the White House. It was World War II that made LBJ an internationalist, like most of the rest of his generation. He fully endorsed the creation of the United Nations as a sign of America's effort to remain engaged with the world, yet he also supported the Truman Doctrine and the growing unilateral American commitment to defend the free world. As the majority leader of the U.S. Senate in the 1950s, he faithfully supported Dwight Eisenhower's cold war policies, sometimes over the vociferous opposition of the president's own party. His support reflected not some deep understanding of international affairs but rather an acceptance of the conventional wisdom about America's role in the world and the principles it needed to protect against communist subversion. Robert Packenham was right in his assessment that the president had "no 'operational' code or Johnson Doctrine for dealing with other nations."[96] Johnson's entire experience had been with domestic legislative affairs. Given that circumstance, it is not surprising that the president reverted to American cold war ideological doctrines and to foreign policy prescriptions which had been in place for a decade

---

[94] Lyndon B. Johnson, *The Vantage Point: Perspectives of the Presidency, 1963–1969* (New York: Holt, Rinehart and Winston, 1971), 464.

[95] Kearns, *Johnson*, 267.

[96] Robert A. Packenham, *Liberal America and the Third World* (Princeton: Princeton University Press, 1973), xviii–xix.

and a half by the time of Kennedy's assassination. His approach might be defined as a superficial moralism based on a general faith in the United States and the institutions it had created, like the United Nations, to preserve peace and freedom in the face of Soviet communism.

While the president assured the General Assembly of America's continuing support, there was no new initiative to enhance the United Nations' role in world affairs, nor to make more active use of it in U.S. foreign policy. At most, the administration was willing to endorse a UN-brokered denouement to the Congolese civil war, and to press member nations to pay their associated assessments. Johnson's representatives at the United Nations—first Adlai Stevenson and then Arthur J. Goldberg, who was appointed following Stevenson's death—pressed delegations to punish the Soviet Union and other states that did not pay their dues. This effort included an attempt under the Charter's provisions to strip those members of their General Assembly vote. But the changing majority in the UN, as well as the recognition that excluding the voice and vote of one of the permanent members would greatly weaken the universal nature of the institution, meant that the U.S. proposal was never likely to pass. The United States gave up its effort in 1965. An exasperated Goldberg told the Security Council:

> If any Member can insist on making an exception to the principle of collective financial responsibility with respect to certain activities of the United Nations,…the United States reserves the same option to make exceptions if, in our view, strong and compelling reasons exist for doing so.[97]

This threat, known as the "Goldberg Reservation," appeared at the time an empty admission of defeat. Broad U.S. financing of the organization had become a permanent element of U.S. policy with both the Kennedy and the Johnson administrations going to Congress regularly for supplemental contributions. By the end of the Johnson years the United States was providing nearly one-third of the UN budget. But, later, during the Reagan administration—when domestic public opinion expressed a strong distaste for the United Nations and its policies—the "reservation" would in fact be exercised. For the first time the United States would withdraw from some agencies of the United

---

[97] Franck, *Nation*, 85–86.

Nations and would refuse to pay its assessment until significant reforms were made.

Financing the United Nations, however, was not a sign that Lyndon Johnson placed a renewed faith in the organization. During the highly secret deliberations surrounding the Cuban missile crisis, Johnson had expressed serious doubt about the effectiveness of international organizations to resolve that dispute, or any other problem between the superpowers, satisfactorily. The practical *détente* that seemed to be emerging in the wake of the Caribbean standoff translated in Johnson's mind into an opportunity to find solutions to problems directly with Moscow, not into a hope for a revitalized and vigorous United Nations.

The most serious item on the president's foreign policy agenda in the weeks following the assassination was Vietnam. Like his predecessors, LBJ perceived this second Indochinese war as a struggle on the periphery with international communism. As early as February 1954, Johnson assured President Eisenhower of his support for the administration's decision to take over the French commitment as long as Vietnam was granted its independence and there were allies in the region to join the United States in the effort. Kennedy had expanded the American policy to hold the line against falling dominoes in Southeast Asia, and Johnson saw no reason to disrupt the continuity. As vice president, he visited Saigon, endorsed the regime, assured politicians there of strong American support, and reported back to President Kennedy on the need to bolster the U.S. effort. He told reporters that deserting Vietnam would mean "the United States, inevitably, must surrender the Pacific and take up our defenses on our own shores."[98]

If Vietnam was not of primary concern to Johnson on the day he became president, it soon would be. One of his first appointments was to make Henry Cabot Lodge the American ambassador to Vietnam. Lodge outlined a grim situation in Indochina. South Vietnam was losing the war. He urged the president to increase American support for the South Vietnamese government while at the same time pressuring Saigon's leaders to undertake reforms that would enhance domestic support for the war. All of the president's principal advisers, holdovers from the Kennedy administration, endorsed Lodge's prescriptions. Secretary of State Rusk particularly encouraged the president to sustain the battle

---

[98] Karnow, *Vietnam*, 250.

against communism, for fear of the consequences a defeat would engender for American policy and prestige around the world.

Other than support for the South Vietnamese military, no one had a formula for reversing the course of the conflict, much less for victory. For a president who was preoccupied with pushing a broad domestic agenda meant to create what he later called the "Great Society," and who put ahead of all other considerations winning an electoral mandate of his own in the 1964 elections, neither an expansion of the war nor a negotiated American retreat was a viable option. During the spring of 1964 his national security adviser, McGeorge Bundy, asked Johnson in a quiet moment, "What is your own internal thinking on this, Mr. President...that we've just got to stick on this middle course?" LBJ responded, "I just can't believe that we can't take 15,000 [American] advisers and 200,000 [South Vietnamese soldiers] and maintain the status quo for six months."[99] The same day he told Senator J. William Fulbright, "We're losing what we're doing, we got to decide whether to send [U.S. ground troops] in or whether to come out and let the dominoes fall."[100] Johnson, however, had no intention of making that decision before the fall elections. Until then the only thing he knew to do was "to do more of the same and do it more efficiently."

Unfortunately, Johnson was not in a frame of mind to find a diplomatic solution in 1964. Pressed by conservative senator Barry Goldwater, the likely Republican presidential candidate, who was calling for military victory in Vietnam, Johnson did not think he could look "soft" on foreign policy. Yet there were signs in both Hanoi and Moscow that a settlement at the conference table was preferable to an escalation of the American military involvement. Immediately following the overthrow of President Diem in November 1963, the Vietcong and North Vietnam floated the idea of a neutralist settlement with the new government.[101] Khrushchev also seemed interested in resolving the matter. Hoping to "contain" China because of the growing Sino-Soviet rift, the Soviet leader feared an expansion of Chinese influence in Southeast Asia at Moscow's expense if the war continued. The costs to

---

[99] Michael R. Beschloss, *Taking Charge: The Johnson White House Tapes, 1963–1964* (New York: Simon and Schuster, 1997), 262–263.

[100] Ibid., 264.

[101] Tom Wicker, *JFK and LBJ* (Baltimore: Penguin, 1969), 189.

the Soviet budget imposed by being Hanoi's primary patron surely would also rise with an escalation of the war.

Secretary-General U Thant was also pressing for a negotiated settlement. He proposed that he quietly organize talks among the principal parties. He met with Johnson in August, following the president's decision to seek authority from Congress to undertake direct American military action against North Vietnam in response to apparent attacks on U.S. ships in the Tonkin Gulf. When U Thant's efforts seemed to bear fruit in October, with a tentative commitment from the North Vietnamese to participate in talks, Secretary of State Rusk dismissed the initiative because it would mean rewarding aggression. U Thant's efforts had the additional unintended effect of undermining his value and merit as secretary-general in the eyes of Washington. Increasingly, he was seen as a critic of U.S. policy and, therefore, not useful to resolving the problem on American terms. Only in support of the U.S. war effort would Johnson consider UN involvement helpful. In May the administration suggested that the U.S. put a peacekeeping or observer group along the Vietnamese-Cambodian border to "stabilize conditions upset by Vietcong operations."[102] In August it also agreed to a Security Council invitation to North Vietnam to participate in the Council's sessions called to hear the American complaint about the Tonkin Gulf incidents. Beyond these small nods to the United Nations, Johnson was unwilling to go. Even when good friends and advisers suggested that he look to the United Nations for a possible diplomatic avenue, he rejected it. Ambassador Stevenson urged a preliminary appeal to the Security Council before the decision to bomb targets in North Vietnam, or at least a convocation of the Geneva Conference to hear an American complaint against Hanoi's violations of the Accords. Johnson rejected the idea and in private ridiculed Stevenson and his proposals as irrelevant.[103] He took much more seriously any recommendation from his old friend and Senate colleague Richard Russell of Georgia. But in June, when Senator Russell suggested that the American people "are [not] so damned opposed to the United Nations getting in there. And I don't think they'd be opposed to [the United States] coming out [then],[104] Johnson

---

[102] Lincoln P. Bloomfield, *The UN and Vietnam* (New York: Carnegie Endowment for International Peace, 1968), 7.

[103] Beschloss, *Taking Charge*, 277.

[104] Ibid., 403.

dismissed the possibility. He told Russell he was looking for a way out of Vietnam along the lines Eisenhower had taken in Korea. That meant threatening the enemy with escalation while controlling the negotiation process without UN interference.

It was the perceived centrality to American national interests of this particular fight on the periphery of the Soviet-American confrontation that made the use of the United Nations so unappealing to Johnson, as it had to Kennedy and Eisenhower. Each cold war president turned to the United Nations when the perceived stakes were low and the possibility of getting a resolution favorable to the United States without direct American participation was high. President Eisenhower left the Congolese war in Secretary-General Hammarskjöld's hands as long as it did not appear that the Soviets might make a major gain in central Africa. When evidence of direct Soviet involvement was discovered, the Administration looked for ways to provide U.S. assistance to the Kasavubu government. Kennedy pursued the same course in the Congo. He also turned to the United Nations when the newly independent government of Indonesia seemed threatened by its former colonial master, the Netherlands, and then in May 1961 when Indonesia invaded western New Guinea. The final agreement to that conflict called for UN administration of New Guinea until appropriate arrangements for its democratic absorption into Indonesia could be made.[105] Johnson himself, in the midst of trying to deal unilaterally with Vietnam, sought UN assistance when fighting broke out on the island of Cyprus, exacerbating tensions between two NATO allies, Greece and Turkey. In March 1964 the administration supported the creation of a UN peacekeeping force to separate the Turkish and Greek Cypriots on the island. Such arrangements, however, were not options for the Vietnamese conflict, at least not until the November elections were won.

Within a span of just a few weeks Nikita Khrushchev was ousted from power in the Kremlin and Lyndon Johnson won a landslide mandate from the American people. Khrushchev's successors—the collective leadership of Leonid Brezhnev, Alexei Kosygin, and Nicolai Podgorny—distancing themselves from the discredited policies of the Soviet leader, increased aid to the North Vietnamese, intensified the propaganda campaign against American imperialism in the war, and

---

[105] For a description of Kennedy's policy in the Indonesian crisis, see Franck, *Nation*, 78.

ceased to look for ways to extricate the United States from the conflict. In
the afterglow of his electoral victory Johnson forgot about the possibility
of using his mandate to withdraw from Vietnam. Instead he thought he
could now use more force to convince Hanoi of the uselessness of its
efforts. Following a Vietcong attack on American barracks at Pleiku on
February 7, 1965, Johnson approved a full-scale bombing plan against
staging areas in North Vietnam in reprisal. The chances for a UN-
brokered peace settlement vanished.

It was only in the late stages of Johnson's presidency that the United
States sought a route out of Vietnam by way of the United Nations. By
then, of course, the United States was dealing from a position of
weakness. Neither the Soviet Union, North Vietnam, nor other
opponents of U.S. policy saw any merit in employing the United Nations
to diminish the likelihood of an American defeat. When the president
asked members of the United Nations at the twentieth anniversary of the
signing of the UN Charter to "individually and collectively...bring to the
table those who seem determined to make war,"[106] there was no
meaningful response. At the end of January 1966 the United States asked
the Security Council to call for immediate unconditional talks, and to
convene a new Geneva Conference, but that was vetoed by the USSR. In
September 1967 U.S. Ambassador Goldberg circulated a draft Security
Council resolution calling for a cease-fire and the withdrawal of foreign
troops from South Vietnam. The Soviets and their allies kept it off the
agenda. In what was the most serious ongoing threat to international
peace in the 1960s, the United Nations was largely ignored and had
almost no impact on the course of events. It, like South Vietnam, was a
victim of the cold war confrontation in an arena where the United States
saw its fundamental interests threatened. In such cases, the United
Nations did not meet its founders' hope as the preserver of world peace.

It is hard today to recall the secondary importance of the Arab-Israeli
conflict in U.S. foreign policy prior to 1967. As with Indonesia, Cyprus,
and the Congo, cold war presidents thought that the Middle East should
be adjudicated by the United Nations. The issues involved were, in their
minds, largely remnants of colonialism and empire. Johnson shared this
perspective. In his speech to the General Assembly in December 1963 he
applauded the United Nations for the peacekeeping work it had done in

---

[106] Bloomfield, *Vietnam*, 8.

the region, citing it as an example of the organization's effectiveness.[107] While the Suez crisis of 1956 had demonstrated the superpower stakes involved in the region, the primary battlegrounds for that contest were Europe, Latin America, sub-Saharan Africa, and Southeast Asia. Berlin, Cuba, the Congo, and Vietnam took precedence. It would not be until the full consequences of the 1967 war were understood, and until the Yom Kippur War of 1973 had produced an oil embargo, and until the geopolitics of President Nixon and his national security adviser Henry Kissinger were in place that the Middle East would become an issue for U.S.-USSR bilateral and strategic policy, not UN multilateralism.

Hostilities mounted between Israel and two of its foes, Egypt and Syria, throughout the spring of 1967. There were armed Israeli-Syrian clashes in April. Egypt's President Nasser made increasingly bellicose statements in the same month. When the Egyptians closed the Strait of Tiran in May, putting a death grip on Israel's economy, war was inevitable. In the midst of the rising tension Johnson wrote to Soviet Premier Kosygin, "It would appear a time for each of us to use our influence to the full in the cause of moderation, including our influence over the actions of the United Nations."[108] As events unfolded over the next several weeks, it became clear that the Soviets were pursuing their own strategic interests in the area by giving undiluted support to the Arab states. Yet the president believed on the eve of war that an appeal to reason and superpower cooperation at the United Nations could avert the disaster. The State Department transmitted a letter to the Israeli cabinet urging the government to resolve the crisis "in a peaceful manner, preferably through the United Nations."[109]

The president had no experience or personal model to guide him, and his first judgment was to let the United Nations solve the Middle East matter. He was reinforced by similar counsel from two Senate leaders: Mike Mansfield and Everett Dirksen. In his *Memoirs*, Johnson says, "As far as possible I wanted the main thrust of our diplomacy [during the 1967 war] to be through the United Nations."[110] In the fall of

---

[107] Lyndon B. Johnson, *A Time for Action* (New York: Atheneum, 1964), 158.

[108] Ibid., 291.

[109] Michael Brecher, *Decisions in Crisis: Israel, 1967 and 1973* (Berkeley: University of California Press, 1980), 113–114. In all, the State Department sent three letters of caution to the Israeli government during this period.

[110] Johnson, *Vantage Point*, 290.

1966 President Johnson had appointed a special study group to look at increasing Soviet influence in the Arab world, but nothing had come of its work by the time the war broke out in June. Thus, his administration, while justifiably worried about renewed violence, did not consider the increasing tension as a matter of high national security. Johnson would be the last president of the twentieth century to believe that this region, as it had been in 1948, was essentially a responsibility of the world's representatives in New York.

On May 16 Nasser asked Secretary-General U Thant to remove from the Sinai the peacekeepers who had been there since the armistice of 1956. Thant acceded. Johnson was "shocked" but launched no strong American initiative to avert war. On May 22 Egypt made good on its threats, closing the Gulf of Aqaba. The president told his advisers, "I want to play every card in the UN...but I've never relied on it to save me when I'm going down for the third time."[111] The Israelis stayed their hand, counting on Johnson to mobilize an international effort to open the gulf and Strait of Tiran. However, this was not a "third time" situation for LBJ; he did little in the way of a strategic American response. Secretary Rusk and Vice President Humphrey both reported to Congress that the United States planned no unilateral move. At most, the president considered U.S. participation in a multilateral naval force to run the blockade. Nothing came of the idea before it was made irrelevant by the outbreak of war on June 5.

Although Secretary-General U Thant had been warning for several months about the rising threat of violence in the Middle East, the United States failed even to consult with the other permanent members of the Security Council. Once challenges to the peace erupted in May, Ambassador Goldberg urged restraint on both sides, finally introducing a draft resolution to that effect on May 31.[112] At 5:09 A.M. on June 5, Dean Rusk called the president to inform him that war had broken out. Johnson's first decision was to approve a message to the Soviets urging the convocation of the Security Council as soon as possible. During the

---

[111] Ibid., 292. Israeli leaders believed at the time that they had the "understanding" of President Johnson if they found it necessary to "embark on war." Chaim Herzog, *The Arab-Israeli Wars* (New York: Random House, 1982), 166. All of the evidentiary documents and statements, however, indicate that the president wanted a peaceful resolution through the United Nations.

[112] Arthur Lall, *The UN and the Middle East Crisis, 1967* (New York: Columbia University Press, 1968), 26–38

days of actual fighting, the United States simply worked for an "immediate cease-fire" without much concern for identifying the aggressor in the conflict, the likely consequences for U.S. policy, or the nature of a future Soviet threat in the area after a cease-fire was in place.

On June 10 President Johnson was called to the Situation Room of the White House for a message from Alexei Kosygin over the hot line. Kosygin accused the Israelis of violating Security Council resolutions. He indicated that a "very critical moment" had arrived and that the Soviet Union would have to take unilateral "necessary actions, including military" to protect its Arab allies if Israel did not desist. Now, with American interests directly threatened, the president did not ask his advisers about possible next steps at the United Nations. Instead he turned to Defense Secretary Robert McNamara and asked, "Where is the Sixth Fleet?"[113] Upon being informed that it was 300 miles from the Syrian coast he ordered a change of course to the east. He knew that Soviet intelligence would note the change and get the message.

The General Assembly convened in special session on June 17 to discuss the war. Representing the Soviet Union, Premier Kosygin traveled to New York. Kosygin's presence in the United States led to a hurriedly arranged summit with President Johnson in Glassboro, New Jersey, diplomatically about halfway between UN headquarters in New York City and the White House in Washington, D.C. Probably unintentionally, the decision to meet Kosygin in Glassboro had the effect of diminishing the apparent importance the United States attached to UN efforts to resolve the Middle East conflict. This was reinforced by Johnson's decision not to attend the special session. He feared that it would lead to pressure for a four-power meeting, since British and French heads of government would also be present. U Thant later remarked that Johnson's actions "by design or coincidence...downgraded the United Nations."[114] It probably was not Johnson's intent to do so, but his actions do indicate that even the events of the previous weeks had not made the Arab-Israeli conflict a central aspect of Soviet-American relations. At the Glassboro summit, much to the president's consternation, Kosygin constantly focused on the Middle East while Johnson tried to engage him in a discussion of arms control. The

---

[113] Johnson, *Vantage Point*, 302

[114] Bailey, *Arab-Israeli Wars*, 253.

president was intent on achieving some progress on a possible strategic weapons agreement, leaving the Middle East to UN deliberations.

Over the next five months the Security Council negotiated and finally passed Resolution 242, which called on Israel to withdraw from occupied territories in return for secure borders and mutual recognition by Israel and her Arab neighbors. Sponsored first by the United Kingdom, and then modified by the United States, the outlines of a settlement were already on the table in July. Ambassador Goldberg saw it as a two-part process. "One immediate, obvious and imperative step is the disengagement of all forces and the withdrawal of Israeli forces to their own territory....A second and equally immediate, obvious and imperative step is the termination of any claims to a state of war or belligerency on the part of the Arab States in the area."[115] The recalcitrance of both the Israelis and the Arabs required strong pressure from both the United States and the Soviet Union on their respective allies to get an agreement. In November the resolution gained the unanimous support of the Security Council. Later, there would be acrimony among the parties over the meaning of 242, specifically concerning whether the resolution required the Israelis to withdraw from all occupied territories or only for those that would not jeopardize Israel's security. Nonetheless, the administration concluded that it had gotten a reasonable settlement without direct intervention. It could now focus on Vietnam and on strengthening relations with Moscow. Regarding the latter, Johnson would seek an arms control agreement before he left office. With Vietnam still defying solution in the summer of 1968, the two sides agreed to a presidential visit to the Soviet Union in October to begin the process toward a strategic arms limitation agreement. The visit was to be announced on August 21, but it never took place, because of the Soviet invasion of Czechoslovakia on August 20. Progress on controlling the weapons of mass destruction had fallen victim to the continuing cold war.

---

[115] General Assembly, A/PV.1554 (1967), 46.

Disarmament and Development

The United Nations is essential because global war is now unthinkable as the result of new and devastating weapons.

—*President Eisenhower to congressional leaders*

Events in Vietnam, Eastern Europe, and the Middle East could leave one believing that the post-1962 *détente* between the United States and the Soviet Union was ephemeral. It was not. A new bilateral *rapprochement* was under way with new trade agreements, an easing of the confrontation in Germany, more cultural and scientific exchanges, and, most important, some progress on arms control. Even the crushing of liberal reform in Czechoslovakia could only slow the thaw, not end it. For both President Kennedy and President Johnson a key element of *détente* was step-by-step arms control.

Central to the "Eisenhower model" spelled out in 1953 was the tenet that agreements on arms limitation were necessary and could be achieved with the help of the United Nations, but only after trust had been established between Moscow and Washington. By the late 1950s the Eisenhower administration refined that argument by pursuing limited arms agreements that might contribute to easing the cold war, not just be a reward for its conclusion. Kennedy and Johnson endorsed that approach, hoping to make significant breakthroughs in arms control even as the Soviet-American confrontation continued. The history of the period, however, confirms that arms agreements came during eras of "good feeling" and improved relations; they did not generate those relations. It also shows that the superpowers' effort at arms control was conducted with only a nod to UN responsibility for disarmament. For the most part, the depths of the cold war made disarmament impossible in the Eisenhower years, and only marginally more probable as tensions eased after the Cuban missile crisis.

Dwight Eisenhower believed in the power of an effective speech. An address by an American president on a matter of critical world significance could set in motion positive forces for change. His "Chance for Peace" speech in April 1953 had been given in that vein. He hoped to do the same regarding disarmament with his "Atoms for Peace" address to the United Nations General Assembly in December of that year. The president was deeply concerned about the arms race and the implications of the confrontation between the two nuclear superpowers. One of Eisenhower's first acts in office was to order a review of the

United States' strategic policy. The results of what became known as "Operation Candor" convinced the president that he must spell out publicly the dangers nuclear weapons presented to the world's population and must also define a course of action which might give hope for the future. The dilemma for the administration was stark. In an effort to keep military spending down, Eisenhower's "New Look" military policy, approved by the National Security Council in October, depended heavily on the H-bomb to deter Soviet aggression. But that dependence was sure to spark an arms race with the Soviet Union, since the Kremlin's leaders could not afford to fall far behind the United States. This prospect meant ballooning national budgets and an increased threat of nuclear war. Eisenhower decided to make a speech "to awaken the American people and the world to the incredible destructive power of the United States' stockpile of nuclear weapons."[116]

During the Truman administration, the United States had put forward the "Baruch plan" to transfer the production and control of fissionable materials to the United Nations without the available use of the veto. It had been a comprehensive approach but was summarily rejected by Stalin as a plot to ensure an American nuclear monopoly. Eisenhower, who as early as 1946 had thought "progressive disarmament" a better strategy,[117] now suggested a partial step toward a less threatening world. He proposed to the General Assembly that the nuclear powers contribute a small percentage of their fissionable stockpiles to a new International Atomic Energy Agency (IAEA), which would be under the ultimate authority of the United Nations but largely independent of its jurisdiction. Over time, as the powers' trust in each other and in the agency developed, more plutonium could be deposited with the United Nations.[118] The president specifically called upon the United Kingdom and the Soviet Union to join the United States in this effort, indicating that the United States would be willing to contribute fissionable materials at a ratio of 5 to 1 of that turned over by the USSR.

---

[116] Eisenhower, *Mandate*, 252.

[117] Pruden, *Partners*, 18.

[118] Address before the General Assembly of the United Nations on the Peaceful Use of Atomic Energy, December 8, 1953, *PPP, 1953*, 813–822. In 1954 the administration suggested that the U.S. contribution to the IAEA would be 100 kilograms of fissionable materials, which could be used in experimental nuclear reactors.

The UN agency would safeguard the plutonium deposits and look for ways to use them for peaceful purposes, such as the generation of electric power. In this way the available weapons-grade plutonium would be reduced and the world would benefit from the positive elements of the nuclear age.

The president was sincere in his proposal, but he was not surprised that Soviet leaders rejected it. Any reduction in nuclear stockpiles, even if it drew more heavily from the American arsenal, would still leave the United States with a significant advantage. The Kremlin leadership, which had only recently exploded its own hydrogen device, could not accept a formula that permitted permanent American dominance in the nuclear field. That the administration did not expect a very positive response from Moscow is demonstrated by the White House's lack of effort to follow up the speech with direct negotiations between the Americans and the Soviets. Dulles' special assistant for atomic energy, Gerard C. Smith, later concluded that "the Administration was ill-prepared to deal with the political and technical details of framing programs and negotiating an international convention"[119] to carry out the president's proposals. In 1954 an IAEA Preparatory Commission was established, consisting of the United States, the USSR, Czechoslovakia, the Vatican, Australia, and India; but little progress was made until 1956. Even the convocation of the first "Peaceful Uses of Nuclear Energy Conference" (PUNE) in the summer of 1955 did not move the proposal forward very much. It was not until 1957 that the IAEA came into existence. It did not obtain the authority to take possession of fissionable materials, but it did develop a "safeguards" system for monitoring nuclear material used for peaceful purposes.

Eisenhower's speech was good propaganda, putting the United States on record in support of significant disarmament. It was the kind of use which his psychological warfare chief C.D. Jackson and UN Ambassador Lodge recommended the United States make of the United Nations. Of course, the United States was not alone in using the United Nations for disarmament propaganda. Since the founding of the Atomic Energy Commission in 1946, the Soviets had scathingly attacked American strategic policies. After Stalin's death Soviet leaders regularly called for "general and complete disarmament," an unrealistic possibility given the hostile international environment of the period. Eisenhower

---

[119] Smith, *Diplomat*, 37.

made clear that no disarmament proposal was acceptable which did not allow for direct inspection of the other side's facilities and nuclear program. This demand was characterized by the Kremlin as little more than an effort to spy on the Soviet Union. During the first decade of the cold war a tit-for-tat attitude developed in which no prospect for genuine arms control presented itself.

Thus, although the Eisenhower model suggested that the United Nations should have an important role in the disarmament effort, the UN's impact in the 1950s was negligible. First, no disarmament was possible until the confrontation between the United States and Russia was muted, and, unfortunately, their relations reached several low points during Eisenhower's first term. Second, even in Eisenhower's conceptualization, strategic weapons policy was too important to America's national interest to be left to the multilateral diplomacy of the United Nations. At most, the United Nations might provide a structural facade behind which the superpowers might reach some partial agreements. The Atomic Energy Commission was replaced in 1952 by the Disarmament Commission, which in turn created a Subcommittee on Disarmament in April 1954, made up of the United States, the Soviet Union, the United Kingdom, France, and Canada. These revisions in bureaucratic structure had the effect of making disarmament largely a subject for secret negotiation by the great powers. Even in that context, however, little more than an exchange of propaganda occurred until mid-1955.

On May 10, 1955, the Soviet delegate to the Disarmament Subcommittee, Jacob Malik, surprised the attending delegations by announcing that the Soviet Union would accept many of the proposals for ground inspections which the United States had been demanding as part of any disarmament agreement. Malik proposed phased disarmament with "control posts at large ports, at railway junctions, on main motor highways and in aerodromes."[120] This was a reversal of the past Soviet position and in another time would have produced a quick American acceptance. The question for Eisenhower, however, was, "Could you believe the Soviet leaders?" The president displayed a curious blend of hopefulness and suspicion[121] when considering his Soviet counterparts' disarmament initiatives. Wanting to move forward

---

[120] W. W. Rostow, *Open Skies* (Austin: University of Texas Press, 1982), 19.

[121] The characterization is H. W. Brands'. See Brands, *Warriors*, 141.

in small ways while always ensuring Western security, he could not bring himself to trust the Soviets.

Malik's proposals came on the eve of a long-awaited four-power summit to be convened in July. The Geneva meeting of the heads of government was the first such gathering since Potsdam in 1945 and raised great expectations that a reversal of the cold war might be possible. Eisenhower wanted to use the meeting as a venue to respond to the Soviet disarmament proposal and to reclaim the American leadership on arms control established in his "Atoms for Peace" speech. He directed his advisers that enforcement and airtight inspection must be bedrock principles of any disarmament program. He also made clear that those factors should be guaranteed by some organization other than the United Nations.[122] A group of advisers headed by Nelson Rockefeller met in Quantico, Virginia during May to draw up proposals for the summit. The group suggested that the president "test" the sincerity of the Soviets by making a series of tough proposals which Soviet leaders could accept only if they were committed to ending the cold war.[123] If they did not accept, then the West would know that it needed to increase its defense budgets and prepare for a long period of confrontation. Among the items in the Quantico Report recommended to Eisenhower was a proposal to have both sides allow unfettered air surveillance of their national territory.

Without forewarning, President Eisenhower sprang the Quantico formulation on the Geneva summit in what became known as his "Open Skies" proposal. He advanced the idea that each side provide complete blueprints of its military establishments to the other. "Next, to provide within our countries facilities for aerial photography to the other country—we to provide you the facilities within our country…for aerial reconnaissance, where you can make all the pictures you choose and take them to your own country to study. We can do the same."[124] The president was arguing for transparency as a "practical step" to avoid a surprise attack or the secret development of nuclear superiority. The Soviets said they would study Eisenhower's idea, but on August 18 they rejected it as nothing but a ruse for American spying. Nonetheless, two

---

[122] President's News Conference of July 6, 1955, *PPP*, *1955*, 677.

[123] Rostow, *Open Skies*, 29.

[124] Statement on Disarmament Presented at the Geneva Conference, July 21, 1955, *PPP*, *1955*, 713–716.

weeks later the president's special assistant for disarmament, Harold Stassen, introduced the proposal in the UN Disarmament Commission. The administration intended to make public relations points, as it had with the "Atoms for Peace" plan, even if little substantive progress was possible. It also stepped up its own surreptitious aerial surveillance of Soviet territory, using high-altitude U-2 spy planes. Flying out of Turkey and crossing some of the most sensitive military regions of the Soviet Union, these flights remained secret until the spring of 1960, when the Soviets downed one of the flights and captured the pilot. According to Soviet propaganda, the U-2 incident confirmed the disingenuous nature of American disarmament proposals.

The UN's disarmament machinery was reduced to near-sterility in Eisenhower's second term. It was dominated by proposals from the small and nonaligned nations of the world, and little of consequence was considered in the official chambers of the United Nations. To be sure, the growing number of new states and the need to maintain influence in the liberated regions of the globe led the superpowers to make organizational concessions to members demanding a role in the disarmament process, but the serious substantive issues were monopolized by the major powers. In August 1959 the Subcommittee on Disarmament was transformed into the Ten Nation Disarmament Committee. In addition to the United States, the USSR, and Great Britain, Bulgaria, Czechoslovakia, Italy, Canada, Poland, Romania, and France were added to the Committee. This provided five votes for the U.S. position and five for the Soviets, which meant that there was little hope of progress. It also meant that, while there was a public display by Moscow and Washington of a willingness to include more members in the deliberations, the vast majority of UN members were excluded. Secretary-General Hammarskjöld complained on several occasions that the UN's responsibility was being undermined by the superpowers' monopolization of the negotiations. By 1961, under pressure from the nonaligned states, the United States and the Soviet Union thought it necessary to reorganize the body yet again as the Eighteen Nation Disarmament Committee (ENDC), adding Brazil, Burma, Ethiopia, India,

Mexico, Nigeria, Sweden, and the United Arab Republic under the chairmanship of the superpowers.[125]

In only one area did the administration seem seriously interested in making some progress on arms limitation, and that was to achieve a test ban covering military explosions above a threshold megatonnage and with sufficient inspection provisions. It was Secretary of State John Foster Dulles who pushed the president particularly hard on this issue. Eisenhower was also under pressure from the Democratic opposition. Adlai Stevenson had made a moratorium on testing and the conclusion of an agreement part of his campaign platform in 1956. Several nonaligned leaders, including India's Prime Minister Nehru, called for a "standstill agreement" as early as 1954, and Soviet negotiators at the 1955 Geneva Conference also proposed a test ban.[126] Without an inspection regime, however, and having little trust in Soviet promises, the administration was prepared to do little beyond continuing the negotiations behind closed doors.

As long as the only serious national security threat to either superpower was its counterpart, the nuclear danger might be grave, but it was manageable. However, following French nuclear tests in 1959, the potential for destabilizing proliferation became a new concern for Washington and Moscow. In February 1960 the United States, joined by Great Britain, proposed a ban on tests above a seismic level of 4.75. All progress was stymied, however, by the collapse of the Paris summit in May. Eisenhower's term ended with no conclusion to the issue. In July 1962 the matter of a test ban treaty was transferred to a subcommittee of the ENDC, where it remained until the crisis in Cuba three months later.

The Cuban missile crisis got rid of many myths surrounding the cold war. Both sides had believed and acted as if they could conduct their global contest on every level as long as they avoided an ultimate nuclear confrontation. The events of October demonstrated that they might not be able to ensure that the outcome they did not want would not in fact occur. The temperature of the heated propaganda between the two sides decidedly diminished following the crisis. For First Secretary Khrushchev, who had "lost" the confrontation with Kennedy, there were

---

[125] ENDC/156, September 14, 1965. See also Office of Public Information (UN), *The United Nations and Disarmament, 1945–1965* (New York: United Nations, 1967), 5.

[126] Jerry Pubantz, "Moscow Agreement of 1963," *MERSH*, Vol. 23, 1981, 83.

really only two choices. He could have accelerated the strategic arms race to overcome the apparent superiority of the United States, or he could seek an accommodation on nuclear arms. Largely for domestic economic reasons, he opted for the latter. In December he indicated that the USSR would welcome a test ban with the kind of inspection procedure being proposed by the United States.[127] Kennedy quickly signaled a desire to reach an agreement. During the spring of 1963 quiet talks were held among U.S., British, and Soviet diplomats in New York, but none of them were conducted as part of the UN effort toward disarmament. The UN was left in the dark on the state of the talks.

The same June day that John Kennedy addressed his audience at American University, the three powers announced the convening of a tripartite conference in Moscow on the cessation of nuclear tests. While there was still some difference among the parties about what type of inspections to allow, in August a partial test ban was signed, prohibiting tests in all environments except underground. With all of its weaknesses and its limited nature, the treaty was the first substantive arms control agreement of the nuclear age, and it had been achieved without the involvement of the United Nations.

At best, it was the shifting voting mathematics of the United Nations that had some impact on the disarmament process. Total membership in the organization grew to ninety-nine by the time of Kennedy's inauguration, with most of the new states emerging from the national liberation movement in the former colonial territories. By 1963 African and Asian states made up a majority of the General Assembly. They quickly rallied to the nonaligned bloc, supporting broader and quicker steps toward disarmament than the superpowers had been willing to undertake so far. President Eisenhower made few concessions to the mounting call for serious disarmament steps. He adhered to his basic strategy of giving lip service to the United Nations regarding disarmament while keeping negotiations in the secret confines of great-power diplomacy. Kennedy and Johnson found the international pressure too severe to ignore. Faced with Soviet competition for influence in Africa, Asia, and Latin America, American policy shifted

---

[127] For a full history of the 1963 Test Ban Treaty negotiations, see the records of the Eighteen Nation Disarmament Committee, and the *Disarmament Document Series* of the U.S. Arms Control and Disarmament Agency.

away from the Eisenhower model and attempted to meet, at least minimally, the third world's demands for arms limitation.

The addition of eight apparently nonaligned or neutral states to the former Ten Nation Disarmament Committee gave the new General Assembly majority an institutional framework in which to press for progress. It seized the opportunity by promoting the conclusion of a nonproliferation treaty.[128] The "nonatomic club" found an ally in Secretary-General U Thant, who urged the American and Soviet governments to respond affirmatively. Outside the United Nations several nations pushed for the creation of nuclear-free zones in central Europe, Africa, and Latin America. On May 25, 1962, the two governments, acceding to the pressure, placed "Measures to Prevent Further Dissemination of Nuclear Weapons" on the ENDC's agenda.[129]

The Cuban crisis suspended the nonproliferation negotiations. The cold war thaw that followed, however, reinvigorated the effort. The conclusion of the Test Ban Treaty moved the proliferation issue to the top of the priority list in Washington and at the United Nations. Negotiations, however, did not move rapidly. The Soviets, deeply fearful of future German revanchism, insisted that any treaty guarantee that the Federal Republic of Germany would never have access to nuclear weapons. As a member of NATO, the Adenauer government in Bonn resented any effort to limit the defense of West Germany. For its part Washington was promoting German participation in a multilateral NATO force (MLF) that would have nuclear capability, always subject to the American president's ultimate authority to control the nuclear weapons. The proposal was unacceptable to the Kremlin, and, consequently, no progress on the proliferation treaty was made until the Johnson administration dropped the MLF idea in 1965.

In 1966 the eight nonaligned nations on the ENDC issued a memorandum calling upon the co-Chairmen to draft a consensus nonproliferation proposal and outlined the provisions necessary to achieve third world support. The weaker states on the committee understood that any agreement which limited the spread of nuclear technology was an inherently "unequal" treaty. It would freeze the gulf between those nations that already possessed these weapons and states

---

[128] In particular, see General Assembly Resolutions 1660, 1664, and 1665 during the Sixteenth Session, *YUN, 1961*, 28–29, 31.

[129] ENDC/First Committee/Document 19, May 25, 1962.

that would be permanently barred from obtaining them. The United Nations' imprimatur was being used to solidify the dominance of nuclear states in world affairs. Consequently, nonaligned states insisted on a balance of mutual responsibilities for nuclear and nonnuclear powers. The group was especially concerned about the "vertical proliferation" represented in the huge arsenals of the superpowers. Any ban on "horizontal proliferation" to nonnuclear states which allowed the United States and the USSR to continue stockpiling nuclear weapons would only exacerbate the gulf between the "haves" and "have-nots."[130] Washington and Moscow were put on notice that to be broadly acceptable, any agreement must meet the demands of the nonnuclear powers. The UN majority for the first time was intruding on the superpowers' monopoly in disarmament negotiations.

A U.S.-Soviet draft nonproliferation treaty was tabled on August 24, 1967. The draft gave formal recognition to the existence of two classes of states in international affairs—those with nuclear weapons as of January 1, 1967, and those without. It barred nuclear signatories from transferring weapons or the technology to build them to nonnuclear states, and it prohibited nonnuclear signatories from acquiring them. The latter group of states were also prohibited from conducting any nuclear tests. One glaring omission from the draft was any system of international control or verification. The Soviets had urged the use of the International Atomic Energy Agency for this purpose. The United States welcomed the IAEA's authority, except in Western Europe—where, it argued, Euratom should provide verification.

Washington found itself in the minority on the inspection issue and had to retreat before strong Third World complaints. It also faced serious criticism that the treaty did nothing about the growing arsenals of the Soviet Union and the United States. A number of delegations, led particularly by Nigeria and Brazil, made it clear that their governments would not sign an agreement which froze their military programs while allowing the superpowers' stockpiling to continue. Without the agreement of the many threshold states in the world, a nonproliferation agreement would be worthless. The Soviet leader Brezhnev and President Johnson found that they needed to make a commitment to move toward limiting their strategic weapons if they wanted the treaty.

---

[130] Jerry Pubantz, "Non-Proliferation Treaty of 1968," *MERSH*, Vol. 25, 1981, 49.

Articles Six and Seven were added, which called upon the parties to "pursue negotiations in good faith on effective measures relating to the cessation of the nuclear arms race at an early date and to nuclear disarmament."[131] For the first time the political clout of third world states in the United Nations forced an American president to make concessions on arms control, which previously would have been only a matter of private negotiation by the superpowers. Disarmament was now not only an east-west issue but also a north-south one.[132] The draft treaty as amended was submitted to the General Assembly in March 1968.

Applauded by Johnson as the most important international disarmament agreement since the dawn of nuclear weapons, the Non-Proliferation Treaty (NPT) became the most significant accomplishment of the United Nations in that regard. Even here, though, no real progress was made until the superpowers submitted their joint draft to the Eighteen Nation Disarmament Committee. The draft was designed not only to protect the superpowers' nuclear interests but also to gain the acquiescence of threshold states in the third world. In the end it accomplished that goal. The United Nations proved a useful vehicle for extracting promises from nonnuclear states not to obtain nuclear capabilities.

Prior to the submission of the joint draft treaty by the USSR and the United States, Lyndon Johnson had attempted to engage the Soviets in talks on strategic arms limitations (SALT). At the Glassboro summit, as we noted earlier, LBJ had pressed Premier Kosygin on the matter only to be deflected by Soviet preoccupation with the Middle East war of 1967. The NPT obligations now, however, made movement on SALT politically imperative for both powers. Eisenhower had never proposed a cap on the superpowers' arms race, but both Kennedy and Johnson, responding to domestic opinion, proposed on several occasions some agreement with Moscow. As early as January 1964, President Johnson proposed to the ENDC a "verified freeze" on arms stockpiling.[133] When he decided, in 1966, to deploy an antiballistic missile defense (ABM) for

---

[131] Ibid., 47.

[132] For a discussion of this aspect of UN disarmament dynamics, see Avi Beker, *Disarmament Without Order* (Westport, Conn.: Greenwood, 1985), 5.

[133] Jerry Pubantz, "Strategic Arms Limitation Talks," *MERSH*, Vol. 37, 1984, 173.

the United States, he coupled the idea with a commitment to pursue private talks with the Russians on strategic weapons. Then, in January 1967, he wrote directly to Kosygin proposing secret negotiations. The president's efforts were motivated in large part by the massive nuclear weapons program under way in the USSR. By the time the United Nations opened the NPT for signature, the Soviet Union was approaching parity with the United States in the number of intercontinental ballistic missile launchers (ICBM). The administration was facing a likely need to undertake a new round of exorbitant spending on missile capability unless it could get an agreement with the Soviets. That prospect was not palatable to a president facing a growing budget deficit, serious domestic economic problems, and the expensive war in Vietnam.

The third world's pressure for strategic arms limitations as part of the NPT was, thus, strangely helpful to the administration. The demands of the United Nations' treaty meant that the two sides were going to have to demonstrate some progress in their talks, or the NPT might not be signed by critical nonnuclear states. In private exchanges during the spring and summer of 1968, Brezhnev and Johnson agreed to begin formal talks on September 30. Sadly, the joint announcement of those talks, scheduled for August 21, was abruptly canceled when Soviet troops poured into Czechoslovakia on August 20, ending the Czech experiment in liberalizing its communist regime. Further progress on strategic arms limitations would not be possible until America's 1968 elections had been held and a new president was inaugurated. The events of 1968 reminded everyone that progress on disarmament and arms control was a function of the cold war temperature in Soviet-American relations and not vice versa, and that promises to the United Nations to move toward a disarmed world could be honored only when essential trust between the United States and the Soviet Union had been established.

Within three months of becoming president, Dwight Eisenhower had spelled out the basic approach of the United States toward the United Nations during the cold war. Battered and revised, it remained the blueprint for nearly two decades. A military man with an aversion to war, Eisenhower could imagine the United Nations in a future time serving the moralist ends his predecessors had envisioned for it. In the cold war he inherited, however, the United Nations would have to be a place of postponed promise until the great contest between communism and the free world was resolved. Until then, the United States must defend its realist interests inside and beyond the institution. Once trust was achieved between Moscow and Washington, the United Nations could be the venue and facilitator of disarmament, which in turn would produce a peace dividend. The resources saved could be used by the UN to feed the hungry, clothe the naked, house the homeless, cure the ill, and finance the underdeveloped.

Eisenhower's model was challenged first in the arena of disarmament, where the need to find small victories in the search for Soviet-American cooperation, a desire to curb the arms race, and the persistent threat of nuclear war led to the test ban treaty, the hot line, a limited agreement on weapons in outer space, and the Non-Proliferation Treaty. These were partial steps, however, that did not discredit Eisenhower's initial formulation. The cold war and its concomitant security demands took precedence over UN interests. Second, and more dramatically, the Eisenhower model was challenged in terms of its final component, aid to the third world. It was in terms of this element that, both bilaterally and through the United Nations, the greatest revisions in American strategy occurred. In a subtle way, though, this change only reinforced the basic cold war view of the United Nations as a secondary institution in U.S. foreign policy. Clearly, of the Soviet-American confrontation, disarmament, and development aid, the last was of least significance to American national security. Thus, it is not surprising that Washington would see it as the arena in which it could make the most concessions. The United Nations was not elevated by that perception but rather patronized. Aid to the less developed countries (LDC) of the world reflected far more specific American cold war interests, a long-term American objection to colonialism, and a short-term American response to the growing political power of the nonaligned movement than it did a return to a moralist recognition of the authority of the United Nations.

In his inaugural address in 1949, Harry Truman told the American people that he believed the United States needed to support the United Nations "as a means of applying democratic principles to international relations."[134] He then outlined several initiatives that his administration would undertake to ensure that those democratic precepts were secured on a global scale. Among those initiatives was a major aid program to

---

[134] *PPP, 1949*, 113.

LDCs in an effort to ameliorate the kinds of human problems which might make a less developed country susceptible to communist subversion. The president couched his proposal as an American responsibility, under Article 56 of the Charter, to promote higher standards of living and to solve the human problems of the less fortunate. In his view, aid through the United Nations was critical to the avoidance of another world war. Known as the "Point Four Program" because of the place it held in his inaugural ordering of proposals, the aid package was submitted to Congress the following June.

Truman's program was part of an American commitment in the Wilsonian tradition to end colonialism. He and his successors regularly condemned European efforts to maintain even limited control over their old imperial possessions. The American liberal creed held that self-determination was an inalienable right of colonial peoples. Throughout the cold war, presidential administrations made no concessions on the advisability of granting independence and sovereignty to the emerging nations. Eisenhower insisted on it in Southeast Asia and in the Middle East, even when holding to that position meant a break in the solidarity of the United States and its allies. He even suggested to Prime Minister Churchill, as the latter approached retirement, that Churchill give a stirring speech in the House of Commons as his swan song on the "rights to self-government" of the peoples in the British Empire.[135] The president's suggestion must have taken the old British imperialist by surprise, for he responded acidly that he would choose another topic rather than defame British efforts to bring "forward backward races and [open] up the jungles." Both Kennedy and Johnson repeated American moralizing about independence, and promoted U.S. financial support as an effort to go beyond containment and to provide a positive response to the national liberation of large swaths of the globe.

If self-determination was the goal, the United Nations was the methodology most likely to succeed in its accomplishment. In Truman's words, the United Nations provided the "procedure and method"[136] to secure the blessings of independence for millions around the world. As a part of the Point Four program, the United States proposed an Expanded Program of Technical Assistance (EPTA) under the jurisdiction of the UN's Economic and Social Council (ECOSOC). Financed by voluntary

---

[135] Boyle, *Correspondence*, 163.

[136] Truman, *Memoirs*, I, 237.

contributions, EPTA commenced operations in 1950 as the UN's single largest program. The United States initially provided 60 percent of the agency's $20 million budget.[137] Even by the time John Kennedy took the oath of office, when many more nations were contributing to the fund, the United States still paid 40 percent of the bills. By the mid-1950s EPTA was dispensing over $25 million annually in more than ninety countries.

Eisenhower's opposition to colonialism was as deep as Truman's, but his commitment of American resources to that end or to the economic development of the newly liberated states was limited by two considerations—the threat of communism and the desire to cut federal spending. Funds for allies in the third world fighting communist subversion or open aggression were forthcoming from the administration. But that diminished what could be spent unilaterally or through the United Nations on the general problems facing less developed states. When counselors suggested a broader American involvement in assistance programs, he would rejoin, "Where are we going to get the money from?"[138]

The strongest advocate in the inner circle for American support of UN development efforts was Ambassador Lodge. He regularly advised the president to expand the American commitment. He was deeply concerned that the changing dynamics brought on by the admission of new members from Africa and Asia would put the United States in a weakened position within the organization unless Washington responded to the obvious needs of the peoples in the Southern Hemisphere. Lodge developed a strong interest in the problems facing the populations of the underdeveloped world, which he never was at a loss to express in sessions with the president, Secretary Dulles, congressional leaders, or other prominent members of the administration. The ambassador endorsed American support for highly visible projects that would win some propaganda points for the United States, and also for what he called "UN multilateral"[139] which would demonstrate the permanence of the U.S. partnership with the United Nations and the LDCs.

---

[137] A. LeRoy Bennett, *International Organizations* (Englewood Cliffs, N.J.: Prentice Hall, 1988), 239.

[138] Rostow, *Open Skies*, 99.

[139] Brands, *Warriors*, 173–174.

Lodge's own visibility in American politics meant that his views received a wide audience; thus there was good reason for Eisenhower to act in accordance with growing public support of development aid. On the other hand, the president faced members of his own party in Congress who strongly opposed any deeper American involvement with UN programs. The conservative Republican senator from California, William Knowland, was particularly outspoken in his opposition to such "internationalist" policies. Thus, the president had to walk a narrow line between the two wings of his supporters in his approach to foreign aid in any form. The outcome was that the administration's record in this area can be divided into two distinct periods marked out by his terms in office.

From 1953 to 1957 the administration did little to expand its support for UN development activities. Faced with concluding the Korean conflict as well as responding to the Soviet strategic challenge and to apparent communist aggression in Southeast Asia, Eisenhower declined to take on his isolationist supporters over new development projects. In his second term, however, the president changed course, enlarging the American effort. The ascendancy of Nikita Khrushchev in Moscow explained part of Eisenhower's shift. The new Communist Party leader, beginning in 1954, showed an interest in the third world that his predecessor, Joseph Stalin, had never demonstrated. Arguing that there was a great "peace zone" which included many third world nations that, while not socialist states, were following "the noncapitalist path of development," he moved to expand Soviet aid programs throughout the underdeveloped world. Under the new strategy Moscow paid special attention to critical states such as India and Egypt. A Soviet deal to sell weapons and expand economic assistance to Egypt in 1955 was particularly worrisome to the Eisenhower administration because it meant the likely growth of Soviet influence in the tense Middle East.

A response to this Soviet assistance was needed, but the form was not obvious. The administration understood that a large part of its aid programs had to be in the form of direct military assistance, but the real question concerned nonmilitary aid. The greatest public relations benefit would come from bilateral aid. Direct assistance would also mean that the United States could have greater control over the expenditure of its funds and could probably expect a higher level of direct influence on the government receiving the aid. Unfortunately, most of the third world nations Eisenhower hoped to influence argued strongly for multilateral aid through the United Nations, so that it would come to them with fewer strings attached. The issue first presented itself in the effort of those nations to establish a Special UN Fund to augment the resources of the 1950 Expanded Program of Technical Assistance.

In 1954 the General Assembly passed Resolution 822, calling for the organization of the Special United Nations Fund for Economic Development (SUNFED). The purpose of SUNFED was to provide capital to underdeveloped countries for infrastructure projects including such things as roads, hospitals, schools, and electric power plants. The assistance was to be provided as grants-in-aid and low-interest long-term loans from resources contributed to the fund by developed nations.[140] By 1955 contributions had already been promised by the Netherlands ($7 million), Denmark ($2 million), and Norway ($1.5 million).[141] The planners hoped, of course, that the United States would make the largest contribution toward the target of $250 million in pledged funds before SUNFED began operations.

The idea of a new funding source for development assistance was good, according to the administration, but the timing was bad. In his "Chance for Peace" speech, Eisenhower had offered to dedicate a percentage of the savings realized through disarmament to the development process. It was premature, therefore, to allocate funds until progress was made on reducing the military arsenals of the superpowers, which in turn could not occur until there was an easing of the Soviet-American confrontation. Many third world delegations saw this American argument as an excuse behind which the administration could hide its general policy of doing little to assist the LDCs. Since disarmament was a slow, distant process, most underdeveloped states contended that development could not wait for arms control. Increasingly they believed that even if disarmament was achieved, little in the way of a peace dividend for development would be made available through UN channels. Given that the USSR supported the creation of SUNFED, albeit with a shift of resources from infrastructure to heavy industrialization projects, the American position put the United States increasingly in a distinct minority opposed to the Fund.

Eisenhower changed his position on SUNFED, and therefore on the timetable and prerequisites of the Eisenhower model, in the spring of

---

[140] *YUN, 1955*, 1.

[141] Ibid., 92.

1956. The administration had underestimated the political weight of the third world when it initially laid out a strategy tying aid to disarmament. Development assistance was now necessary on its own merits because the cohesiveness and importance of the LDCs could not be ignored, at least not without creating an opening for the Soviet Union. Despite congressional opposition to any large contribution, the administration reluctantly moved toward support of the new organization. The General Assembly established SUNFED in December 1957, with a promise from the United States to make contributions equaling two-thirds of what all other nations gave.[142]

The last months of Eisenhower's term in office were marked by increasingly strong statements about the need for the world community to expand development programs. While he would make no additional commitment of U.S. dollars to the SUNFED, he urged other states to increase their contributions. He also encouraged the United Nations to extend its programs to parts of Asia and Africa as yet untouched by development efforts. Having broken the link between disarmament and development, Eisenhower supported new types of aid, including the establishment of the Food and Agriculture Organization. By 1960 the United States became the leading force among developed states encouraging the United Nations to respond to the impoverishment endemic to a large portion of the globe.

President Kennedy saw no reason to reverse the course of U.S. policy inherited from Eisenhower. If anything, the new president was even more concerned about the problems of the third world and their probable negative impact on American fortunes in the struggle with Moscow. He took a special interest in Africa, surprising African leaders with his detailed knowledge of their countries and the problems they faced. As he assessed American national interests, he was willing to consider expanding aid to nonaligned nations, even to those that had been critical of U.S. policies. Shedding the ideological perspectives of the previous administration, the president looked upon development assistance as a valuable instrument for winning friends in the third world. During his brief time in office, John Kennedy developed a close working relationship with some of the "lions" of the nonaligned and socialist movements in Africa, among them Kwame Nkrumah of Ghana and Sekou Touré of Guinea.

---

[142] Pruden, *Partners*, 214.

President Kennedy was much more enamored with bilateral aid than with multilateral aid because he thought about development assistance as an instrument of a realist foreign policy. Through direct loans, grants, and credits the United States could influence government decisions in the countries critical to U.S. interests. It could also ensure that the aid was directed at projects the administration believed would contribute to stability and growth. He regularly asked Congress to increase the budget for development programs and agencies, saying that American "assistance to its less fortunate sister nations" was not only "a matter of international responsibility," but also "in our national interests."[143] Kennedy and his advisers were not as interested in the high-visibility projects promoted by Lodge, Dulles, and Eisenhower for their propaganda value. Rather, they were advocates of a then-popular development theory that emphasized modernization as a route to nation-building. Not just capital and investment projects were needed; all social structures in third world states must be reformed. The United States must involve itself in long-term projects to change the way populations saw and participated in government, the economy, and social development. Two months after becoming president, Kennedy sent his foreign aid proposals to Capitol Hill. He told the legislators that the purpose of his proposals was not "negatively to fight communism," but rather to "make a historical demonstration that in the twentieth century...in the southern half of the globe as in the north—economic growth and political democracy can develop hand in hand."[144]

The president's penchant for bilateral programs administered from Washington led to the centralization of American aid efforts in a newly created Agency for International Development (AID) and in several Kennedy-supported diplomatic and bureaucratic initiatives. During less than three years in office the administration launched the Alliance for Progress, a dramatic effort at economic assistance in Latin America; the Food for Peace Program, which in an eighteen-month period, under the leadership of George McGovern, distributed more supplies than Herbert Hoover's efforts had been able to accomplish in ten years of assisting victims of World War I; and the Peace Corps. The last of these best represented Kennedy's belief in the long-term and social revolutionary

---

[143] Special Message to the Congress on Free World Defense and Assistance Programs, April 2, 1963, *PPP, 1963*, 294.

[144] Schlesinger, *Thousand Days*, 545.

nature of the development process. Kennedy called upon Americans to volunteer their talents and time to serve in third world countries, side by side with nationals in the painstaking work of transforming societies. Kennedy made development policy a central element of U.S. foreign policy, separate from the fortunes of disarmament or the confrontation with the Soviet Union.

This change in U.S. development policy did not translate into a boom for UN programs and institutions. The emphasis on bilateral assistance eclipsed efforts at the United Nations and the president's urging the UN to focus on limited practical steps toward development. He was wary of grand strategies, which might well fail. In the context of the first "Decade of Development" then under way, Kennedy cautioned the United Nations about the danger of raising expectations when the resources, will, and capability were not there to accomplish declared goals. He addressed the General Assembly in September 1963, during what he acknowledged was a "pause in the cold war." The recent *détente* allowed new development initiatives. He urged the delegates to create a world center for health communications at the World Health Organization, to establish regional medical research centers in the third world, to create a global system of satellites for communications and weather monitoring, and to undertake worldwide conservation and farm productivity programs.[145] But he made no specific offer of American financial assistance in these projects.

It is understandable that the slain president's successor, Lyndon Johnson, might approach economic assistance as an aspect of U.S. foreign policy to be judged and pursued on its own. Kennedy detached it completely from the disarmament effort, which the administration pursued on a separate track, leading to the Test Ban Treaty of 1963. He also saw it as intertwined with the Soviet challenge in a far more complex and indirect way than Eisenhower. Late in his term, Kennedy told Congress that helping the less fortunate of the world was "the most challenging and constructive effort ever undertaken by man on behalf of freedom and his fellow man."[146] For Johnson, who hoped to sustain the continuity of Kennedy's policies and who was uniquely attuned to the social and economic problems of disadvantaged people, the expansion of

---

[145] Address before the 18th General Assembly of the United Nations, September 20, 1963, *PPP, 1963,* 696.

[146] *PPP, 1963,* 296.

development aid was naturally appealing, either directly from Washington or multilaterally through the United Nations.

After just twenty-five days in office, Johnson addressed the General Assembly. He emphasized the importance of the UN's fight against hunger, poverty, and disease. He compared the plight of the world's destitute populations to the plight of Americans during the Great Depression of the 1930s. His performance was vintage Johnson. This president, who came from a desperately poor part of Texas and made his political career by promoting vast domestic social development programs, now recommended a "New Deal" for the world.[147] He applauded the UN for its "Decade of Development" and its maintenance of agencies and programs that alleviated the suffering of people around the globe.

During his five years in office Johnson expanded American efforts, both through the United Nations and unilaterally, out of a personal conviction that such actions were important on their own merits, not primarily as tactics in the cold war. Particularly following his victory at the polls in 1964, he forwarded to Congress for its approval a number of new programs and increases in foreign aid spending. He once mused to his biographer, Doris Kearns, after leaving the Presidency, that if he could become the world's dictator he could transform the human condition:

> Every hungry person would be fed, every ignorant child educated, every jobless man employed. And then I [would know that] I could accomplish my greatest wish, the wish for eternal peace.[148]

Through economic largesse the United States could make the world a different place, and in so doing defend its national interests *and* achieve the universal good it had always sought.

Those things that had been part of his own personal travail were especially close to Lyndon Johnson's heart. The hunger so prevalent in the underdeveloped world moved him to seek additional congressional funding for America's role in the Food and Agriculture Organization and for food contributions to the Alliance for Progress, to Asian and

---

[147] Johnson, *A Time for Action*, 158–163.

[148] Kearns, *Johnson*, 202.

African food programs, and to specific LDCs facing shortages. He also encouraged multilateral efforts to improve water supplies and electricity throughout the third world, just as he had fought during the 1930s and 1940s for rural electrification on the farms of the American South, and for water diversion projects from the Colorado River to West Texas.[149] The formula for global peace and prosperity was no different, in his mind, from the domestic solution, because people were people, and they were motivated politically and otherwise by the same needs, incentives, and ambitions. The "American" solution at home, consequently, could work anywhere.

Johnson's focus on the development process as an independent variable in world affairs and his laudatory remarks concerning the UN's role did not mean, however, that the United Nations was the sole or even the primary vehicle for economic and social development. Always attuned to public opinion, the president was aware of the growing negative sentiments in the American body politic toward the United Nations and foreign aid.[150] The steady erosion of the American majority in the General Assembly led to regular criticisms of the United States in that body and to votes that U.S. policy and public opinion did not support. Faced with a backlash among voters, LBJ had to find artful ways to enlarge U.S. assistance to the underdeveloped states without endangering his base of support in Congress or in the nation at large. His strategy was to emphasize the efficiency and effectiveness of UN programs, to promote regional economic development outside the UN machinery, and to expand American unilateral projects where it could be demonstrated that U.S. help would make the recipient nation quickly independent of outside support.

At the United Nations he endorsed the third world's demand for greater inclusion in the decision-making organs. Four days before his

---

[149] Johnson could be outright melodramatic in his description of the problems plaguing the world and of the need for an international solution. Talking to an audience in rural West Virginia in 1966 about the global need for usable water, he said, "Either the world's water needs will be met, or the inevitable result will be mass starvation in the world, mass epidemics in the world, mass poverty greater than anything you have ever known before." Remarks at the Dedication of the Summersville Dam, Summersville, West Virginia, September 3, 1966, *PPP, 1966*, 946.

[150] See his remarks to the General Advisory Committee on Foreign Assistance Programs, March 26, 1965, *PPP, 1965*, 334.

first address to the General Assembly, that body voted overwhelmingly to enlarge the Security Council's membership from ten delegates to fifteen. The new nonpermanent members were meant to give the Council a broader geographical and political representation, diluting the dominance of the permanent five and representing the interests of the many new states admitted since 1945. Although the United States abstained from voting, Johnson subsequently lobbied Congress to approve the amendment to the Charter, as well as to ratify an enlargement of the Economic and Social Council from eighteen to twenty-seven nations.[151] Johnson argued that the revisions were "realistic" and "equitable," given the huge growth in UN membership. He asserted that the expansion of the two Councils would give them new vitality by recognizing that the United Nations must serve "the large *and* the small, the rich *and* the poor—for the peace of one area is but part of world peace, and the prosperity of one country is but an element of the world's well-being."[152] To make the United Nations more effective in promoting prosperity, the administration urged it to merge its assistance programs. Responding to the idea, the United Nations combined the Special Fund for Economic Development (created in 1958) and the Expanded Program for Technical Assistance (created during Truman's presidency) into the United Nations Development Program (UNDP) in 1965. The president in turn asked Congress to augment the U.S. contribution to UNDP in proportion to other nations' allocations.

The reform of UN structures eased the political problems Johnson faced with the public and with third world countries, but it did not convince him that the United Nations should be the channel for delivering the bulk of U.S. aid to recipient states. For that, he concluded, regional organizations and agreements provided the longest-lasting benefit. He believed that the world was not ready for the "global solutions" which the United Nations symbolized, and he fully understood that individual nations could not withstand the political upheaval generated by an American cutback in giving brought on by incipient isolationism at home. Thus he outlined a new approach in his 1966 State of the Union Address, telling Congress that his foreign policy was committed "to help build those associations of nations which reflect

---

[151] Special Message to the Senate on Amendments to the United Nations Charter, April 6, 1965, *PPP, 1965*, 387–389.

[152] Ibid., 390. It should be noted that the italics were Johnson's.

the opportunities and necessities of the modern world....We will take
new steps this year to help strengthen...the regional organizations of the
developing continents."[153] Expanding the regional principle which had
kept the peace in Western Europe for twenty-five years and which
President Kennedy had initiated in Latin America through the Alliance
for Progress, Johnson envisioned raising the standard of living in the
third world by devising a strategy "somewhere between a world
community and a system based on narrow nationalism."[154]

He commenced his efforts with a trip to Latin America in April,
where he endorsed a cooperative planning process among the United
States and the governments of the Western Hemisphere. After nine
months' work the group arrived at a broad program of development
assistance and self-help projects for the region. To support the initiative,
Johnson requested $1.5 billion from Congress. Despite the size of the
request, Johnson thought he had devised a strategy which would make
the United States only a "junior partner" in the development process,
meeting criticisms at home while providing the needed aid. President
Johnson followed up his success in Latin America with similar proposals
for sub-Saharan Africa and Asia.

In Africa the president was particularly impressed with the work of
the Organization of African Unity (OAU). African states had already
taken the lead in developing regional solutions to the problems of the
continent in ways the Organization of American States had never done.
Thus it was important for the United States to work with the OAU.
Johnson pressed the World Bank to organize a donors' committee of
developed states which would work closely with the OAU on African
issues. The committee met for the first time in 1967; its membership
consisted of the United States, the United Kingdom, Italy, Belgium, and
Canada.

In Asia Johnson intended to live up to American promises in the
SEATO Treaty, which called not only for regional defense but also for
economic development to raise the standard of living in the area. In this
setting LBJ even saw a possible way out of Vietnam. On several
occasions the president publicly called upon North Vietnam to make
peace and, thus, become eligible to participate in the economic
renaissance of Asia. He promised broad American aid to Hanoi and the

---

[153] Johnson, *The Vantage Point*, 348.

[154] Ibid.

entire region if Ho Chi Minh would settle the war. Until that day the administration was prepared to push ahead with its noncommunist partners in regional development projects. Johnson's most important goal was the completion of plans for the Asian Development Bank, which began operation in late 1967. The original capitalization for the bank was $1 billion, with the United States subscribed for 20 percent of the total.[155] In the Far East the United States joined with South Korea, Nationalist China, Malaysia, and several other nations to form the Asian and Pacific Council (ASPAC), which committed itself to promoting regional prosperity through freer trade and assistance programs.

Johnson's regional approach was not intended to eliminate UN efforts, but it focused U.S. attention and energies elsewhere than on the agencies and specialized bodies of the UN. Just as the responsibility for disarmament had largely been removed from the UN because of monopolization by the superpowers, development became largely a matter for the donor states working directly with regional groupings and individual nations. As the largest donor, the United States could determine the success or failure of any new initiative. The Johnson administration was willing to pursue a "Great Society" on a world scale, including increased contributions to UN efforts, but it was also ready to bring about a new, prosperous world order directly from Washington.

*   *   *

The cold war perverted the founders' dream for the United Nations. The UN could not be a universal collective security system in a world dominated by ideologically antagonistic superpowers. American presidents, faced with the demands of national security, pursued both hope and neglect in their policies for the United Nations. Lincoln Bloomfield rightly characterized the United States–UN policy from 1953 to the election of Richard Nixon in 1968 as divided between "ideal and reality."[156] The difficulty arose from seeing the UN as two entities: an idealized vision of a qualitatively better world, and an arena for the contest between east and west. The first image promoted a desire to see

---

[155] Message to the Congress Transmitting 20th Annual Report on U.S. Participation in the United Nations, March 9, 1967, *PPP, 1967*, 297.

[156] Lincoln P. Bloomfield, *The United Nations and U.S. Foreign Policy* (Boston: Little, Brown, 1967), 4.

the United Nations succeed, while the second often led U.S. administrations to avoid, manipulate, or even condemn the United Nations' efforts. Largely created by the United States for "higher" purposes, the United Nations became a tool sometimes to be used, sometimes to be confronted, sometimes to be ignored.

Arms control best demonstrated this phenomenon. Certainly the United States' interest in a nuclear-free world, or at least a world in which nuclear weapons did not create a balance of terror, was one moral end toward which all cold war presidents thought the United Nations might work. Yet the Test Ban Treaty, the Non-Proliferation Treaty, the preparations for SALT, and the various limited safeguards against the use of nuclear weapons after 1962 were all a result of direct negotiation between the United States and the Soviet Union. Additionally, they came only in the wake of the most serious nuclear confrontation the two sides had during the cold war, the Cuban missile crisis. The most important success achieved by the United Nations in arms control was the Non-Proliferation Treaty of 1968. Even here, however, no real progress was made until the superpowers submitted a joint U.S.-Soviet draft in 1967.

Whether U.S. policy in the United Nations sought the moralist ends for which the institution was created, or sought some self-interested goal, or ignored the body altogether turned on a number of factors. One was the perceived strategic importance of any particular issue to American interests. During the cold war there was an inverse relationship between the gravity of the challenge to U.S. national interests and the willingness of American administrations to take the case to the United Nations. With the sole exception of the Korean War, in which the Truman administration actively sought UN endorsement and participation, the United States government largely excluded the United Nations from events that presented a strategic challenge to America. When strategic interests seemed remote, the United States was far more amenable to multilateral solutions, sometimes with little U.S. leadership. That was Eisenhower's approach in the Congo, and it was Johnson's immediate response to the Six Day War.

Margaret Karns and Karen Mingst have argued that changes in the "instrumentality and influence" of the United Nations in American foreign policy are explained partially by changes in presidential administrations.[157] To the extent that moralism and realism are part of the policy-maker's perceptual makeup, each president certainly brings to the office a unique set of theoretical and psychological precepts. Eisenhower was a military man with an abiding desire for world peace. He deeply feared the arms race, with its implicit vision of a nuclear Armageddon. He wanted to cut wasteful spending on the wages of war and transfer the world's resources to the fight against hunger and want. Yet to place American trust in the United Nations to achieve these goals was folly during an era of distrust between the superpowers, because the United Nations, in spite of all of its promise, was necessarily flawed by the reality of the veto. The "Eisenhower model" provided a schema which left the most serious matters to U.S.-Soviet determination while holding out hope for a future United Nations that could deal with disarmament and development. Kennedy was far more a "realist" who saw things in geopolitical terms. He nonetheless held the liberal faith in an ultimate world built on cooperation and justice. The United Nations was part of that world; but until that vision could be realized, the organization would have to serve more practical purposes. Most important, it could represent the interests of the weaker nations of the world while the superpowers used it as a venue for contest and limited negotiation. Johnson brought his passion for domestic transformation to the world stage. He married the New Deal aspirations of his Rooseveltian origins with the general hope of his predecessors for a better world through American leadership and international cooperation.

All of American cold war policy reflected the tension between moralism and realism produced at the intersection of Americans' permanent belief in the universal appeal of their political values, their internationalism, and the often contrasting security needs of a great power faced with an implacable foe. This faith sustained a recurring belief that there remained a glimmer of promise in the United Nations. It could, under the right circumstances, live up to its founders' hope and find a cooperative and peaceful solution to difficult international problems. As Lyndon Johnson put it, "Above all, our commitment to the

---

[157] A full study of the issues that the United States has been willing to pursue in the United Nations can be found in Margaret P. Karns and Karen A. Mingst, eds., *Multilateral Institutions*. A priority listing of issues can be found in their included article, "The United States and Multilateral Institutions: A Framework for Analysis," 15.

United Nations is an expression of faith which has illuminated the entire history of our country: a faith that the creative powers of democracy and human reason can overcome the evils of tyranny and violence."[158] Conversely, the tribulations of cold war, the national liberation movement that produced new UN members often critical of U.S. policy, and a United Nations that seemed unable to resolve some of the great challenges of the day without direct and unrestricted American leadership weakened public support for the organization. Without that support no president could or would encourage an expansion of UN responsibility over those things important to American national interests. The full promise of the United Nations would have to await a more auspicious time.

---

[158] *PPP, 1967, 297.*

4

The Realists' Ascent

The postwar period in international relations has ended....[Henceforth] our objective in the first instance is to support our *interests*.

—*President's Report to Congress*
February 18, 1970

Do we leave the memory only of the battles we fought, of opponents we did in, of the viciousness we created, or do we leave possibly not only the dream but the reality of a new world?

—*Richard Nixon*
Toast at a meeting with Prime Minister Tanaka, July 31, 1973[1]

Richard Nixon was the omnipresent, if most controversial, politician of post–World War II America. After returning from service in the war, he captured a congressional seat in the election of 1946 and a Senate seat from California in 1950, and then ran in five national elections (a feat matched only by FDR), winning four of them—1952 and 1956 as vice president, and 1968 and 1972 as president, losing only by a hairbreadth to JFK in the presidential race of 1960. In 1962 he lost a bitter campaign for governor of California and promptly announced to the media, which he considered overly hostile, that he was finished with politics. But by the close of the decade he was back in Washington as the new president.

Although he was considered a political conservative, Nixon presided over a massive increase in federal government authority in our social and economic life, removed the dollar from the international gold standard, and imposed wage and price controls. Although he had been raised a Quaker, he authorized, in December 1972, a devastating and sustained bombing attack on North Vietnam *after* his national security adviser had assured the nation that peace in Vietnam was "at hand." Although he was a "hawk" in military matters, he arranged an American retreat from Southeast Asia and "balanced" weapons reduction agreements with our most dangerous adversary, the Soviet Union. Although he had established a reputation in his early political career as a

---

[1] *PPP, 1973,* 674.

zealous anticommunist, he opened the diplomatic door to the Soviet Union and China, heralding the celebrated thaw of *détente*. Although he won a sweeping election victory in 1972 (garnering all electoral votes except those in Massachusetts and the District of Columbia) he became, within less than two years of that triumph, the only president in our history to resign under the cloud of imminent impeachment. Despised and discredited, Richard Nixon persistently arose from what appeared to be his certain public demise, until, at his death in 1994, he was praised publicly by the most prominent Republicans *and* Democrats of the time.

As president, Nixon signed bills that provided for revenue sharing; for expanded federal entitlement programs such as Medicare, Medicaid, and Social Security; for wage and price controls; and for the Environmental Protection Agency, the Occupational Safety and Health Administration, and the Consumer Products Safety Commission. On the recommendation of his adviser Daniel Patrick Moynihan, he proposed an innovative welfare policy, the Family Assistance Plan, which, had Congress approved, would have guaranteed an annual income to all poor families. These activist programs have led some scholars to argue that Nixon's lasting legacy rests in domestic policy.[2]

But the president himself certainly saw his long public career as a benefaction to the nation in the field of foreign affairs. Of his ten published books (which mark him as one of the most prolific writers among our presidents), eight were about international affairs, and a ninth, his memoirs,[3] contained extensive commentary on foreign policy. Nixon believed that he had brought about an essential transition from the *idealist*-driven policies of his predecessors to a more *realistic* international posture that met the undeniable challenges of a dangerous world.

By choosing a Harvard professor, Henry Kissinger, as his national security adviser, Nixon signaled his proposed new direction. Kissinger, from a German-Jewish background, had immigrated from Germany to the United States as a young man. He studied and taught at Harvard and had been an adviser to the governor of New York, Nelson Rockefeller. Kissinger's Ph.D dissertation had been an approving study of nineteenth-century balance-of-power diplomats. Kissinger had long

---

[2]   Joan Hoff, *Nixon Reconsidered* (New York: Basic Books, 1994), 4.

[3]   *RN: The Memoirs of Richard Nixon* (New York: Grosset and Dunlap, 1978). Hereafter cited as *RN*.

lamented the Wilson-inspired moralism of American diplomacy.[4] His *realist* views not only conformed to Nixon's thinking but derived from a prominent academic tradition of which he was a part, and which included such contemporary savants as Hans J. Morgenthau and George Kennan.[5]

Kissinger always understood the limits of his realism. On October 8, 1973, amidst the confusion of both a new and dangerous Middle East crisis and the accelerating Watergate scandal, he gave a speech at a Pacem in Terris Conference in Washington, where he conceded the nation's imbedded Wilsonianism: "This country has always had a sense of mission. Americans have always held the view that America stood for something above and beyond its material achievements. A purely pragmatic policy provides no criteria for other nations to assess our performance and no standards to which the American people can rally." The new secretary of state then proffered his consistent demur, warning: "But when policy becomes excessively moralistic it may turn quixotic or dangerous."[6] And that, Kissinger was convinced, was the ongoing challenge to the crafting of a sensible American foreign policy.

Nixon shared this concern, even if the president's feelings about Wilsonianism were more complicated. "I have always had a very high regard for Woodrow Wilson," he often said, usually adding the caveat, "I think that Wilson's policy doesn't work in the real world."[7] But in one of his last televised interviews, Nixon returned to his lifelong enchantment with the League's founder, telling Brian Lamb of CSPAN that Wilson was one of the giants of the century, and distinct in being

---

[4] Henry Kissinger, *American Foreign Policy* (New York: Norton, 1969); see especially "An Inquiry into the American National Interest," 91–92. In his later work *Diplomacy*, however, Kissinger acknowledges the overwhelming importance of idealism in foreign policy to the American people. Without a commitment to America's exceptionalist values, he asserts, it would have been impossible to sustain America's defense of the West throughout the long cold war.

[5] Hans J. Morgenthau, *In Defense of the National Interest* (New York: Knopf, 1951); *Politics Among Nations* (New York: Praeger, 1967); and *A New Foreign Policy for the United States* (New York: Praeger, 1969). George F. Kennan, *American Diplomacy, 1900–1950.*

[6] Henry Kissinger, *Years of Upheaval* (Boston: Little, Brown, 1982) 447–448.

[7] C. L. Sulzberger, *The World and Richard Nixon* (New York: Prentice Hall, 1987), 28.

both a "great professor" and a "great leader," that is, both "a man of *action* and a man of *thought*"—a priceless combination.[8] Clearly Nixon regarded Wilson as an exemplar for himself.

Although there were differences among realists of the 1970s, certain essential lines of thought were pertinent to a new effective foreign policy. First, realists concluded that a universal ideology, such as communism, might not be as important a factor in motivating individuals and governments as previous policy-makers had argued. Indeed, they argued, *nationalism* may be the most important factor in the contemporary world. Among communist states themselves, there were great differences in both national aims and ideology. Thus realists would see China and Russia not as being closely aligned because both were ostensibly Marxist-Leninist states but rather as potentially suspicious and fearful of each other because of their competing national interests. Nixon and Kissinger expected to take advantage of this particular "reality," to play the two off against each other.

Second, according to these realists (as we have seen in earlier chapters), a nation should pursue its *interests*, not conduct diplomacy on the basis of a globalist, moralistic ideology. That is, a country should understand its limitations and its own economic and defense needs, and avoid a foreign policy devoted, for example, to spreading "human rights" or "democracy."

Third, 1970s realists tended to look at the world in terms of a balance of powerful forces, rather than as a competition among transcendent ideologies or, alternatively, the convergence of international politics in multilateral rapport. For example, Nixon and Kissinger were of the opinion that arms agreements could succeed if the countries negotiating them perceived that there was "parity" between them, that both sides had equivalent military strength.

In this regard, some realists accepted the fact and value of *spheres of influence*. Thus, the Nixon-Kissinger team tended to center its attention on the balance among the great powers—chiefly the Soviet Union, China, and the United States—believing that decisions made by and among these dominant players, with their own national interests and spheres of influence, were the most consequential decisions in world politics. This is why, often, the Nixon administration thought it could find a resolution

---

[8] CSPAN, *Booknotes*, February 23, 1992; found on the CSPAN website at *www.booknotes.org*

of the most pressing problems—the war in Vietnam, the India-Pakistan crisis, and so on—in its relations with the great powers of China and Russia.

Moreover, by the early 1970s there seemed to be mounting evidence that the United States was no longer the dominant world player it had been. We were unable to subdue a small distant Southeast Asian people. Inflation was becoming an ominous and persistent accompaniment to America's global overextension. By midsummer 1971, the United States recorded its first trade imbalance since 1894, weakening the dollar against foreign currencies. The economy was stagnating, and dissent against foreign adventure was intensifying. We seemed on the verge of what would be called, though surely prematurely, an "age of limits." The new realist foreign policy, the president and his national security adviser agreed, was based on sound political science and would help the country adjust to its new, less affluent, and less dominant role in the world.[9]

Thus did Nixon, an early, apparently ideologically driven, cold warrior, break with the bipolar view of the world and proclaim realism as the basis of our foreign policy. An important speech to Congress in 1970 marked the transition: "The postwar period in international relations has ended....International Communist unity has been shattered...by powerful forces of nationalism....[From now on] our objective in the first instance is to support our *interests.*"[10]

Where in this new configuration did the United Nations fit? At first the administration said little about the UN, apart from noting that the General Assembly, though ineffective, contained a growing number of third world nations who used the United Nations as a forum to fume against the United States.[11] On the central questions of American foreign policy inherited by the administration, the president simply did not consider the United Nations a factor in their resolution. The Nixon-Kissinger approach to the preoccupying problem of Vietnam, called

---

[9] Walter LaFeber, *America, Russia, and the Cold War, 1945–1975*, 3rd ed. (New York: Wiley, 1976), 264–272. According to John Stoessinger, Kissinger's favorite book while he was a student at Harvard was Oswald Spengler's *The Decline of the West*; Stoessinger, *Henry Kissinger: The Anguish of Power* (New York: Norton, 1976), 7.

[10] First Annual Report to the Congress on United States Foreign Policy for the 1970s, February 18, 1970, *PPP, 1970*, 116–117.

[11] Stoessinger, *Kissinger*, 168.

"Vietnamization," was as *unilateral* in its nature as Kennedy's and Johnson's policies had been. Approaches to China and the Soviet Union, including arms negotiations, likewise took place outside any multilateral forum. The Johnson administration may have been forced by the UN's nonnuclear members into arms limitation talks with the USSR as the price for a multilateral nonproliferation treaty, but Richard Nixon intended to exclude all actors other than the superpowers from future negotiations. The same approach underlay America's controversial international economic policies, and Nixon's attitude toward Latin America, culminating in the controversial overthrow of the Allende government in Chile. The president's UN policy itself became the dependent variable in his overall strategy, changing to complement his sweeping initiatives on the world stage.

The following pages will examine the connection between the Nixon administration's realist foreign policy and its approach to the United Nations by focusing, not on chronology, but on particular themes or issues that faced the administration. We will proceed with a look at the administration's overall relationship with the United Nations, then consider the impact on policy-making of three matters distinct to the Nixon years—the extraordinary dramas of the year Nixon was elected (1968), the Watergate scandal, and the insular style of diplomacy characteristic of Nixon's White House. We will follow these discussions with accounts of specific foreign policy challenges and developments.

Nixon and the UN

Nixon, like Kennedy, was an internationalist, a product of the immediate post–World War II transformation in America's outlook on the world. As a freshman member of the House of Representatives, Nixon traveled to Europe with a congressional group to investigate the economic plight of the continent and to assess Europe's need for aid. His political advisers in California and the overwhelming majority of his constituents opposed any financial assistance. Yet the young Republican ended up a strong advocate of the Marshall Plan of 1947 and of extensive aid to Europe, explicitly supporting the postwar bipartisan Truman-Vandenburg internationalist policy.[12] One year later he attended the Republican convention in Philadelphia, where he supported the governor of Minnesota, Harold Stassen, for the presidential nomination

---

[12] *RN,* 48–51.

over the front-runners Robert Taft and Thomas Dewey; by 1952, he had completely dismissed Taft as the party standard-bearer, in large part because the Ohio senator had an "isolationist streak" and thus was unlikely to be able to deal with "serious international challenges." Nixon preferred Eisenhower, who was supported by "liberal" internationalist elements of the party.[13]

Nixon's internationalist convictions never wavered, but his thoughts about the United Nations and about multilateralism went through significant permutations. "I was elated," he wrote many years later, "when both the United States and the Soviet Union supported the founding of the United Nations. As an admirer of Woodrow Wilson I felt that we had made a serious mistake in not joining the League of Nations, and I believed that the UN offered the world's best chance to build a lasting peace."[14]

But the former secretary-general Kurt Waldheim would remember that "Nixon had little regard for the United Nations."[15] Nixon at one point maintained that the League of Nations and the United Nations had been "tragic failures." "The United States," he would add, using realist language, "cannot submit issues affecting its interests to a body so heavily prejudiced against it....[As far as the United States is concerned] world peace is inseparable from national power. No foreign policy goals, whether strategic, geopolitical, or related to human rights, can be achieved without the application of national power."[16] He certainly found that "the popular idea that the United Nations can play a larger role [than it already plays] in resolving international conflicts is illusory." He approved of onetime UN Ambassador Jeane Kirkpatrick's assessment that "multilateral decision making is complicated and inconclusive...[and] characteristically ineffective." But, he insisted, "This does not mean that the United Nations should be thrown on the scrap

---

[13] Ibid., 71–85.

[14] Ibid., 45.

[15] Kurt Waldheim, *In the Eye of the Storm: A Memoir* (Bethesda: Adler and Adler, 1986), 117. Waldheim continued: "However, I am obliged to say that in the field of foreign policy, one could not but appreciate his knowledge, vision, and skill. Of the four presidents with whom I have dealt, he was the best prepared for his diplomatic responsibilities."

[16] Richard Nixon, *1999: Victory Without War* (New York: Simon and Schuster, 1988), 21–22.

heap of history"; it just means that the United States must understand its responsibility to take a leadership role in its activities. "We should enlist U.N. support for our policies but not put the U.N. in charge of them."[17]

The United States ambassadors to the United Nations in previous administrations often had been political heavyweights. The post carried cabinet rank. As we have seen in earlier chapters, presidents from Truman through Johnson had given quite public attention to the United Nations and the role of their personal representative in the UN. Nixon sought to downplay the organization in his foreign policy. His first ambassador was Charles Yost, a holdover Democrat. Then in 1971 he appointed George Bush as Yost's successor. This appointment, however, was purely a product of politics and the administration's disdain for the United Nations. The White House had encouraged Bush to run against Senator Yarborough in the 1970 Texas senate race. He had already lost one race for the office in 1964. During that campaign he suggested that the United States consider withdrawing from the United Nations if the UN replaced the Nationalist Chinese delegation with one from Mao Zedong's government.[18] Secure as a two-term congressman six years later, Bush was enticed into a second effort by the promise of an important appointment in the administration should he not be successful in his election bid. When Bush left the post in 1973, he was succeeded by John Scali. Scali was a well-known diplomatic reporter who had played a minor role in the private negotiations with Soviet interlocutors during the Cuban missile crisis. However, he did not have the stature of Henry Cabot Lodge, Eleanor Roosevelt, Adlai Stevenson, or Arthur Goldberg.

At the swearing-in of Ambassador Bush, the president offered the following observation: "There are those who look at the United Nations' record over the last 25 years and appropriately point out that the world still has a lot of problems and a lot of crises. Cabot Lodge used to say, 'Let us suppose that we had not had the United Nations. How many more problems and how many more crises would we have had?'"[19] By implication, his remarks seemed to give some credit to the United Nations for the maintenance of peace in the cold war. Yet his

---

[17] Richard Nixon, *Beyond Peace* (New York: Random House, 1994), 30–32.

[18] Nicholas King, *George Bush: A Biography* (New York: Dodd, Mead, 1980), 54. David Mervin, *George Bush and the Guardianship Presidency* (New York: St. Martin's, 1996), 17.

[19] Item 76, *PPP, 1971*, 346.

appointments to the UN and his emphasis on unilateral American actions demonstrated otherwise. Nixon, preferring to conduct policy out of the White House, and sharing in the general growing public disenchantment with the United Nations,[20] appointed individuals who were unlikely to bring much attention to the United Nations and were not disposed to act independently of White House control.

Henry Kissinger's relationship with the United Nations was, at least on the surface, bumpy. With a growing third world majority in the 1960s and 1970s, the United Nations appeared to Kissinger to have descended into meaningless tirades aimed at the "first world." The roughest days came after Nixon's resignation and in the early moments of the Ford administration. In 1974 the General Assembly invited the Palestinian leader Yasir Arafat to address the body. Only four nations opposed the invitation, the leading dissenter being the United States. By November 1974 the United Nations had granted the Palestine Liberation Organization observer status.[21] U.S. Ambassador John Scali was authorized to begin criticizing "rhetoric over negotiation" and to lambaste the oratorical "tyranny of the new majority." Developing nations (former colonies, economically "underdeveloped," and often called "third world" countries) responded with yet another antiwestern resolution, the "Charter of Economic Rights and Duties of States," passed overwhelmingly by the General Assembly on December 12, 1974.[22] Among other rights in the resolution's long list was the right of nations to "nationalize, expropriate, or transfer ownership of foreign property." Secretary-General Waldheim believed that this resolution represented a new low in relations between north and south (industrialized nations and developing nations).[23]

On July 14, 1975, the secretary of state delivered an address in Milwaukee, where he derided "the alignment of the nonaligned" at the United Nations and suggested that the UN "depart the scene." The Ford administration then replaced Scali with the erudite if acid-tongued

---

[20] For a general discussion of the public mood regarding the United Nations in the 1970s, see Joseph R. Harbert, "The U.S. Role in International Institutions: A Redefinition," *U.S. Policy in International Institutions, Defining Reasonable Options in an Unreasonable World*, edited by Finger and Harbert, 1–4.

[21] GA Resolution 3237, November 22, 1974, *YUN, 1974*, 227.

[22] Ibid., 402-407. This was GA Resolution 3281.

[23] Waldheim, *Eye of the Storm*, 115.

Daniel Patrick Moynihan, who was expected to spearhead a more confrontational presence in New York.[24] The new ambassador's outspokenness soon drove U.S.-UN relations to their nadir. Speaking in California at one point, Moynihan referred to President Idi Amin of Uganda as a "racist murderer" and added that "it was no accident that the OAU [the Organization of African Unity] had elected Amin as their president." (Actually, the post was filled in random rotation.) His remarks so angered several African nations that their delegations to the United Nations may have been more inclined to vote for resolutions strongly opposed by the United States. Kissinger, who lamented Moynihan's impolitic imputation, certainly thought this was the case.[25] The most infamous of these resolutions was one equating Zionism with "racism," which passed the General Assembly by a large majority on November 10, 1975.[26]

Given the public posturing toward the United Nations, it is nevertheless worthwhile to observe that after Kissinger became secretary of state in the fall of 1973, his actions belied a learning process which granted the world body a more important role in some aspects of world affairs. He gave his very first speech as secretary to the General Assembly. He invited the members of the United Nations "to move with us from *détente* to cooperation, from coexistence to community," and he proceeded to call for a UN-sponsored World Food Conference.[27] The conference took place in November 1974, just months after Nixon's resignation and barely into the Ford administration. At the conference, Kissinger, with Ford's blessing, pledged U.S. aid and policies to improve worldwide food distribution and proposed a World Food Council to funnel food and money to poorer nations. By 1976 the World Food Council was coordinating food deliveries to several needy countries annually. Then, in the spring of 1976, the secretary made a well publicized tour of Africa, during which he firmly supported eventual black majority rule in southern Africa; pledged to work to repeal the Byrd Amendment, which allowed imports into the United States of

---

[24] Moynihan's own descriptions of his tenure as ambassador can be found in his book *A Dangerous Place* (Boston: Little, Brown, 1978).

[25] Stoessinger, *Kissinger*, 165–169.

[26] GA Resolution 3379, November 10, 1975, *YUN, 1975*, 599-600. For Moynihan's full, outraged assessment, see *A Dangerous Place*, 169–199.

[27] Kissinger, *Years of Upheaval*, 447.

Rhodesian chrome in violation of UN sanctions; urged independence for Namibia under UN supervision; and called for an end to apartheid in South Africa, a long-term UN goal.[28]

During the five and a half years of his truncated presidency, Nixon delivered two revealing addresses to opening sessions of the United Nations: those of 1969 and 1970. He was careful in these remarks to harmonize the realism of his foreign policy to the ears of his listeners (the word "realistic" and "realism" surfaced repeatedly in these two addresses). In 1969 he rued the tendency of "many countries...to withdraw from responsibilities, to leave the world's often frustrating problems to the other fellow and just hope for the best." Rather, he insisted, we must recognize that "we are maturing together into a new pattern of interdependence....We have entered a new age....For the first time ever, we have truly become a single world community." While "It would be dishonest...to pretend that the United States has no national interests of its own, or no special concern for its own interests,...our most fundamental national interest is in maintaining that structure of international stability on which peace depends, and which makes orderly progress possible." Specifically, he underscored the primary role of the United Nations in the Middle East conundrum—maintaining that Security Council Resolution 242 was the indispensable undergirding of any just settlement. He also affirmed support for the UN-sponsored arms control negotiations at Geneva, pledged "the strongest support" for the upcoming UN Conference on the Environment, and hinted that he expected China to join the United Nations soon.[29]

His address at the twenty-fifth anniversary session of the General Assembly disclosed a collateral, if rather overlooked, link between his long-held internationalism and his commitment to a policy of realism: "The fate of more than $3^1/2$ billion people today rests on the *realism* and candor with which we approach the great issues of war and peace, of security and progress....I...speak with you today not ritualistically but *realistically*; not of impossible dreams but of possible deeds." While the challenges facing the world "have made more compelling than ever the central idea behind the United Nations," it would not be *"realistic"* (a term he used in three successive paragraphs) to assume that simple personal relationships between heads of governments, or "better mutual

---

[28] Stoessinger, *Kissinger*, 172.

[29] September 18, 1969, Item 365, *PPP, 1969.*

understandings," or the denial of "power" in international relations can solve our problems. "Power is a fact of international life." Nonetheless, the United States was prepared to move ahead vigorously with the United Nations in (1) internationalizing foreign aid by placing larger shares of American assistance under impartial international agencies like the World Bank and the UN Development Programme; (2) advancing the UN's "capacity for peace-making, settling disputes before they lead to armed conflict, and its capacity for peacekeeping, containing and ending conflicts that have broken out;" and (3) sustaining the "uniquely equipped" United Nations in its "central role" to clean up the world's environment and control the world's population explosion; indeed, the United States would "continue to support the rapid development of U.N. services to assist the population and family planning programs of member nations."[30]

These positions reflected enlightened internationalist Republicanism in the early 1970s. It was a position that would not outlive Nixon's years in the White House by very long. Future leaders of the Republican Party would deride even the limited role Nixon assigned the United Nations. For example, Republican Jesse Helms, Chair of the Senate Foreign Relations Committee at the end of the 1990s, would demonstrate great discomfort with Nixon's concept of the United Nations in American foreign policy.[31]

At the same time, Nixon's public words often seemed to mask different private views. Robert Gates, who served five consecutive presidents, has noted of Nixon that his "public words and private actions" were often in opposition.[32] And late in life, Nixon shared with a confidante this view about UN speeches: "I've done the UN a few times. Worthless, but the media love that fluff."[33]

* * *

---

[30] October 23, 1970, Item 377, *PPP, 1970.* Italics added.

[31] See Chapter 6.

[32] Robert M. Gates, *From the Shadows: The Ultimate Insider's Story of Five Presidents and How They Won the Cold War* (New York: Simon and Schuster, 1996), 571.

[33] Quoted in Monica Crowley, *Nixon in Winter* (New York: Random House, 1998), 69.

There is one other specific UN-related matter that impinges on the history of the Nixon administration: the two-term tenure of Kurt Waldheim as secretary-general. Waldheim was one of the first candidates for secretary-general to openly campaign for the post. The UN Charter provides that the Security Council forward a name to the General Assembly, which then chooses the new secretary-general. That is, secretaries-general are chosen so as to satisfy the appearance of democracy, but they must be fully acceptable to each of the permanent members of the Security Council. When U Thant's term was coming to a conclusion in late 1971, two candidates emerged as most prominent: Waldheim of Austria and Max Jakobson of Finland. The Nixon administration initially supported Jakobson, who believed that U.S. Ambassador Bush would stick with him to the very end. But in the Security Council, the Soviet Union vetoed Jakobson (some thought because he was Jewish and the Soviets were assuaging their Arab friends). The United States backed away from its position, and Waldheim's name went to the General Assembly, which dutifully chose him, even though he was known to have served, as had many other Austrians, in the German army during World War II. The Nixon administration, pleased with Waldheim's work, particularly in the Middle East, let him know that it would support him for reelection, which in fact it did. Waldheim even campaigned for a third term in 1981, and again the United States supported him. But this time the Chinese provided the veto and the Austrian's long service came to an end. Much later, in 1986, when Waldheim was running for president of Austria, the World Jewish Congress made public well-substantiated charges that in his youth he had been a member of at least two Nazi organizations, and that he had served for most of World War II as a second lieutenant, assigned to a German unit in the Balkans, where he had participated in rounding up Jews for deportation to Auschwitz. Among other revelations appearing in the *New York Times* and on *ABC News*, was the fact that in February 1948 the War Crimes Commission, just as it was about to disband, had placed Waldheim's name on a list of war criminals. The file subsequently came to be stored in overlooked UN archives.[34] Waldheim had successfully concealed this information for almost forty years.

---

[34] See Robert Edwin Herzstein, *Waldheim: The Missing Years* (New York: Paragon House, 1989). See also Stanley Meisler, *United Nations: The First Fifty*

This exposé certainly did nothing to help the reputation of the United Nations. As Brian Urquhart, who served as undersecretary-general during the 1970s, has written: "Waldheim, emerging as a living lie, has done immense damage not only to his own country but to the United Nations and those who have devoted, and in some cases sacrificed, their lives for it....The Waldheim episode is above all an indictment of the way in which governments, and especially the great powers, select the world's leading international civil servants."[35]

The United States not only was one of those great powers, but through two administrations (Nixon's and Carter's) had worked, sometimes very closely and sympathetically, with Waldheim. Indeed, this tarnished public servant, carrying enormously damaging baggage, had, a disapproving Urquhart has said, performed "rather better" than he had anticipated.[36]

1968

The year of Nixon's election to the presidency was possibly the most traumatic in the postwar era. It began in January with the Tet lunar new year holiday, when the Vietcong enemy simultaneously attacked the major cities of South Vietnam, infiltrating even the American embassy in Saigon. Even if, as defenders of Johnson's Vietnam policy argued, the offensive was a desperate gamble on the part of the Vietcong, and ultimately a military loss, it represented a public relations disaster for policy-makers wishing to carry the war forward. For some years the opposition to the war had increased among Americans, and Tet seemed the last straw to the growing number of doubters.

Within just over a month, the antiwar Democratic candidate Eugene McCarthy challenged the president in the first primary of the campaign season, in New Hampshire. McCarthy embarrassed the president by winning a surprising 42 percent of the vote. On the last day of March, Johnson announced that he would not seek reelection, throwing the Democratic Party into disarray, as both Senator Robert Kennedy and Vice President Hubert Humphrey now entered the race.

Years (New York: Atlantic Monthly Press, 1995), 185–203.

[35] Brian Urquhart, *A Life in Peace and War* (New York: Harper and Row, 1987), 227–228.

[36] Ibid., 228.

Also in March, the president's commission appointed to study the causes of recent urban rioting (the National Advisory Commission on Civil Disorders), issued a careful, disturbing report, widely disseminated, detailing the continuing inequality and racism of American life.[37] Less than a month later, on April 4, 1968, civil rights leader Martin Luther King, Jr. was assassinated in Memphis, Tennessee, an event that triggered yet more inner-city violence. In Los Angeles, on June 5, while celebrating his victory in the California primary, Senator Robert Kennedy died from another assassin's bullet.

Both political conventions thereupon took place within tense urban settings. Blacks rioted in Miami where the Republicans nominated Nixon. In Chicago, antiwar protesters besieged the city. Six thousand armed troops arrived to patrol the streets and parks, as television recorded the chaos and the Democrats met in a tense and confrontational convention to nominate Hubert Humphrey. The United States, consumed in domestic turmoil and division, hamstrung in Southeast Asia, then looked on in virtual incapacity and dismay as Soviet armed forces invaded Czechoslovakia in August, overthrew its moderate *communist* reform government, and announced the "Brezhnev Doctrine," or the right to use force to defend and maintain "socialism" in neighboring countries.

By the fall election there was yet another candidate, the governor of Alabama, George Wallace, whose two principal issues were unrestrained prosecution of the war in Vietnam and the maintenance of a segregated society at home. He received a surprising 13.5 percent of the vote in November.[38] Exit polls showed that voters favoring military escalation in the war were twice as numerous as those favoring unilateral withdrawal.[39] Humphrey and Nixon each received about 43 percent of the vote; the tally was so close that Nixon's victory was not certain until the morning after the election.

Richard Nixon was elected by a minority of voters to lead a country in perilous disarray, rent asunder over racial and diplomatic issues, frozen in the international community, looking very much like a nation

---

[37] *Report of the National Advisory Commission on Civil Disorders* (Washington, D.C.: U.S. Government Printing Office, 1968).

[38] Daniel A. Mazmanian, *Third Parties in Presidential Elections* (Washington, D.C.: Brookings, 1974).

[39] LaFeber, *America, Russia, and the Cold War*, 264.

in precipitous decline. And for the entirety of his troubled term he would face a Congress dominated by the opposing Democratic Party.

Nixon and Watergate

Any consideration of Richard Nixon's place in American history, whether in his dealings with the United Nations or with any other matter, must take account of the Watergate scandal, insofar as the scandal indicates a style of governing that affected his entire presidency. Nixon became the first, and so far the only, president to resign from office. Whatever long-term influence he may have had on America's relationship with the United Nations, the consequences of this grandest of all scandals also had an impact, both immediate and long-term, on the way the United States approached world affairs and on its relationship to the United Nations.

There is a certain irony in the fact that, as Nixon fell from grace—from 1973 to his resignation in 1974—pundits announced that the presidency in recent times had become "imperial," that is, beyond or above the control of normal constitutional or institutional constraints.[40] The charge has persisted in some quarters into the late twentieth century. Such a claim is of interest to this study, given our regard for America's role in the larger world, and the truism that the president is, by constitutional mandate, the country's foreign policy leader. It is thus useful to remember that, within less than two years from an overwhelming electoral victory, within a year and a half after he had risen to the highest poll ratings of his long career (January 1973, at the moment of the Paris peace agreement on Vietnam), Richard Nixon, under pressure from Congress, the courts, and an independent media (all provided for in the Constitution) left office a humiliated man. Moreover, it is difficult to find in the ensuing presidencies of Gerald Ford and Jimmy Carter much evidence of an "imperial presidency." Even the popular Reagan found himself reasonably restrained by opposition Democrats in Congress and by the Iran-Contra scandal. The president may be the most important player in the formulation and conduct of America's diplomacy, but as we can see throughout this study, he can be effective only by playing within the game's rules, provided in the intricate constitutional system bequeathed by our

---

[40] Arthur M. Schlesinger, Jr., *The Imperial Presidency* (Boston: Houghton Mifflin, 1973).

nation's founders. And, as we have noted in the introduction to this book, that constitutional system—with its role for Congress, occasionally the courts, and the individual states, certainly the voters, and often the competing political parties and unfettered media—provides the environment within which the United States responds to international affairs and international organizations such as the United Nations. That Nixon at times tried end runs may have done serious damage not only to his legacy, but also to the subtle play of political forces in that intriguing if complex sport called American politics.

The "Watergate" scandal received its name from an apartment complex in Washington, D.C. Here, in June of 1972, operatives working for the campaign to reelect the president burglarized the offices of the Democratic National Committee in an attempt to tap the phones, photograph various files, and prepare to covertly undermine the Democrats' ability to conduct an effective election campaign. In the ensuing unfolding of the scandal, a congressional hearing, an investigation by a "special" prosecutor, and revelations from concealed tape recordings of private conversations within the White House divulged a series of offensive secret activities originating with Mr. Nixon. These activities included drawing up an "enemies" list, planning to use tax audits to harass those enemies, discussing clemency for the Watergate burglars, and making efforts to cover up the involvement of the White House in the growing crisis.

By the summer of 1974, actions by both Congress and the courts had severely checked the president. On July 24, the Supreme Court (which had four justices appointed by Mr. Nixon) unanimously rejected the president's contention that he could withhold sixty-four tapes subpoenaed by the special prosecutor, one of which clearly recorded the president planning a cover-up. By the end of July, after the Judiciary Committee of the House of Representatives had agreed on three articles of impeachment, Mr. Nixon found himself with few options but to resign. Although subsequently pardoned by President Ford for any offenses he "may" have committed, Mr. Nixon had bestowed on his reputation the word "Watergate," which became synonymous with a growing perception of the Nixon administration as lawless, secretive, and arbitrary. A man who had begun his second term seemingly unassailable was now in disgrace and out of office.[41]

"Nixinger" Diplomacy

The covert nature of the Watergate scandal mirrored in some respects the style of diplomacy that Nixon and his closest adviser, Henry Kissinger, brought to the White House. This is not to say that secret activities, bypassing normal channels of decision-making, had not taken place, for example, in Johnson's or Kennedy's administration, but the Nixon White House brought a refinement, pursuing calculated tactics for developing policy and carrying it out in a way that centralized diplomatic authority in the White House; this administration used "back-channel" negotiations outside the purview of traditional institutions (including the State Department and the United Nations), did things in secret, and attempted to deal with the world unilaterally rather than multilaterally.

The Nixon administration's style of diplomacy has drawn considerable criticism.[42] The president's reliance on trusted staff members, particularly Kissinger, resulted in secret diplomacy often bypassing an out-of-the-loop State Department, headed by William Rogers. Enthusiasm for secrecy, covert action, and manipulation seemed to bring the president and his national security adviser together.[43] Kissinger, with the president's concurrence, quickly established himself in the White House as the main focus for foreign relations. His

---

[41] For chronology and documents, see *New York Times*, *The End of a Presidency* (New York: Bantam, 1974); and Stanley I. Kutler (ed.), *Watergate: The Fall of Richard M. Nixon* (St. James, N.Y.: Brandywine, 1996). See also Stanley I. Kutler (ed.), *Abuse of Power: The New Nixon Tapes* (New York: Free Press, 1997).

[42] See, for example, Stephen E. Ambrose's three-volume study of Nixon, particularly the last two volumes, *Nixon: The Triumph of a Politician, 1962–1972* (New York: Simon and Schuster, 1989), and *Nixon: Ruin and Recovery, 1973–1990* (New York: Simon and Schuster, 1991); Tad Szulc, *The Illusion of Peace: Foreign Policy in the Nixon Years* (New York: Viking, 1978); and William Bundy, *A Tangled Web: The Making of Foreign Policy in the Nixon Presidency* (New York: Hill and Wang, 1998). For friendlier assessments, see Sulzberger, *The World and Nixon*; and Stoessinger, *Kissinger*.

[43] Ambrose has written that the two shared a love of "secrecy and surprise, a strong sense of contempt for the bureaucracy, for established methods, for regular procedure. They were born conspirators." *Nixon*, II, 233.

appointment as "special assistant," not simply "national security adviser," was symbolic. He established working groups to coordinate policies around the world, and, though not confirmed in his office as a cabinet member would have to be, set out to be the most consequential (and most famous) national security adviser in our history. By September 1973, Kissinger would replace Rogers at State while retaining his own position as national security adviser, and thus bring an even tighter coordination of foreign policy under his direction. He maintained this dual position into the Ford administration, until, under increasing attack from the conservative wing of the Republican Party, Ford removed Kissinger from his position on the National Security Council (NSC), replacing him with Brent Scowcroft.[44]

Joan Hoff (who coined the term "Nixinger") speaks of Nixon's "basic aprincipledness." She finds unsuitable his tendency not to fully reveal himself in his public actions.[45] For example, although he chose his long-time confidant Rogers to head the Department of State, the president had every intention of having the White House function as the State Department. By centralizing foreign policy in the White House and creating a kind of closed system in the NSC, the administration conflated policy and action. Moreover, Nixon and Kissinger even bypassed the NSC if they believed it necessary.[46] For example, *both* the NSC system and the State Department were basically ignored in deciding such important matters as (1) "Vietnamization," (2) the "Nixon Doctrine," (3) the secret talks with North Vietnam, (4) the president's "New Economic Policy," (5) covert intervention in Chile, and (6) the president's trip to China in 1972.[47]

Moreover, as the administration advanced its policy of *détente* with the Soviet Union, it continued the tightly controlled methods originally established. Kissinger had made early contact with the Soviet ambassador, Anatoly Dobrynin, and through so-called "back-channel," secret dealings with Dobrynin and others, he and the president circumvented not just domestic institutions but also our close allies in NATO. In such wise did the administration plan the celebrated

---

[44] Gerald R. Ford, *A Time to Heal: The Autobiography of Gerald R. Ford* (New York: Harper and Row, 1979), 325–326.

[45] Hoff, *Nixon Reconsidered*, 3.

[46] Ibid., 157–158.

[47] Ibid., 162.

presidential trip to Moscow in 1972 and develop its breakthrough advances in the Anti-Ballistic Missile (ABM) and Strategic Arms Limitations (SALT I) agreements with the Soviet Union.

Nixon's predecessors, presidents Kennedy and Johnson, had proposed the control of strategic weapons and their delivery vehicles (SNDVs) on several occasions. Nearly all these proposals were made in the setting of multilateral disarmament negotiations. In particular, both presidents used the Eighteen Nation Disarmament Committee (ENDC) as the forum for new initiatives.[48] As we saw in Chapter 3, LBJ raised the issue with Premier Kosygin at the 1967 Glassboro Summit. Johnson understood that the two powers were unlikely to gain much support for their joint draft nonproliferation treaty if they did not demonstrate some progress on the "vertical" proliferation represented by their growing stockpiles.

The "Nixinger" style of diplomacy redirected American efforts at arms control away from even the limited multilateral context used by previous administrations. In March 1969 the White House announced that it would go ahead with the deployment of an ABM system. Undertaken largely as a "bargaining chip" in direct negotiations with the Soviets, the controversial defensive system could be dismantled if a strategic weapons agreement was reached. In November the two sides began direct bilateral talks on an agreement.

The thirty months of U.S.-Soviet negotiations that followed were conducted outside the normally accepted institutions and procedures of arms control decision-making. Alternating between Helsinki and Vienna, the American and Soviet delegations made no effort to keep UN organs informed on progress. They also used highly secret "back channels" for sensitive communications between the Kremlin and the White House. In April 1972 Kissinger made a secret visit to Moscow to end a deadlock on the number of submarine-launched ballistic missiles (SLBMs) each side would be allowed to keep.[49] In May, a Moscow summit between Nixon and Leonid Brezhnev capped the process. An ABM Treaty and a Five-

---

[48] Jerry Pubantz, "Strategic Arms Limitation Talks," *MERSH*, Vol. 37, 1984, 173.

[49] Ibid., 177

Year Interim Offensive Weapons Agreement were signed by the two parties.[50]

Examples abound of the unilateralism implicit in Nixinger diplomacy. U.S. policy was as brazen in Chile as anywhere. With the election of a socialist, Salvador Allende Gossens, as president in 1970, despite secret funding of his opponents by the CIA, the White House became involved in a covert attempt to destabilize the new government. Allende nationalized U.S.-owned copper mines and expropriated property of the International Telegraph and Telephone Corporation. Following these actions, the Nixon administration ended economic aid and tried to influence international financial institutions like the World Bank and the Inter-American Bank to deny Chile credit. No effort was made to take America's dispute with Allende to the United Nations or to negotiate with the Chilean government through UN channels. Nixon, taking a page from his mentor President Eisenhower, who had toppled the Guatemalan regime in 1954 without recourse to the international community, turned to covert means to bring down Allende.

Although the Allende government lasted through another election (increasing its popular vote to 43 percent in the congressional election of 1972), domestic opposition grew, fed by demonstrations and strikes. The White House's so-called "Forty Committee" had approved almost $9 million in secret funds, to be dispensed chiefly to Allende's political enemies, between 1970 and 1973. In September 1973, a military coup overthrew the president, and Washington immediately recognized the new government, led by General Augusto Pinochet. The coup ended forty-one consecutive years of democratic government in Chile, the longest period of any South American nation.[51] As for the United Nations, whatever concern there may have been among its members,

---

[50] For the most complete collection of SALT materials, see *SALT Handbook: Key Documents and Issues 1972–1979*, edited by Roger P. Labrie (Washington, D.C.: Arms Control and Disarmament Agency, 1979). Soviet periodicals with extensive commentary on the SALT negotiations are *Mirovaia Ekonomika I Mezhdunarodnye Otnosheniia, Krasnaia Zvesda,* and *Voennaia Mysl'*. See also Gerard Smith, *Doubletalk: The Story of the First Strategic Arms Limitation Talks* (Garden City, N.Y.: Doubleday, 1980); Thomas W. Wolfe, *The SALT Experience* (Cambridge, Mass.: Ballinger, 1979); John Newhouse, *Cold Dawn: The Story of SALT* (New York: Holt, Rinehart and Winston, 1973); and Strobe Talbott, *Endgame: The Inside Story of SALT II* (New York: Harper and Row, 1979).

[51] Szulc, *Illusion of Peace,* 720–724. Szulc uses data from Senate hearings.

debate over Chile's fate remained embedded in various UN bodies' resolutions of complaint. Neither Washington nor its new friends in Pinochet's government in Santiago paid much heed.[52]

At Guam, in the summer of 1969, the president announced, unexpectedly, the "Nixon Doctrine," intended to limit U.S. involvement in future small wars. We would henceforth provide only arms, advisers, and financial aid—not troops—to friends engaged in such conflicts.[53] The Nixon Doctrine, coupled with "Vietnamization," was designed to turn over the war effort in Southeast Asia to the South Vietnamese, while removing American ground troops and making more use of American air power. In the late stages of the Johnson administration, LBJ had sought some UN "good offices" as a possible way out of Vietnam. Nixon's Vietnamization plan assumed that Ho Chi Minh would soon see that he could get a better deal with the Americans than with a strengthened and determined South Vietnamese regime. To work, Nixon's stratagem could not in any way suggest that the United Nations might at some propitious moment step in, allowing the influence of its members to temper possible future peace terms. Vietnamization denied any possibility of a UN-brokered end to the war.

Washington's international economic policy wavered between the centralized tactics described above and a more open and traditional diplomacy. Nixon, who had developed an interest in international trade as a practicing attorney in the early 1960s, appointed capable, internationally oriented advisers such as John Connally, George Shultz, and Peter Peterson as cabinet officials in the Treasury and Commerce departments. These advisers, unlike the ill-fated Rogers, played a central role in international economic policy. The difference may have been that Kissinger was not as informed or as interested in economics as in what he considered larger political matters.[54] One result was the "New Economic Policy," announced in August of 1971.

Responding to a variety of economic challenges, Nixon called a weekend meeting at Camp David for August 13–15. Among the fifteen people in attendance were advisers and cabinet officials (including Connally, Shultz, and Peterson), Federal Reserve Chairman Arthur

---

[52] *YUN, 1973*, 174–175; *YUN, 1974*, 677–678, 687.

[53] For details, see Report to Congress, February 25, 1971, Item 75, *PPP, 1971*, 222–228.

[54] Stoessinger, *Kissinger*, 155.

Burns, staff from the Council of Economic Advisers, and other economists and business leaders. Two concerns were paramount in these private discussions: the sluggish domestic economy, with the menace of inflation; and challenges to the dollar in international exchange. Since the Bretton Woods Conference of 1944 (which had created the International Monetary Fund and the World Bank), currencies had been based on a regularized exchange rate. The U.S. dollar, the base currency after the war, was linked to gold. In the week before the Camp David gathering, the British ambassador had appeared at the Treasury Department to ask that $3 billion be converted into gold. Nixon's advisers feared that if the United States acceded, other countries might have come forth for further conversions, severely damaging the dollar's standing and creating a run on American currency.

After presiding over two days of concentrated discussion, the president made his surprise announcement on Sunday evening, August 15. The "New Economic Policy" imposed temporary wage and price controls, and—more important in the long run—peremptorily ended the gold connection to the dollar and brought us the system of international currency flotation we have today.[55] The "Nixon shocks" permanently transformed the Bretton Woods international monetary and trading systems, which, like the United Nations, were an integral part of the postwar world. The president made these decisions with no international or multilateral consultation.

Vietnam and Nixon

Nixon, of course, did not initiate U.S. involvement in Vietnam, and certainly did not authorize the expansion of U.S. ground forces there. In the end, in fact, he disengaged the country from that unfortunate adventure. Yet the trauma of Vietnam, ruinous to Lyndon Johnson's place in history, also tainted Nixon's term in office.

During the campaign of 1968, Nixon had promised that he had a plan, unstated at the time, to resolve the Vietnam quandary. That plan became *Vietnamization*, which essentially meant reducing American ground forces while increasing bombing raids. As we have seen above, the "Nixon Doctrine" was a codicil to Vietnamization.

Public negotiations to end the war had begun just before the election of 1968 and continued in Paris after Nixon assumed office. In the

---

[55] *RN*, 518–520.

meantime, and conforming to the new "back-channel" techniques, Kissinger in 1969 began a series of secret negotiations with Xuan Thuy, the principal representative from North Vietnam. This two-tracked set of talks proceeded for some time. In the interim, in an attempt to stop the movement of North Vietnamese troops, Nixon ordered the secret bombing of neutral Cambodia, and eventually, in May 1970, the invasion of that country, replacing the government of Prince Sihanouk with a pro-American general, Lon Nol.

The Cambodian offensive ignited nationwide protests from college students who opposed the war. At Kent State University, four protesters were killed when panicky National Guardsmen fired into a crowd at an antiwar rally. In 1975, the tragedy deepened as American forces and diplomats left Southeast Asia, and as a weakened Cambodia was taken over by the communist Khmer Rouge, who would visit upon that unhappy land one of the worst episodes of genocide in history.

Antiwar sentiment became a powerful force within the Democratic Party. By the time of the Democratic convention in Miami Beach in 1972, Senator George McGovern of South Dakota, popular with opponents of the war, had amassed enough delegate votes in the primaries to ensure his nomination to run against Nixon. Meantime, peace negotiations continued on the two-track basis. On October 26, 1972, within days of Nixon's overwhelming reelection victory, Kissinger put the final nail in the McGovern campaign by announcing, "Peace is at hand."[56] But, partly because of South Vietnamese recalcitrance, talks came to a standstill.

The president decided on an abrupt and savage act to break the deadlock. In mid-December, he ordered what critics called a "carpet bombing" of North Vietnam. These intense bombing raids persisted unabated over eleven days during the Christmas season.

Kissinger and the new Vietnamese negotiator, Le Duc Tho, signed the Paris Peace Accords on January 23, 1973. The final agreement was in most particulars identical to what could have been achieved prior to the Christmas bombing. Moreover, in its essentials, the agreement basically returned the situation in Vietnam to the settlement described in the

---

[56] *New York Times*, October 27, 1972, 1, 18.

Geneva Accords of 1954.[57] As in those accords, no perceptible role was assigned to the United Nations. Order was to be restored through agreement of the principal parties without the interference of the universal collective security system. For their efforts, Kissinger and Le were awarded the Nobel Peace Prize in 1973.

In late April 1975, less than a year after Nixon's departure from office, his successor, Gerald Ford, would preside over the humbling departure of all American personnel from Vietnam and Cambodia.[58] North Vietnam forces easily made their way into Saigon, soon to unify the country under their direction. The Americans had lost almost 60,000 dead in this longest of all our wars; the Vietnamese, millions. The world's worst war since Korea ended in a way that testified to the near irrelevance of the United Nations.

There is little doubt that as the United States persisted in its unilateral prosecution of the war, its indifference to the United Nations, and to the sentiments of many delegations in that organization,[59] further eroded relations between third world nations and Washington. Secretary-General U Thant, worried about the spread of the conflict, had pressed for negotiations to end the war and had criticized U.S. bombing

----

[57] The full Paris Peace Accords of 1973 are in *New York Times*, January 25, 1973, 15–17; the negotiated agreement as revealed in late October 1972 by the North Vietnamese, can be found in *New York Times*, October 27, 1972, 19; and the "Final Declaration" of the Geneva Accords of 1954 is in *New York Times, The Pentagon Papers* (New York: Bantam, 1971), 49–52.

[58] Ford, *Autobiography*, 250–257.

[59] Delegations to UN bodies did occasionally voice concerns about U.S. involvement in Vietnam. For example, in an overwhelming vote on November 29, 1972, GA Resolution 2932A, without mentioning specific countries, "deplored" the use of napalm and "other incendiary weapons in all armed conflict." The resolution seemed directed at U.S. actions in Southeast Asia, but the United States simply abstained in the vote; *YUN, 1972*, 18–19. Also, the secretary-general always extended his "good offices" to the parties to the conflict, but the United States ignored the offer; Ibid., 155. The secretary-general was invited, in accordance with Article 19 of the Paris peace agreement of 1973, to witness and acknowledge the official signing of the treaty at an international conference on Vietnam held in Paris in late February and early March, 1973. See *YUN, 1973*, 103.

raids in the North.[60] U Thant's successor, Kurt Waldheim, had, in his first year in office, issued a public statement urging the cessation of U.S. bombing raids.[61] In both instances, the Nixon administration either reacted with sharp disapproval or ignored the entreaties. As U Thant ruefully conceded, "The United Nations as an organization has been powerless to intervene" in Vietnam.[62]

India and Pakistan, 1971

One of the few episodes in which the Nixon administration showed some interest in UN involvement was a dangerous clash between India and Pakistan in late 1971. Even here, though, the president vacillated between encouraging UN action and avoiding the world body for fear that it might complicate superpower politics.

In 1947 a partition of the Asian subcontinent had created India and Pakistan out of the imperial domain formerly controlled by Great Britain. The division, and the ensuing flood of refugees from one of the new countries to another, resulted in bloody clashes between Muslims and Hindus. Additionally, Muslim Pakistan was separated into an eastern and western region, each bordering the larger India.

By the early 1970s strains between Pakistan and India had become commingled with even larger geopolitical tensions. In October 1962, open hostilities had broken out between China and India over contested boundaries in the Himalayas, and bitterness persisted for the following decade. Further complicating the picture were armed border clashes in 1969 between China and the Soviet Union along the Amur river. Thus, with the Nixon administration's overtures to the Chinese, along with its apparently charitable attitude toward Pakistan, India began to worry about a U.S.-China-Pakistan alignment and sought closer relations with the Soviet Union as a counterbalance. The Soviets, with their own worries about a China-U.S. rapprochement, responded positively, and on August 9, 1971, the two countries signed the Soviet-India Friendship Treaty.

---

[60] Press statements, May 5, 1970, and November 23, 1970, *Public Papers of the Secretaries-General of the United Nations; U Thant, 1968–1971*, VII (New York: Columbia University Press, 1977), 353, 379. Hereafter cited as *PPSG*.

[61] Waldheim, *Eye of the Storm*, 117.

[62] *PPSG, U Thant*, 41.

Meantime, feuds between the two geographic areas of Pakistan quickened, and by 1971 India decided to take advantage of these differences to split its neighboring adversary into two less powerful countries, thus removing the presence of pro-Chinese Pakistan on its eastern frontier. Pakistan was led by General Aga Muhammed Yahya Khan and was at odds with the impoverished eastern half of the country, which considered itself exploited by the larger and more affluent west. In 1971 riots against Yahya Khan broke out in the east. Yahya Khan sent in troops, bloodshed spread, refugees flooded into India, and in December the Indian army invaded East Pakistan and defeated the general's forces. Threats to invade western Pakistan receded, and by 1972, encouraged by India, the east had broken away to become Bangladesh, destined to be one of the poorest countries in the world.

When the crisis was accelerating during the summer of 1971, the Nixon administration, wishing to avoid confrontation between the Pakistan army and East Pakistanis, and desirous of keeping the Indians out of the conflict, urged Yahya Khan to call for a UN-supervised program of relief in the poverty-stricken east. In mid-July the Pakistan government agreed with the proposal but India rejected any use of UN agencies or the injection of the Security Council into the matter.

Full war broke out in late November. Urged by the U.S. ambassador, Joseph Farland, President Yahya Khan requested that the United Nations send observers to the Pakistani side of the line and take over refugee facilities in East Pakistan. Early in the war virtually all affected sides—the United States, the Soviet Union, India, even Pakistan—seemed reluctant to call for a discussion of the crisis in the Security Council, leading Kissinger to write later, "It was a sad commentary on the state of the United Nations when a full-scale invasion of a major country was treated by victim, ally, aggressor, and the other great powers as too dangerous to bring to the formal attention of the world body pledged by its Charter to help preserve the peace."[63]

Of course, the United States was as guilty of procrastination as anyone, and as late as early December, when the Security Council finally convened, Washington was still considering a unilateral approach to the crisis. It was at this moment that the journalist Jack Anderson published pilfered, and damaging, remarks from a secret meeting of Kissinger's Washington Special Action Group, proposing a "tilt toward Pakistan."

---

[63] Henry Kissinger, *White House Years* (Boston: Little, Brown, 1979), 894.

But as the war quickly spread, and the United States began to fear an Indian invasion of West Pakistan, the administration turned increasingly to the United Nations.

On December 4, Ambassador George Bush supported a resolution before the Security Council calling for a cease-fire and a *withdrawal* of armed forces from the current battle lines. Vetoed by the Soviet Union, the proposal was carried to the General Assembly, where, three days later, under the "Uniting for Peace" formula,[64] it passed by 104 to 11 votes. In a matter of days, Washington had become fully engaged with the United Nations in trying to resolve this troublesome and perilous situation.

On December 9, President Yahya Khan, under threat of a full invasion from India and responding to Nixon's importuning, conceded East Pakistan's secession and accepted the General Assembly's cease-fire resolution.[65] But it was too late: India was on the march, and New Delhi rejected the UN call for a cease-fire. The United States now began working on a new UN resolution to effect a cease-fire *in place* throughout the subcontinent, hoping that the Soviet Union would accede to this modification in the Security Council. Kissinger worried that if this did not work, an agreement to a cease-fire by the Pakistani commander in the east would immediately open the possibility that India would mobilize for full war in the west. While Ambassador Bush was hard at work to bring the Soviets in line in the Security Council, the administration sent a naval task force through the Strait of Malacca into the Bay of Bengal.

The crisis finally subsided on December 16, when Pakistani forces in East Pakistan surrendered, and the Indian prime minister, Indira Gandhi, conceivably on the understanding that the Soviet Union was joining the United States in its Security Council efforts, offered an unconditional cease-fire in the west.[66] Moreover, India had achieved its ultimate objective of removing a hostile Pakistan from its eastern border.

---

[64] See Chapter 2 for an explanation of "Uniting for Peace."

[65] *RN*, 528.

[66] Confirmed in Security Council Resolution 307, December 21, 1971; the USSR abstained but did not veto. *YUN, 1971,* 161.

The next day the UN-decreed cease-fire between India and Yahya Khan's forces went into effect.[67]

Pakistan had been sundered in two, and the subcontinent would remain a flashpoint for the future. But, for the time, a wider war had been avoided. In the halls of the United Nations, stalwart efforts by the United States had produced Soviet-American cooperation and a multilateral resolution to a tough problem.

China

Nixon may well be judged in the long term for his diplomatic initiative with China. In retrospect, his approach to the Middle Kingdom is not as curious as some at the time thought. During his political exile in the 1960s, Nixon had spent considerable time thinking through major foreign policy challenges. His musings on China were revealed in an article he wrote in 1967 in *Foreign Affairs*.[68] He summarized his views by saying, "We simply cannot afford to leave China outside the family of nations." In his address before the General Assembly in 1969 he said, "Whenever the leaders of Communist China choose to abandon their self-imposed isolation, we are ready to talk with them in...[a] frank and serious spirit." [69]

But revealing our receptiveness to mainland China's eventual entrance into the international community would have a serious impact on our traditional policy toward China. Since Mao Zedong's communist victory in the civil war against Generalissimo Chiang Kai-shek in 1949, the United States had firmly maintained recognition of Chiang's Nationalist regime, exiled on the island of Taiwan, as the legitimate government of China. We continually supported the seating of Taipei's representative as the permanent Chinese member of the United Nations, and opposed any effort to allow Mao's government into the organization. The intransigence of this policy derived from the fractious political debate that had raged after 1949, when Republicans accused the Truman administration of "losing" China. Nixon had been part of this political attack. The ensuing rise of "McCarthyism," the "red scare" of the 1950s, and China's support for North Korea in the Korean conflict all

---

[67] For two differing interpretations of the story see Kissinger, *White House Years*, 861–914; and Ambrose, *Nixon*, II, 482–485.

[68] "Asia After Vietnam," *Foreign Affairs* 46 (October 1967): 121–124.

[69] September 18, 1969, Item 365, *PPP, 1969,* 728.

cast the government of the mainland as our bitterest enemy. Inexorably, Nixon's new approach to China would collide with that tradition.

On November 22, 1970, the president sent a memorandum to his national security adviser. "On a very confidential basis," he began, "I would like for you to have prepared in your staff—without any notice to people who might leak—a study of where we are to go with regard to the admission of Red China to the United Nations. It seems to me that the time is approaching sooner than we might think when we will not have the votes to block admission."[70]

Meantime, Chinese and U.S. diplomats began secret talks in Warsaw, Poland. In March 1971, the Chinese invited an American Ping-Pong team to visit. At the same time, secret arrangements were under way to send Kissinger to Beijing. All this while, the State Department, mostly unaware of these developments, prepared for the annual vote to retain Taiwan's seat at the United Nations. In July, 1971 Kissinger himself showed up in Beijing, after vanishing briefly from a visit to Pakistan.

These dramatic events were but a prelude to the carefully arranged trip the president took to China in February 1972. Here he met with the aging Mao and signed the "Shanghai communiqué" whereby the United States recognized that Beijing had "sovereignty" in China and that both Chinese governments claimed Taiwan (thus disavowing a "two-China" policy, with one China on the mainland, another on Taiwan). Both sides agreed to strive for a "peaceful resolution" of the Taiwan dispute.[71]

In the midst of these remarkable events, and while Kissinger was preparing for his second trip to China in late 1971, the annual UN debate regarding China commenced. Kissinger later admitted, "Our opening to Peking effectively determined the outcome of the UN debate, although we did not realize this immediately."[72] Nixon saw the vote as "inevitable."[73] But all the while, the State Department had been scrambling to keep up with events while protecting our stated position.

As we have noted, the configuration of membership in the United Nations had begun to shift, adding such a large number of formerly colonized nations that by the 1960s they had become a majority in the

---

[70] *RN*, 545.

[71] Joint Statement Following Discussions with Leaders of the People's Republic of China, February 27, 1972, Item 71, *PPP*, 1972, 376–379.

[72] *White House Years*, 770.

[73] *RN*, 556.

General Assembly. These new, poorer third world countries were interested less in cold war alliances and disputes than in their own social and political development. They tended to be socialist economically and authoritarian politically. They were embittered by the wealth of the Northern Hemisphere nations, and they tended to be antagonistic to U.S. actions in Southeast Asia and Latin America and suspicious of Washington's apparent reluctance to impel an end of racial segregation and repression in southern Africa. Third world delegations began to push for mainland China's membership in the United Nations. In fact, the unseating of the U.S.-supported Taiwan government and its replacement by Beijing had become almost a cathartic uniting tactic.

Since 1961 the United States had reacted to pressures to seat the People's Republic by a procedural technique. Beginning with the second term of the Eisenhower administration, recall, the United States had always submitted a resolution making any proposal to change China's representation an "Important Question," which, according to the UN Charter, required a two-thirds vote to succeed. Thus there were always two votes in the General Assembly, one on the "Important Question" resolution and a second on whether or not to seat the People's Republic. As late as 1969 the "Important Question" resolution had passed: 71 for, 48 against, 4 abstaining. But support for the American position was clearly eroding, and the State Department, with Secretary Rogers' approval, had begun considering shifting to a "two-China" policy in an attempt to keep Taiwan in the United Nations, while also allowing the mainland to become a member. Of course, this approach was inconsistent with the policy now developing in the White House, which would result in the Shanghai communiqué. Nonetheless, the president allowed Rogers to go ahead and develop the dual-representation formula, which would seat the People's Republic of China as the permanent member of the Security Council while allowing the Nationalist government to remain in the General Assembly. Beijing gently rebuffed the idea. Meantime, Kissinger took off for another trip to China, where he would be during the UN vote. Secretary of State Rogers warned that the national security adviser's visit to the People's Republic would doom U.S. efforts to keep Taiwan in the United Nations,[74] and indeed it did. Allies of the United States who had previously supported

---

[74] Doug Wead, *George Bush, Man of Integrity* (Eugene, Ore.: Harvest House, 1988), 144.

keeping the communist Chinese out could now see little value in
maintaining that position while Washington made its own peace with
the mainland regime. In October 1971, the Albanians presented their
annual resolution to admit the People's Republic and expel Taiwan.[75]
The die was cast, and the result was one of the most humiliating defeats
for the United States in the United Nations—concurrently abetted by one
of the most renowned of postwar American policy shifts.

The historic UN vote took place on the evening of October 25, and
the eight-hour meeting, "tense and emotion-filled," according to the *New
York Times*,[76] spilled over into the morning of October 26. The vote on the
resolution presented by Albania and twenty other nations came with
"dramatic suddenness" and took the American delegation, headed by
Ambassador George Bush, by surprise. More quickly than the Americans
had anticipated, a roll call vote was taken on the "Important Question"
issue at 9:47 P.M., and for the first time, it was lost: 59-55-15. When the
electric tally boards showed that the proposal had been defeated,
pandemonium broke out. The chief Tanzanian delegate, Salim Ahmed
Salim, led his colleagues in a victory jig, and delegates around the
General Assembly floor jumped up and applauded. Ambassador Bush
slumped visibly. The General Assembly then defeated a subsequent vote
to postpone until the next day consideration of the final resolution to
expel Taiwan. The Nationalist delegation left the hall. The third vote of
the session, to remove Taiwan and seat Beijing, passed 76-35-17. The
General Assembly adjourned at 11:20 P.M., but the rejoicing delegates did
not leave the building; they headed to the delegates' lounge for a toast.
Ambassador Bush called the evening a "moment of infamy."[77] The
president prepared for his historic visit to mainland China. Nixon's
gyrations on the admission of China reinforced the realist perspective
that the United Nations was a place where states defended their
interests; they did not attempt to change the world there.

It is arguable that China's entrance into the United Nations, even if it
embarrassed the United States, resulted in more positive consequences
than critics would have admitted in the immediate aftermath of the vote.
China proved reluctant and circumspect in casting vetoes in the Security

---

[75] Kissinger, *White House Years*, 771–783.

[76] *New York Times*, October 26, 1971, 1.

[77] For full coverage of the voting, see several articles, Ibid., 1,10. See also *RN*,
556–557.

Council. Its first veto was cast against the admission of Bangladesh following the India-Pakistan war. Furthermore, it participated quietly yet responsibly in various UN-related conferences on disarmament, development, the environment, terrorism, the seabed, and finances. And, as Nixon himself pointed out many years later, China cooperated with the United States in many instances, including, crucially, by not using its veto in the Security Council during the Persian Gulf War of 1991, when George Bush was president.[78] John Stoessinger has evaluated China's role in the United Nations in this way: "China's entry into the United Nations signifies the first time in her history that she has been compelled to deal with other states on the basis of sovereign equality."[79] The realist Richard Nixon would surely find that assessment agreeable, for, if true, it highlights a consummation of his carefully timed China policy.

Yom Kippur

The Middle East has been a high-profile foreign policy concern for the United States, and for the United Nations, since the establishment of Israel in 1948. Because of the realist demeanor of Nixon's diplomacy, however, the American approach to this volatile area was more than subtly different from that of the immediately preceding period. Eisenhower, Kennedy, and Johnson had avoided American overinvolvement in the region. Not until the denouement of the 1967 war had demonstrated the centrality of the area to the Soviet-American confrontation did the United States seek to manipulate events in the Middle East directly. Every president prior to Nixon had hoped to leave the management of Middle East issues to the United Nations. By the time the Nixon-Ford years had ended, some three years after the pause in the 1973 Middle East war, Secretary of State Kissinger had engineered a military disengagement between the Egyptians and the Israelis on the Sinai peninsula (January 1974) and a similar agreement between the Israelis and the Syrians on the Golan Heights (May 1974). On September 4, 1975, in Geneva, Kissinger successfully cobbled together an acceptable buffer zone in the Sinai, originally to be maintained by U.S. civilian technicians stationed between the antagonists. The exhausting "shuttle diplomacy" that Kissinger used to bring about these modest but important steps, and to provide "good offices" for adversaries unwilling

---

[78] Nixon, *Beyond Peace*, 123.

[79] Stoessinger, *The United Nations and the Superpowers*, 53.

to talk directly to one another, had begun in the immediate aftermath of the 1973 war.

October 6 was Yom Kippur, the Day of Atonement, the holiest day of the year for Jews. Nixon was in Key Biscayne, Florida, relaxing, and Kissinger was at the Waldorf Towers in New York to attend the opening session of the United Nations. Early that morning, Assistant Secretary of State Joseph Sisco awoke Kissinger with urgent news from the Middle East. Syria and Egypt had attacked Israel from two fronts. For three days the Arab coalition advanced; Egyptians crossed the Suez Canal, forced hundreds of Israeli troops to surrender, and recaptured land in the Sinai seized from them in the Israeli victory of 1967. Syria, in the north, nearly broke through Israeli defenses in the Golan Heights. The assumption of Israeli invincibility was severely, possibly permanently, damaged.

The United States was Israel's major supporter and arms supplier. At the same time, the president and the secretary of state viewed the Middle East as a more complex issue than simply maintaining the survival of the Jewish state. Each wished to sustain and improve good relations with moderate Arab states, not least because of the petroleum exports that emanated from the area; for like reason, the Americans wanted long-term balance and stability in the region, and the avoidance of permanent crises that might bring in outside forces, most ominously the Soviet Union. Indeed, Washington had been pleased a year earlier when President Anwar Sadat of Egypt had removed 10,000 Soviet advisers from his country. Finally, Nixon and Kissinger wanted the United States to play the dominating role in bringing a settlement to the troubled area. Curiously, they believed that the immediate crisis offered a fleeting opportunity. Nixon would later say, "Despite the great skepticism of the Israeli hawks, I believed that only a battlefield stalemate would provide the foundation on which fruitful negotiations might begin."[80] The administration prepared to make full use of the United Nations to exploit what it hoped would be a fortunate standoff.

During the first days of the war, Washington did not want a prolonged, acrimonious debate in the General Assembly, nor did it favor an immediate cease-fire resolution in the Security Council, which would have been disadvantageous to the Israelis and not accepted by them. Rather, the Americans supported convening the Security Council, where they hoped to draw the Soviets into a joint response. Although Kissinger

---

[80] *RN*, 921.

privately contacted Ambassador Dobrynin about this, all sides, including the United States, seemed to want a delay. At least this was the case in the very early days of the war. At the United Nations, U.S. Ambassador John Scali pursued dilatory "consultations" in the hope that the Israelis would soon turn the military tide. By the second day of the war (Sunday, October 7) Egypt had established a line across the Suez Canal, and the Syrians were well into the Golan Heights, so each felt the surge and pride of victory and neither was ready to deal. Their Soviet friends in the United Nations were thus also not yet ready to be drawn into a Security Council resolution.

Meantime, and encouragingly, President Sadat had made contact with the Americans through his national security adviser, Mohammed Hafiz Ismail, who had previously established a relationship with Kissinger. The secretary of state, impressed by Sadat, was convinced that "we were dealing with a statesman of the first order."[81] By Monday, October 8, Soviet President Leonid Brezhnev let it be known that he was prepared to work in cooperation with the United States.

The tide of battle began to turn when Washington responded positively to an urgent plea by Israeli Prime Minister Golda Meir for military aid. Within the next two days, Israel moved against Syria, and a U.S. airlift began. Still, Egypt and the Soviet Union resisted a cease-fire resolution in the Security Council. But by October 16, Egypt, now under duress in the field, again made contact. Kissinger responded by recommending a cease-fire in place to be followed by "talks under the aegis of the secretary-general with a view to achieving a settlement in accordance with Security Council Resolution 242 in all of its parts."[82]

The next day the president met with a delegation of foreign ministers from Saudi Arabia, Morocco, Algeria, and Kuwait and told them: "I will work for a cease-fire, not in order to trick you into stopping at the cease-fire lines, but to use it as a basis to go on from there for a settlement on the basis of Resolution 242....we will work within the framework for Resolution 242."[83] At this stage, however, Prime Minister Meir demurred, specifically rejecting any linkage of Resolution 242 with a cease-fire. Kissinger, now convinced that "without Resolution 242, there

---

[81] *Years of Upheaval*, 482.

[82] Ibid., 530.

[83] Ibid., 535.

would be no legal basis for any future negotiations,"[84] doggedly pressed ahead, turning again to the Security Council. By October 18 an opening appeared as the Soviets offered a draft resolution calling for (1) a cease-fire in place, (2) withdrawal of Israeli forces to borders implied in Resolution 242 (by which they meant to signal Arab nations of their support for the pre-1967 borders), and (3) beginning consultations on a peace agreement.[85] Immediately, Nixon sent Kissinger to Moscow to take advantage of the Russian initiative.

Kissinger and Leonid Brezhnev produced a draft resolution on October 21, accepting the first and third of the Soviet proposals for a cease-fire in place and the initiation of negotiations for a just and durable peace, but altering the second provision to a more equivocal call for the implementation of UN Resolution 242 in all its parts. The carefully calibrated compromise became Security Council Resolution 338 when it passed the Council at 12:50 A.M., October 22. Momentarily, all sides accepted.

Then the cease-fire unraveled, as each contestant prevaricated and accused the other of violations. Now a new crisis was layered over the existing one, as Brezhnev conveyed to New York a scheme calling for sending a joint U.S.-Soviet military force to the Middle East to enforce the UN resolution, implying that if the Americans did not join in, he would intervene unilaterally. Nixon immediately responded that the proposal was unacceptable, hastily let Sadat know that the United States would veto such a suggestion in the Security Council, and countered Soviet threats with a worldwide military alert. The crisis seemed to be spinning out of control.

But the president also let it be known that Washington would support inserting between the antagonists an expanded UN truce supervisory force of noncombatant personnel.[86] Early on the morning of October 25 a message arrived from Sadat, who said that he would ask the United Nations, not the United States and the Soviet Union, to provide an international peacekeeping force. The Security Council, ignoring the Soviet suggestion of the previous day, then passed Resolution 340, calling for a "return" to the original cease-fire lines as provided in Resolution 338, and for an augmentation of international

---

[84] Ibid., 593.

[85] *RN*, 930.

[86] Ibid., 938–939.

observer personnel in the area to monitor compliance. Nixon called off the alert and cabled Brezhnev, proposing that "at this time we leave the composition of the UN Observer Force to the discretion of the Secretary-General....We do not believe it necessary to have separate observer forces from individual countries operating in the area."[87]

Within the Security Council, then, the crisis eased. The Israelis, regrouped and hoping to deliver a final telling blow to the Egyptians, reluctantly, and under pressure from the Americans, accepted the UN denouement. Nixon's hope for a "stalemate" had materialized. However, the territorial character of the cease-fire had trapped the Egyptian Third Army behind enemy lines. Responding to the United States, Israel agreed on "talks" to solve the problem. Egypt, never having recognized the legitimacy of Israel, now bent. Sadat's confidant, Hafiz Ismail, let Kissinger know that Egypt would accept direct talks "to discuss the military aspects of the implementation of Security Council Resolutions 338 and [the follow-up] 339 of October 22 and 23, 1973." The talks, he insisted, must take place under UN supervision at a specific spot, and a complete cease-fire must be in effect two hours before the meeting. Israel, averse to UN Resolution 242, and fearing further diplomacy that might enshrine its principles, accepted.[88]

At 1:30 A.M. on Sunday, October 28, under the watchful eye of staff from the United Nations Truce Supervisory Organization, Israeli and Egyptian military representatives faced one another in the Sinai. It was the first time in the twenty-five years of Israel's history that high ranking officials from the two nations had ever met for direct talks. They did so under the auspices of UN observers. This UN-guided rendezvous also set the stage for Kissinger's subsequent, and ultimately fruitful, shuttle diplomacy throughout the Middle East.

On December 21, 1973, Secretary-General Kurt Waldheim called a meeting in Geneva. Wary foreign ministers from Egypt, Jordan, Israel, and the USSR (but not Syria) joined an American delegation to hear the secretary of state (who had once written that "History is the memory of states,"[89]) refine and elaborate his familiar realism: "Respect for the

---

[87] Ibid., 940–941.

[88] Kissinger, *Years of Upheaval*, 601–610.

[89] From Kissinger's published dissertation, *A World Restored*; quoted in Stoessinger, *Kissinger*, 7.

forces of history does not mean blind submission to history."[90] The Yom Kippur war had educated Kissinger and had left the ashes from which he would rise to the heights of his tireless Middle East diplomacy.

That Kissinger would finish off his service in the executive branch shuttling about the Middle East is noteworthy, given his professed unfamiliarity with the area at the beginning of Nixon's term.[91] The president, on the other hand, was mindful of the painful history of this region, and, for example, had a more sanguine view of UN Resolution 242 than Kissinger. During his speech to the General Assembly in 1969, Nixon had found it propitious to "point up anew the urgency of a stable peace" in the Middle East. "The United States continues to believe that the U.N. cease-fire resolutions define the minimal conditions that must prevail...[and that] the Security Council resolution of November 1967 [242] charts the way to that settlement."[92] Kissinger would also come around to this view, following the drama of October 1973.

President Ford's Interregnum

After Nixon left office and Gerald Ford assumed the presidency in August 1974, Kissinger continued to play the most important role in foreign relations. President Ford's first public statement included a reassurance to the American people and world leaders that he intended to continue Nixon's foreign policies under Kissinger's firm guidance. The new president demonstrated the same willingness to go it alone in international affairs. He did so, for example, in May 1975, when Cambodia seized an American cargo vessel, the *Mayaguez*. He did not seek a Security Council session or use UN back-channel routes to negotiate a release of the ship. Ignoring the War Powers Act, passed in 1973 over President Nixon's veto, by which Congress gained authority to limit or approve the president's power to engage in undeclared war, Ford ordered an assault to free the crew. As it happened, by the time of the rescue attempt all the Americans had been released. And since thirty-eight Americans would lose their lives in the pointless attack, Ford came in for some criticism and derision at home and in UN bodies.[93]

---

[90] Ibid., 195.

[91] *White House Years*, 914.

[92] Item 365, *PPP, 1969,* 727.

[93] Ford, *Autobiography,* 275–284.

Ford, however, was more open than Nixon to the possibilities of multilateral diplomacy. While the Soviet-American relationship might be central to world affairs, it could be managed through larger collective efforts than simply bilateral superpower interactions. The president's biggest success with this approach was the Helsinki Conference in August 1975. This meeting, sought for some time by the Soviet Union, represented perhaps the primary multilateral accomplishment of *détente*, with ramifications few foresaw at the time. In Helsinki, Finland, tension between East and West seemed to ease more than ever as thirty-five nations from Europe and the Americas met in what was called the European Security Conference. This was largest meeting of European heads of state since the Congress of Vienna in 1815. The conference produced a far-reaching treaty effectively ending border disputes that had festered since World War II. All sides agreed to respect the political divisions that then existed. The United States tacitly recognized East Germany by joining its representatives at the negotiating table. In the same spirit, in September 1973, as plans were proceeding for the Helsinki meeting, East and West Germany were admitted to the United Nations.

These steps seemed to confirm a rigid stabilization of existing cold war borders. But in fact, the Soviet Union, eager to complete a comprehensive agreement with so many nations, made an eventful concession in the language of Helsinki's "Final Act." The frontiers were described as "inviolable" instead of what the Soviets preferred—"unchangeable." Such wording seemed to preserve the prospect of a peaceful change in the borders at a later date, including the theoretical reunification of Germany, which in fact took place in 1990.[94]

Moreover, Western nations won from Moscow guarantees regarding human rights within the Soviet sphere of influence, including the right of emigration. Contained in the third section of the Final Act, these so-called "basket three" provisions furnished a source of support in international law for dissident groups throughout Eastern Europe to challenge pro-Soviet regimes. The "Final Act" also provided for regular follow-up meetings of the participating nations to monitor the progress of the Helsinki accords. This mandate tended to maintain public pressure for implementation of "basket three" guarantees regarding

---

[94] F. Stephen Larrabee, "Some Gains for the West," *New York Times*, August 1, 1985, 21.

human rights, trade union freedoms, human contacts, and the free flow of information.

When Ford addressed the conference, he restored idealism to the rhetoric he used to emphasize Helsinki's stipulations about human rights: "The founders of my country did not merely say that all Americans should have these rights, but all men everywhere should have these rights."[95] Some commentators have seen the Helsinki accords as a crucial stepping-stone to the end of the cold war. If so, this represents a singular triumph of cooperative diplomacy for the Ford administration.

Yet Ford had little time to bask in any glory. A stagnant economy and criticism of his pardon of Nixon kept him reeling. He would suffer most from conservatives within his own party, who now criticized Kissinger as being too soft on the Soviet Union, resisted the extension of the SALT treaty agreed to by Ford and Brezhnev at a summit in Vladivostok late in 1974, and reacted negatively to the Panama Canal treaties, which were designed to return the canal to Panamanian control. The most prominent conservative assailant within Republican ranks was the governor of California, Ronald Reagan. The governor gave every evidence that he was planning to run against Ford for the 1976 nomination. He mounted a highly visible attack on realist foreign policy and détente, the twin pillars of "Nixinger" diplomacy.[96] In response, Ford removed Kissinger as national security adviser (but kept him as secretary of state) and ceased using the now damaged word "détente" while nonetheless maintaining his conviction of its value. Even so, he barely won the nomination at Kansas City against the up-and-coming Reagan. The Republican Party was deserting the moderate internationalism that had sustained idealists like Eisenhower and realists like Nixon and Ford. The new Republicanism would create an even more threatening challenge to the fortunes of the United Nations than either Eisenhower's benign neglect or Nixon's active distaste ever had.

---

[95] Address in Helsinki, August 1, 1975, Item 459, *PPP, 1975,* 1078.

[96] Ford, *Autobiography,* 373–374. Ford saw Reagan's public criticism as "inflammatory and irresponsible."

5

Two Sides of Idealism

> When my time as your President has ended...I would hope that the nations of the world might say that we had built a lasting peace, based not on weapons of war but on international policies which reflect our own precious values.
>
> —*Jimmy Carter*
> *Inaugural Address, 1977*

> Mr. Gorbachev, tear down this wall!
>
> —*Ronald Reagan*
> *At the Brandenburg Gate, Berlin, June 12, 1987*

Jimmy Carter came to the presidency as a virtual unknown. As late as the spring of 1973, while serving as governor of Georgia, he appeared on a popular television show—*What's My Line?*—where a panel of four celebrities tried to determine guests' occupations. They could not guess his.[1] He is generally considered a failure as president. The journalist Haynes Johnson has referred to his tenure as a "tragedy."[2] This common negative assessment is due in part to his being one of three elected presidents to that time in the twentieth century denied reelection. Two earlier holders of the office lost under extreme circumstances: William Howard Taft in 1912, facing not only his Democratic opponent Woodrow Wilson but also the strongest third-party challenge ever mounted in a national campaign (when former president Theodore Roosevelt also ran); and Herbert Hoover, who lost to Franklin Roosevelt in 1932 in the midst of the worst economic depression in U.S. history. But George Bush's unsuccessful attempt at reelection in 1992 poses the question whether single-term presidencies in the twentieth century should be considered as unusual as observers thought when Carter lost in 1980.

---

[1] Peter G. Bourne, *Jimmy Carter: A Comprehensive Biography from Plains to Postpresidency* (New York: Scribner, 1997), 384.

[2] Haynes Johnson, *In the Absence of Power: Governing America* (New York: Viking, 1980), 321. Johnson pointed out that the Carter presidency "had not been destroyed or disgraced. No great scandal had stained his administration. No great war-and-peace, boom-or-bust issue divided the nation." Mistakes were "little," "personal," and "self-inflicted." 278, 316, 317.

It was after his presidency that Carter gained new and growing respect, as he and his wife Rosalynn, zestfully pursued good works and wrote best-selling books. After leaving office, the former president established the activist Carter Center in Atlanta and traveled the world as an invited official observer at crucial elections in developing countries, often arranged by the United Nations, and as an independent negotiator resolving seemingly insoluble international problems.[3]

Ronald Reagan ascended to the presidency after a long career as an actor in movies and television, followed by two terms as governor of California, the most populous state in the union. He was one of the most widely recognized public figures of the second half of the twentieth century, and he was a very popular president. Reagan was the oldest person ever elected chief executive, and when he left the White House in 1989, he retired quietly in southern California, debilitated by Alzheimer's disease.

Both Carter and Reagan rejected the "realism" espoused by the Nixon and Ford administrations. Each articulated a need to return to the moral roots of the nation's beginnings and to emphasize in our foreign policy the idealistic strains of the American experience. Beyond that similarity, however, each saw his assignment quite differently. Carter, a serious and reflective Christian, believed in the necessity of redemption for our own country and its people, much in an Old Testament way. He saw "human rights" as universal in the sense of being equally applicable to friends and foes, Americans and foreigners. But Reagan saw America as a shining "city on a hill," a realized example for the rest of the world to emulate. The problem, Reagan insisted, was not ourselves or our friends. The problem was international communism.

Carter evinced a much greater interest in international organizations and multilateral diplomacy than his immediate predecessors had. He announced his firm support for and commitment to the United Nations. Reagan, as signaled in his initial appointment of Jeane Kirkpatrick—a critic of the UN—as the permanent representative in New York, saw the United Nations much as Daniel Patrick Moynihan had—a meeting place for unworthy scoundrels and opponents of the United States. Yet, curiously, Reagan, in each of the final six years of his eight-year term,

---

[3] See Douglas Brinkley, *The Unfinished Presidency: Jimmy Carter's Journey Beyond the White House* (New York: Viking, 1998); and Rod Troester, *Jimmy Carter as Peacemaker: A Post-Presidential Biography* (Westport, Conn.: Praeger, 1996).

spoke at the UN's annual opening session, and he took his speeches quite seriously. Carter, with uncommon verve, spoke twice to the organization in his very first year in office, then never again.

Carter's hopes for the expansion of human rights, for world peace, and for an end to cold war confrontations faded away in his last years of office as revolutionary Iran besieged the U.S. embassy in Teheran and took American hostages, and as the Soviet Union invaded Afghanistan. By the end of Carter's term, confrontation, not cooperation, seemed the hallmark of international affairs. Reagan, who initiated an enormously expensive military buildup, called the USSR an "evil empire," and approved covert (and sometimes probably illegal) military interventions in third world countries, ended up presiding over the effective end of the cold war.

These preliminary remarks, though true, mask a more complex set of contingencies than might first appear from a simple recording of differences between the two presidents. To deal with each administration in the challenging and kaleidoscopic environment of the times is the task of the following pages.

*   *   *

Jimmy Carter came to the highest office in the land in the aftermath of Watergate, Vietnam, and the activist presidencies of Nixon, Johnson, and Kennedy. In many respects his election represented a backlash against a strong presidency. As he entered the White House, he had to face a Congress less pliant than in the recent past and more determined to chart an independent course. Elected in part because he was an "outsider," separated from the perceived venality of Washington, he had to deal with "insiders" in the Congress, the bureaucracy, and the media. Whatever liability this situation posed, his administration did achieve some notable successes in domestic affairs. Unemployment declined during Carter's term; Congress passed the first comprehensive energy bill in our history (introduced by Carter in early 1977 and ultimately passing eighteen excruciating months later); by early 1980 Congress finally approved the president's plan to deregulate petroleum and impose a massive windfall profits tax on oil companies; two new departments—energy and education—were created, fulfilling campaign promises; and Congress passed the president's landmark civil service reform bill, the first such reform since 1883. Indeed, President Carter's relations with Congress were, given the resurgence of congressional independence, reasonably good.[4]

While Americans tend to remember the anguish of the Iranian hostage crisis and the Soviet incursion into Afghanistan, Carter could also cite accomplishments in foreign affairs. He skillfully guided the Panama Canal treaties through the Senate; he normalized relations with China; he brought the Israelis and Egyptians together in the Camp David Accords; and he markedly improved America's relations with developing countries, particularly in Africa.

Carter and Foreign Policy

Carter's approach to diplomacy quickly became evident. He, like Nixon before him, was determined to control foreign policy decisions from the White House. He was what would be called a "hands-on" president in almost every aspect of executive leadership. He studied issues carefully before making final decisions, and observers often portrayed him as an extremely well-informed president, even the details of any topic.[5] His press conferences revealed an intelligent leader who was both thoughtful and knowledgeable.

The president surrounded himself with capable foreign policy advisers who sometimes disagreed with one another.[6] But he was always willing to make final decisions. As secretary of state he named a New York lawyer, Cyrus Vance, a graduate of Yale and Yale Law School who had served in many government posts. Vance and his wife Gay became close friends of the Carters.[7] Initially at least, Vance seemed to mirror the president's own views regarding a more idealistic foreign policy. For example, Vance saw international organizations, like the United Nations,

---

[4] Jimmy Carter, *Keeping Faith: Memoirs of a President* (New York: Bantam, 1982), 88. *Congressional Quarterly Weekly,* January 16, 1988, shows that in his relations with Congress Carter compares quite favorably with his predecessors and with President Reagan.

[5] Zbigniew Brzezinski, *Power and Principle: Memoirs of the National Security Adviser, 1977–1981* (New York: Farrar, Straus, Giroux, 1983), 94. UN Undersecretary-General Brian Urquhart said that Carter was "remarkably well informed." Brian Urquhart, *A Life,* 278.

[6] Gaddis Smith, *Morality, Reason, and Power: American Diplomacy in the Carter Years* (New York: Hill and Wang, 1986), 35–45.

[7] Carter, *Keeping Faith,* 51.

as able to "provide the most effective setting for resolving international disputes and for broadening the realm of international cooperation."[8] Vance worked diligently and effectively with the United Nations and with the secretary-general to further U.S. goals. His trusted and able deputy, Warren Christopher, would stay on as deputy secretary of state under Edmund Muskie following Vance's resignation. Christopher became the key Washington official in the Iranian hostage crisis, and some years later President Clinton would choose him as secretary of state.

Harold Brown, president of the California Institute of Technology, became the secretary of defense. Carter thought him a sophisticated scientist and a competent manager. Moreover, the president believed that the Pentagon "needed some discipline," and that Brown was the man to bring it.[9]

As national security adviser Carter chose Zbigniew Brzezinski, whom he described as "perhaps the most controversial member of my team."[10] Like Kissinger, Brzezinski was an immigrant from central Europe (Poland), a graduate of Harvard, and a professor at an Ivy League university (Columbia). Also like Kissinger, Brzezinski lamented the impact of Wilsonian moralism on U.S. diplomacy and gave considerable thought to the question of blending "a concern for moral principle with the imperatives of national power." He noted Carter's "genuine dedication to principle" and "high intelligence with occasionally surprising naiveté."[11] On more than one occasion he indicated to the president that he understood Carter's desire to go down in history as "a President Wilson," but always insisted that "before you are a President Wilson you have to be for a few years a President Truman." And early on he worried that Vance, whom he saw as a "Wilsonian," would be "overly concerned with the United Nations."[12]

With David Rockefeller and others, Brzezinski had founded the Trilateral Commission in the early 1970s. The commission was a think

---

[8] Cyrus Vance, *Hard Choices: Critical Years in America's Foreign Policy* (New York: Simon and Schuster, 1983), 435.

[9] Carter, *Keeping Faith*, 55.

[10] Ibid., 51.

[11] Brzezinski, *Power and Principle*, 23.

[12] Ibid., 23, 432, 520.

tank of major business and academic elites that pondered the dominating and important international connections between Europe, North America, and Japan. Brzezinski invited Carter, who was then governor of Georgia, to join the commission, and an intellectual friendship formed.

Brzezinski's National Security Council was staffed with young Ph.Ds, like Michael Oksenberg for China issues, Robert Pastor for Latin America, and William Quandt for the Middle East. The smallest regional office was for the United Nations and South Africa.[13] Vance's State Department would concentrate on these two areas.

Given his energy and intelligence, and his foreign policy team, the new president's foreign policy prospects looked promising. And Carter set out to do as much as possible as fast as possible. But, as one critic has pointed out, he may have "tried to do too much too quickly."[14] For example, Carter had pledged during the campaign to remove American troops from South Korea. The Americans had been there, technically as United Nations troops, since the cease-fire in the Korean War of the early 1950s. Proponents of the American presence argued that the troops were necessary to keep the North Koreans passive, and, in a larger sense, to demonstrate the projection of American power and influence in a volatile East Asia. Carter, who considered the government of South Korea's president, Park Chung Hee, morally repugnant, insisted that the troops were no longer needed. At a press conference on January 26, 1977, he indicated that he would abide by his campaign promises. But opposition from General John K. Singlaub, the third-ranking army officer in Korea, whom Carter subsequently removed, and from both Republicans and some powerful Democrats in the Senate, including John Glenn of Ohio, Sam Nunn of Georgia, and even the liberal Hubert Humphrey of Minnesota, along with the quieter resistance of Japan, caused the president to defer the decision indefinitely.[15]

Of equal boldness were the decisions to discontinue production of the B-1 bomber and abort plans to produce and deploy the so-called neutron bomb. The Pentagon wanted the B-1 to replace the aging fleet of B-52s. Its many opponents found the new bomber much too expensive, and unnecessary in the age of intercontinental missiles. Carter sided with

---

[13] Smith, *Morality, Reason, and Power*, 39.

[14] Burton I. Kaufman, *The Presidency of James Earl Carter, Jr.* (Lawrence: University Press of Kansas, 1993), 37.

[15] Ibid., 47–48.

the critics and announced the discontinuation of the program at a press conference in late June of 1977. Secretary of State Vance called the cancellation "one of the most courageous and politically costly defense decisions of his presidency."[16]

The neutron bomb was an enhanced-radiation weapon that allowed the killing of humans without destroying surrounding structures. By early 1978 Carter had decided to defer production and deployment of the weapon in the European theater, where it was considered a balance against the considerable manpower advantage held by the Soviet Union. In this instance, he angered domestic hawks and some European allies.[17] But here again, unlike in Korea, he stuck to his decision.

Whatever merits there were in these presidential decisions, the political fallout—indeed, the international fallout—might have been considerably less had Carter been able to match his actions with simultaneous trade-offs from our clearest adversary, the Soviet Union, or had he awaited a substantive agreement on SALT II. But the president had decided to move ahead in these decisions quickly and unilaterally, seeking little in the way of congressional feedback, and nothing in the way of Soviet concessions.

*   *   *

Carter's handling of the Panama Canal treaties was more adroit. The manner in which the canal through the isthmus of Panama had originated had occasioned a strain between the United States and Latin America that had outlasted moments of cordiality (such as Franklin Roosevelt's "good neighbor" policy) and continued into the 1970s. Theodore Roosevelt was president in 1901 when a presidential commission had reported in favor of constructing a canal route through Nicaragua. But a bankrupt French canal company, bogged down in a project in the Colombian province of Panama, now lobbied hard for the United States to opt for the route the company had been unable to complete and buy it out. Roosevelt determined on the Panama route and sent several warships into the area in late fall 1903, with the odd authorization to aid in stopping any Colombian officials who might wish to land in the isthmus with "hostile intent." Of course, Panama was part

---

[16] *Hard Choices*, 57.

[17] Carter, *Keeping Faith*, 225–229; Vance, *Hard Choices*, 67.

of Colombia. Nonetheless, there was hardly any official resistance to a Panamanian "revolution" that took place in a brief three days in early November. The United States quickly recognized the new government and welcomed to Washington its ambassador, the Frenchman Philippe Bunau-Varilla, whose last job had been with the French canal company. Within days, Bunau-Varilla signed a treaty with Secretary of State John Hay, allowing the United States to build and administer a canal through the isthmus. No Panamanian ever signed the treaty, and the provisional government ratified it under threat of the withdrawal of American military protection. The canal remained under U.S. operation for most of the twentieth century; but in 1964, partly in response to Panamanian riots protesting the presence of the United States, negotiations began with the aim of returning sovereignty over the Canal Zone to Panama. Each administration from Johnson through Ford carried forth the negotiations, and by the time Carter entered the presidency, two separate treaties had been ironed out that provided for Panamanian sovereignty in 2000, and for the perpetual neutrality of the Canal Zone, guaranteed by both Panama and the United States.

Supporters of the treaties included an impressive array of distinguished Americans, such as former secretaries of state Dean Rusk, a Democrat, and Henry Kissinger, a Republican; liberals such as George McGovern and Ted Kennedy; and the conservatives William F. Buckley, Jr., and George Will; as well as a politically conservative movie star, John Wayne.[18] But opposition was strong. In the Senate its center was very conservative members like Jesse Helms of North Carolina and Strom Thurmond of South Carolina. But the most important and zealous opponent was former California governor, Ronald Reagan.

Polls initially showed an overwhelming opposition to the treaties. Carter faced the issue head-on. He worked hard with the Senate; enlisted the vocal endorsement of a wide range of well-known and respected Americans, both Republican and Democrat; took questions on a nationwide radio hookup; and went one-on-one with swing voters in the Senate. By early spring of 1978, public opinion moved in the president's direction; a majority now favored the treaty. When the Senate ratified the two treaties in mid-April 1978, each passed by the same margin: 68 to 32,

---

[18] See John Wayne, "Listen, Pardner, Let's Back That Treaty," *Los Angeles Times*, October 28, 1977, Part II, 11; and William F. Buckley, Jr., "Why Not Make It Unanimous?" *Los Angeles Times*, January 27, 1978, Part II, 7.

only one vote more than the required two-thirds majority.[19] Carter had demonstrated impressive presidential leadership in the face of seemingly overwhelming odds. An important collateral benefit was the now budding realization among Latin Americans and many in the third world that this president might be a friend, indeed might be serious about his pronouncements.

Carter, Human Rights, and the UN

This fresh perception by the third world was to be enhanced by Carter's early approach to the United Nations.

Two related factors pervade Carter's relationship with the UN: one was his public commitment to human rights, the other his determination to respond with sensitivity to the concerns of the underdeveloped world.

In his inaugural address Carter had said that "our commitment to human rights must be absolute."[20] At a town meeting in Clinton, Massachusetts, in March 1977, he added, "I want our country to be the focal point for deep concern about human beings all over the world."[21] And in a commencement speech at Notre Dame University on May 22, 1977, while outlining the major themes of his foreign policy, he proclaimed America's commitment to human rights as "fundamental."[22]

Carter's persistent engagement with the motif of human rights derived in part from his religious background and from the connection of his religious convictions with the civil rights movement he had observed firsthand in his native South. A revealing statement in his memoirs illustrates the conjunction of his religion and the civil rights movement with his international idealism:

> To me, the political and social transformation of the Southland was a powerful demonstration of how moral principle should and could be applied effectively to the legal structure of our society....The same lesson has been learned many times in our dealings with other nations....In recent history, President Harry Truman was the strongest and most effective advocate of human

---

[19] For full coverage, see *New York Times*, April 19, 1978.

[20] *PPP, 1977,* I, 2.

[21] Ibid., 385.

[22] Ibid., 958.

rights on an international scale. His encouragement of the formation of the United Nations and his steadfastness in the face of great pressure as he quickly recognized the new nation of Israel were vivid demonstrations of American influence at its finest.[23]

But America, Carter believed, had strayed from that earlier idealism. In recent years we had forfeited our most effective way to challenge threats from totalitarian ideologies. By playing with the same "lack of rules as the evildoers," including both the Soviet Union and even pro-West dictators, we had made serious mistakes. In Vietnam, Cambodia, Chile, and elsewhere, insidious covert operations by the CIA, lying at the highest level of government, and playing power politics at the expense of moral principle, had left American diplomacy depraved and understandably unpopular. Carter rejected the claim that we had to choose between "idealism and realism, or between morality and the exertion of power."[24] A nation could be realistic in international affairs *and* moral. Indeed, it was imperative for the United States to be exactly that, because, "Ours was the first nation to dedicate itself clearly to basic moral and philosophical principles...a revolutionary development that captured the imagination of mankind."[25]

Carter carefully studied human rights reports from Amnesty International and from the United Nations. In early discussions with the Soviet ambassador Anatoly Dobrynin, the president, to the ambassador's chagrin, stressed his expectation that the USSR would live up to the UN Charter, the Universal Declaration of Human Rights, and the Helsinki Accords. And on March 1, 1977, in a good-faith demonstration of his own compliance with the human rights provisions of the Helsinki Accords, he lifted travel prohibitions on American visitors to Cuba, North Korea, Vietnam, and Cambodia. He appointed Patricia Derian, a civil rights lawyer from Mississippi, as assistant secretary of state for human rights, and he authorized Warren Christopher to establish the "Christopher group" in the State Department to make certain that U.S. human rights positions were fulfilled in the nation's foreign policies. One result was that more careful attention was paid to U.S. voting on

---

[23] *Keeping Faith*, 142.

[24] Ibid., 142–143.

[25] Acceptance speech, July 1976; see excerpts Ibid., 144.

multilateral loans from international banking institutions like the World Bank. The United States now more frequently voted against or abstained on loan proposals to countries perceived as unfriendly to human rights, irrespective of whether the countries were aligned with or against our international adversaries. By October of his first year in office, the president, at the United Nations, signed the UN covenants on Civil and Political Rights and on Economic, Social and Cultural Rights.[26]

This flurry of activity on behalf of the Carter administration's self-proclaimed morality led to a conservative backlash within the United States. In 1979, Jeane Kirkpatrick, who would become Reagan's ambassador to the United Nations, lashed out in an article entitled "Dictatorships and Double Standards," suggesting that the Carter people did not understand the reality of world affairs. There were, Kirkpatrick insisted, clear differences between friends who were "authoritarian" and communists who were "totalitarian." Unfortunately for U.S. foreign policy, Carter had merged and confused the two.[27]

Carter, however, had applied his own deeper Christian meaning to the issue of human rights and morality. He believed that he had come into office at a moment when Americans, repelled by the sordid politics in their midst, desired a return to "first principles." Like Wilson, whose inaugural address he most admired, he too wished to call for "national repentance." His original choice for a biblical citation at his inaugural was from II Chronicles 7:14: "If my people, which are called by my name, shall humble themselves, and pray, and seek my face, and turn from their wicked ways; then will I hear from heaven, and will forgive their sin, and will heal their land." Worried that this passage might be a bit too strong for his listeners, the new president nonetheless stayed with the King James version of the Old Testament, and a more subtle play on the theme of redemption, by citing Micah 6:8: "What doth the Lord require of thee, but to do justly, to love mercy, and to walk humbly with thy God."[28] For Carter, America had to be good itself in order to pursue good internationally. To start we had to reject the immediate past by returning to "first principles." This eventually turned out to be an unappetizing prescription for many Americans.

---

[26] Ibid., 144–146. Smith, *Morality, Reason, and Power*, 51–54.

[27] Jeane Kirkpatrick, "Dictatorships and Double Standards," *Commentary* (November 1979), 34–45.

[28] *PPP, 1977*, I, 1. Carter, *Keeping Faith*, 19–20.

Carter's own interior struggle to merge his religious convictions with his political ambition had framed his public persona. And in this respect he was more interestingly recondite than many remember. For example, in the mid-1960s, a friend, responding to Carter's anguish at reconciling religious faith and a life in politics, lent this dedicated Southern Baptist a copy of the anthology *Reinhold Niebuhr on Politics*. In many respects, Niebuhr, a professor at Union Theological Seminary in New York, was one of the foremost philosophers of what would become a "realist" outlook on international affairs. An early socialist, he split from the movement during the Second World War over the issues of pacifism and nonintervention. In the late 1940s he joined other prominent liberals in founding the anticommunist Americans for Democratic Action. His writings on the relationship of moral values, Christianity, and politics led the realist guru Hans Morgenthau to call him "the greatest living political philosopher of America." Niebuhr's criticism of Woodrow Wilson for steadfastly adhering to principle in the face of reality was interpreted by Carter as, "We must always combine realism with principle."[29] Carter called the little book of Niebuhr's essays that he had borrowed "my political Bible," and long after he had left the presidency he continued to cite the book approvingly in his writings.[30]

*   *   *

The so-called third world—the earth's poorest nations, formerly colonies, usually situated in the Southern Hemisphere—represented a focus unusually susceptible to Carter's moral convictions. Like segregated black Americans in his native South, third world peoples had seemingly been left aside as the rest of the world charged into modernity. These recently colonized people had understandable grievances against their former masters and against the vagaries of international economics. A true Christian would surely be sensitive to those grievances. Moreover, the third world, through a fortuitous set of historical circumstances, had come to represent the majority of voices in the UN General Assembly. Whatever their grievances, they would now be heard on the international stage.

---

[29] Bourne, *Jimmy Carter*, 171–172.

[30] Jimmy Carter, *Living Faith* (New York: Random House, 1996), 110.

The growth in UN membership, which began with Eisenhower's agreement to sixteen new admissions in 1955, swelled the body to 146 nations by the time Carter came to office, with the dominant majority in the General Assembly coming from the third world. We have noted in earlier chapters the impact on the United States of this demographic shift in UN membership.[31] Mainland China's admission to the United Nations in October 1971 signified the United States' first major defeat in the UN. By the middle of the 1970s the new majority, originally called the "Group of 77," but now much larger, seemed to be running roughshod over the First World, and was particularly antagonistic to the United States. The Nixon and Ford administrations, as we have seen, had to contend with a General Assembly that ignored Washington's wishes, invited the Palestine Liberation Organization's leader Yasir Arafat to address it, granted the PLO official observer status, and passed the anti-West "Charter on the Economic Rights and Duties of States." All this while, the developing nations were crafting a plan they called the "New International Economic Order," by which they meant a system of financial and trade readjustments that would result in a substantial transfer of existing wealth from the rich nations of the Northern Hemisphere to the poorer nations in the south. Needless to say, no industrialized nations went along with the scheme. Then, in November 1975, a low point was reached as the new majority gleefully passed the infamous resolution declaring Zionism "a form of racism and racial discrimination."

The previous administration had initially reacted to these events with antagonism, and with the appointment of Ambassador Moynihan; but Carter followed an alternative course. He would improve relations with the new majority by placing third world matters at the heart of his foreign policy, listen to and address seriously the concerns of these up-to-now ignored peoples, attract them to the new American point of view, and thus bolster international support for American initiatives around the world. And he planned to use the United Nations as the place for performing this seduction.

His first, and perhaps most important, gesture was to appoint Andrew Young as ambassador to the United Nations. For Young—a veteran civil rights activist and former Congressman from Georgia—the appointment carried with it the prestige of a cabinet position. He was the

---

[31] See also Stoessinger, *The United Nations and the Superpowers*, 26–54.

first African-American to serve in this post, a symbolic event that did not go unnoticed among the numerous African nations with whom he enthusiastically dealt. Young's appearance at the United Nations caused an emotional uplift both in the U.S. delegation and in the halls of the General Assembly. He became an active and visible presence, voicing the loftiest tenets of the new administration. In just his first year in office, he gave numerous well-covered addresses before the General Assembly, the Security Council, and the Economic and Social Council; overseas at special UN conferences, such as the Economic Commission for Latin America; and as special invitee at meetings throughout the third world. Everywhere he underscored the administration's commitment to those reforms most compatible with third world sensibilities. He emphasized that in Africa the key problem was not communism but racism; he called for independence for Rhodesia (Zimbabwe) and Namibia; he attacked apartheid in South Africa and urged mandatory sanctions on the minority white-ruled regime; he recommended "equitable participation of developing countries in global economic decision-making," insisted that "we are rebuilding our people's support for the United Nations and for our common effort of building a more equitable international economic system," and mesmerized foreign audiences with stories of the civil rights movement.[32] UN Undersecretary-General Brian Urquhart observed that the peripatetic Young was "often greeted as if he were one of the Beatles."[33]

Young's unquestioned impact on UN-U.S. relations came to an end with an unfortunate and imprudent action. In the late summer of 1979, while the Carter administration was struggling to implement the Camp David accords between Israel and Egypt, Young attended a brief meeting in New York that included the Palestine Liberation Organization's permanent observer to the United Nations, Zehdi Terzi. In mid-August, Young, trying to deflect any misunderstanding regarding the encounter, informed the Israeli ambassador to the UN, Yehuda Blum, about the meeting. The government of Israel reacted negatively, the news got out, and a considerable public relations stew ensued. American Jewish leaders reacted against what they saw as a violation of Kissinger's now

---

[32] Lee Clement (ed.), *Andrew Young at the United Nations* (Salisbury, N.C.: Documentary Publications, 1978). The two direct quotes are on pp. 66 and 72.

[33] Urquhart, *A Life*, 277.

five-year-old promise not to acknowledge the PLO.[34] Young, under pressure, resigned, to be replaced by his deputy, Donald McHenry, who became the second African-American to serve in the post.

At McHenry's swearing-in in September 1979, Young, ever the trouper, remarked that "never has the United Nations had the kind of commitment from the President of the United States and from the Secretary of State and the entire State Department that it has in this administration."[35]

Indeed, there was more to Carter's engagement with the United Nations than just Young's appointment. Shortly after assuming the presidency, Carter invited Secretary-General Kurt Waldheim to the White House for an official visit. He informed Waldheim and Waldheim's closest assistant, Brian Urquhart, that he was anxious to appear before the United Nations as early as possible, a request that seemed delightfully "unusual" to these UN leaders. Waldheim, who thought that Carter "visibly wanted to upgrade the role of the United Nations and its secretary-general," worried about attendance at an abrupt, off-cycle meeting of the United Nations. He need not have been concerned. On the evening of March 17, 1977, Waldheim introduced the new president to a General Assembly Hall overflowing with receptive delegates. It was, said the secretary-general, "a most impressive event."[36]

The president told an enthralled audience that he intended to bring to the world "a more open foreign policy" and always "speak frankly" about U.S. aims. He spoke of his desire to effect "deep reductions" in strategic arms and to "pursue a broad, permanent *multilateral* agreement on the cessation of nuclear testing" [emphasis added]. "The basic thrust of human affairs," he maintained (clearly speaking to the third world majority), "points toward a more universal demand for fundamental human rights. The United States has a historical birthright to be associated with this process." Although American ideals "have not always been attained," even in the United States, the current administration would demonstrate its full commitment by signing, and then seeking congressional approval of, the UN covenants on economic, social, and cultural rights, and on civil and political rights; by urging the

---

[34] Carter, *Keeping Faith*, 491. *New York Times*, August 15, 1979, A1, 6–8.

[35] "Remarks at the Swearing In of Donald McHenry," September 23, 1979, *PPP, 1979*, II, 1717.

[36] Kurt Waldheim, *Eye of the Storm*, 140, 145. Urquhart, *A Life*, 278.

Senate to ratify the Genocide Convention and the Treaty for the Elimination of All Forms of Racial Discrimination; by lifting all travel restrictions on Americans; by working to help "developing countries acquire fuller participation in global economic decisionmaking"; and by fully complying with UN sanctions "against the illegal regime in Rhodesia."[37] The next morning, Carter signed House Resolution 1746, which reestablished the embargo against the purchase of chrome from Rhodesia. At the signing, the president said, "This puts us back on the side of support for the United Nations...on the side of what's right and proper."[38]

Carter returned to the United Nations in early October to speak at the opening of the Thirty-Second General Assembly. His message remained on target, and he now specified his intention to address and effect the transition to majority rule in Zimbabwe and Namibia, to use Security Council Resolutions 242 and 338 to bring resolution to the Middle East conundrum, and to recognize the "legitimate rights of the Palestinian people."[39] Never had a U.S. president spoken so directly to third world concerns.

Following his morning address, Carter hosted a working lunch at the U.S. mission for officials of African nations, where he spoke of America's "need to understand your special problems and your special hopes and dreams and aspirations."[40] His busy day at the United Nations continued at a meeting with members of the U.S. delegation and the American staff of the UN Secretariat, and, in the evening, at a working dinner which he hosted for officials of Western and Eastern European nations. The next morning, still in New York, Carter met with Foreign Minister Moshe Dayan of Israel, and the two issued a joint statement declaring that Security Council Resolutions 242 and 338 "remain the agreed basis for the resumption of the Geneva Peace Conference" on the Middle East. He then spoke at the Economic and Social Council chamber of the UN, where he signed the international human rights covenants, as he had promised in March he would do, and then returned yet again to

---

[37] Address Before the General Assembly, March 17, 1977, *PPP, 1977*, I, 444–451. For extensive coverage, see *New York Times*, March 18, 1977, A1, 10–11.

[38] March 18, 1977, *PPP, 1977*, I, 452.

[39] Address Before the General Assembly, October 4, 1977, *PPP, 1977*, II, 1715–1723.

[40] Ibid., 1724.

the U.S. Mission across First Avenue for a working lunch which he hosted for officials of Asian nations.[41]

Despite all this, Carter's revitalized UN policy often produced frustratingly little progress. To head the delegation to the UN's Law of the Sea Conference, Carter appointed Elliot Richardson, a moderate and respected Republican. In 1973, Richardson had resigned as President Nixon's attorney general when he was pressured to fire Archibald Cox, the independent counsel investigating Watergate. The United States, with Richardson's leadership, participated with 148 other nations in negotiating a Law of the Sea agreement, but President Reagan later refused to sign it.[42]

The Non-Proliferation Treaty of 1968 eventually obtained over 100 signatories; and Congress, responding to Carter's urgings, did pass the Nuclear Non-Proliferation Act of 1978. But India, which detonated a test bomb in 1974, never joined the treaty, and some other potential nuclear nations stayed away as well. Meantime, by the end of the Carter administration, when the world looked much more inhospitable to the United States, Washington found itself back in the business of selling and supplying arms, deviating from the president's earlier expressions to the United Nations.[43]

Possibly the most heart-wrenching paradox confounding the administration's UN policy had to do with the contested credentials of the Cambodian delegation following Vietnam's incursion in late 1978. As the Americans left Southeast Asia in the spring of 1975, communist forces in both Vietnam and Cambodia quickly took control from former U.S.-backed governments. In Cambodia, the Khmer Rouge communists captured the capital, Phnom Penh, in mid-April 1975. The new government, headed by the notorious Pol Pot, evacuated all cities and towns, sending virtually the entire population out to clear jungles and forests. The barbarous policies of the Khmer Rouge resulted in one of the worst cases of genocide in history, as some 1 million Cambodians were killed by their own government. The situation became more awkward when Vietnamese forces invaded in late 1978 and by early January of 1979 captured Phnom Penh. Suddenly, *communist* Vietnam now

---

[41] Ibid., 1725–1737.

[42] Smith, *Morality, Reason, and Power*, 59. For the Law of the Sea agreement, see March 15 to May 7, 1976, *YUN, 1976*, 73.

[43] Smith, *Morality, Reason, and Power*, 60–61.

controlled most of what had previously been *communist* Cambodia. The respite from the brutal Khmer Rouge rule brought by the Vietnamese invaders was welcomed in many quarters, but the clear fact of the military incursion of one neighbor into another created a complicated issue for the United States and other nations in deciding who really represented Cambodia in the United Nations. China supported the seating of Pol Pot's regime, now pushed to the rural hinterland of Cambodia. So too did the former leader of Cambodia, the revered Prince Norodom Sihanouk, who was settled in Beijing, where he denounced the Vietnamese invasion. Some, like India and the Soviet Union and its allies, favored seating the Vietnamese-supported Heng Samrin government in Phnom Penh. For the United States, to oppose the Pol Pot regime would be to countenance an invasion of an independent country by our own recent enemy; furthermore, to do so would have been siding with Moscow, Hanoi, and Havana. Alternatively, to accept Pol Pot's regime as the legitimate representative of the Cambodian people would place the United States on the side of one of history's worst violators of human rights. In the fall of 1979 the issue came before the General Assembly. On Pol Pot's side were the Chinese and the Association of Southeast Asian Nations (ASEAN), which included Indonesia, Malaysia, the Philippines, Thailand, and Singapore. The Carter administration had been purposely cultivating ASEAN, seeing these nations as a key to stability and progress in east Asia.

Strong opposition to seating the Khmer Rouge government surfaced within the administration. Patricia Derian, the State Department's director of human rights; Anthony Lake, from the National Security Council; and Donald McHenry, our ambassador to the United Nations, all argued against it. Meantime, our allies in the European Community and in Japan urged the seating of Pol Pot's regime. Our new (and first) ambassador to Beijing, Leonard Woodcock, cabled to the State Department, recommending that we agree to the seating of the Pol Pot government on the narrowest of grounds; and assistant secretary of state for east Asia, Richard Holbrooke (who would be appointed UN ambassador in 1999), agreed. In certainly one of the hardest of the "hard choices" facing Secretary of State Vance and the administration, the

United States held its nose and allowed the seating of the offensive Pol Pot government.[44]

Carter, China, and the USSR

In its dealings with China and the Soviet Union, the Carter administration, even given the president's early suggestions that he would fully engage the United Nations and concentrate on multilateral and cooperative policies, tended, like those that had preceded it, to act unilaterally, apart from UN environs. Nonetheless, American treatment of China and Russia did have repercussions within the larger international community, did affect our posture in the United Nations, and—as we will see below—resulted in the playing out of consequential issues within the UN.

* * *

Nixon had initiated the opening with China, but he had not officially normalized relations with Beijing. Although the United States regularly dealt with the People's Republic of China in its capacity as a permanent member of the Security Council, Washington continued, at least technically, to recognize the regime on the island of Taiwan. Once again Carter moved forcefully to resolve an unsettled policy, while at the same time underscoring U.S. interest in courting the third world.

The president intended to exchange ambassadors with the People's Republic of China at the most feasible time. In May 1978, he sent Brzezinski to Beijing where the national security adviser met with Foreign Minister Huang Hua. The two reaffirmed the basic principles of the Shanghai communiqué and agreed on a common "position on global and regional hegemony," a not very subtle reference to the Soviet Union, much favored by the Chinese, and fittingly appropriate to Brzezinski's own predilections. After visiting the Great Wall, just as Kissinger had done before him, Brzezinski met with Vice Premier Deng Xiaoping, the acknowledged leader of the Communist Party and of the People's Republic. They agreed privately on procedures to effect normalization between the two countries. Upon his return, Brzezinski appeared on the television interview program *Meet the Press*, where he criticized Russian

---

[44] See Vance, *Hard Choices*, for a full assessment from the administration's point of view.

policy in Africa, thus magnifying the apparent anti-Soviet nature of America's renewed coziness with China. Secretary of State Vance, at work on several fronts in southern Africa (including within the United Nations, where Moscow's acquiescence was courted) and seeing SALT negotiations still at a sensitive point, found the remarks unhelpful. Indeed, Vance had advised against Brzezinski's trip, believing that it would send a confusing message about who spoke for the administration on foreign policy. For the moment, tension between the State Department and the NSC threatened to cause a schism within the administration.[45] Carter let Brzezinski know of his displeasure over the affair. The process of normalization then proceeded with more contributions from the State Department. Still, following successful secret negotiations between America and China (conducted in Beijing by Leonard Woodcock as liaison), the final announcement of normalization was made, contrary to Vance's advice, without previous consultation with Congress.[46] At 9 P.M. on December 15, 1979, the president made the surprise announcement that we would exchange ambassadors with China, and that, the very next month, Deng Xiaoping would become the first leader of the People's Republic ever to visit the United States.

Washington elevated Woodcock to ambassador, changed its embassy in Taipei to a "foundation," and abrogated its Mutual Defense Treaty with Taiwan. Although several members of Congress rankled at the lack of consultation that had accompanied these striking developments, and although Senator Barry Goldwater tried unsuccessfully to have the courts overturn the decision to abrogate the defense treaty, the final judgment the American people gave to Carter's breakthrough in China seemed to accord with Secretary Vance's: "It will remain one of the enduring achievements of the Carter years."[47]

*   *   *

The Chinese-American rapprochement did not play well in Moscow. In fact, it may have added to a series of vexations that clouded Washington's relations with the USSR. The historian Gaddis Smith has suggested that Carter's policies toward the Soviet Union were

---

[45] Brzezinski, *Power and Principle*, 209–220. Vance, *Hard Choices*, 114–116.

[46] Vance, *Hard Choices*, 118.

[47] Ibid., 119.

incompatible with one another.[48] For one, he wanted to work with Moscow to address problems in places like the Middle East and southern Africa and to eliminate nuclear weapons. (He had said in his UN speech of March 15, 1977, that he preferred "deep reductions" in strategic arms, beyond what was then on the table.) Yet by publicly insisting on the maintenance of human rights everywhere, he had angered the Soviets, especially when he wrote to dissidents like Andrei Sakharov (pledging support of human rights worldwide), welcomed other dissidents to the White House, and openly criticized the Russians for violating the Helsinki Accords. Finally, his cooperative stance was measured by the Soviets against his appointment of Brzezinski, whose perceived hard-line views worried Moscow.

Into this capricious mix the administration forwarded its first proposals for arms negotiations. SALT I was scheduled to expire in October 1977. Three years earlier, Ford and Leonid Brezhnev had reached a modest agreement at Vladivostok on ceilings of strategic missile launchers for both countries. Carter felt that the Vladivostok understanding was much too limited. He wanted a broad improvement in relations with the Soviet Union that would extend beyond SALT II and include resuming talks in Vienna about mutual and balanced reductions of conventional forces, a comprehensive test ban such as he had mentioned in his UN address, and limits on weapons transfers. And, to repeat, he hoped that Moscow would participate cooperatively in alleviating problems in the Middle East and in southern Africa.[49]

In his first meeting with Anatoly Dobrynin, Carter took the ambassador by surprise by spelling out his inclination to go forward with SALT II talks but including much more dramatic cuts. He also called for prior notification of any test missile launchings, a comprehensive test ban, demilitarization of the Indian Ocean, and "deep cuts in total nuclear weapons" in a new SALT III treaty.[50] The president had sent a long letter to Brezhnev detailing these propositions and adding proposals for full access to divided Berlin and the complete upholding of all "basket three" human rights provisions of the Helsinki

---

[48] Smith, *Morality, Reason, and Power*, 66.

[49] Brzezinski, *Power and Principle*, 159.

[50] Carter, *Keeping Faith*, 217.

Accords.[51] He then sent Vance to Moscow to present these extensive overtures formally.

Vance arrived in Moscow in late March 1977, accompanied by his arms negotiation adviser, Paul Warnke. The Americans presented Carter's agenda to Brezhnev and Foreign Minister Andrei Gromyko. The perplexed and suspicious Russians rejected the American blueprint on the spot and insisted that the two sides return to the much more modest Vladivostok framework of understanding.[52] Carter's sweeping early initiative had come to an abrupt dead end. The president returned to building on the accords achieved by his predecessors. Talks were conducted in Geneva and through back channels between Washington and Moscow.[53] Verification issues generated by the loss of American listening posts in revolutionary Iran held up agreement until 1979. In the end, however, the seizure of American hostages in Teheran in November of that year, and the Soviet invasion of Afghanistan the following month, scuttled any chance of ratification by the Senate. The entire exercise in arms negotiations by the Carter Administration, conducted without reference to UN machinery or interest in disarmament matters, came to naught.

While the SALT negotiations went on, events conspired to affect further disappointment. The United States' official recognition of China in early 1979 caused the Soviets some anxiety. In the same year, a week before the president departed for Vienna to meet with Brezhnev to consummate the painstakingly negotiated SALT II agreement, the administration announced that it would proceed with development of the so-called MX intercontinental ballistic missile (a highly sophisticated mobile delivery weapon). Vance reluctantly supported these decisions despite some lingering worries.[54] Brzezinski, more inclined to play tough with the Russians, hailed the recognition of China and the MX as providing a "proper strategic and geopolitical context for our forthcoming meeting with Brezhnev" in Vienna.[55]

---

[51] Brzezinski, *Power and Principle*, 153–154.

[52] Vance, *Hard Choices*, 18. Smith, *Morality, Reason, and Power*, 76.

[53] Pubantz, "Strategic Arms Limitation Talks," 182.

[54] Ibid., 114–116, 137–138.

[55] Brzezinski, *Power and Principle*, 338.

The edgy leaders of the two superpowers met that June and signed SALT II. But sentiment in the U.S. Senate was not on the side of approval. Liberals believed that the agreement had not gone far enough; conservatives feared that it had given too many advantages to the Russians. The president prepared a vigorous campaign for ratification. He was far from assured of the necessary two-thirds vote when, on December 27, 1979, the Soviet Union invaded bordering Afghanistan.

Afghanistan, an Islamic country of some 20 million people, was one of the earliest members of the United Nations, joining the organization in 1946. Historically sensitive to the influence of its larger northern neighbor, which considered it a buffer against Iran and Pakistan, Afghanistan had been beset by recent instability. In 1973 Muhammad Daoud led a coup overthrowing the monarchy. He established a republic, which became friendly with anti-Soviet Pakistan and Iran (at that time ruled by the pro-American shah). In April 1978, Marxist army officers overthrew Daoud. Moscow signed a friendship treaty with the new government in December. The following February, as Iranian militants besieged the U.S. embassy in adjacent Iran, Islamic rebels in the Afghani capital of Kabul kidnapped and killed the U.S. ambassador, Adolph Dubs. Vance found these alarming concurrent developments "surreal," as, undoubtedly, did the American people.[56] But worse was to come. The Soviets, clearly unhappy with the ineffective government in Kabul, continued to try to manipulate the internal politics of the country. Ultimately they despaired. In the last week of 1978, the Russians rushed military forces into Afghanistan, allegedly to support the prime minister, Amin Hafizullah, who was subsequently himself murdered, after which Afghanistan's former UN ambassador, Babrak Karmel, took over the country as, in effect, a Soviet puppet.[57]

Carter called this episode "the most serious international development" of his presidency.[58] His response was swift and severe. He placed sanctions on the invaders, including an embargo on exports of American grain and electronic equipment. He withdrew Americans from the Moscow Olympics. In his state of the union address on January 23, 1980, he announced the so-called Carter Doctrine, committing the United States to the defense of its friends, the oil sea lanes, and its "national

---

[56] Vance, *Hard Choices*, 342.

[57] Ibid., 384–387. Smith, *Morality, Reason, and Power*, 219–222.

[58] Carter, *Keeping Faith*, 473.

interests" in the Persian Gulf region.[59] Finally, he suspended SALT II from consideration by the Senate, effectively ending his tireless pursuit of an arms agreement. The failure to ratify SALT and to pursue even more far-reaching agreements on nuclear arms control was, the president said, "the most profound disappointment of my presidency."[60] This peace-loving man's goals for accommodation with the Soviet Union were a shambles. The cold war, which he had hoped and believed was over, was back in full force.

In the altered international atmosphere, the president turned to the United Nations, where he proceeded to push hard for a condemnation of the invaders. Immediately after the incursion, fifty-two member states requested a meeting of the Security Council. The gathering took place on January 5–9, 1980, but because the Soviets held the veto, the Council was unable to act on an overwhelmingly approved resolution deploring the invasion.

Once again using the "Uniting for Peace" procedure, first devised during the Korean War, supporters carried the condemnatory resolution to the General Assembly. It "strongly" deplored the armed intervention, insisted on an "immediate withdrawal" of Russian forces, and called on the Security Council to consider all ways and means to see to the resolution's implementation. In the great hall of the General Assembly, on January 14, the resolution passed by a vote of 104 to 18, with 18 abstentions. The only negative votes were from the USSR and its closest allies. The Chinese delegation—both in the Security Council and later in the General Assembly—supported the United States' position.[61] As the president later remarked, "This was the first time such an action had ever been taken against one of the leading nations of the world."[62] It may be worth noting that by 1988 the Soviet Union had met all the conditions of the resolution and had left Afghanistan. But that is a later story.

Breakthrough at Camp David

Among the flurry of activities Carter pursued in the early days of his term, none was more important to him than his Middle East strategy.

---

[59] *PPP, 1980–1981*, II, 194–202, see particularly 197.

[60] Carter, *Keeping Faith*, 265.

[61] *YUN, 1980*, 299, 307.

[62] Carter, *Keeping Faith*, 475.

Carter had thought deeply and comprehensively about it. His diary entry for March 7, 1977, reads, "I've put in an awful lot of time studying the Middle East Question."[63] His memoirs contain more pages dealing with this topic than with any other, and one of his more impressive post-presidential books is about the Middle East.[64]

Carter's initial objective was to seek a resuscitation of the UN-sponsored all-party Geneva conference that had met under U.S.-Russian tutelage during Kissinger's last days in office and then had ceased to carry on. He proposed a joint Soviet-American invitation to reconvene the conference. In February, 1977, he sent Secretary of State Vance to the Middle East to probe possibilities for Geneva, and in early March he met in Washington with Israeli Prime Minister Yitzhak Rabin. The president's long-term aims were (1) to secure undeviating acquiescence to UN Resolution 242 as the basis of settlement; (2) to ensure Israel's security in the region (and to convince Israelis of that commitment); (3) to resolve the issue of who owned the land in dispute; and (4) to bolster the rights of "Palestinians" (that is, those Arabs who lived—and whose ancestors had lived—in the geographic area of the Palestine mandate administered by Britain during the interwar period, many of whom had been displaced during the founding of Israel in 1947 and in the 1967 war).[65] In fact, Carter's position on the Palestinian question was much advanced from that of previous presidents. Brzezinski even worried that the president was too forward in his public stance.[66] As a candidate, Carter had expressed the view that a final settlement of the Middle East question would have to take into account recognition of the Palestinians as a people and a nation with a place to live and a right to chose their own leaders. During an interview on his flight to the special UN meeting in New York in March 1977, he had defended his use of the phrase Palestinian "homeland."[67] At a press conference on May 12, 1977, reporter Helen Thomas persisted with the question, "Mr. President, do you think that Israel should accept the Palestinian homeland if the

---

[63] Ibid., 269.

[64] *The Blood of Abraham* (Boston: Houghton Mifflin, 1985).

[65] Carter, *Keeping Faith*, 279.

[66] Brzezinski, *Power and Principle*, 96.

[67] *New York Times*, March 18, 1977, A 10.

Palestinians or PLO accept the fact of Israel?"—to which the president responded "The answer...is yes."[68]

These views may have attracted resistant Arabs, including Palestinians, into more serious consideration of peace talks; but whatever the prospects were for progress in the Middle East, they seemed to receive a damaging blow with the election of the very conservative Likud government in the Israeli parliamentary elections of May 17. The new prime minister, Menachem Begin, believing that the Bible documented Israel's right to virtually all of Palestine, would prove to be a tough negotiating adversary for the president. Begin and his foreign minister, Moshe Dayan, came to Washington in July, where the two sides sparred over various matters. The Israelis, suspicious in the first place of some of the language of Resolution 242, indicated that they would prefer not to use it as a basis for negotiating. They were particularly concerned that Carter had seemed to "widen" the meaning of the resolution with his remarks about "Palestinians," a word that Begin resisted using. Israel also balked at a Geneva conference cosponsored by the USSR.[69] Deadlock seemed certain. And then something quite dramatic happened.

Though condemned at the time by most Arab leaders, a surprise visit by Egypt's president Anwar Sadat to Israel in November 1977 provided the spark for movement in the negotiations. Sadat became the first Arab leader to acknowledge the state of Israel overtly. In an emotional setting he addressed the Knesset (Israel's parliament) and expressed his desire to have peace between the two nations.[70] But the goodwill that flowed from this extraordinary gesture was not in itself sufficient to bring very old rivalries and entrenched positions to a final agreement. That took the indefatigable and singular efforts of Jimmy Carter.

Matters were not made easier in March 1978 when Begin ordered an invasion of Lebanon in retaliation for attacks on Israeli land from guerrillas in the southern regions of that tormented country. In the attack, Israel had used American-supplied cluster bombs. Carter was

---

[68] *PPP, 1977,* I, 861.

[69] Moshe Dayan, *Breakthrough: A Personal Account of the Egypt-Israel Peace Negotiations* (New York: Knopf, 1981), 18–19, 66–70. See also William B. Quandt, *Camp David: Peacemaking and Politics* (Washington, D.C.: Brookings, 1986), 72–77, 80–81.

[70] Sadat's speech to the Knesset (November 20, 1977) is in Quandt, *Camp David*, Appendix C, 345–355.

irate, and the United States took the lead in proposing to the Security Council Resolution 425, which condemned the invasion.[71]

Determined not to let the momentum provided by Sadat's visit slow down, Carter invited Sadat and Begin to convene at Camp David, the presidential retreat in rural Maryland. Both accepted, and meetings commenced on September 5, 1978. They lasted thirteen days. Carter was personally engaged in these talks. He shuttled from one leader to the other with proposals and counterproposals. He would not let the parties leave until they had reached an accord. In the end, the two antagonists agreed to two documents: first, a historic peace agreement between Israel and Egypt, by which the two nations would exchange ambassadors and the Israelis would return occupied portions of the Sinai peninsula to Egypt; and second, a "Framework for Peace," based on UN Resolutions 242 and 338, detailing procedures to complete a comprehensive peace for the region. The "Framework" called for negotiations involving the United States, Egypt, Israel, and Jordan for the express purposes of granting a "homeland" to the Palestinians and securing the borders of Israel. Those talks would not be conducted under the auspices of the United Nations or the Geneva conference but would be closely orchestrated by the United States.

The Egyptian-Israeli peace was quite acceptable to the Israelis, and it was a national triumph for Sadat. But the "Framework" was absolutely crucial for Sadat, who could not leave Camp David without having gained concessions for the wider Arab world and particularly for the Palestinians. Final approved treaties were scheduled to be completed within three months. But they were not. In the ensuing months, the situation was complicated on the American side by the Iranian revolution and the SALT talks, and little was done to bring the agreement to fruition. Indeed, the parties quibbled, Begin backpedaled, and the Middle East suddenly looked not like the triumph perceived in September but like on of Carter's typical fiascos.

The key to the "Framework for Peace" was in the language of the treaty. That language conformed to earlier points that the UN had insisted on, added progressive new details to the process of settlement, and created a new momentum that, despite periodic setbacks, continued on through the next decade and a half, at least up to the Oslo accords of 1993.

---

[71] March 19, 1978, *YUN, 1978,* 312.

In March 1979, Carter invited himself to Cairo and Jerusalem. Once again he used considerable personal pressure to force the parties back to the table. In the process he promised substantial military aid to both countries. Finally, official agreement was reached, and appropriate ratifications took place in each country. On March 26, 1979, at the White House, with Carter between them, Sadat and Begin signed the two documents, the first such pact between an Arab country and Israel since Israel's founding over thirty years earlier. [72]

We must recall that Begin's Likud government had entered the original talks with the Carter administration with qualms about using Resolution 242 as the basis for any negotiation. This was because the resolution denied the right to acquire territory by war and called for a withdrawal of Israeli forces from such territory so acquired. Additionally, the Israeli government's historic position had been that there were no such people as "Palestinians"; rather, there were Arabs in the region who could reasonably be expected to live in countries then in existence, such as Jordan. Sadat, understandably, not only wanted to reclaim Egyptian land conquered by Israel in the 1967 Six Day War, but also wanted to effect an Israeli withdrawal from other occupied areas—the Gaza Strip, the West Bank of the Jordan River, and if possible the Golan Heights—and achieve some acknowledgment of the rights of Palestinians. Carter, as we have seen, shared with Sadat the view that Israel would have to retreat from some territory and that Palestinians deserved recognition as a people and the right of self-government. At the same time he maintained that the United States would persist in its support of Israel's security and press the obligation for its neighbors to recognize Israel's legitimacy and sovereignty. The president believed that these aims were consistent with Resolution 242, which, in turn, was the absolutely necessary underpinning of any settlement.

---

[72] Stanley Meisler, *United Nations,* 197. Much controversy surrounded the Camp David accords. Palestinians and most Arab nations rejected them as conceding too much to Israel and as being anti-Palestinian. The Israelis would subsequently interpret the accords as allowing them to maintain an expansive state, a position rejected by both Sadat and Carter. Meisler, a journalist, has added another twist by criticizing Carter for diminishing the role of the United Nations in the Middle East, which had once been its main province. But Camp David was a breakthrough. And a careful consideration of both the meaning and the implications of the two accords answers many of the criticisms.

In the "Framework for Peace" Carter had made certain of the requisite use of UN Resolution 242: [73]

> The agreed basis for a peaceful settlement of the conflict between Israel and its neighbors is U.N. Security Council Resolution 242 *in all its parts*....To achieve a relationship of peace, in the spirit of *Article 2 of the U.N. Charter*, future negotiations between Israel and any neighbor prepared to negotiate peace and security with it, are necessary for the purpose of carrying out all the provisions and principles of Resolutions 242 and 338....The parties are determined to reach a just, comprehensive, and durable settlement...through the conclusion of peace treaties based on Security Council Resolutions 242 and 338 *in all their parts*. [italics added]

Resolution 242 stressed "the inadmissibility of the acquisition of territory by war;...[the] withdrawal of Israeli armed forces from territories of recent conflict; termination of all claims of states of belligerency and respect for and acknowledgment of the sovereignty, territorial integrity and political independence of every state in the area and their right to live in peace within secure and recognized boundaries free from threats or acts of force." Sadat and Begin agreed to all of this.

The Palestinian question had been addressed in furtive and opaque language in 242, which spoke only of "a just settlement of the refugee problem." This wording had always distressed Palestinians and their supporters. But the "Framework" added flesh to the bare bones of 242:

> Egypt and Jordan and the representatives of the *Palestinian people* should participate in negotiations on the resolution of the *Palestinian problem in all its aspects*....Egypt, Israel and Jordan will agree on the modalities for establishing the *elected self-governing authority* in the *West Bank and Gaza*. The delegations of Egypt and Jordan may include Palestinians from the West Bank and Gaza or *other Palestinians* as mutually agreed....The solution from the

---

[73] All relevant documents regarding the Middle East negotiations during the Carter administration are in Vance, *Hard Choices*, Appendix II, 463–497; the "Framework for Peace" is at 464–468. The same documents, plus full analysis, can be found in Quandt's extensive case study, *Camp David*; documents are in the appendix section, 341–383.

negotiations must also recognize the *legitimate rights of the Palestinian people* and their just requirements. [italics added]

Begin's right-wing Likud government had accepted the word "Palestinian" and conceded the "legitimate rights" of the "Palestinian people." On paper at least, this was a movement forward. In fact, despite all kinds of logjams down the line, there would be no turning back on the advanced principles provided by Camp David, including the elevation of the Palestinians to a place of primary concern.

Importantly, the "Framework" called on the United Nations Security Council to endorse the peace treaties and to ensure that their provisions were carried out. Rather than finessing the United Nations, Camp David built on the juridical basis of UN resolutions and forwarded the process begun in 1967 in the Security Council. That is, Camp David was in a direct trajectory from UN Resolution 242.

Finally, with a peace treaty between Egypt and Israel, and the return of the Sinai, the most dangerous potential military enemy of the Israelis was neutralized. No longer would Israel have to fear a two-front war. There were two long-range implications from the peace treaty. Israel could negotiate from a more secure position, and the other Arab states—and the Palestinians—eventually would have to consider negotiations as more likely to achieve their aims than was the prospect of a war against Israel.

Of course, while Egypt and Israel exchanged ambassadors and entered a new, if sometimes troubled, relationship as coequals, peace did not break out all over the rest of the Middle East. Rejectionists among Palestinians and the Arab states condemned the "Framework." The Begin government resisted following through on crucial details of the accord. The Middle Eastern untidiness would remain for some years. But, to reiterate: Camp David resulted in (1) peace between Israel and Egypt; (2) the recognition of Israel by the largest Arab nation in the region; (3) the elevation of the Palestinian question into the diplomatic discourse of the Middle East; (4) a new balance of power that, in the long run, made war less rational than negotiation for achieving a settlement; and (5) the reassertion of the importance of the United Nations as the juridical source for a future settlement.

Carter and Africa

Of the many diplomatic predicaments in sub-Saharan Africa, three in the southern part of the continent were of the most immediate interest to both the United Nations and the United States by the late 1970s. One was in Rhodesia, named for the English imperialist Cecil Rhodes, but soon to be renamed Zimbabwe. Another was in Southwest Africa (to become Namibia). A third was in the largest and most prosperous of the countries, South Africa. The United Nations had taken many formal actions to influence the situation in each of these countries, including numerous resolutions calling for majority (black) rule in each, demands for full independence from minority or outside powers, and, in the case of South Africa, assertive demands for an end to apartheid—the system of racial segregation and denial of political rights to nonwhites that left a minority white government in full control. As we have seen above, the Carter administration stated plainly its support for UN positions in southern Africa. The particular situation in each area when Carter entered office was as follows.

South Africa was a country with a richly diverse population of some 27 million, the overwhelming majority of which were from different black ethnic groups. The Cape of Good Hope, in the southern part of the country, had been settled by Dutch immigrants in the seventeenth century. Britain seized the Cape in 1808, during the Napoleonic Wars, following which the Dutch trekked north to found two new settlements. Britain subdued the Dutch, then called Boers, in the Boer War of 1899–1902 and unified the entire country under its rule as the Union of South Africa. In 1948, the Afrikaners (the modern name for the Boers) had wrested control of the internal government from the less numerous English. The Afrikaners' National Party officially instituted the policy of apartheid. In 1961 the Union of South Africa declared independence from Britain, becoming the Republic of South Africa, effectively ruled by a single party. From the 1960s on, UN responses to these developments reflected the growing voice of third world nations. A Security Council resolution in April 1960 "deplored" South African apartheid, called on the government there to abandon the policy, and instructed the secretary-general to work with South Africa to uphold all principles of the UN Charter. The United States spoke and voted in favor of the resolution.[74] In 1962, with the United States in the minority, the General

---

[74] *YUN, 1960.* 147.

Assembly established a Special Committee Against Apartheid to review South African policies; and in 1970, the General Assembly, again contrary to the United States' wishes, denied credentials to the South African delegation.[75]

"Southern" Rhodesia, a country of some 7 million people, had been controlled by Cecil Rhodes' British South Africa Company from the late nineteenth century until Britain took over official colonial administration in 1923. In November 1965, the prime minister of the dominant minority white population, Ian Smith, declared independence from the United Kingdom. London termed the act illegal and demanded a broadening of voting rights to bring eventual majority black rule to the country. The Security Council condemned the unilateral declaration, and, urged by Britain, the Council then imposed sanctions, including arms and trade embargoes.[76]

Southwest Africa, the size of California, was sparsely populated, with about one million inhabitants. It had been a so-called protectorate of Germany from the late nineteenth century up to the First World War, being one of that country's few overseas colonial possessions. With Germany's defeat in World War I, the League of Nations granted Britain's Union of South Africa a "mandate" over the territory. By the 1960s, the now independent country of South Africa continued to control the area, even in the face of a guerrilla insurrection led by the South-West Africa People's Organization (SWAPO) and growing demands in the international community that the country be independent. The UN General Assembly's Resolution 1514 of December 14, 1960—the "Declaration on the Granting of Independence to Colonial Countries and Peoples"—remained the oft-cited source for dealing with Southwest Africa. In October 1966 the General Assembly voted to terminate South Africa's mandate there, and in early 1976 the Security Council, by a unanimous vote, called for elections under UN supervision.[77]

---

[75] GA Resolution 1761, November 6, 1962, *YUN, 1962*, 99–100; GA Resolution 2636, November 13, 1970, *YUN, 1970*, 153–154.

[76] SC Resolution 216, November 12, 1965, *YUN, 1965*, 132; SC Resolution 232, December 16, 1966, *YUN, 1966*, 116–117; and SC Resolution 253, May 29, 1968, *YUN, 1968*, 152–153.

[77] GA Resolution 1514, December 14, 1960, *YUN, 1960*, 49–50; GA Resolution 2145, October 27, 1966, *YUN, 1966*, 605–606; SC Resolution 385, January, 30, 1976, *YUN, 1976*, 782.

Two other matters are of relevance. In 1974 there had been a revolution in Portugal, one of the last remaining colonial powers with possessions in Africa. The next year, Portugal's new government liquidated its African empire, which meant that two nations near the affected areas discussed above—Angola in the west, and Mozambique in the east—were now independent and would presumably soon be ruled by black majorities. Thus the remaining minority white-ruled regimes in South Africa and Rhodesia found themselves more isolated than they had been just a few years earlier.

The United States had been perceived by many in the world as insensitive to the legitimate demands of the black majority in southern Africa, especially when the Senate had refused to go along with certain portions of the UN's sanctions. Particularly galling was the Byrd Amendment, which allowed Americans to ignore the embargo on importing Rhodesian chrome. Moreover, conservative senators, led by Jesse Helms of North Carolina, evinced an open sympathy for white rulers in Africa. Secretary of State Kissinger, as we have seen in Chapter 4, opposed the Senate's defiance of UN sanctions, and toward the end of his tenure he traveled throughout southern Africa, assuring those he met that the United States favored majority rule and would work to repeal the Byrd Amendment. Kissinger's late activity represented a helpful prelude for the Carter administration's more conspicuous approach.

Carter, as we know, addressed the African situation in his early speech to the United Nations and authorized Ambassador Young to play a principal role in rebuilding African's confidence in the United States. In the spring of his first year in office, the president outlined his intentions regarding southern Africa in a wide-ranging interview with a group of publishers, editors, and broadcasters.[78] In Rhodesia he pressed for majority rule and encouraged the British to take a leadership role with substantial American backing and cooperation; he saw the United Nations as playing the major role in Namibia (Southwest Africa), again with strong U.S. support; and as for South Africa, he insisted on the end of apartheid. He also viewed South Africa as a key to addressing the other outstanding issues in the southern part of the continent. He urged Pretoria to help resolve the issues of Zimbabwe and Namibia, but only according to international demands. And he meant to play tough with South Africa, as revealed in American support for a Security Council

---

[78] April 15, 1977, *PPP, 1977*, I, 646–647.

resolution in November 1977 placing a mandatory arms embargo on the country until it met UN prescriptions.[79]

By March of 1977 the president had persuaded the Congress to repeal the Byrd Amendment, and he prepared to work with the British to produce an acceptable outcome in Rhodesia. Then, Ian Smith of Rhodesia placed an obstacle into the mix. He announced an "internal solution" which would involve including in the government Bishop Abel Muzorewa, a Rhodesian black, and his followers. Smith would remain prime minister for an interim period, and his white supporters would retain considerable power in the new political configuration. The plan would have effectively excluded the more numerous supporters of Robert Mugabe and Joshua Nkomo, who were both engaged in guerrilla resistance to the white government. The British Foreign Office, and the Labour government in London, saw Smith's proposal as a sham. The so-called "frontline states" (black-ruled nations adjacent to Rhodesia) rejected Smith's scheme outright. But in Washington, Brzezinski at first leaned toward the "internal solution."[80] Conservatives in the Senate were also interested; Senator Helms invited Smith to visit the United States in October 1978 to explain his proposal. Helms introduced legislation to suspend sanctions against Rhodesia as a show of support for the internal settlement.[81]

Vance and his colleagues in the State Department intended to stick with the United Nations and go along with the British. London and Washington now jointly pressed for an "all-parties conference" at Geneva. The secretary of state and the president, with the invaluable contribution of Warren Christopher, who worked closely with friendly senators, circumvented Helms and the conservatives by developing a compromise whereby the sanctions would be lifted by December 31, 1978, *if* the president determined that Smith's government had demonstrated a willingness to attend an all-parties conference and to accept a new government following free, internationally supervised elections. Smith, resistant, demurred, and the sanctions remained.[82]

---

[79] SC Resolution 418, November 4, 1977, *YUN, 1977*, 61–62.

[80] Brzezinski, *Power and Principle*, 140.

[81] Smith, *Morality, Reason, and Power*, 140–141. Vance, *Hard Choices*, 290–293.

[82] Vance, *Hard Choices*, 293.

Carter's support for the UN's isolation of the Rhodesian regime was tested first by the conservatives' victories in the 1978 American congressional elections, and then by Margaret Thatcher's election as prime minister of Great Britain in May 1979. For a moment, the situation looked bleak. However, Thatcher, who was initially intrigued with the "internal settlement," gradually came to be persuaded by members of her Foreign Office to oppose it. Her commitment to the all-parties conference was crucial, and in the first week of August 1979, at a Commonwealth conference in Lusaka, she announced a proposal in line with the Anglo-American position as it had developed when Labour was in office. Thatcher committed Britain to majority black rule, the removal of white privileges from the Rhodesian constitution, and free and fair elections under British authority and Commonwealth direction.[83]

The Thatcher government invited all parties to Lancaster House in London, where, after three months of talks, all participants signed an agreement providing a temporary restoration of British rule in Rhodesia, followed by free, open, and internationally observed elections and then by independence.

In late December 1979, at the successful conclusion of the Lancaster meeting, the Security Council, with U.S. endorsement, lifted all sanctions on Rhodesia.[84] By April 1980, Robert Mugabe had been chosen as the first democratically elected prime minister of newly independent Zimbabwe. The following August, Mugabe visited Washington. At a White House reception, President Carter warmly welcomed the prime minister, spoke of the occasion as an "exciting time in our country's history and the history of the world," and congratulated Zimbabwe on its new membership in the United Nations.[85]

*   *   *

No such successful denouement occurred in Namibia during Carter's presidency, but the efforts made by the president and his secretary of state did lay the groundwork for future progress. Early in his term, Carter, who believed that a breakthrough in Namibia might stimulate more rapid change elsewhere in southern Africa, sent Vice

---

[83] Ibid., 298.

[84] SC Resolution 460, December 21, 1979, *YUN, 1979*, 217.

[85] August 27, 1980, *PPP, 1980–1981*, II, 1579–1580.

President Walter Mondale to meet with the prime minister of South Africa, B. J. Vorster, in Vienna. The vice president underscored Washington's dedication to political and social change throughout southern Africa, including the end of apartheid in South Africa. Of immediate concern, Mondale said, was the independence of Namibia, a demand grounded in America's commitment to basic human rights.[86] Washington chose to move in tandem with the United Nations. The administration made clear its support for Security Council Resolution 385, passed in the last year of Ford's term, calling for South Africa to withdraw from Southwest Africa and for elections under UN supervision.[87] A "Contact Group" was formed—made up of Canada, France, the Federal Republic of Germany, the United Kingdom, and the United States—to work with South Africa, SWAPO, and the United Nations to implement Resolution 385.[88] Donald McHenry, at the time Andrew Young's deputy at the United Nations, became chairman of the Contact Group.

Defying Resolution 385, Pretoria convened the "Turnhalle conference" (so named for the hall in Windhoek—Namibia's capital—where the meeting took place) in late 1976. South Africa tried to engineer its own version of an "internal settlement" in Namibia, thus disregarding UN demands. The so-called Democratic Turnhalle Alliance (DTA) included several carefully defined black ethnic groups but excluded members of SWAPO, the guerrilla group (made up chiefly of Ovambos, the majority ethnic group in the country) which had been resisting South African rule. SWAPO's leader, Sam Nujoma, rejected the legitimacy of ethnic-based parties and the DTA. He was joined in his opposition by all neighboring black-ruled states. SWAPO and its allies insisted on a UN-conducted resolution. Pretoria wanted to administer its own settlement, preferably excluding any UN or SWAPO participation. The aim of the Contact Group was to move the negotiations clearly to the UN position and subvert the "internal settlement," but to provide enough South African participation to ensure the regime's acceptance of an eventual solution.

Focused negotiations brought heartening progress by late summer of 1977. The South Africans grudgingly agreed to the appointment of

---

[86] Vance, *Hard Choices*, 265.

[87] January 30, 1976, *YUN, 1976*, 782.

[88] Waldheim, *Eye of the Storm*, 103–104.

Ambassador Maarti Ahtisaari, a Finnish diplomat, as the UN's special representative to prepare for UN participation once all the other details could be ironed out. Then Sam Nujoma, at UN headquarters in New York, agreed to the principle of free elections, a UN-supervised transition, and—as concessions to Pretoria—a South Africa-appointed administer-general and a cease-fire in the guerrilla war once the transitional procedures were in place.[89] But there negotiations froze. South Africa resisted any UN peacekeeping forces, and SWAPO would not move until such forces showed up.

In February 1978, the Contact Group invited delegations from both SWAPO and South Africa to New York for talks at the United Nations. But disagreements continued to afflict the discussions. In May, South Africa launched a large-scale attack on SWAPO bases and Nujoma broke off all discussions. Now the Contact Group began to put added pressure on Pretoria. South Africa allowed Ambassador Ahtisaari to come to Windhoek in early August to make preliminary plans for setting up the United Nations Transition Assistance Group (UNTAG). But on September 28, the ruling South African Nationalist Party named Defense Minister Pieter Botha, an opponent of any concessions on Namibia, as the new prime minister. The following day, the Security Council adopted Resolution 435, cosponsored by the United States. It authorized the secretary-general to arrange a transition and elections under UN mandate, and it declared all unilateral South African measures in Namibia null and void.[90] South Africa ignored Resolution 435 and proceeded to hold its own internal election in Namibia in December. SWAPO stood by the original UN plan and refused to move.

When Carter left office, there was no independent Namibia. Vance, who had worked so steadfastly on the Namibian question, could comfort himself only with the observation that, with UN Resolution 435, a "framework" was firmly in place for an eventual settlement.[91] In fact, Vance proved prescient, for, in full accord with UN Resolution 435, Namibia became an independent majority-ruled nation in May 1990.

In February of that same year, the new prime minister of South Africa, Frederik W. de Klerk, ordered the release of the black nationalist

---

[89] Vance, *Hard Choices*, 280–282.

[90] *YUN, 1978*, 915–916. See Vance, *Hard Choices*, 307–311, and 501, which has the full text of the resolution.

[91] Vance, *Hard Choices*, 313.

leader Nelson Mandela, who had been incarcerated for almost three decades. A year later, de Klerk, in compliance with UN resolutions, announced the end of all apartheid laws. Mandela would be elected the first black president of South Africa. Within just over a decade from Carter's reelection defeat, Zimbabwe, Namibia, and South Africa were all independent, ruled by democratic majorities, and full members of the United Nations; and apartheid was a curse of the past.

The Iranian Hostage Nightmare

Iran had once been the heart of the great Persian Empire. In the seventh century, Arabs brought to the Persians the Islamic faith, which displaced the indigenous Zoroastrianism. By the nineteenth century, Iran had become a pawn in the imperial competition between Britain and Russia, which were both trying to influence the ruling native dynasty. During World War II, Mohammad Reza Pahlavi, with British collaboration, replaced his abdicating father as shah, and in 1945 Iran become one of the charter members of the United Nations. As the cold war hardened, the new shah, facing a Soviet threat to the North, tilted toward the West. Washington considered Iran a major source of petroleum, a key listening post, and a defense barrier against Soviet intentions. Following the CIA's overthrow of the Mossadegh government in the early 1950s, the shah pursued a vigorous policy of modernization and secularization, seeking to "westernize" his nation.

Early in his presidency, Carter had met with and toasted the shah as a valued friend. It was a friendship that would soon be sorely tested. In early 1978 conservative religious leaders of the majority Shiite Muslim faith, resentful of the shah's secularism, joined with unhappy students, merchants, and dissident political opponents in growing complaints about the shah's rule and about the presence of some 50,000 Americans training the Iranian military and operating the oil fields. More secular opponents condemned the Shah's violations of human rights in the treatment of his subjects. The burgeoning opposition united around a curious Islamic religious figure—Ayatollah Ruholla Khomeini, an eighty-year-old exile living in France. Street demonstrations accelerated. In early September the shah announced martial law; troops fired on civilian protesters, killing hundreds. In late December 1978, the shah appointed Shapour Bahktiar as prime minister and then, in the face of growing revolt, left the country. The following February, Ayatollah Khomeini returned victoriously from Paris, ordered the arrest of

Bahktiar, who fled the country, and appointed his own prime minister, Mehdi Bazargan. An "Islamic republic" imposed conservative, antiwestern religious rule on Iran, and Americans began leaving.

In late October 1979, Carter made the costly decision to admit the exiled and now cancer-ridden shah into the United States for medical treatment. This action triggered an explosion of anger in Teheran, where the Ayatollah accused Washington of plotting another attempt to reinstall the shah and urged Iranians to take to the streets in protest against the "great Satan Carter." On November 1, a million irate Iranians marched on the U.S. embassy (called by Khomeini "a nest of spies"). Hundreds stormed the compound, and on November 4 they seized the embassy and imprisoned the sixty-nine Americans there. The Ayatollah seemed to approve the capture, and his government was unwilling to arrange the release of the Americans.

The Carter administration chose to use international institutions to end the crisis, and, in due course, to isolate the Iranian government. At the International Court of Justice, the United States won a quick decision that Iran had acted illegally and must immediately return the hostages and pay compensation. Washington then froze Iranian assets in the United States and presented its case to the UN Security Council. In the interim, Teheran released a few of the hostages, including all the women and African-Americans.[92] The remaining captives were to be held a long time.

Meantime, Secretary Vance and the assistant secretary of state for Near Eastern Affairs, Harold Saunders, began meeting in private with Kurt Waldheim at the secretary-general's home in New York. At first Vance hoped that Waldheim would be the intermediary in delivering a statement to the Iranian foreign minister, Abolhasan Bani-Sadr, which would begin negotiations to end the impasse. But Bani-Sadr, possibly because he had been in contact with Waldheim, was dismissed in late November, though he reappeared in January as Iran's new president.[93] Vance and the Americans persisted in trying to find a useful role for the secretary-general, and on December 4 the United Nations Security Council, by a unanimous vote, approved Resolution 457, urgently demanding the immediate release of the hostages and the use of the

---

[92] Ibid., 377–378. Smith, *Morality, Reason, and Power*, 199–201.

[93] Carter, *Keeping Faith*, 467. Vance, *Hard Choices*, 378–379. Waldheim, *Eye of the Storm*, 2.

secretary-general's "good offices" to carry out the resolution and to mediate a solution. The Council reinforced its initial action on December 31, with Resolution 461, restating the demands of 457 and "deploring" the continued detention of the hostages.[94] The United States was also prepared to urge international sanctions against Iran. However, following the breakdown in U.S.-Soviet relations as a consequence of the Afghan invasion, Washington was uncertain about a Russian vote for sanctions in the Security Council. The USSR had sided with all other Council members for Resolution 457, but less than a week after storming into Afghanistan, Moscow abstained on Resolution 461, allowing it to pass.

In accordance with the UN's resolve, Secretary-General Waldheim left for Teheran on New Year's Eve, 1979. The visit was to be, in the secretary-general's own words, a "nightmare." He met in eerie settings with the new foreign minister, Sadegh Ghotbzadeh, and the new president, the erstwhile foreign minister, Bani-Sadr, but he found both of them taciturn and uneasy and could elicit only rote demands that the shah be returned to Iran for trial. Waldheim had a troubling sense of chaos in Teheran and actually feared for his own life.[95] When he returned in early January 1980, he reported to the Security Council and then flew to Washington to brief Carter, with whom he continued to work closely during the long crisis.[96] On January 12, the Security Council voted sanctions on Iran, but the now disaffected Soviet Union vetoed the resolution. The United States imposed its own sanctions and invited all other nations to join it.[97]

Although it was now time for the presidential campaign to begin and Carter was a candidate for reelection, he secluded himself in the White House and announced that he would not campaign until the Iranian hostages were returned. The Americans held out hope that the United Nations could arrange something to end the crisis. Waldheim appointed a UN commission to go back to Iran in March, but nothing came of the trip. Then, in desperation, Carter authorized a secret rescue attempt. He made the decision at a National Security Council meeting in

---

[94] *YUN, 1979*, 311–312.

[95] Waldheim, *Eye of the Storm*, 1–11.

[96] Ibid., 156–157. Carter, *Keeping Faith*, 478.

[97] Vance, *Hard Choices*, 400.

mid-April, while Vance was away on vacation. Vance, wholly opposed to the mission, stayed at his post only until the operation had been completed, then resigned. On April 24, eight helicopters flew from the carrier *Nimitz* through a dust storm into a staging area in the Iranian desert. Two disabled helicopters, attempting to turn back, collided with each other and with a transport plane. The crash killed eight servicemen, and Carter aborted the mission.[98] The president, humbled by the failed mission and by the resignation of a valued friend who had shared his earlier idealistic visions, appointed Senator Edmund Muskie of Maine the new secretary of state, and hoped for the best.

In late July, the shah died. Then, in September, Iraq, taking advantage of the apparent disarray in Iran, attacked its neighbor, initiating a ferocious decade-long war. By fall, indirect and still Byzantine negotiations commenced that would eventually result in the exchange of the American captives for Iran's frozen assets. A specially convened State Department group, working under Deputy Secretary of State Warren Christopher, managed the American effort and dealt for the most part with the Algerian embassy in Washington, which represented Iranian interests following the break in diplomatic relations in April 1980.[99] After his defeat in November, Carter worked with his accustomed diligence to free the fifty-two imprisoned diplomats. With Algeria acting as broker, Iran's assets were unfrozen, and the hostages were returned at the very moment that Carter's successor entered the presidency.

* * *

Jimmy Carter had entered the Oval Office in 1977 believing that he could change the course of U.S. foreign policy by putting America on the side of history's momentum. Integral to his vision was the effective use of the United Nations in the resolution of international challenges. Multilateral cooperation, American leadership, and a commitment to human rights were the key to a new era of peace.

By 1980, most of Jimmy Carter's hopes lay in ruins. His last year in office had begun ominously enough, with a troublesome inflation that

---

[98] Ibid., 409–413.

[99] See Warren Christopher et al., *American Hostages in Iran: The Conduct of a Crisis* (New Haven, Conn.: Yale University Press, 1985).

had risen to double digits, with Senator Edward Kennedy preparing to mount a damaging challenge for the Democratic nomination, and with the hostage crisis a nightly embarrassment on television news. The Soviet Union had just invaded Afghanistan, the cold war had resumed, and SALT had been removed from the Senate's consideration. The president seemed to be in a kind of political purgatory, clearly susceptible to the humiliating defeat he would suffer in the fall. What Carter thought he could cite as a success in early 1980 was the recently elevated position of the United States within the United Nations. Pro-American resolution after resolution seemed to be passing in the General Assembly and in the Security Council. addressing a leadership conference on civil rights late January, the president opined:

> The tremendous votes that took place recently in the United Nations contradict the historical tone, when the small nations and the new nations and the weak nations and those who represented populations with black and brown and yellow people supported our position with our hostages in Iran and who condemned the Soviet Union for their invasion of Afghanistan. That would likely not have been the case a few years ago.[100]

That there was a notable shift from hostility to support among third world nations in the United Nations is indisputable. The change is made evident by comparing the major UN resolutions of the turn of the year from 1979 to 1980 with actions during the worst moments of U.S.–UN relations during the mid-1970s. For example, a careful analysis of the vote on each relevant resolution during these two periods shows that the preponderant number of third world nations who had voted for the most egregious earlier resolutions—those calling for a Charter of Economic Rights and Duties, for according observer status to the PLO, and for declaring Zionism as a form of racism—voted in support of the United States both in the General Assembly and, if serving in the Security Council, there as well. This was true, most importantly, on two key

---

[100] January 27, 1980, *PPP, 1980–1981*, I, 224.

issues: the invasion of Afghanistan and the Iranian hostage crisis.[101] Moreover, in addition to more favorable voting patterns in the United Nations, there may have been collateral advantages to the United States resulting from the altered relationship with the third world.

In the middle of October 1980, Iran's recently appointed prime minister, the hard-line Mohammad Ali Rajai, came to New York to seek UN help in condemning Iraq for its brutal invasion. Before this trip, the prime minister had never been outside of Iran. The Majlis (the Iranian parliament) had chosen him as a counter to the perceived moderation of President Bani-Sadr and Foreign Minister Ghotbzadeh, each now in disfavor with Ayatollah Khomeini.[102] Ali Rajai certainly expected some sympathy from what he thought would be friendly third world nations. In fact, there is every evidence that he believed these countries sympathized with Iran's hostile actions against the United States. But the reception for the Iranian envoy was unexpectedly cold. Secretary-General Waldheim explained to him that as long as Teheran held the American hostages, in violation of international law and UN resolutions, he could expect little commiseration from member states. Waldheim's admonition was corroborated in a "steady round of reprimands" directed at Ali Rajai from all quarters of the United Nations.[103] The chastened prime minister returned home on October 19 with an unanticipated report of his visit to New York. Within days of his return, Iran designated Algeria as the official intermediary with the United States to solve the crisis. From that time forward, Teheran evinced every intention to end the deadlock. The individuals most closely involved on the American side in the final negotiations believe that the key to

---

[101] Compare the votes for GA Resolution 3237, November 22, 1974 (observer status for the PLO), *YUN, 1974,* 227; GA Resolution 3281, December 12, 1974 (Charter of Economic Rights and Duties), *YUN, 1974,* 402–407; and GA Resolution 3379, November 10, 1975 ("Zionism is a form of racism") with SC Resolutions 457, December 4, and 461, December 31, 1979 (demanding release of the hostages), *YUN, 1979,* 311–312, and with GA Resolution ES-6/2, January 14, 1980 (deploring Soviet intervention in Afghanistan), *YUN, 1980,* 307.

[102] Harold Saunders, "Beginning of the End," in Christopher, *American Hostages,* 288–289.

[103] Waldheim, *Eye of the Storm,* 165. The quoted remark is by Warren Christopher, in *American Hostages,* 8.

settlement was Ali Rajai's visit to the United Nations.[104] Waldheim has written: "In my opinion this was the turning point in the Iranian hostage crisis. Rajai was visibly shocked by the luke-warm reception he received in New York, not only by the Western Representatives but also by his friends from the Third World."[105] Warren Christopher agreed, pointing out that "countries we often have thought to be our antagonists within the U.N. system helped mightily and perhaps decisively to let Iran know that, for its own sake, it should resolve the crisis."[106] Algeria, which a few years earlier had been the leader of the anti-American coalition in the United Nations, was of crucial help. The Algerian ambassador in Washington, Redha Malek, proved to be a man of enormous "stature" during the last days of the crisis, and officials of an Algerian delegation remained in Teheran from December 30, 1980, until January 20, 1981, when they escorted the American hostages home.[107]

Thus, the purposeful strategy of courting the third world and elevating the status and importance of the United Nations may have paid some dividends. But these hard-won achievements among Third World peoples and in the halls of the United Nations probably offered only minimal solace to Jimmy Carter on inauguration day, 1981, as he watched a beaming Ronald Reagan replace him in the White House.

Reagan and the UN: Phase One

In 1984 the Heritage Foundation, a conservative think tank in Washington, D.C., published an anthology entitled *A World Without A U.N.*[108] The authors commended the Reagan administration for its innovative and conservative policies, particularly in foreign affairs, and at the same time proposed that, given the new administration's inclination to question former conventions, it rethink the United States'

---

[104] See, for example, in Christopher, *American Hostages*, the remarks by Harold Saunders at 291, and Gary Sick at 168. Saunders was assistant secretary of state for the Near East and South Asia and head of the Iran Working Group during the crisis. Sick was chief assistant to the national security adviser during the crisis.

[105] Waldheim, *Eye of the Storm*, 165.

[106] *American Hostages*, 8.

[107] Ibid., 291.

[108] Burton Yale Pines, ed., *A World Without a U.N.: What Would Happen If the U.N. Shut Down?* (Washington, D.C.: Heritage Foundation, 1984).

membership in the United Nations. If the United States were to withdraw, such an act conceivably could complement the Reagan foreign policy and might not be as devastating as the UN's supporters argued. The foreword to this book was written by Charles M. Lichenstein, former alternate U.S. representative to the United Nations, who, in September 1983, had become renowned for proclaiming at a meeting of a UN committee that UN delegates should "seriously consider removing themselves and this organization from the soil of the United States....We will put no impediment in your way and we will be at dockside bidding you a fond farewell as you set off into the sunset."[109]

For some observers, the Heritage Foundation's anthology mirrored the attitude of the Reagan administration. Undersecretary-General Brian Urquhart thought that in Reagan's Washington the United Nations "sometimes seemed to be seen exclusively as a target of contempt and ridicule and as a minor prop in the ongoing extravaganza of American public life."[110] And Reagan, determined to reverse Carter's brand of international idealism, chose conservative foreign policy advisers whose hostility to the United Nations, and for that matter to multilateral activity generally, was unquestioned. The president picked Alexander Haig as his secretary of state. Haig—a professional military man and a hardened cold warrior who had served as President Nixon's last chief of staff—characterized the United Nations, "with its vociferous anticolonialist coalition of Third World and Marxist members," as "ineffective."[111] William Casey, a political confidant of the new president, moved into the directorship of the CIA. Casey, who had served during the Second World War in the Office of Strategic Services (the precursor to the CIA), set out to rebuild the CIA's covert intelligence capabilities. The director shared with the appointed secretary of defense, Caspar Weinberger, a hawkish attitude toward the Soviet Union, a desire to augment defense expenditures, and an inclination to go it alone in international matters. The CIA chief particularly liked Jeane Kirkpatrick,

---

[109] Ibid., ix.

[110] Brian Urquhart, *A Life*, 1987), 370.

[111] Alexander M. Haig, Jr., *Caveat: Realism, Reagan, and Foreign Policy* (New York: Macmillan, 1984), 270.

the administration's ambassador to the United Nations.[112] Kirkpatrick, a professor of international affairs and American foreign policy at Georgetown University, had attracted Mr. Reagan's attention as he geared up for the 1980 election campaign. Reagan, who initiated contact with Kirkpatrick in 1979, in a Christmas letter, was dazzled with the professor's *Commentary* article in November of that year; she had criticized President Carter for not understanding the difference between the unequivocal evil of totalitarian dictators in places like the Soviet Union and China and more benign and friendly "authoritarian" dictators like General Pinochet of Chile.[113]

During her four-year tenure at the United Nations, Kirkpatrick proved a forceful advocate of Reagan's philosophy of foreign affairs. She perceived her role as adversarial, similar to that of Ambassador Daniel Patrick Moynihan during Ford's presidency. Her remarks and votes, within the General Assembly and sometimes in the Security Council as well, usually were in opposition to the majority. Sometimes she found herself alone on issues, or joined by very few—on several occasions only by Israel. Among the many speeches she gave as ambassador were those with titles such as "Standing Alone" and "The Problem of the United Nations."[114]

While the ambassador directed Washington's offensive in New York and gave numerous speeches around the country, the president avoided speaking to the United Nations during his first year in office. When he did speak—in 1982, before a special session of the General Assembly devoted to disarmament—he sprinkled his remarks with harsh criticisms of the Soviet Union and confirmed that the United States was engaged in a unilateral arms buildup of unprecedented size.[115] The traditional annual presidential United Nations proclamations for 1981 and 1982 made clear the views of the administration as they were being articulated by Kirkpatrick. The brief 1981 proclamation revealingly spoke to the

---

[112] Robert M. Gates, *From the Shadows: The Ultimate Insider's Story of Five Presidents and How They Won the Cold War* (New York: Simon and Schuster, 1996), 219.

[113] Peter Hannaford, ed., *Recollections of Reagan: A Portrait of Ronald Reagan* (New York: Morrow, 1997), 78–80.

[114] Jeane J. Kirkpatrick, *The Reagan Phenomenon—and Other Speeches on Foreign Policy* (Washington, D.C.: American Enterprise Institute, 1983), 79–91, 92–98.

[115] *PPP, 1982,* I, 784–789.

"values and ideals that *originally* inspired the United Nations," and the 1982 proclamation asserted that "the U.N. has been misused," and that in consequence "today's world is too often fraught with strife, division, and conflict."[116]

The Reagan administration proceeded to withdraw from The United Nations Educational, Scientific, and Cultural Organization (UNESCO) and to reject the Law of the Sea Treaty, which, according to Secretary-General Waldheim, had been "laboriously crafted over a period of many years with the concurrence of U.S. delegations representing earlier American administrations."[117] The administration also endorsed a legislative proposal named for its initiator, Senator Nancy Kassebaum of Kansas. The so-called "Kassebaum Amendment" called for a cut in U.S. contributions to UN special agencies and a 15 percent reduction in the UN staff. And in 1985 the president signed a congressional act lowering the American contribution to the total UN budget from 25 percent to 20 percent.[118]

In addition to Ambassador Kirkpatrick's tough view of the United Nations, her equally hard-line thoughts on the Soviet Union, an arms buildup, Central America, southern Africa, and the Middle East were shared in the early Reagan administration by influential presidential advisers. Haig, Weinberger, Casey, and Kirkpatrick all had a deeply suspicious attitude regarding the Soviet Union and undoubtedly welcomed the president's zealous public criticisms and his characterization of the USSR as an "evil empire."[119] In his very first press conference, Reagan charged that "the only morality [the Soviets] recognize is what will further their cause, meaning they reserve unto themselves the right to commit any crime, to lie, to cheat, in order to attain [global domination]."[120] The "evil empire" speech, given in the spring of 1983 before a meeting of the conservative National Association of Evangelicals, was followed up within days by the president's

---

[116] *PPP, 1981*, 905–906; *PPP, 1982*, II, 1154. Emphasis added.

[117] Waldheim, *Eye of the Storm*, 228.

[118] See Chapter 6.

[119] The "evil empire" speech was made on March 8, 1983. See Ronald Reagan, *An American Life* (New York: Simon and Schuster, 1990), 569–570.

[120] Quoted in Charles A. Hantz, "Ideology, Pragmatism, and Ronald Reagan's World View: Full of Sound and Fury, Signifying...?" *Presidential Studies Quarterly* XXVI (Fall 1996): 945.

impromptu announcement on national television of his intention to develop a futuristic defense shield covering the entire United States, which he called the Strategic Defense Initiative (SDI), soon dubbed "Star Wars" by the media and critics. Meantime, the Reagan administration went forward with plans initiated at the end of the Carter years to deploy medium-range missiles in Western Europe. Moscow reacted by walking out of all arms control talks at the end of 1983. As the election campaign of 1984 took place, the president found himself being criticized by his political opponents as the only chief executive since Herbert Hoover not to have met with his Soviet counterpart. It is no wonder that there was a cool, argumentative meeting between Foreign Minister Andrei Gromyko of the Soviet Union and the newly appointed secretary of state, George Shultz. In this three-hour meeting, held at the U.S. mission to the United Nations in September 1982, Gromyko called U.S.-USSR relations "politically tense," and pointedly asked Shultz whether Washington wanted "peaceful coexistence or confrontation."[121]

If the international community's hopes for serious progress on disarmament seemed dashed by the growing tension between Moscow and Washington, the new arms race made matters even worse. The president's Strategic Defense Initiative, estimated by some observers to require outlays of from $100 billion to $1 trillion, was to be added to the already considerable increase in military spending sponsored by the administration. In addition to expenditures to bolster existing military activities, the president and his secretary of defense, Caspar Weinberger, presided over an armaments program that favored development of the B-1 bomber (canceled by Carter) and the MX mobile missile, all in addition to SDI. One long-term consequence of the expensive defense buildup was an exploding national budget deficit (made more severe by a simultaneous policy of tax reductions). Indeed, one of Reagan's clearest legacies was the federal debt, which, during his two terms, tripled the total national debt accumulated over the entire two centuries preceding his presidency.

Central America also felt the sting of Washington's revived cold war mentality. The government of El Salvador, sustained by Washington with advisers and $5 billion in aid during the eight years of Reagan's presidency, spent most of the money and training in a desperate effort to

---

[121] George P. Shultz, *Turmoil and Triumph: My Years as Secretary of State* (New York: Scribner, 1993), 122.

defeat a guerrilla insurrection in a seemingly unending civil war. In neighboring Nicaragua, on the other hand, the United States backed the revolutionaries (called "Contras"), here fighting the government of the left-leaning Sandinista party. According to historian Walter LaFeber, Casey's CIA "built the Contras virtually from scratch" to conduct what was called "low-intensity conflict."[122] The CIA also mined Nicaraguan harbors, in violation of international law. When Nicaragua took its grievance before the International Court of Justice in The Hague, the Reagan administration refused to argue the case, denying the court's jurisdiction.[123]

Although polls showed that Americans were perplexed as to which government we were supporting and which we opposed in Central America, most grasped that the administration had returned to an older policy of trying to dominate the political destiny of the region. The rationale for this policy was that it was needed to check the expansion into the Caribbean and Central America of Soviet-influenced communism. Two consequences of the policy were, first, the unremitting violence visited upon these unhappy countries, and second, the Iran-Contra scandal, which we discuss below. It should be worth noting at this point that in the early 1990s, after Washington had ended its vigorous intrusion into Central America, elections took place in Nicaragua and El Salvador under the scrutiny of UN observers. From a certain perspective, the peaceful resolution of political problems under UN supervision proved more positive than the military solution sought by the Reagan Administration. In Nicaragua, the party that challenged the Sandinistas actually won the presidency in 1990, while the Sandinistas, accepting the outcome of the election, remained an opposition political party. In El Salvador, the right-wing Arena Party won the presidency in an open election in 1994, but a coalition of leftist parties retained considerable support and won impressive political victories in subsequent years. If these poor countries eventually prove that they can live and prosper, and avoid conflict, in a peaceful, competitive political environment, perhaps they will give credence to the notion that the international approach of the United Nations is preferable

---

[122] Walter LaFeber, *Inevitable Revolutions: The United States in Central America*, 2nd ed. (New York: Norton, 1993), 300.

[123] Ibid., 301.

in such situations to the unilateral military approach tried by the United States in the 1980s.

The administration's policy toward Afghanistan likewise reflected its cold war stance and its commitment to what was called "low-intensity conflict," that is, anticommunist combat that Washington would abet secretly with money and weapons without introducing American ground forces. In an effort to thwart the Soviet Union in Afghanistan, the CIA covertly funded anticommunist guerrillas there. These *mujahidin*, Islamic fundamentalists, were based in neighboring Pakistan. They happily accepted American weapons, training, and economic assistance. Once the Russians were gone, by the end of the 1980s, these heavily armed *mujahidin* fell into bloody factional disputes, and many joined in international terrorist activities aimed at the United States.

In southern Africa there was a reversal of Carter's diplomacy, at least until Secretary of State Shultz finally began to direct the policy during Reagan's second term. In the spring of 1981, Ambassador Kirkpatrick set the stage for the new approach in several statements at the United Nations and in public addresses.[124] She criticized the UN's role in southern Africa, said that Washington was more concerned about Cuban influence in Angola than it was about South Africa's iniquities, and insisted that the Democratic Turnhalle Alliance created by South Africa in Namibia be given equal consideration with SWAPO, contrary to the UN's preference.[125] The policy took on a more nuanced tone with the appointment of Chester Crocker as assistant secretary of state for African Affairs in June 1981. Crocker had written an article in *Foreign Affairs* the winter before his appointment recommending a policy of "constructive engagement" with the white government of South Africa. He described the new policy as engaging South Africa to help foster a "regional climate conducive to compromise and accommodation."[126] Because Crocker recommended dealing more sympathetically than Carter had

---

[124] See Kirkpatrick, *Reagan Phenomenon*, particularly the following speeches: "Southern Africa, Namibia, the United Nations, and the United States," "Southern Africa: Fair Play for Namibia," and "Southern Africa: Fair Play for South Africa," 155–168.

[125] For details of the Namibian situation, see above (the section on the Carter administration's policy).

[126] Chester A. Crocker, *High Noon in Southern Africa: Making Peace in a Rough Neighborhood* (New York: Norton, 1992), 74–82.

done with the white regime of P.W. Botha, Reagan found the approach attractive. But the president seemed to commiserate even more with southern Africa's white rulers than Crocker did. By 1986 disagreements surfaced between the White House and Congress about how to deal with South Africa. A majority in the legislative branch wished to place sanctions on Pretoria for ignoring UN resolutions, most of which had been favored by the Carter Administration. Reagan opposed sanctions, and when Congress placed some on South Africa by passing the Anti-Apartheid Act in 1986, he vetoed the bill. In the East Room of the White House, in July 1986, he delivered a strong defense of his policy to an audience from the World Affairs Council and the Foreign Policy Association. The speech, written by a conservative White House aide, Patrick Buchanan, never mentioned the United Nations, any UN resolutions, or any connection between the United Nations and southern Africa. Though briefly criticizing apartheid, the speech was given over chiefly to rejecting sanctions, praising President Botha, presenting a sensitive historical view of white involvement in South Africa, and insisting that, given black-on-black violence and the "communism" of the African National Congress, the minority white government had every right to maintain internal order. The president reminded his audience of the "strategic importance" of South Africa and of the need to cultivate good relations with the existing South African government in order to resist Soviet intrusion in the area.

In the most curious portion of the speech, Reagan maintained that we could not and must not try to "transplant our ideas and institutions" to South Africa.[127] This odd assertion was precisely the converse of Reagan's most consistent message—that America's democratic ideals and institutions were superior to any others and adaptable everywhere in the world. The president, throughout his two terms in the Oval Office, argued for a unilateral idealism that envisioned the United States as the guardian of universal principles. A God-blessed nation, America needed to lead the world in a battle for the "good." In that battle, Reagan—unlike Truman or Eisenhower—saw little meaningful role for the United Nations. In fact, the UN had become part of the problem, infected by the influence of the Soviet Union and other authoritarian regimes. American moralism—which had originally created the idea of a universal collective security system, had led Roosevelt and Truman to

---

[127] *PPP, 1986*, II, 984–988.

place their trust in a new United Nations and had moved Carter to see new possibilities in a revived UN—now was put to the task of repudiating the organization and, alternatively, calling Americans to the challenge of changing the world on their own. It seemed that in the case of South Africa, we needed to accept and support nondemocratic institutions because they were appropriate to the internal situation and because they served the "higher" interest of blunting the spread of pernicious communism. Listening to the speech, a dejected Shultz waited in vain for a hint of moderation or any acknowledgment that blacks in southern Africa had serious grievances. Shultz was a supporter of, among other UN initiatives, Resolution 435, which the former secretary of state, Vance, had worked on with such diligence, and he grew more morose when he observed that "the President's delivery demonstrated that he was fully in tune" with what he was saying.[128]

For a while it appeared that yet another complete reversal of Carter's policy would take place, this one regarding China. Until Reagan's highly publicized visit to China in 1984 restored good feelings, relations with Beijing were frosty. During the 1980 campaign Reagan had criticized Carter's normalization with China, and particularly the cavalier way he thought Taiwan had been treated. Once in office he hinted that he might restore full relations with Taiwan, and he promised to sell weapons to the Taipei government. Reagan described Taiwan as a "loyal, democratic, longtime ally." Even Secretary of State Haig felt that the Chinese had reason to be distressed.[129]

The Middle East, Reagan, and the UN

Jimmy Carter had remodeled Washington's approach to the Middle East to concentrate on regional and local problems and grievances. That is, he had removed the discourse about the Middle East from the cold war framework, which he felt had masked the real problem and had made any diplomatic movement difficult. The Camp David accords were a product of this alteration in approach. While the Reagan administration insisted that it would follow up on Camp David, Reagan's early attitude once again reflected a harsher cold war view. Secretary of State Haig, for example, sought to ignore the Israeli-Palestinian issue and concentrate on convincing Israel and the

---

[128] Shultz, *Turmoil and Triumph*, 1122.

[129] Haig, *Caveat*, 198–200; see also Reagan, *American Life*, 361.

conservative Arab states, such as Saudi Arabia, Jordan, and Egypt, to join an American-brokered alliance designed to resist Soviet influence in the Middle East. Undoubtedly this stance, which oversimplified the Middle East problem as a contest between the United States and the USSR, created three difficult challenges. First, the Israelis seemed to have come to the conclusion that the United States would approve aggressive actions they decided to take to protect themselves and to remove the Palestine Liberation Organization from any credible role in the area. Second, Palestinians and their allies reasonably came to believe that the United States was not a disinterested middleman but rather pro-Israeli. Third, the overlay of a competitive East-West alliance system seemed to reject a substantive role for the United Nations, and in fact ignored long-standing UN prescriptions for the area.

Problems began to develop when the Israeli government, led by the conservative Likud party, annexed the Golan Heights in December 1981, despite a protest by the United States. Taken from Syria during the Six Day War of 1967, the Golan was considered by most Arab states to have been included in UN resolution 242, which insisted on the return of conquered land. In the meantime, in conversations with their American counterparts, Israeli officials made no secret of their intention to invade Lebanon in order to quell the guerrilla attacks emanating from the southern region of that country, and to neutralize the PLO, whose headquarters were in Beirut. At the funeral of the Egyptian president Anwar Sadat in the fall of 1981, for example, Prime Minister Begin explicitly informed the secretary of state of plans to strike at Lebanon. Haig answered that if Israel did so "you're on your own," and the topic was dropped.[130] In May 1982, Israel's defense minister, Ariel Sharon, visiting the State Department, sketched for Haig a military campaign that would extend all the way to Beirut. Israeli forces would join with the Phalange, a Christian militia group fighting Islamic opponents and PLO guerrillas, to control and dominate the country's capital city;[131] in the event, the Phalange-Israeli combination would destroy the PLO's elaborate infrastructure. This is precisely what Sharon soon attempted to

---

[130] Haig, *Caveat*, 326–327.

[131] Ibid., 335.

do, probably believing that the United States had given him a "green light" to proceed.[132]

Thus, on June 6, 1982, following initial skirmishes of the previous day, Israel—"goaded," according to Haig, "by bombardment of her northern settlements by Palestinian gunners and by terrorist attack...at home"—launched a full-scale invasion of Lebanon and headed to Beirut to rout the Palestinians.[133] Within days, Israeli forces had advanced to the outskirts of Beirut and occupied most of the southern half of the country.

As the invasion ensued, the president was in Europe for meetings with the G-7 (the seven most affluent industrial nations). He made a brief statement from France, urging "restraint on all parties in Lebanon."[134] Earlier, on June 5, Ambassador Kirkpatrick had voted with the unanimous majority for UN Security Council Resolution 508, calling for an immediate cease-fire; the next day she did the same for Resolution 509, demanding that "Israel withdraw all its military forces forthwith and unconditionally to the internationally recognized boundaries of Lebanon."[135] Suddenly, Washington had realized the value of the United Nations, or at least of the Security Council. And by mid-June, the United States supported, first, Resolution 511, extending the mandate of the UN Interim Force in Lebanon through the middle of August; and, second, Resolution 512, calling on all parties to respect the rights of civilians and support the humanitarian work of the UN Relief and Works Agency for Palestinian refugees.[136] Withdrawal and respect for the rights of civilians—demands which the Israelis would resist—became the focus of Israeli-U.S. tension in coming days and, along with a change in the leadership of the State Department, gradually worked a delicate change in Washington's attitude toward the Middle East.

But in the interim, confusion seemed to be the mode of operation in the crisis. Haig, at a press conference in New York on June 19, demanded

---

[132] See the coverage in the *New York Times* for July 1, 1982, and particularly the opening question and answer of the president's press conference, at page 14.

[133] Haig, *Caveat*, 317.

[134] June 6, 1982, *PPP, 1982*, I, 732–733.

[135] *YUN, 1982*, 450.

[136] Ibid., 450–451.

that all "foreign forces" leave Lebanon,[137] a demand well beyond the UN resolutions, which named only Israel. The implication of Haig's remarks was that Washington wanted the PLO and Syria out as well. This, of course, was the very reason the Israelis said they had invaded in the first place. Then, Haig, with the president's approval, instructed Kirkpatrick to veto any resolution in the United Nations that (1) called on Israel alone to withdraw and (2) imposed sanctions on Israel for not withdrawing.[138]

The seeming confusion derived in part from the president's mind-set regarding the Middle East. Unlike Carter, who studied the situation with student-like fervor, Mr. Reagan, in this as in many things, had views that were much simpler, almost generic. Even long after the events, as he composed his memoirs, Reagan revealed thinking that must have affected his policy-makers. His perceptions deserve a closer look. In the memoirs, he explained the Lebanese situation in the following way. First, Israel had long been harassed with "hit and run" attacks across "its" borders by "PLO terrorists." Second, there was, Reagan believed, legitimate concern about the presence in Lebanon of Syrian forces fighting the Phalange, which he approvingly referred to as a "Christian militia." Israel, a small country, "surrounded by enemies," and unduly pressured by the international community to make concessions, had always to be cognizant that "without the West Bank, Israel was so narrow in places that a cannon shot could be fired all the way across the country." Even more ominously, "the Soviet Union was eager to exploit any opportunity to expand its influence" in the Middle East, and it must be stopped. The other enemies in the area, ripe for alliance with the Soviets, were the "Palestinian extremists" and the "radical Muslim fundamentalists."[139] Opponents to be confronted were, then, "extremist" Palestinians, "fundamentalist" Muslims, and the Soviet Union. Surely it is not unfair to summarize the president's overall concept as the simplest combination of the views of (1) the Likud party, (2) conservative Christians who come close to seeing the Middle East in apocalyptic, crusader-like terms, and (3) hard-line cold warriors. Within that framework, the United Nations must have seemed like an adversary. And to resolve any of the difficulties in the Middle East by trying to

---

[137] Haig, *Caveat*, 343.

[138] Ibid., and see *YUN, 1982*, 451.

[139] Reagan, *American Life*, 412, 414–415, 418.

redress the grievances Mr. Reagan suggested in the above remarks would have required a shift from the policy pursued by Carter, and, frankly, from the policy ultimately pursued by his own State Department.

As in many things in the 1980s, Mr. Reagan's initial, instinctual reading of the world faded in the face of events and new advisers. This appears to have happened in regard to the Middle East. First, and crucially, for a host of reasons Haig resigned during the crisis. He was gone by June 25, 1982, and was replaced by George Shultz, whose perspective on the Middle East was, to say the least, different. But tragedy was to strike before a newer policy could offer any evidence of success.

In early June, Shultz had phoned Reagan's chief of staff, William Clark, to voice his serious concerns over the invasion. When he came into the administration in the summer of 1982, he found an unappetizing situation. He was particularly worried that Ambassador Kirkpatrick's ideas on the Lebanese incursion had won out in the White House. Kirkpatrick, according to Shultz, welcomed the "deathbed confession of the PLO," and urged that the United States leave the Israeli forces alone in Lebanon and "let the military drama play out," a view right in line with the Likud.[140] Kirkpatrick's anti-Palestinian position, with which the president agreed—at least at first—boiled up in an irate rejection of a French-British proposal in the United Nations to revise Resolution 242 to recognize the "legitimate rights of the Palestinian people" including their right of "self-determination,"[141] even though very similar language had been used in the Camp David accords.

Against this background it is necessary to say that Shultz, though in no way a proponent of the PLO, saw any resolution of the Middle East problem as impossible unless it dealt with the grievances of the Palestinians. In this respect, he deviated from most of the president's original advisers and, indeed, from the sentiments of the president himself. As a consequence, Shultz began the torturous work of seeking Israel's withdrawal from Beirut and the simultaneous withdrawal of an intact PLO. Shultz and his special envoy in Lebanon, Philip Habib, worked out a plan for the PLO to evacuate the capital city under the protection of a multinational force made up of French, Italian, and

---

[140] Shultz, *Turmoil and Triumph*, 48.

[141] Ibid., 51.

American marines. In late August, the PLO left, and then the multinational force withdrew. On September 1, the president made a major announcement, articulating a new Middle East policy that had the clear imprint of his new secretary of state. He proposed a formula of "peace in exchange for territory," with Israel giving up the West Bank, which would become a Palestinian "homeland" to be confederated with Jordan.[142] For the first time an American proposal struck a positive chord with the Arab world, which endorsed the Reagan's autonomy plan at the Fez conference as a good first step. The Israeli government, however, rejected it outright.

Shultz continued to pursue his plans. But before he could accomplish any aims, disaster hit Lebanon again. Bashir Gemayal, the Phalange leader who had just been elected president, was assassinated. Meantime, Israeli forces had not left, and by mid-September they had occupied Muslim West Beirut. With their Phalange allies, the Israelis had earlier hoped to liquidate the PLO before it could leave town, but Yasir Arafat and his followers were gone, assured that the Palestinians remaining behind would be protected by the multinational forces. The latter, however, were withdrawn shortly after the PLO's departure. Now the Phalange militia entered two Palestinian refugee camps in the area of Beirut occupied by their Israeli allies and conducted a bloody massacre, killing many Palestinians in the camps. Shultz was sickened at the news[143] and arranged a return of the multinational force for an indefinite stay. In all of these actions the United States organized its efforts through direct negotiations with its allies. There was no thought of turning the matter over to an augmented UN peacekeeping force or to UN administration directly.

The returning marines were unpopular in Lebanon, particularly among Shiite Muslims and Syrians, who increasingly saw them as siding with the Maronite Christians. The situation was made more difficult because the United States never made explicitly clear what the purpose of its presence was, and it came to be more and more involved in the civil war that now raged. On April 18, 1983, a suicide bomb exploded at the American embassy in Beirut. Sixty-three people died, including seventeen Americans. The marines found themselves acting in ways that

---

[142] "A New Opportunity for Peace in the Middle East," September 1, 1982, U.S. Department of State, *Bureau of Public Affairs*, Current Policy No. 417.

[143] Shultz, *Turmoil and Triumph*, 104–105.

appeared to be aligned with the Christian militias in the expanding war, even shelling Muslim positions in the Shouf mountains outside of Beirut. On Sunday, October 23, a truck bearing a load of TNT backed into the U.S. marine barracks near the Beirut airport. The suicide bombers killed 241 marines and navy personnel as they slept. It was a disaster for the United States. Reagan was constrained to remove the remaining American marines early the next year. The United States Middle East policy was a shambles and would begin to recover only toward the end of the Reagan presidency.

Reagan and the World

While Reagan always insisted that he was "realistic" in foreign policy, he constantly enunciated unmistakably "idealist" beliefs about the world. Long after the president had dismissed Alexander Haig, he praised Haig for having forwarded "our new policy of realism and peace through strength." Realism, he said in a speech on January 16, 1984, meant that "we must start with a clear-eyed understanding of the world we live in."[144] Yet Reagan had been at the forefront in criticizing Henry Kissinger's conduct of diplomacy according to those very principles of realism. In fact, Reagan's many speeches on international affairs consistently expressed the straightforward view that the world would be a better place if everyone simply changed behavior and followed the path charted by the United States to bring about private enterprise and democratic rights. One of his favorite citations was a sermon by John Winthrop in 1630 declaring that the Puritan community in New England was a "city on a hill," commanding the moral heights above all other societies. Reagan undoubtedly saw Winthrop's sermon as the first enunciation of what others would call "American exceptionalism." Whenever the United States stood accused of being a bully in the world, Reagan could justify such behavior as the understandable action of a peculiar and morally sensitive nation, grounded in principles of the Christian faith, market economics, and American-defined democracy. The idea that the United States was distinct and exceptional, while at the

---

[144] Reagan, *American Life*, 361, 591.

same time having a mission to convert the world to our ways, was a theme never far from Reagan's lips.[145]

But, however elemental Reagan's public pronouncements often seemed, some mystification was created by his sometimes vitriolic hard-line expressions on the one hand and his geniality on the other. Here was a man who could say, regarding bombing raids in Vietnam in 1965, "We could pave the whole country and put parking stripes on it and still be home by Christmas,"[146] or joke into an open microphone prior to a public address that he had just ordered the bombing of the Soviet Union, which would soon be completely destroyed; yet he could demonstrate a most amiable presence before those who found his outlandish remarks disturbing, even menacing. UN Undersecretary-General Brian Urquhart, suitably dismissive of what he believed to be Reagan's pugnacious bearing toward the world, found it "absolutely impossible not to like Ronald Reagan."[147]

Reagan, who had joined the United World Federalists at the end of World War II, deplored the doctrine of "Mutual Assured Destruction" (MAD) that had developed over the years as a U.S. deterrent doctrine.[148] His refusal to see any merit in MAD probably underlay, ironically, both his proposed SDI and his eventual expeditious acceptance of disarmament proposals once they came seriously from Mikhail Gorbachev. According to his biographer Lou Cannon, Reagan's uncomplicated ideas about world cooperation may have been inspired by some of his favorite movies. Indeed, one of these, the science fiction film *The Day the Earth Stood Still* (1951), in which the peoples of the world must cooperate in order to defy a Martian attack, was one of Reagan's favorites. On occasion, the president would pencil in thoughts from the film that he wished to add to speeches crafted by others. Usually, he was persuaded to omit these emendations, but, according to Cannon, his

---

[145] See, for example, "Remarks at a Luncheon of the World Affairs Council of Philadelphia," October 15, 1981, *PPP, 1981*, 937–944, especially at page 938; the president's statement at the First Plenary Session in Cancun, October 22, 1981, Ibid., 980–982; and his various speeches before the United Nations, cited throughout this chapter.

[146] Lou Cannon, *President Reagan: The Role of a Lifetime* (New York: Simon and Schuster, 1991), 197.

[147] Urquhart, *A Life*, 357.

[148] Cannon, *Reagan*, 62.

advisers reluctantly yielded when he added a section from the alien invasion story of the movie to his UN speech in 1987. "In our obsession with antagonisms of the moment," he intoned, "we often forget how much unites all the members of humanity. Perhaps we need some outside, universal threat to make us recognize this common bond. I occasionally think how quickly our differences worldwide would vanish if we were facing an alien threat from outside this world. And yet, I ask you, is not an alien force already among us? What could be more alien to the universal aspirations of our peoples than war and the threat of war?" According to Cannon, this speech reveals "Reagan at his most idealistic."[149]

To "reckon with Reagan,"[150] then, especially in the realm of foreign affairs, poses challenges to the student of international relations and of the United Nations. If, as we must surmise, Reagan was swayed by advisers while at the same time retaining a core, if simple, set of "idealistic" values, then the advisers become as important as the president in the evaluation of the administration's foreign policy. With this in mind, we are struck with the fact that there were fully six successive, and often quite different, national security advisers during Reagan's eight-year term: Richard Allen, William Clark, Robert McFarlane, John Poindexter, Frank Carlucci, and finally Colin Powell. Likewise noticeable was the turnover in chiefs of staff, from James Baker to Donald Regan (Regan started as treasury secretary and he and Baker, privately between themselves, decided to switch jobs and then told the compliant president) to the former senator Howard Baker (although the assistant chief of staff, Michael Deaver, may have been as influential as anyone else). All this would suggest a bewildering inconsistency in the direction of foreign affairs; and, indeed, for some critics, that was precisely the nature of Reagan's foreign policy—inconsistency. But two considerations intervene for the historian; one, the occasional leadership initiatives of the president; and, two—perhaps more important—the doggedness of George Shultz.

The president appears to have taken charge of one difficulty during the unsettling days of Israel's invasion of Lebanon—he fired Secretary of

---

[149] Ibid., 61–64. The full text of the speech to the United Nations in 1987 can be found in *PPP, 1987*, 1058–1063.

[150] The phrase is Michael Schaller's. See his *Reckoning with Reagan; America and Its President in the 1980s* (New York: Oxford University Press, 1992).

State Haig. Haig's problems were many. For one, he did not get along with the White House staff, which he felt always ignored him. More important was his behavior in the immediate aftermath of the assassination attempt on the president in the spring of 1981. At a press conference while the president was in the hospital, Haig had announced, "As of now, I am in control here, in the White House."[151] The president, and most of his staff, found Haig's actions at this time unacceptable. More important, however, was that the president and Haig simply did not see eye to eye on certain matters. Haig was initially upset that Reagan had named Vice President Bush as chair of a special group to coordinate with the NSC in managing international crises. He demonstrated a vocal anger at and jealousy of the White House staff and, according to the president, carried turf battles "too far." The president found that Haig, while he was secretary of state, did not want anyone else, including Reagan himself, to influence foreign policy. By the time Reagan fired Haig, he had noted in his diary that "the only disagreement was over whether I made policy or the Secretary of State did."[152] The public statements of June 25, 1982, announcing the removal of Haig, lacked the cordiality of the numerous other dismissals of the Reagan years. Haig incourteously noted in a public letter to the president: "In recent months it has become clear to me that the foreign policy on which we embarked together was shifting from that careful course which we had laid out." The president, in turn, curtly announced Haig's resignation and the appointment of George Shultz.[153] Shultz immediately set out to reenergize and reformulate the president's approach to the world, and in his quest he would elevate the position of the United Nations.

Shultz had been mentioned as a possible secretary of state following Reagan's election in November 1980. But the mention probably came from pundits associated with the more international wing of a party now apparently on the outs with the new and more conservative Reagan. Thus, Haig's appointment had originally appeared understandable. Shultz came to the White House's attention again when he phoned Chief of Staff William Clark to voice concern over Israel's invasion of Lebanon

---

[151] Haig, *Caveat*, 160; Haig went on to say, however, "pending return of the vice president."

[152] Reagan, *American Life*, 255, 271, 361–362.

[153] *PPP, 1982*, I, 819–820.

in early June, 1982. At the time, Shultz was president of Bechtel Corporation, a multinational firm with extensive international connections, including some in the Arab world. This alone made him suspect to several conservative, nationalist Republicans, as well as to some liberal, pro-Israeli Democrats. Shultz came from a privileged background: he was born in midtown Manhattan; his father had worked on the New York Stock Exchange and had taken care that his son receive the most prestigious education, studying at Princeton for a bachelor's degree and finishing up a Ph.D. in economics at the Massachusetts Institute of Technology. In between, Shultz served as a marine in the Second World War. He went on to become a member of Eisenhower's Council of Economic Advisers and a dean at the University of Chicago, and to hold three cabinet posts under Richard Nixon.[154] By most measures, Shultz was the definition of what political sociologists sometimes call the "power elite" in America.

The new secretary of state was confirmed by the Senate on July 14, after extensive testimony before the Senate Foreign Relations Committee, where he revealed a more measured approach to the Middle East than had been obvious during the summer's crisis there. He made clear his view that while Israel's vital security must be maintained, other equally important aspects of the crisis must be addressed by the United States, including the political aspirations of the Palestinians, which had to be met, and the concerns of the Arab nations in the region. Finally, he insisted that any resolution to the crisis would have to win the endorsement of the international community.[155]

At first, Shultz's approach to the Middle East proved ineffective. As we have seen above, by 1984 U.S. troops had been compelled to leave Lebanon, and Reagan's initiative of September 1, 1982 (initiated by Shultz), had gone nowhere. Shultz would return to the Middle East conundrum with more success at the close of the Reagan years.

In the meantime, he turned to other matters, including efforts to abate the revived cold war and to establish a constructive dialogue between Washington and Moscow. The most heartening development, prior to the ascendancy of Mikhail Gorbachev, took place with the United Nations as serviceable backdrop. The year was 1984, and it did

---

[154] Shultz, *Turmoil and Triumph*, 20–27.

[155] Extensive excerpts from Shultz's testimony can be found in *New York Times*, July 14, 1982, A1, 8.

not seem promising; there was a presidential election in the United States and the Soviets had snubbed the Los Angeles Olympics, leading the Eastern bloc in a boycott. But, using third parties, Foreign Minister Andrei Gromyko let Shultz know that he was interested in meeting the president.[156] Shultz, who was receptive, told Reagan of the gesture in mid-August, 1984. According to one insider, conservatives in the administration "were scared to death at what Reagan might do" if he met with Gromyko.[157] At a gathering of the National Security Council on September 18, Shultz suggested that Gromyko be invited to Washington and that the administration consider offering to pursue an actual weapons agreement. Weinberger balked and told the president he should be tough and talk to the foreign minister from an assured position of strength. Reagan "gently but firmly put the Secretary of Defense in his place," and, to Shultz's satisfaction, told the assembled advisers: "We must follow the Gromyko meeting with specifics and make concessions."[158]

The UN General Assembly session of 1984 offered an opportunity to bring about the rendezvous. Gromyko usually showed up at the opening session. With this in mind, Reagan, following consultations with Shultz, issued an invitation for the foreign minister to follow up his appearance in New York with a visit to the White House. The president then went to work on his own speech for the General Assembly.[159] In the GA's Great Hall on September 24, the president made a significant departure in manner and theme from his earlier UN addresses. Shultz called it "constructive, even conciliatory."[160] While half the speech was given over to the usual benign laundry list of U.S. positions in much of the world, the more spirited second half dealt with Soviet-American relations. And, in contrast to prior remarks, the president had "not a word of criticism for the Soviet Union."[161] He mentioned several areas of cooperation, or proposed cooperation, including institutionalizing

---

[156] Shultz, *Turmoil and Triumph*, 480–481.

[157] Gates, *From the Shadows*, 324.

[158] These quotations are from notes taken by Robert Gates, who was in attendance at the meeting. Ibid., 325.

[159] Reagan, *American Life*, 603–605.

[160] Shultz, *Turmoil and Triumph*, 482.

[161] Ibid.

regular ministerial or cabinet-level meetings on a "whole agenda of issues" and agreeing to reduce weapons stockpiles. He promised to increase grain available for purchase by the USSR. "As I stand here and look out from this podium," the president said, "I can see the representative for the Soviet Union—not far from the representative of the United States....There's not a great distance between us." Satisfied, even exultant, he concluded his address with the idealistic words of Thomas Paine: "We have it in our power to begin the world over again."[162]

Reagan had used the United Nations to set the tone for his meeting with Gromyko, scheduled for four days later, September 28. He evinced an uncommon interest and spent time preparing for this encounter, the first on such a high level since the Soviets had invaded Afghanistan in 1979. The meeting was cordial and was followed up with Gromyko's visit to the State Department the next day. Then, on November 22, 1984, both countries announced that Shultz would meet with Gromyko in Geneva in early January for wide-ranging discussions. The ice, frozen for some four years, was breaking. Within half a year it would proceed to melt with the coming of Mikhail Gorbachev. But, in the meantime, dark clouds were circling the Reagan administration, and the subsequent downpour would seriously divert attention from international matters.

Iran-Contra

Secretary of State Shultz, as we have seen, began his career in the State Department faced with a problem in the Middle East that he did not relish. Similarly, he found that "Central American policy was a swamp."[163] Little could he realize in 1982 how the two regions would be star-crossed and would involve the Reagan administration, and the country, in a damaging scandal.

On November 3, 1986, *Al Siraa*, an Arab-language magazine in Beirut, broke a story that the United States had negotiated an arms-for-hostages deal with Iran. Reagan, of course, had denounced Iran during the election campaign of 1980. Moreover, by federal law (the Arms Export Control Act), the United States was precluded from providing any weaponry to Iran. Finally, as Shultz noted in his memoirs, this

---

[162] "Address to the 39th Session of the UN General Assembly," *PPP, 1984*, II, 1355–1361. For the cited quotes, see pages 1359–1361.

[163] Shultz, *Turmoil and Triumph*, 322.

"massive, secret White House operation" was "totally" contrary to the long-standing U.S. policy of resisting terrorism.[164]

Al Siraa revealed that Robert McFarlane, former NSC chief, and others, including Colonel Oliver North of the NSC, had clandestinely traveled to Teheran in September of 1986 to expedite the deal. The operation, apparently the brainchild of CIA Director William Casey, McFarlane, and North, arranged for the United States to sell arms secretly to Iran, which was locked in a brutal war with its neighbor, Iraq. In exchange, the Iranians were supposed to use their influence to help free American hostages held by pro-Iranian terrorists in Lebanon. Only one hostage was ever released; the others were detained throughout this episode. The profits generated by these arms sales were to be diverted as military aid for the Contras, far away in Nicaragua. That diversion, too, was illegal, violating the Boland Amendment, a congressional law. The diversion was also unconstitutional, since the entire enterprise bypassed the right of Congress to appropriate funds and was carried out apart from even the normal channels of foreign policy decision-making, which would typically include the constitutional officers of the State Department and the Defense Department.

Although the arms-for-hostages deal had been discussed (and resisted) at high levels in the administration, the diversion of funds to the Contras was apparently the scheme of Colonel North.[165] When the media found out about the affair, North shredded hundreds of documents but was unable to destroy all of them, and one document linked the White House to the plan. A special presidential commission, the Tower Commission (named for the former senator John Tower), issued a report highly critical of Reagan's handling of the affair; a special prosecutor (Lawrence Walsh) brought several indictments; and Congress conducted a lengthy investigation in the summer of 1987. President

---

[164] Ibid., 789.

[165] Reagan's diary entry for December 7, 1985, notes a discussion about arms for hostages. The president says that Shultz, Weinberger, and Regan opposed the plan and pointed out that it was illegal, but then says that the plan "apparently is going ahead." The president also acknowledged that the Israelis would be middlemen in the arms exchange. Earlier, Reagan had authorized Casey to undertake a program of covert operations to help the Contras, who, the president insisted, were resisting the export of Marxist revolution in the hemisphere. Reagan, *American Life*, 510, 474. North, at least, took these discussions and events to indicate that the president fully knew of and supported his plans.

Reagan insisted that he remembered little of this; Colonel North, in his autobiography, insists that "President Reagan knew everything."[166] Although there were clear and serious violations of law and of the Constitution, no somber call for impeachment was heard in the land. Colonel North faced charges in court and was subsequently convicted, but his sentence was suspended as a consequence of his earlier immunized testimony before Congress.[167]

Gorbachev

Despite the gravity of the Iran-Contra scandal, Reagan left office as one of the most popular presidents in history.[168] If he surfaced from scandal so unscathed, it may have had as much to do with the rise of Mikhail Gorbachev as with anything. While there is a conservative refrain insisting that Reagan alone planned and accomplished the end of the cold war,[169] one has some difficulty imagining the dramatic international events of the late 1980s without according considerable weight to the strategy, skill, and determination of Gorbachev. Archie Brown, who has done a careful study of the Reagan-Gorbachev period, points out that Reagan's early policy of harshness actually hardened the Soviet Union. Moreover, it was not Reagan who brought Gorbachev to power, but rather internal Soviet politics; and, in the end, Brown persuades, the "Gorbachev factor" was much more decisive in ending the cold war.[170]

As we noted earlier, critics had pointed out that, for his entire first term, Reagan was the only president in half a century not to meet with

---

[166] Oliver North, with William Novak, *Under Fire: An American Story* (New York: HarperCollins, 1991), 12.

[167] A comprehensive study of the Iran-Contra scandal is Theodore Draper, *A Very Thin Line: The Iran-Contra Affairs* (New York: Hill and Wang, 1991). See also Lawrence E. Walsh, *Iran-Contra: The Final Report* (New York: Random House, 1994), and *The Tower Commission Report* (New York: Random House, 1987).

[168] Reagan's approval rating at the end of his term was 63 percent, exceeded only by Franklin Roosevelt's 68 percent. Adriana Bosch, *Reagan: An American Story* (New York: TV Books, 1998), 332.

[169] Peter Schweizer, *Victory: The Reagan Administration's Secret Strategy That Hastened the Collapse of the Soviet Union* (New York: Atlantic Monthly Press, 1994).

[170] Archie Brown, *The Gorbachev Factor* (New York: Oxford University Press, 1996), 227–228.

his Soviet counterpart. But, in fairness, as the president once said, it was not easy to plan meetings when Soviet leaders were dying off at such a rapid pace. The dour President Leonid Brezhnev, who had headed the USSR for almost two decades, died in 1982. He was followed briefly by Yuri Andropov, dead by 1984; and then by Konstantin Chernenko, who was gone by the spring of 1985. It was at this point that a much younger man, Gorbachev, ascended to the position of party leader.

Gorbachev was a graduate of the law program at Moscow State University. On a fast track, he had joined the Communist Party at the age of twenty-one; and in 1980, at only forty-nine, he had become a full member of the Politburo. He had traveled more widely than any of his immediate predecessors, leading delegations to Canada in 1983 and Great Britain in 1984, where he impressed Western leaders. His cosmopolitanism was aided by the presence of his wife, Raisa, a professor of philosophy at Moscow State University. Upon his rise to the highest position in the USSR, Gorbachev initiated two sweeping reform programs: *glasnost* ("openness") encouraged full discussion and debate about virtually every conceivable element of Soviet public policy and history; and *perestroika* was a movement to reform the Soviet economy and make it more effective. Among his most important appointments was his choice of a reformer, the Western-oriented Edvard Shevardnadze, as foreign minister. Also, Gorbachev opened himself up to foreign correspondents in ways unheard of for a Soviet leader.

Time magazine published a lengthy interview with him in early September, 1985. Here, Gorbachev urged an end to the "vicious circle" of arms buildups and announced a Soviet moratorium on nuclear explosions. He asked that the United States join in a "complete ban on nuclear tests" and agree to provisions for the "prevention of an arms race in space." To the question whether his proposals were mere "propaganda," he responded: "Then you Americans could take revenge by doing likewise. You could deal us yet another propaganda blow, say, by suspending the development of one of your new strategic missiles. And we would respond with the same kind of 'propaganda.' And so on and so forth." Gorbachev's rejoinder to the oft-cited contention that Reagan had spent so much that the Soviets, unable to do the same, simply had to give in reflected further his wry and accessible demeanor, and his awareness of the excessive American budget deficit: "We would prefer to use every ruble that today goes for defense to meet civilian, peaceful needs. As I understand, you in the U.S. could also make better use of the money consumed nowadays by arms production."[171]

Gorbachev charmed the world. Prime Minister Margaret Thatcher of Great Britain found him to be a "man we can work with." Even Jeane Kirkpatrick was won over, seeing Gorbachev as a "man of history." According to Shultz, "Gorbachev impressed everyone, and the result was a certain Gorbachev euphoria in the air."[172] Shultz himself was not immune. Once, after CIA Deputy Director Robert Gates gave a pessimistic speech about Gorbachev's prospects at home, Shultz phoned him, irate. The Secretary may even have asked the president to dismiss Gates for that *faux pas*.[173] Gorbachev reciprocated Shultz's respect. He found Reagan's views sometimes "bizarre," and, because of the president's "dislike for detail" agreed to let Shevardnadze and Shultz work things out in more extensive discussions. Gorbachev came to see Shultz as someone who "genuinely wanted to sustain the dialogue...a serious man of sound political judgment...[and] a far-seeing person."[174]

At the same time there was a reciprocal appeal between the two major world leaders. Reagan would later write, "It's clear that there was a chemistry between Gorbachev and me that produced something very close to a friendship."[175] The two met officially five times, exceeding by far the encounters by any of their predecessors. These included the summits in Geneva (November 1985), Reykjavik (October 1986), Washington (December 1987), Moscow (June 1988), and Governor's Island, New York (December 1988). Two additional meetings followed Reagan's retirement: in June 1990 at the birthplace of the United Nations in San Francisco, and in Moscow in September 1990. About twenty letters between the two were exchanged in the last three and a half years of the Reagan's presidency, and Reagan warmly cites lengthy chunks of this correspondence in sections of his autobiography.

A high-water mark of sorts was reached late in Reagan's second term, when Gorbachev came to the United Nations to give one of his most important speeches. On December 7, 1988, Gorbachev met Reagan

---

[171] *Time* (September 9, 1985): 23, 25.

[172] Shultz, *Turmoil and Triumph*, 532.

[173] Gates, *From the Shadows*, 443–444.

[174] Mikhail Gorbachev, *Memoirs* (New York: Doubleday, 1995), 407, 409, 440.

[175] Reagan, *American Life*, 707.

on Governor's Island in New York Harbor. It was the last official summit between the two leaders. Following it, the Russian leader addressed a full gathering of the United Nations, not far away, on the larger island of Manhattan. Secretary Shultz was there, alternately mesmerized and pleased by the novel substance of the speech (there was no mention of Marx, for example) and by the universal accord which greeted the speaker.[176]

Gorbachev had long thought that "it was high time to make use of the opportunities provided by this universal organization."[177] In his address in the General Assembly hall, Gorbachev expressed respect "for the United Nations Organization, which is increasingly manifesting itself as a unique international centre serving the cause of peace and security." He saw the United Nations as crucial for twenty-first-century advances in peacekeeping, development, environmental reform, disarmament, and moving from an "armaments economy" to a "disarmament economy." His other important themes were democracy, human rights, and ending the arms race. He insisted that no society, given modern technology, can be "closed." The world economy, he said, "is becoming a single entity." Then, in a memorable gesture, he rejected denying any nation "the freedom of choice, regardless of the pretext or the verbal guise in which it is cloaked....Freedom of choice is a universal principle. It knows no exceptions."[178] Archie Brown has said that this last statement at the United Nations "paved the way for the independence of the countries of Eastern Europe."[179]

The end of the cold war became obvious with the peaceful liberation of Eastern Europe. The benefits accruing from the cold war's demise were many, including cooperation between Washington and Moscow in addressing some of the most intractable problems in the world. And the United Nations, as Gorbachev hoped, proved more often than not to be the forum for that cooperation.

---

[176] Shultz, *Turmoil and Triumph*, 1106–1107.

[177] Gorbachev, *Memoirs*, 442.

[178] Gorbachev, *Address to the United Nations, New York, December 7, 1988* (Moscow: Novosti Press Agency Publishing House, 1988), 3, 5, 10, 27.

[179] Brown, *The Gorbachev Factor*, 307.

Reagan and the UN: Phase Two

Meantime, the Iran-Contra scandal had played an ironic role as a catalyst in the growing cordiality of the two superpowers. Partly as a consequence of the scandal, those advisers most hostile to the Soviet Union were gone or replaced. By 1987 William Casey was dead, felled by a brain tumor; gone, too, were John Poindexter from the NSC and Donald Regan from the White House staff. Kirkpatrick and Haig had long been out of the picture. Vernon Walters replaced Kirkpatrick at the United Nations in the spring of 1985. Left now were Howard Baker as chief of staff; William Webster at the CIA; Frank Carlucci, heading the NSC and then taking over the Defense Department from Weinberger; and Colin Powell, following Carlucci as NSC chief. These were no hard-liners, but moderates. With them in place, Shultz moved into the ascendancy in foreign affairs. There was a new acceptance of the notion that the United Nations might be a useful instrument for defusing conflicts in the Middle East, Asia, and Africa. Results were quick to come.

The Iran-Iraq war had been going on for almost a decade, following the Iraqi's aggression in 1979. Death rates and carnage were high, particularly for the Iranians, and neither side seemed on the verge of victory. It became clear with the administration of Gorbachev in Moscow that there could be cooperation among the major powers in addressing the crisis in the Gulf. Shultz convinced Reagan that the United States should work through the United Nations to take advantage of the cooperative spirit. In July 1987, Shultz traveled to New York for informal discussions with Secretary-General Javier Perez de Cuellar and the representatives of the permanent members of the Security Council. An intense three-hour meeting revealed a common concern for the crisis and a shared commitment to resolve it. That very day, July 20, the Security Council unanimously passed Resolution 598, calling for a cease-fire and the withdrawal of belligerents to internationally recognized borders, and deploring the bombing of civilian populations. It also threatened unspecified retaliation against the combatants if they did not agree to a cease-fire. As Shultz noted approvingly, the resolution was adopted under the authority of Articles 39 and 40 of Chapter VII, "the UN Charter's most powerful provision."[180] Iran, angry that the international community had not found Iraq to be the aggressor in the war, criticized

---

[180] Shultz, *Turmoil and Triumph*, 931–932.

the resolution, which nonetheless contained an acknowledgment of Iran's concerns in Operative Clause 6, which authorized the secretary-general to consult with both belligerents in about convoking an impartial body to determine the responsibility for the conflict.[181] Teheran, now interested, invited Perez de Cuellar to visit in mid-September and explain Resolution 598. Within days, Iran informed the secretary-general that it would act within the "framework" of 598. Yet the war dragged on for almost a year. Finally, both sides acceded to a UN settlement, and on August 9, 1988, again by unanimous vote, the Security Council approved Resolution 619, setting up a UN Iran-Iraq Military Observer Group to implement the cease-fire and withdrawal. By August 20, UN observers were in place to monitor the now effected cease-fire.[182] Even crusty Caspar Weinberger saw these developments as an impressive success for the United Nations.[183]

A more publicized compact, this one between the Soviet Union and the United States, came to fruition on the following December 8. Gorbachev came to Washington to sign the carefully crafted Intermediate Nuclear Forces agreement, which provided for the dismantling of tactical nuclear weapons deployed by both sides. This treaty, the first real "disarmament" agreement in the twentieth century since the Washington Naval Conference of 1921–1922, was opposed by several conservative Republicans, including Senator Dan Quayle and Senator Jesse Helms, who feared the denuclearization of Europe. But the president stuck with it, signed the treaty in a highly publicized session with Gorbachev, and then guided it through Senate approval the following spring.[184] Reagan noted in his memoirs his approval of Gorbachev's hopeful remark: "May December 8, 1987, become a date that will be inscribed in the history books."[185]

The situation in Afghanistan had exacerbated U.S.-Soviet relations since late 1979, when Brezhnev had authorized an invasion of the country. The Soviets and their clients were trying to subdue the country,

---

[181] *YUN, 1987,* 223.

[182] *YUN, 1988,* 194–195.

[183] Casper Weinberger, *Fighting for Peace; Seven Critical Years in the Pentagon* (New York: Warren, 1990), 399, 424.

[184] Cannon, *Reagan,* 778–779.

[185] Reagan, *American Life,* 699.

while *mujahidin* rebels, stationed in friendly Pakistan and supplied by the Americans, carried on the sanguinary resistance. Gorbachev had indicated a sincere desire to withdraw and to resolve the problem, and had written an article in *Pravda* in 1987 recommending that the United Nations might help bring disengagement and a cease-fire, using the permanent members of the Security Council as guarantors of the cease-fire. Meantime, Diego Cordovez, an assistant to Secretary-General Perez de Cuellar, had worked quietly but effectively to mediate the conflict and to find ways the United Nations could facilitate removal of Soviet troops.[186]

Shultz appreciated and supported the work of the United Nations in seeking to provide a means for a diplomatic resolution. He welcomed Gorbachev's announcement, in early February 1988, that Moscow would begin a withdrawal from Afghanistan by the following May and complete it within ten months. But Gorbachev also asked that the United Nations sponsor peace talks between Pakistan and the Soviet-influenced Afghani regime, so as to avoid further bloodshed once Soviet troops were gone. Portentously, Foreign Minister Shevardnadze, who also favored disengagement, had once told Shultz of the USSR's worries: "A neutral, nonaligned Afghanistan is one thing, a reactionary fundamentalist Islamic regime is something else."[187]

At the Palais des Nations in Geneva, a four-part agreement was reached on April 14, 1988. Afghanistan and Pakistan were the principal signatories, with the United States and the USSR becoming guarantors of the pact. The Soviets began their withdrawal and completed it by the following February. Some fifty UN observers, under the UN Good Offices Mission in Afghanistan and Pakistan, monitored and verified the withdrawal.[188]

The newfound friendship between Moscow and Washington helped as well in ushering in a successful solution to an old problem in southern Africa. By late summer, 1988, all parties consented to simultaneous withdrawals of forces by Cuba and South Africa from, respectively, Angola and Namibia. This opened the way for full implementation of Security Council Resolution 435, originally passed during the Carter

---

[186] Karen A. Mingst and Margaret P. Karns, *The United Nations in the Post–Cold War Era* (Boulder, Colo.: Westview, 1995), 80–81.

[187] Shultz, *Turmoil and Triumph*, 987.

[188] *YUN, 1988*, 184–188; Mingst and Karns, *United Nations*, 81.

years. Now the resolution could go into effect and provide for a UN Angola Verification Mission and the placement of the United Nations Transition Assistance Group (UNTAG) in Namibia to help with the conversion to independence. In Geneva, in mid-November 1988, the Angola-Namibia accords were concluded; on December 22, Shultz represented the United States at the United Nations for the official signing of the historic accord, creating an independent Namibia.[189]

In the last days of the Reagan administration, the indefatigable secretary of state returned to the most stubborn of issues, the issue that had brought him into the government in 1982. In 1987 the *intifada* had begun in the West Bank and the Gaza Strip, areas heavily populated by Palestinians but controlled and administered by Israel. The intifada was a persistent, widely supported Palestinian uprising against Israeli occupation. It created a new situation. In June 1988, Bassim Abu Sharif, a close aide of Yasir Arafat's, circulated an essay in English, indicating the PLO's readiness to accept, and negotiate directly with, Israel.[190] Several Palestinian leaders in the West Bank and Gaza evinced support for Abu Sharif's statement. At the end of July, King Hussein announced that Jordan would cut all legal and administrative ties to the West Bank. There was, then, by late summer 1988, considerable and interesting activity around the Israeli-Palestinian issue, much of which seemed to suggest the possibility of positive movement. Added to this was the new friendliness between the Soviet Union and the United States, which made senseless any continuing interpretation of the Middle East problem as part of the cold war.

In the fall of 1988, the PLO representative at the United Nations, Zehdi Terzi, informed the Security Council that he would request a visa for Yasir Arafat to come to the annual meeting. By treaty with the United Nations, the United States had agreed not to block such visas unless a security risk was involved. At the same time, U.S. law forbade representatives of the PLO from visiting unless the secretary of state recommended an exception. Almost everyone told Shultz—seemingly under no political pressure now that George Bush had been elected and the Reagan team was virtually a lame duck—to accede to the visit. The CIA, the FBI, former presidents Carter and Ford, and even President-Elect Bush all said to go ahead. But on November 26, Shultz announced

---

[189] Mingst and Karns, *United Nations*, 82; Shultz, *Turmoil and Triumph*, 1127.

[190] The essay is in *New York Times*, June 22, 1988, Section I, 27.

his rejection of the request. Secretary-General Perez de Cuellar; the Pope; the incoming secretary of state, James Baker; and even conservative columnists like William F. Buckley, Jr., all criticized the decision. Those who were overjoyed were the Israeli government, Israeli lobbying groups in the country, and the pro-Israeli members of Congress. For them, Shultz was suddenly a trusted friend.

But what Shultz had done was a subtle and adroit finesse. He had neutralized opposition to any serious forward movement in the Israeli-Palestinian situation. With the most strident Israeli supporters now on his side, and completely cognizant of the significant momentum that had taken place since early summer, he now engineered a stunning démarche. On December 2, he contacted the Swedish ambassador to the United States. As it happened, Sweden was at that very moment hosting a meeting between the PLO and some prominent liberal American Jews, unsympathetic to the position of the Israeli government. Shultz told the ambassador that if the PLO wished to open dialogue with the United States, it would have to meet specific American conditions as outlined in a speech the Secretary had given in September. The Swedish ambassador, Count Wilhelm Wachtmeister, returned with a statement produced in Stockholm between Arafat and the Swedish foreign minister, Sten Andersson. Shultz told the ambassador that "without a doubt" the statement met all American conditions. Still, Shultz required that Arafat read and sign the statement in a public forum. Arafat did precisely that at Geneva on December 14. By this "official" proclamation of the Executive Committee of the Palestine Liberation Organization, the PLO declared that it was "prepared to negotiate with Israel...on the basis of UN resolutions 242 and 338," that it sought "to live in peace with Israel and other neighbors and to respect their right to exist in peace within secure and internationally recognized borders," and that it condemned "individual, group and State terrorism in all its forms, and will not resort to it."[191] The words were exactly those Shultz had demanded. Arafat was completely willing to accede, because he would achieve the preeminent goal of recognition by the United States.

Late in the afternoon of December 14, the president agreed to all that Shultz had done and authorized him to make a public statement announcing that Washington would now begin a dialogue with the PLO. Within a matter of days, Shultz had sustained a wide-ranging

---

[191] The document can be found in Shultz, *Turmoil and Triumph*, 1042.

condemnation for his refusal to allow Arafat to attend the United Nations in New York, only to announce to the world the astounding news that Washington now recognized, and would deal a face-to-face, with the PLO. The Middle Eastern challenge had come a long way from the desperate days of summer 1982.[192]

In fact, in the Persian Gulf, in arms negotiations, in Afghanistan, and in southern Africa, as well as in the Middle East, the world had come a long way since Reagan's inaugural. This in no way means that the world then, or in the near future, would verge on utopia. Indeed, in each area outlined just above, severe problems and challenges persisted. What seems clear is that the original cold war approach of the Reagan administration proved much less effective than the more multilateral, UN-linked methods of the late years. Bolstered by the historic appearance of Mikhail Gorbachev, moderates in the administration, led by Secretary Shultz, were able to make use of international organizations, chiefly the United Nations, to make at least some success. On the last pages of his memoirs, Shultz features his ready enchantment by Gorbachev at the United Nations in December 1988. Certainly he came to see the United Nations as the crucial setting for his most impressive accomplishments.

That Reagan would increasingly be influenced by his secretary of state and the other moderates around him may not be surprising. From his speech to the United Nations in 1984—which, as we have seen above, signaled a change in attitude—on through his final speech at the General Assembly in 1988, one can sense a rising appreciation of the United Nations. After his first year in office he did not miss a chance to speak to the UN, and his enthusiasm seemed to grow.

One of his very last official speeches was his address to the General Assembly on September 26, 1988. He told the audience that he found the United Nations "a better place...[and] so too, is the world." With that kind of genuine if theatrical affection only Reagan could mount, he acknowledged delegates from every corner of the world and concluded: "Thank you for your hospitality over the years. I bid you now farewell."[193]

---

[192] The full story is Ibid., 1033–1043; also of use is the coverage for these dates in the *New York Times*.

[193] *PPP, 1988*, II, 1224–1225.

6

The New Moralists

The United States has always played a twin role to the United Nations, first friend and first critic.

—*President Clinton*
September 1993

Marsaxlokk Bay on the east coast of Malta is normally a haven for affluent tourists vacationing on warm Mediterranean waters. It is not an idyllic place to be when strong storms blow in, as one did on December 2 and 3, 1989. The seas were whipping up sixteen-foot waves; the rain fell in torrents, driven by sixty-mile-per-hour winds. Through the downpour a visitor could make out two warships ominously at anchor in the bay. One was the American cruiser *Belknap*. The other was the USSR's *Slava*. Tugboats worked steadily to keep the two ships from crashing into each other under the dire conditions. On the *Belknap* George Bush waited unsuccessfully for the seas to calm in hope of making the 1,000-yard trip to the Soviet ship. In port Mikhail Gorbachev, aboard the Soviet cruise liner *Maxim Gorky*, prepared for his anticipated meetings with the president of the United States.

Such was the improbable setting for what would be the formal conclusion to the cold war. For the third time in the twentieth century, an era in international affairs had come to an end. Like Woodrow Wilson at Versailles and Franklin Roosevelt at Yalta, President Bush hoped to resolve any remaining issues between the major adversaries and to commence a new period in world politics. He called his trip to this island—where FDR had met with Winston Churchill forty-four years earlier—a "great and noble undertaking," thus recalling Dwight Eisenhower's words on D-Day as the invasion began. History was in the making.

In the end the two presidents were forced to meet several times on the *Gorky*. At the conclusion of the two-day meeting, while no grand alliance had been hammered out, the leaders spoke of "partnership" on a large number of world issues.[1] They also signed several bilateral agreements. The new world order had begun rather inauspiciously.

---

[1] Cohen, *Cambridge History*, 243.

The process of change had been under way for several years by the time George Bush and Mikhail Gorbachev met in Malta. The latter had transformed Soviet foreign policy since coming to power in March 1985. As a consequence of mounting difficulties in the USSR and in its client states, as well as the change in direction produced by Gorbachev's policy of *perestroika*, Soviet control over Poland, East Germany, Hungary, Romania, Bulgaria, and Czechoslovakia progressively disappeared in 1988 and 1989. Just three weeks before the Malta meeting, gleeful Germans tore down the Berlin Wall, the most dramatic symbol of the cold war. Independence movements gained strength in the non-Russian republics of the Soviet Union, most particularly in the Baltic States, leading to the dissolution of the USSR itself following an attempted coup in August 1991.

President Bush had the opportunity to mold U.S. foreign policy at a transforming moment in international affairs. He described it well, shortly after his return from Malta, to a joint session of Congress:

> There are singular moments in history, dates that divide all that goes before from all that comes after....1945 provided the common frame of reference, the compass points of the postwar era we've relied upon to understand ourselves. And that was our world, until now. The events of the year just ended, the Revolution of 1989, marks [sic] the beginning of a new era in world affairs.[2]

Bush envisaged the United States as a leading force in the new world because of the values it espoused. Asserting his version of American exceptionalism, he told Congress that the country was "not just a nation but an idea, alive in minds of people everywhere." He went on, "Our aim must be...a great and growing commonwealth of free nations."[3]

To organize his concept of how the United States might express its exceptionalism in the international arena, President Bush repeatedly returned to what he described as a "New World Order" (NWO). First employed in the face of Iraq's aggression against Kuwait in the summer of 1990, the term would come to encapsulate the administration's approach to world affairs. Meaning at a minimum a commitment to

---

[2]   State of the Union Address, 1990, *PPP, 1990*, I, 130.

[3]   Ibid., 130, 133.

maintain the traditional principles of international law and the UN Charter, the NWO meant, for Bush, a world "where diverse nations are drawn together in common cause to achieve the universal aspirations of mankind—peace and security, freedom and the rule of law."[4]

The New World Order was not a grand strategy equivalent to "containment," "détente," or the Carter, Reagan, and Truman doctrines. Rather, the president sought pragmatic opportunities to manage incremental change. While the effort to develop a new relationship with the USSR was paramount on the agenda, the Bush administration also sought, cautiously, to remold old alliances, international organizations, and friendly coalitions to the benefit of American interests. Instead of promoting a "vision" for the post–cold war period, Bush employed his extensive contacts, personal international friendships, and talented advisers to "cope" with individual challenges to the new order.[5]

Bush's new world order included an expanded role for the United Nations. From his first days in office, gone were the vilifications and condemnations of the institution that had been heard so often during President Reagan's administration. Bush, the first president to have served as the U.S. permanent representative to the United Nations, often noted the successes achieved by UN agencies. He lauded the organization for its fight against drug trafficking. In his first nationwide address, the president urged the Senate to ratify the UN Antidrug Convention. He also called for the creation of an international force to combat drug cartels. On the eve of his election he promised to strengthen the International Atomic Energy Agency (IAEA), given its record of successful performance. He strongly endorsed the Non-Proliferation Treaty (NPT).

President Bush's endorsement of UN activities reversed the downward spiral in U.S. policy toward the organization. Regularly

---

[4] Address Before a Joint Session of the Congress on the State of the Union, January 29, 1991, *PPP, 1991*, I, 74.

[5] There is much in the literature on President Bush's cautious and conservative internationalism. It presents a picture of Bush trying to avoid pitfalls by "doing no harm." See, for example, Stephen R. Graubard, *Mr. Bush's War* (New York: Hill and Wang, 1992), 90–91; David Mervin, *George Bush and the Guardianship Presidency*, 8, 175; Michael R. Beschloss and Strobe Talbott, *At the Highest Levels* (Boston: Little, Brown, 1993), 4; and John B. Judis, "Foreign Policy, New World, Old Vision," *Eyes on the President, George Bush: History in Essays and Cartoons*, edited by Leo E. Heagerty (Occidental, CA: Chronos, 1993), 47.

throughout his term he sought new ways to utilize the organization. In his first address to the General Assembly, he told the delegates, "The UN is moving closer to the ideal....The possibility now exists for the creation of a true community of nations built on shared interests and ideals."[6] On the eve of war with Saddam Hussein, he told the American people that there was a real chance at an order in which a credible United Nations could use its peacekeeping role to fulfill the promise and vision of its founders.[7] To support the UN's peacekeeping efforts the president established a permanent peacekeeping curriculum at the American military academies and offered assistance for multinational training of UN personnel. On the policy level, Bush suggested that nuclear proliferation should become a concern of the Security Council, even recommending that the enforcement mechanisms of Chapter VII be used against violators. Clearly, the president conceived of the United Nations as an important element in the construction of the new world order emerging from the demise of cold war hostilities. In cooperation with the USSR and the other permanent members of the Security Council, Bush saw an opportunity for the United States to move world politics toward an era of stability, relative peace, and American principles on a global scale. Bush's new world order with an active United Nations augured a revived *multilateral moralist impulse* in American foreign policy.

President Bush's UN Odyssey

George Bush's relationship with the United Nations was characterized by many ironies. He began his political career highly critical of the institution, but he would "rediscover"[8] the UN at its moment of greatest promise since 1945. In fact, he would be responsible for much of that promise. A president not given to grand theorizing, he would describe a new world order based on globalized American values, and he would do more than any past president to employ the United Nations to actualize his concept. He would serve eight years as vice-

---

    [6] Address to the 44th Session, September 25, 1989, *PPP, 1989,* II, 1248–1249.

    [7] *PPP, 1991,* I, 74. When asked at a meeting of the Economic Club of New York for a definition of the NWO, the president noted the value of UN peacekeeping. See "Remarks and a Question-and-Answer Session at a Meeting of the Economic Club in New York, New York," *PPP, 1991,* I, 123.

    [8] The term is Robert Gregg's. See Robert W. Gregg, *About Face? The United States and the United Nations* (Boulder, Colo.: Lynne Reinner, 1993), 1.

president in an administration that spent more time dismissing than praising the United Nations. Yet he would use this period to strengthen his personal ties to the diplomatic corps and to the political leaders who populated the UN system. Appointed to the United Nations as a novice in foreign policy-making, he ultimately would be, by virtue of his election to the Oval Office, the most illustrious of the U.S. ambassadors to serve in that post. Bush had come to the United Nations in 1971 under the realist tutelage of Kissinger and Nixon, who both disdained the institution, but as president he would attempt to use the organization in ways none of his mentors would have thought advisable. In his early career he believed that the United Nations had not lived up to his own view of it as the "last best hope for peace," but he would see the post–cold war world as a setting in which the UN was poised to carry out the mission envisioned by its founders.

During his years in active political life prior to 1971, George Bush had held no special sympathy for the United Nations, nor had he seen it as an embodiment of the American liberal democratic mission in the world. His political experience was completely in the domestic arena. An admirer of Theodore Roosevelt and a Republican supporter of Richard Nixon's *realpolitik* foreign policy, Bush seemed an unlikely proponent of UN activism. Nonetheless, as president he repeatedly sought to alter international affairs through the Security Council. He actively sought the involvement and leadership of the United Nations in many American foreign policy initiatives. By so doing, he enhanced the visibility and the authority of the institution to the point of creating self-limiting restraints on American foreign policy.

George Bush was the first president to have served at the United Nations. He knew its inner workings better than any of his predecessors. As we described in Chapter 4, Richard Nixon appointed Bush ambassador in 1971 with little expectation that he would draw much attention to the UN. Bush took up his new responsibilities at a difficult moment for U.S. interests in the United Nations, and many in the administration considered him unqualified for the job. Secretary of State William P. Rogers thought of him as a "lightweight," and the mission staff in New York expected little in the way of significant leadership. The U.S. delegation found itself increasingly in the minority on important issues. The collapse of old colonial empires and the subsequent addition of new member states meant that a coalition of third world and socialist governments could pass resolutions hostile to the United States' positions and interests. Bush faced a growing "politicization" of UN agencies and bodies, which seemed to undermine the original intent of those organizations.

In fact, George Bush proved to be adept at the politics and intrigues of UN life. A fast learner with great personal warmth, he quickly organized a hardworking staff[9] and developed good relationships with the professionals in the mission and with important foreign delegations. What would later be called Bush's "Rolodex diplomacy"[10] was a conscious strategy to develop personal ties to his peers on the Security Council and in the General Assembly.[11] In particular, he focused on close friendships with the Soviet delegate Jacob Malik and the head of the Chinese delegation, even after Mao's representatives were seated.

As Michael Duffy and Dan Goodgame have noted, Bush viewed diplomacy through a "prism of personality."[12] The headquarters in New York provided a place to meet people on an even plane and to accomplish things through the intricacies of interaction. His future secretary of state, James A. Baker, later concluded that Bush had learned the benefit of personal contacts during his UN tenure.[13] It may also be

---

[9] Bush tended to use career foreign service officers and experienced government officials. His chief aides were Christopher Phillips and W. Tapley Bennett, Jr. Bennett had served as ambassador to the Dominican Republic. Bush appointed Bernard Zagorin, a longtime Treasury official, to the Economic and Social Council.

[10] Bruce W. Jentleson, *With Friends Like These: Reagan, Bush, and Saddam, 1982–1990* (New York: Norton, 1994), 232.

[11] Seymour Maxwell Finger, *Your Man at the UN* (New York: New York University Press, 1980), 216. Finger had served fifteen years at the U.S. mission when Bush arrived in 1971. He calls Bush "certainly one of the best-liked U.S. permanent representatives to serve at the U.N." Nicholas King, who served as Bush's press officer at the United Nations, also notes Bush's affability as his greatest strength. See King, *George Bush*, 65. Personality, both his own and that of people with whom he interacted, played a critical part in George Bush's conduct of diplomacy and governance. See George Plimpton, *The X Factor: A Quest for Excellence* (New York: Norton, 1995), 94.

[12] Michael Duffy and Dan Goodgame, *Marching in Place: The Status Quo Presidency of George Bush* (New York: Simon and Schuster, 1992), 53. The UN protocol officer at the time referred to Bush as the "Perle Mesta of the U.N." See Fitzhugh Green, *George Bush: An Intimate Portrait* (New York: Hippocrene, 1989), 123.

[13] James A. Baker, *The Politics of Diplomacy* (New York: Putnam, 1995), 10.

said that Bush found the United Nations a congenial place in spite of his preconceived notions about its lack of value to U.S. interests. His two years pursuing friendly persuasion in New York left him with a more nuanced view of the merits of diplomacy at the United Nations. He could see possibilities for utilizing the institution and could appreciate accomplishments of the organization that had not been apparent to him as a politician from Texas. Twenty years after his arrival in New York, the president's contacts from that period would serve him well as he held together a fragile coalition to confront Saddam Hussein. It would be natural for him to consider the United Nations an appropriate venue and instrument for the United States' efforts at multilateral action.

Whatever its merits as a vehicle for personal diplomacy, the United Nations in the early 1970s was not a place George Bush found friendly to American foreign policy. The anti-American majority in the General Assembly meant that the ambassador would be fighting a losing battle on many contentious issues. The most serious issue was the perennial matter of Chinese representation. Abandoning the United States' longtime support for the Nationalist government on Taiwan, the Nixon administration had decided to promote a "dual representation" scheme; and Bush, who had campaigned in 1964 for withdrawal from the organization if Mao's government was seated, now found himself as a loyal team player pushing for its admission. The new position was part of a general change in U.S.-Chinese relations orchestrated by Nixon and Kissinger. The ambassador found no support for that position and was relegated to escorting the Taiwanese representative from the General Assembly Hall as the vote went overwhelmingly against Nationalist China and the United States.[14]

Bush's two years at the United Nations left him with a mixed impression of the institution. His victories were few. The only significant one was the reduction of the American contribution to the UN budget from 31.5 percent of the total to 25 percent. He achieved acceptance of the new assessment ceiling by demonstrating to other delegations that their contributions would not have to increase as a result of it. But even this effort was undertaken in response to a growing hostility among the American public toward the UN. In his own words:

---

[14] See Chapter 4.

> The United Nations...proved by and large a great disappointment....In the crucial area of peacekeeping the UN fell far short of the world's hopes for it. It showed little ability to prevent wars. And once wars had started, it showed little ability to stop them.[15]

Bush admitted that the UN was a good place for international negotiations and debate, but he contended that it had become "a forum for the practitioners of terror and violence and for their propaganda."[16] In particular, he decried "bloc voting" in the General Assembly.

Then, and on many occasions in the future, Bush expressed the view (noted above) that the United Nations had failed to live up to its promise as the "world's last great hope for peace."[17] His criticism of the institution was often presented in juxtaposition with this phrasing, reflecting a deep-seated, if inappropriate, personal, understanding about the purposes of the UN. A member of the World War II generation and the son of an internationalist moderate Republican senator from Connecticut, Bush had hoped for a United Nations as Roosevelt, Truman, and many in their administrations had described it.[18] Bush judged the United Nations against the baseline of 1945. In the 1940s and 1950s the American dominance of the institution guaranteed a symmetry between expectations and performance. One might actually believe that the activities of an international organization could be substituted for hardball international politics.[19] Bush's efforts in Republican politics in Texas, his induction into foreign policy by the Nixon administration, and his experience at the United Nations itself all contributed to his disaffection regarding the UN's value to U.S. interests in the 1970s.

In Bush's view the only real successes of the United Nations were to be found in the marginal areas of economic and social policy. In spite of

---

[15] Wead, *George Bush*, 143.

[16] Ibid., 144.

[17] See, for example, George Bush, *Looking Forward: An Autobiography* (New York: Bantam, 1987), 117.

[18] Secretary of State Cordell Hull, for example, called the UN "the fulfillment of humanity's highest aspirations and the very survival of our civilization." See Franck, *Nation*, 9.

[19] For a discussion of how the generation of 1945 the United Nations, see Ibid., 7–9; and Thompson, *Political Realism*, 68.

"inefficiencies and infighting," agencies such as the World Health Organization (WHO) and the High Commissioner for Refugees (UNHCR) had a valuable role to play. He believed they had worked well because ideology had affected their work less noticeably than it had the more political bodies. Aside from these accomplishments, though, the United Nations had not lived up to the founders' hopes. He later wrote that the UN "is and always will be a reflection of, rather than a solution to, the tensions that exist in the world."[20]

Given his considered view of the United Nations, it is not surprising that Ambassador Bush worked to diminish its role in American foreign policy. From the days of Adlai Stevenson, the U.S. ambassador had been a member of the president's cabinet. At the close of his tenure in New York, Bush recommended to President Nixon that the practice be ended.[21] The United Nations was, in his view, only a small part of the global chessboard on which the United States had to pursue its goals. Given the makeup of the membership when he left in 1973, Bush could not see much reason for Washington to invest any great effort in its UN policy.

There is little to suggest that Bush had revised this realist view prior to his inauguration as president in January 1989. In 1987, in his autobiography, Bush acknowledged, "Like most Americans who had idealistic hopes for the United Nations when it was created in 1945, I'd undergone a sea-change in attitude by the 1970s. As the 'last best hope for peace' the U.N. was another light that failed."[22] All this makes it even more interesting that he used the organization so extensively during his White House years. Just two years later, as president, Bush set a new course. Unlike his mentor in foreign policy, Richard Nixon, Bush expressed no distaste for the UN. In fact, along a continuum described by Henry Kissinger as ranging from "geopolitical" to "idealist,"[23] Bush increasingly pursued policies toward the idealist end of the spectrum. His decisions, particularly those involving the United Nations, reflected a seemingly unconscious intellectual journey between the two great traditions of American foreign policy—from "realism" to "idealism." As

---

[20] Frank, *Nation*, 116–117, 248.

[21] Ibid., 248.

[22] Bush, *Looking Forward*, 108.

[23] Kissinger, *The White House Years*, 915.

with Franklin Roosevelt's changing attitudes, Bush's presidency and its
relationship to the United Nations provide a reaffirmation of the power
of the idealist tradition, and insight into the impact of events, context,
and institutions on the thinking and policies of presidents.

One explanation for the apparent shift in George Bush's estimation
of the United Nations lies in his perception that the organization had
changed dramatically by 1989.[24] As a result of the collapse of
communism and of a maturing attitude among developing states, the
United Nations could now be a venue in which American interests could
be defended and pursued effectively. A far friendlier atmosphere existed
for U.S. initiatives, including growing support from the Soviet Union
and China for those efforts.

But President Bush's increasingly positive language about the
United Nations and his willingness to turn to it in the first instance of
crisis during his term also suggest that he had more than a realist's view
of the UN's merits. In his speech to the General Assembly in 1989 he
noted that a "true community" of nations was emerging. Three years
later, addressing the same group, he would define that community as
based on "respect for principle, of peaceful settlement of disputes,
fundamental human rights, and the twin pillars of freedom: democracy
and free markets."[25] His words, no longer Nixonian, were reminiscent of
Woodrow Wilson and the foreign policy tradition associated with
Wilson. Moralism was once again an enhanced element of U.S. policy
regarding the United Nations.

Professor Rebecca Bjork tells us that "reality is discursively
constructed," that human beings use language to define internally for
themselves situations, events, and material conditions. They use symbols
and terminology to make sense of experiences, to create a worldview
that can provide predictability and a basis for action."[26] The "New
World Order," with its new emphasis on multilateralism and an

---

[24] This is the view held by President Bush's national security adviser,
General Brent Scowcroft. See his remarks in the transcripts of the Hofstra 10th
Presidential Conference: "George Bush, Leading in a New World," Hofstra
University, April 17, 1997.

[25] *U.S. Department of State Dispatch*, Vol. 3, No. 39, September 28, 1992,
721–724.

[26] Rebecca S. Bjork, *The Strategic Defense Initiative* (Albany: SUNY Press,
1992), ix–11.

expanded role for the United Nations, did these things for George Bush. Early in his term he told his staff, "I want to do something important in world affairs." The rubric of the new world order gave him a framework within which to do this. The United Nations, provided one of the vehicles.

President Bush's NWO incorporated American exceptionalism and Wilsonian internationalism into a "New Moralism." It went beyond the unilateral moralism of Ronald Reagan's "city on the hill." The new moralism increasingly conveyed a commitment by the United States to manage change in the post–cold war era through the United Nations. Beyond serving as the aloof model of universal values in a corrupt world (George Washington's concept), the United States now not only would participate actively in world affairs through democratic institutions (Wilsonianism), but would seek to lead a global community in a "new partnership...based on consultation, cooperation and collective action,...a partnership united by principle and the rule of law,...a partnership whose goals are to increase democracy, increase prosperity, increase peace, and reduce arms."[27] In this new partnership the United Nations could be "the world's parliament of peace."[28] This was a long journey from Bush's Nixonian realism of 1971 and 1972. It was far more reminiscent of Francis Fukuyama's "end of history"—a managerial world. In such a setting, while the United States as the sole remaining superpower might lead the world community, it would also be constrained by a need to maintain consensus in the global partnership.

President Bush's gravitation toward the new moralism occurred with each new foreign policy challenge that confronted his administration. Additionally, the decision-making process he followed and the choices he made had the effect of enhancing the prestige and public authority of the United Nations. This in turn meant that the United States needed to take UN dynamics into consideration in its foreign policy decisions. By the end of his term the president was even willing to contemplate U.S. military forces acting "under the full

---

[27] "Address Before the 45th Session of the United Nations General Assembly in New York," October 1, 1990, *PPP, 1990,* II, 1332–1334.

[28] Ibid.

authority of the United Nations,"[29] a step, he argued, that might be necessary to make the world safe for American values.

President Bush's Use of the UN

The watershed event in George Bush's development of the new moralism and his use of the United Nations was the Gulf War. Prior to the invasion of Kuwait in August 1990 there were signs that President Bush was willing to use American power on behalf of moralist values. In the same month that he met with Gorbachev in Malta, he had unilaterally ordered military action in the Philippines to protect the democratically elected Aquino government from yet another attempted coup, and he had sent troops into Panama to overthrow and arrest General Noriega, who was reputedly deeply involved in drug trafficking. The war against Saddam Hussein, however, provided the opportunity to mobilize a partnership with the permanent members of the Security Council and to use the UN in the service of the new world order.

The occupation of Kuwait directly threatened American interests in the Gulf region, it endangered a significant proportion of the world's oil supply, and it placed several of the United States' allies under immediate threat. Saudi Arabia, in particular, faced the possibility of Iraqi aggression. That the president would have to respond went without question. That Bush decided on a massive reversal of the Iraqi's action by any means necessary came as a surprise to many, including the leadership in Baghdad.

The president immediately attempted to mobilize the United Nations. In the early hours of August 2, he ordered Ambassador Thomas Pickering to request an emergency meeting of the Security Council and to obtain a resolution of condemnation, demanding the withdrawal of Iraqi forces. Over the next three months the administration sought and obtained ten Security Council resolutions directed at the isolation of Iraq and at preparing the legal groundwork for military action.

Bush's efforts had two significant institutional consequences. The focus of action, which had been largely centered in the General Assembly during the cold war, now shifted to the Security Council. While the founders might have believed that the Council would have

---

[29] Remarks at the United States Military Academy in West Point, N.Y., January 5, 1993, *PPP, 1992–1993*, II, 2229.

primary responsibility for peace and security in the world, the use of the veto meant that most things the United Nations wished to accomplish had to be done circuitously, through the Assembly. From 1950 to 1990, even in the context of open aggression, efforts to stop the fighting had to be pursued through such devices as the Uniting for Peace Resolution initiated by the Truman administration in 1950, or Chapter VI of the UN Charter, which allowed for the insertion of peacekeeping forces. The enforcement mechanisms of Chapter VII were largely unusable, given the superpowers' confrontation. Having presided during the burial of the cold war, President Bush now made a concerted effort to mobilize the Security Council as the primary instrument for challenging Saddam.

Second, within the Security Council the administration sought to maintain a consensus among the five permanent members. Surely the possible use of the veto made consultation essential. Bush achieved the ten resolutions he sought by securing the support, or at least the abstention, of the other four permanent members on each of the proposed measures. His efforts had the effect of creating a council within the Council. As Wendell Gordon has noted, "Increasingly, the substantive discussion of Security Council resolutions [occurred] only among the five permanent members…without much contribution by other countries."[30] A "cabal" system of Council decision-making emerged which persisted well after the conclusion of the Gulf crisis. The president's administration was willing to make concessions and alter policy proposals in order to maintain the record of no vetoes being cast, not only in the Gulf War but later, on matters related to Somalia, Bosnia, and Haiti.

At the urging of the United States, the Security Council condemned the invasion (Security Council Resolution 660), declared null and void the annexation of Kuwait (Security Council Resolution 662), imposed economic sanctions on Iraq (Security Council Resolution 661), established a naval blockade (Security Council Resolution 665), and—most important—on November 29 adopted Resolution 678, giving Iraq forty-eight days to withdraw or face military retaliation. For only the second time in history, member states were authorized to use "all necessary means…to restore peace and security in the area." The resolution legitimized the decision of the United States and its coalition

---

[30] Wendell Gordon, *The United Nations at the Crossroads of Reform* (Armonk, N.Y.: Sharpe, 1994), 35.

partners to drive Iraq out of Kuwait if the deadline was not met. Forty-five years after its founding, the United Nations was acting as Roosevelt and Truman had hoped it would.

The United Nations was instrumental to the president's coalition-building. According to Secretary of State James Baker, Bush saw the UN as the "first stop" if the administration was going to succeed in gaining global support.[31] From his first meeting with his advisers in the wake of the invasion, Bush was adamant about achieving multilateral support.[32] Over the first thirty days of the crisis Bush spoke personally with sixty-two heads of government. He also initiated a plethora of diplomatic contacts and travel missions by his senior aides in an effort to create massive support for U.S. policy. Ultimately he put together a coalition of thirty-five nations contributing 200,000 troops to U.S. forces already in Saudi Arabia. All of these were to act under UN authority.

On the eve of war in January 1991, President Bush addressed the American people. He said it was important to follow one's "inner moral compass" and to end Saddam Hussein's threat to "the peace and democracy of the emerging new world order;…this long dreamed vision we've all worked toward so long."[33] While his national security adviser, Brent Scowcroft, was outlining the crisis as "the first test of our ability to maintain global or regional security in the post–cold war era," the president was telling the American people that this was "an opportunity to stand up for what's right and condemn what's wrong, all in the cause

---

[31] Baker, *The Politics of Diplomacy*, 278.

[32] General Colin Powell, Chairman of the Joint Chiefs of Staff, recollects the president saying, "Whatever we do, we've got to get the international community behind us." See Colin L. Powell, *My American Journey* (New York: Random House, 1995), 464.

[33] *PPP, 1991*, I, 95.

of peace."[34] For Bush the fight was about more than oil and regional influence. It was about the NWO. It was about avoiding the mistakes of the past when aggression threatened the world system. Remembering both the 1930s and Vietnam,[35] Bush intended the United States to respond strongly and to do so in concert with the major powers as represented in the Security Council.

Harry Truman sought endorsement of the United States' action by the Security Council during the Korean crisis of 1950. It was the only time prior to the Gulf War that the enforcement provisions of Chapter VII had been activated. Once he had that imprimatur, Truman conducted the war in Korea as if it were an American affair. The United Nations provided the symbolic facade; the United States provided the policy. While there are some who see in President Bush's efforts a replay of Truman's strategy to create a "multilateral shield"[36] for an American war, there was a clear difference in Bush's willingness to employ UN mechanisms to conduct the war and the trusteeship of Iraq afterward. Bush was also committed to going after the cooperation of the USSR and the other great powers even if that meant limiting the United States' goals and tactics. There was no possibility of Soviet support in Korea,

---

[34] Address to the Nation, August 8, 1990, *PPP, 1990*, II. Scowcroft and Bush's other senior advisers (Powell, Baker, and Secretary of Defense Richard Cheney) came from the realist school of foreign policy. Only Baker regularly advised conducting U.S. policy in concert with the United Nations. Baker was on a diplomatic visit to the USSR when Iraq launched its invasion, and he spent most of the night on the phone to Bush and Scowcroft, emphasizing the value of the United Nations in this instance. See Beschloss and Talbott, *At the Highest Levels*, 245; also Baker, *The Politics of Diplomacy*. Others, particularly Scowcroft, worried about the limitations on the United States' freedom of action that could result from overuse of the United Nations. On several occasions he and Cheney recommended unilateral action.

[35] For an analysis of Bush's internal motivations for his response to the Iraqi's provocation, see Alex Roberto Hybel, *Power Over Rationality* (Albany: SUNY Press, 1993), 9. Also see Bjork, *The Strategic Defense Initiative*; and Duffy and Goodgame, *Marching in Place*, 178.

[36] The term is Phyllis Bennis'. See Phyllis Bennis, *Calling the Shots: How Washington Dominates Today's UN* (New York: Olive Branch, 1996), xiv. Bennis quotes John Bolton, the administration's Undersecretary for International Organization, as saying that the success of the United Nations during the Gulf War was due to the United States' decision to employ the institution for practical purposes. In 1994 he put it succinctly, "When the United States leads, the United Nations will follow."

and Truman never considered being restricted in his decision-making even when close allies like Britain and France raised concerns.

Throughout the conflict, President Bush "sweated out" Security Council votes, fearful that a permanent member would veto a vital resolution. Beyond his concern about a negative vote, Bush also hoped, through those resolutions, to enmesh the other great powers in the effort against Iraq. His advisers regularly cautioned against depending too deeply on the United Nations because it might well limit the United States' latitude in the crisis. Secretary of Defense Richard Cheney noted, however, "Bush had enormous respect for the [UN]. He was frankly willing to go a lot further in order to build support within the United Nations than some of us in the Cabinet who frankly wouldn't have devoted as much time to it."[37] Ignoring Cheney's advice, the president engaged in what might be called "micro-leadership,"[38] a concerted and continuous effort to cajole individual Security Council members, to define immediate objectives for allies, and to develop strategies all parties could assent to and willingly carry out.

Bush's micro-leadership of the international effort involved regular consultation with world leaders, compromises on policy in an effort to maintain consensus, and delay in the execution of force against Iraq in order to allow allies and neutrals to find face-saving ways out of the confrontation. Bush kept in regular contact with President Gorbachev, including a summit at Helsinki in September, and endorsed Soviet efforts to find a diplomatic solution prior to the UN's deadline for withdrawal. The administration even attempted last-minute negotiations directly with Iraq in January 1991 to reassure its nervous partners in the coalition. The president clearly wanted his counterparts at the United Nations to understand that he had gone "the extra mile" to find a resolution more acceptable to them than the use of military force.

This had the hoped-for consequence of keeping the international community largely supportive of Bush's leadership. It also had the effect of making the United Nations critical to the resolution of the problem.

---

[37] Richard Cheney, remarks in the transcripts of the Hofstra 10th Presidential Conference: "George Bush, Leading in a New World," Hofstra University, April 18, 1997.

[38] For a discussion of Bush's use of the United Nations as a form of "micro-leadership," see Jarrod Wiener, "Leadership, the United Nations, and the New World Order," *The United Nations and the New World Order*, edited by Bourantonis and Wiener, 44–50.

The UN would provide the institutional structure through which legitimacy and "burden-sharing" would be achieved. As a further consequence, there would be a natural expectation that after the crisis, the United Nations would play a central role in implementing any penalties against Iraq. The successful military operation in February 1991 forced Saddam Hussein to accept the loss of Kuwait and direct UN involvement in Iraq's internal affairs. A near-trusteeship status was imposed on Iraq.

The war ended with Saddam Hussein still in power in Baghdad. The American expectation had been that, having suffered two humiliating wars—first with Iran and then with the United States—and having absorbed overwhelming damage to the civilian infrastructure in both conflicts, the regime would not be able to survive. The administration openly called for the Iraqi military to seize power. As the coalition's assault routed Iraqi forces in February 1991, there were also calls for the United States to march to Baghdad and depose the dictator. Neither eventuality occurred. In the latter case, George Bush explained that he had halted offensive operations on February 28 without destroying the regime because the United Nations had not authorized the removal of Saddam Hussein. Instead, the president looked to the United Nations to impose such conditions on Iraq that the regime would not be able to meet them and thus would not be able to survive politically. The administration was acknowledging that its use of the United Nations had created self-imposing limits on what the United States could or would do in the Gulf War.

In the spring of 1991 the Security Council created a Sanctions Commission to monitor the isolation of Iraq and eventually to sell its oil, the revenues from which were to be distributed via a UN escrow account to cover humanitarian needs and to repay Kuwait for its losses (Security Council Resolutions 706 and 712).[39] The border between Iraq and Kuwait was to be redetermined by a UN Iraq-Kuwait Observation Mission (UNIKOM). Most important, the Security Council created the Special Commission on Iraq (UNSCOM). The commission was authorized to inventory and monitor Iraq's weapons programs. It undertook to destroy Hussein's arsenal of weapons of mass destruction and to negate any possible revival of the regime's development of nuclear weapons. When the Iraqi government balked at demands from the commission, President

---

[39] *YUN, 1991*, 207–208.

Bush unhesitatingly used air strikes to back up the UN's efforts. The Security Council ordered the commission to take responsibility for monitoring Saddam's treatment of his own citizens.

Of particular concern was the protection of the Kurdish and Shia populations. In April, following Hussein's brutal repression of uprisings, Operation Provide Comfort began to establish safe zones for groups threatened by the government in Baghdad. Extensive relief operations were launched to assist refugees in northern Iraq. Undertaken to limit the flow of Kurdish populations into neighboring Turkey, the international community's program set a precedent for humanitarian intervention in the domestic affairs of a state without the consent of the central government.

The war had ended with a dramatic victory for the United Nations and the U.S.-led coalition. It also left the United Nations with ongoing challenges to redress the damage caused by the war, and to assure the region that Saddam Hussein would no longer threaten his neighbors. In Bush's view the war had been about more than oil, U.S. interests, and the balance of power in the Gulf. In response to a college student's letter in January, the president wrote that if the UN and the United States did not stand up to Iraq, Saddam Hussein's "lawlessness" would threaten the peaceful and democratic world that now seemed within reach.[40] The conflict was about "right versus wrong." In Bush's view the invasion of Kuwait and the response it engendered enhanced the new promise of the United Nations. He told the General Assembly that the UN was coming closer "than ever before" to realizing the deepest hopes of its founders. Bush noted that those who created the United Nations "were intensely idealistic and yet tempered by war."[41] In the new and different world that had emerged since 1989 the founders' idealism could be reinvigorated and the United Nations could become the center for international collective security. As the American people celebrated the end of the fighting, the president reported to Congress:

> Twice before in this century, an entire world was convulsed by war. Twice this century, out of the horrors of war, hope emerged for enduring peace. Twice before, those hopes proved to be a

---

[40] *PPP, 1991,* I, 25.

[41] Address Before the 45th Session of the United Nations General Assembly in New York, October 1, 1990, *PPP, 1990,* II, 1330.

distant dream, beyond the grasp of man. Until now, the world we've known has been a world divided—a world of barbed wire and concrete block, conflict and cold war. *Now we can see a new world coming into view…a world where the United Nations, freed from the Cold War stalemate, is poised to fulfill the historic vision of its founders. A world in which freedom and respect for human rights find a home among all nations."* [italics added][42]

*   *   *

The conclusion of the Gulf War left the administration and the United Nations in a moralist euphoria. There seemed little in the new world order that could not be handled through adroit utilization of the UN. To highlight the central role of the United Nations, and particularly of the Security Council, the first Heads of Government Council meeting was convened in January 1992. The Prime Minister John Major of the United Kingdom chaired the session, calling it a "turning point in the world and at the United Nations." The mood of consensus among the great powers had relegated to distant memory the 279 vetoes cast during the cold war. Bush and his colleagues directed Secretary-General Boutros Boutros-Ghali to prepare recommendations on ways of strengthening the UN and making it more efficient in "preventive diplomacy" and peacekeeping. The Council asked that Boutros-Ghali's report be submitted no later than six months hence.

The secretary-general published his recommendations in June. Entitled *An Agenda for Peace*, the report outlined the most ambitious program for efforts at peacekeeping ever undertaken by the UN. Boutros-Ghali suggested that the United Nations needed to identify "at-risk" states and act early to avoid the collapse of state sovereignty and internal order. He proposed that military forces be placed at the disposal of the United Nations for rapid action in times of crisis. The report outlined problems in the less developed countries and the need for a humanitarian, political, economic, and military response by the UN. As a result of the report, new terms such as "preventive diplomacy," "state-building," and "peacemaking" entered the lexicon of potential UN activities.

---

[42] Address Before a Joint Session of the Congress on the Cessation of the Persian Gulf Conflict, March 6, 1991, *PPP, 1991,* I, 220.

There was a growing "institutionalization" of the United Nations in American foreign policy during George Bush's last year in office. In the Gulf War, the president had demonstrated the viability of the United Nations. In its aftermath, the procedures and structures of the United Nations increasingly seemed to be appropriate venues for decision-making, even if that meant some limitation on unilateral action, or if it meant that outside actors such as the secretary-general would set the agenda for international attention and action.

An *Agenda for Peace* was not dramatically different from an emerging "Bush Doctrine" in U.S. foreign policy. Enshrined as the new world order, the doctrine envisioned a liberal and internationalist America willing to lead a multilateral coalition of great powers through UN auspices on behalf of ending aggression in the third world, solving disputes by peaceful negotiation, and directly intervening to ameliorate humanitarian disasters. The new moralism envisioned a "better" world and sought to bring it about through UN mechanisms.

In the flush of victory, even old intractable problems seemed open to collective solution. As part of the effort to hold the Gulf coalition together, the Bush administration gave strong hints that when the war ended a new U.S. initiative would be launched to resolve the Arab-Israeli conflict. The president indicated that the United Nations would have a role in a new comprehensive approach to negotiate an agreement. As U.S. ambassador to the United Nations, Bush had seen firsthand the anti-Israeli bias of the organization during the 1970s, culminating in the "Zionism is racism" resolution shortly after his departure. Nonetheless, he now believed that events and attitudes had shifted sufficiently to allow a significant UN role in any settlement. Secretary of State Baker shuttled between capitals in hope of a breakthrough, an effort culminating in the Madrid conference. Bush urged the full participation of the United Nations in the conference, a position adamantly opposed by the Israeli government. In the end the UN was granted a meager "observer" status. George Bush had found that—for all of the United States' new moral authority in the Middle East—external geopolitical pressures continued to impinge on the United States' freedom of action.

Two international trouble spots in 1992 seemed more appropriate settings than the Middle East for the imposition of UN solutions. They were in Yugoslavia and Somalia. Yugoslavia had experienced a steady unraveling during the previous decade. The collapse of communism, the revolts in Eastern Europe, increasing economic difficulties, and the inability to establish effective national leadership to replace the longtime dictator Tito (Josip Broz), who had died in 1980, led to the rise of ethnic independence movements in all of the subnational units of the federal state. While the United States and its European allies would have preferred the maintenance of a unified state in the Balkans, it became clear in 1991 that Yugoslavia was likely to fall apart. Slovenia and Croatia were the first to declare their independence. The central government, headed by the Serb nationalist Slobodan Milosevic, first sought to hold the nation together by force, and then tried to carve out Serbian enclaves in Croatia through a policy of "ethnic cleansing." Europe experienced civil war and atrocities not witnessed since the Holocaust.

When Bosnia, under Muslim leadership, declared its independence, Sarajevo became the target of an attack by Bosnian Serbs with Milosevic's help, and Croatians sought to keep large tracts of land out of the hands of the Bosnian government. By 1992 Yugoslavia had become a microcosm of the ethnic strife and antidemocratic politics evident in parts of the former Soviet Union, Eastern Europe, and the Middle East. Self-determination was becoming a nightmare for which the Great Powers, the United Nations, and the world community at large had little solution.

While there was great pressure on the administration to intercede in Yugoslavia, the Bush White House sought to limit U.S. involvement. Still preoccupied with the aftermath of the Gulf War, the president first suggested that the Balkan crisis was a "European problem" for Europeans to solve. To the extent that the United States might become involved, it would have to be in support of initiatives by the European Community or through multilateral efforts under UN auspices or the Conference on Security and Cooperation in Europe (CSCE). At the urging of the British and French governments the Security Council imposed on all parties to the dispute the first Chapter VII arms embargo in Europe.[43]

By August 1992 it was clear that the European Community's efforts had failed. Even UN humanitarian teams were under attack. In response,

---

[43] For a list of all UN resolutions on Yugoslavia passed during the Bush years, see John Tessitore and Susan Woolfson, *A Global Agenda: Issues Before the 47th General Assembly of the United Nations* (New York: University Press of America, 1992), 12–16.

the United States proposed a division of labor, with the Europeans focusing on political matters and the United Nations undertaking peacekeeping responsibilities. In October a UN Protection Force (UNPROFOR) was created to oversee any cease-fire achieved and to establish policies to ease ethnic tensions. Bush also persuaded the Security Council to pass a resolution authorizing states to undertake "all necessary means" to deliver humanitarian aid.[44] Bush was particularly concerned about protecting civilians in Sarajevo and surrounding Muslim towns. It is worthy of note that the administration sought the same wording as it had in the Gulf conflict. The formula provided wide latitude for actions the United States and its allies legitimized by the United Nations. The resolution also demanded access to all camps, prisons, and detention centers in an effort to halt crimes against humanity. The president indicated that he would also seek the Security Council's approval of a war crimes tribunal.

On August 6, Bush raised the possibility of using force in Bosnia to deliver humanitarian relief supplies. In particular, he suggested that NATO airpower might be used. He also revealed that his administration had been engaged in lengthy behind-the-scenes negotiations at the United Nations concerning Bosnia. Among other considerations was the use of troops to close the alleged death camps run by Bosnian Serbs. However, the essential requirement, according to Bush, was a consensus among all of the major powers. The United States would not act alone, but if the United Nations passed a resolution, he promised that it would be implemented.

Because no consensus could be reached, Bush was unable in the waning days of his presidency to create a Gulf-style coalition to deal with the Bosnian conflict. Russia, France, and Great Britain opposed anything beyond the establishment of a war crimes authority in The Hague and the imposition of economic sanctions against Milosevic's regime. Paris and London had a substantial number of peacekeepers on the ground in the Balkans and feared reprisals against their nationals if the United Nations took harsher action. Russia's president, Boris Yeltsin, concerned about nationalist opposition at home, did not wish to endorse strident measures against Russia's historical allies, the Serbs.

---

[44] Statement on the United Nations Security Council Vote on Humanitarian Aid to Bosnia, August 13, 1992, *PPP*, 1992–1993, II, 1353.

Pictures of atrocities, presidential election politics, and international requests brought strong pressure to bear on the Bush White House in the summer of 1992 to undertake unilateral action in Bosnia, given the apparent impotence of the world community. On June 8 President Alija Izetbegovic of Bosnia appealed to Bush for air strikes to relieve the Serbian bombardment of Sarajevo. The president and his senior advisers were wary of becoming involved in the mountainous terrain of the Balkans, and in the age-old ethnic controversies that lay at the heart of the fighting. The chairman of the Joint Chiefs of Staff, Colin Powell, was particularly cognizant of the differences between the Balkans and the Gulf region, arguing that the kind of quick victory achieved in the war with Iraq was not possible in Bosnia. The administration feared a Vietnam-style engagement with no clear objectives, an open-ended commitment, and no obvious way to extricate U.S. troops. Thus the Bosnian nightmare, which in moralist terms appeared to be the type of crisis best resolved through the UN, in fact demonstrated the limitations of the new moralism. While the president was willing to seek a multilateral solution, and to consider using U.S. power on behalf of human rights in a civil war, realistic concerns about the efficacy of American efforts and the costs of such an undertaking in the end stayed George Bush's hand. The euphoric belief in the possibility of conflict management through the United Nations, born in the Gulf crisis, receded dramatically with the growing war in the hills around Sarajevo.

In Bosnia "the facts" frustratingly made the exercise of the new moralism impossible. They did not, however, make the conditions any more acceptable. Moralist presidents historically have been leaders driven by a sense that "it should not be so."[45] They have espoused certain values or principles for all human beings, rather than for a single group. They have been in this sense *universalists* or *globalists*. The preservation of "human rights" has been the primary motivation for moralist occupants of the White House. Each has attempted to push the international community into action to preserve or enlarge those rights. For Woodrow Wilson the cause was self-determination. President Carter sought to end repressive regimes. President Bush focused on the need for

---

[45] For a seminal work on the motivational forces at work in leaders guided by either moralism or realism, see Herz, *Political Realism and Political Idealism*. For this particular quote, see 31.

humanitarian relief and a safe haven for innocent civilians caught in the midst of collapsing states or ethnic or religious strife.

Bush, like his predecessors, first sought a multilateral response, then looked to America's own resources. The inability to find a politically acceptable strategy to alter the "facts" on the ground in Bosnia did not dissuade the president from supporting UN and European peacekeeping efforts. It did present, for the first time since the Gulf War, the truth that there were very real limits to what could be achieved by this approach. Bosnia would remain a critical agenda item well into President Clinton's term.

The same week the Security Council passed the U.S.-sponsored resolutions on Bosnia, Bush ordered American aircraft to transport a 500-man UN force to Somalia to guard relief efforts there pursuant to Security Council Resolution 751. Largely owing to clan conflict following the overthrow of Siad Barre's dictatorship, Somalia had devolved into near-anarchy. UN and private relief efforts were regularly harassed by private armies, making it impossible to transport food, medicine, and other necessary supplies out of the port city of Mogadishu to the towns and villages in the countryside. Efforts to reestablish political order and a central government had produced few positive results. During the cold war either the Soviet Union or the United States had been a major donor of foreign aid to the Siad Barre regime, guaranteeing stability if not democracy. The end of the superpower contest, however, had greatly diminished the preoccupation with the Horn of Africa. Attention having shifted elsewhere, the Somali people were left to the political ambitions of warlords and their followers.

Secretary-General Boutros-Ghali was the prime mover in mobilizing the world community to deal with the problems in Somalia. Boutros-Ghali, as a former foreign minister of Egypt, took a special interest in African affairs, and he attempted to focus world attention on the growing instability on the continent. His predecessor, Javier Perez de Cuellar, had launched the first relief efforts in the wake of the Ethiopian famine of the late 1980s, but it would be Boutros-Ghali who would seek the active intervention of the sole remaining superpower in the Somali morass. At his initiative, Resolution 751 in April 1992 established UNISOM I, a small peacekeeping contingent for Somalia. The force was limited to fifty unarmed observers, at the insistence of the United States, which was concerned about the legal and financial aspects of the operation.

During their summit in May 1990, Gorbachev and Bush had taken note of famines in Saharan and central Africa, and they issued a joint call for an "international conference of governments under the auspices of the UN on settlement of conflict situations in the Horn of Africa."[46] However, the invasion of Kuwait by Saddam Hussein in August and the attempted coup in Moscow a year later left little desire to get involved with African problems. It was only with the convening of the Heads of Government Security Council summit in January 1992 and the nearly concurrent passage of the first Council resolution on humanitarian relief in Somalia[47] that the president focused anew on the problem.

After the Six Day War in 1967, the Horn of Africa had become critically important to the protection of vital sea lanes between the oil-rich Persian Gulf and the West. Much geopolitical importance was attached to the United States' effort to maintain influence in the area. By 1992, however, the United States had few critical national interests that needed defending in Somalia or neighboring states. With the exception of a growing Iranian influence in the region, few anti-American trends were under way. Thus, George Bush's decision to intervene in Somalia cannot be explained in realist terms. It was a logical, nearly pristine, extension of his new moralism.[48]

Following his decision to airlift UN aid workers to Somalia, Bush attempted to use what he later called the "Gulf pattern" of diplomacy to deal with the crisis. To lay a basis for that strategy, he directed his UN ambassador to seek the Security Council's authorization for additional measures. In his speech to the General Assembly in October, Bush signaled that the United States would play an increased role in UN peacekeeping. The Pentagon was directed to develop plans for action in Somalia. By November, the Department of Defense, the National Security Council Deputies' Committee, and other key elements of the U.S. government were prepared for operations.

---

[46] *PPP, 1990*, I, 755.

[47] Security Council Resolution 733. See Letter to Congressional Leaders on the Situation in Somalia, December 10, 1992, *PPP, 1992–1993*, II, 2179.

[48] For a full discussion, see Stephen F. Burgess, "Operation Restore Hope: Somalia and Frontiers of the New World Order," Paper Presented at the Hofstra 10th Presidential Conference: "George Bush, Leading in a New World," Hofstra University, April 19, 1997.

His advisers still counseled caution. They made much the same arguments that were used to limit involvement in Bosnia. There was a serious likelihood that the United States would be entrapped in a civil war with little chance of successfully resolving the difficulties and with mounting open-ended costs. Early fall 1992 found "mountains of wheat piled up in warehouses [in Mogadishu], and people starving and dying inland."[49] UNISOM I was proving incapable of providing security for the food supplies or their effective movement to established feeding stations. By November, estimates ran as high as half a million Somali dead from civil war, famine, and disease. Nearly 25 percent of southern Somali children under five years of age had died. The pictures broadcast by CNN and other western news outlets made a compelling impact on American public opinion.

Just prior to Thanksgiving, following his defeat for reelection, Bush decided to act. Armed with a letter from Secretary-General Boutros-Ghali requesting U.S. action, the president urged the Security Council to invoke Chapter VII. On December 3 the Council passed Resolution 794, officially finding the circumstances in Somalia to be a threat to international peace and security. The resolution endorsed the offer "by a member state" to put together an international force to protect humanitarian relief. For the first time the United Nations had subcontracted out a peacekeeping operation.[50] While the mandate had been given by the Security Council, a primarily American-led task force (UNITAF) would conduct the operation.

On December 10, Bush notified Congress of his decision to insert U.S. forces into Somalia as part of an international effort at humanitarian relief. French, British, Italian, Belgian, Canadian, and Moroccan troops augmented the U.S. invasion force. Later troop contributions would be made by eight additional nations. Bush conveyed to the American people his hope that U.S. forces would be out of Somalia by the time Bill Clinton was inaugurated in January. He called upon local warlords to put up no resistance to the intervention. The administration envisioned a

---

[49] John L. Hirsch and Robert B. Oakley, *Somalia and Operation Restore Hope* (Washington, D.C.: United States Institute of Peace Press, 1995), x.

[50] For a discussion of this new approach to peacekeeping, see Winrich Kühne, "Fragmenting States and the Need for Enlarged Peacekeeping," *Documents on Reform of the United Nations*, edited by Paul Taylor, Sam Daws, and Ute Adamczich-Gerteis (Aldershot: Dartmouth, 1997), 56.

"hand-off" of command and control responsibilities to the United Nations once law, order, and effective food distribution had been reestablished. According to Secretary of Defense Cheney, after a UN command was in place the United States would maintain a 1,300-man "quick response team" along with a Marine expeditionary unit to ensure no regression in the situation. It would also contribute 4,000 troops to the operation under UN command.[51]

Bush's decision to commit troops was a demonstration of how far he had come in his growing acceptance of the authority and role of the United Nations in the post–cold war world. Using the enforcement provisions of Chapter VII, the president was willing to intervene in the internal affairs of a sovereign state without any prior request from its reputed leaders. Humanitarian intervention in what Boutros-Ghali would call an "at-risk" state was now an acceptable international response to ensure the new world order. In realist terms, a stronger case could have been made at that moment for U.S. intervention in Bosnia. Yet the president decided that only the United States could ensure the immediate distribution of food and other necessary materiel to the Somali population, and that "Operation Restore Hope" could be completed without serious opposition.

In 1988, the year George Bush won the presidency, there were fewer than 10,000 UN peacekeepers on duty in world hot spots, costing the UN $364 million annually.[52] As Bush entered his last year in the White House, the number was still less than 11,500. By June 1992 the number of peacekeepers had risen to 44,000, and it would approach 80,000 shortly after President Clinton's inauguration. The total cost would also rise dramatically, to $4 billion a year. The new world order was being policed by UN-authorized peacekeeping forces largely initiated by U.S. efforts in the service of humanitarian needs around the world. In December the United Nations established the Office of Humanitarian Affairs Coordination to oversee the many operations under way.

During his last two months in office George Bush gave two important speeches that explained his view of the United Nations in the new world order. The first was given at Texas A&M University, the

---

[51] Hirsch and Oakley, *Somalia*, 109.

[52] Staff Report, "Reform of the United Nations Peacekeeping Operations: A Mandate for Change," *Committee on Foreign Relations*, United States Senate, 1993 (Washington, D.C.: Government Printing Office, 1993), viii.

future site of his presidential library. The second was at the United States Military Academy in January. They offer insights because they were given at a time when no political considerations needed to be imputed to them. They were valedictory statements by a soon-to-be former president trying to leave his mark on history.

To his audience at Texas A&M the president made the strongest statement of his public life about the exceptional nature of America's role in the world. One "truth" seemed clear: "America remains today what Lincoln said it was more than a century ago: the last best hope of men on Earth."[53] It was equally clear that American leadership was essential for the NWO, "just as such an order is essential to us." He suggested that the nation's future success depended on building a world in harmony with the principles of democracy, the rule of law, and global community. He concluded that while some would "dismiss this vision as no more than a dream," critics should "consider the last four years when a dozen dreams were made real [largely owing to] American moral force."[54]

In his speech to the U.S. Military Academy, he contended that it might be necessary to place American troops in peacekeeping operations under UN authority in order to fulfill the mission of making the world more compatible with American values. While he cautioned "That a nation's sense of idealism need not be at odds with its interests, nor does principle displace prudence,"[55] he also defended the use of force in the service of UN directives. He cited Somalia as a case where the lack of American action would have morally "scarred the soul of our nation."

The United States commitment to the United Nations arose from the moralist tradition in American foreign policy. President Bush gravitated toward that tradition with each new foreign crisis that confronted his administration. The Gulf War and the challenges of the unfolding new world order gave a moderate pragmatist choices that had not presented themselves since the days of Harry Truman. The choices Bush made had the effect of enhancing the prestige and authority of the United Nations. This in turn meant that, increasingly, the United States needed to take UN dynamics into consideration in its foreign policy decisions. It became an essential ingredient of every decision to maintain the great powers'

---

[53] "Remarks by the President at Texas A&M University," December 15, 1992, Office of the Press Secretary, White House.

[54] Ibid.

[55] Military Academy, *PPP, 1992–1993*, II, 2229.

consensus in the Security Council. By January 1993 George Bush had moved from his earlier cynical view of the United Nations to the perspectives of its founders.

President Clinton:
The New Moralism and the Demands of Politics

Ironically, popular support for the United Nations diminished after the extraordinary victory in the Persian Gulf. The realization that Saddam Hussein would remain in power and that a lengthy military commitment by the United States and the UN would be needed in the area tarnished the American image of the predicted new world order. The new responsibility of protecting Iraq's minority populations from the central government, the inability of UN inspectors to eliminate Baghdad's military arsenals, and the high costs of a permanent security shield contributed to the rapid diminution of approval ratings for Bush's UN policy.

The quick emergence of other international problems in the wake of the war also diminished the willingness of Americans to pursue an activist agenda. With growing ethnic and political strife in Yugoslavia, the states of the former Soviet Union, sub-Saharan Africa, and the Caribbean, the electorate sensed that there might not be acceptable, affordable multilateral solutions. The turning point in public opinion came with the overthrow of the democratically elected Haitian government in September 1991. In spite of U.S. condemnations and its efforts to obtain OAS and UN measures against the leaders of the military coup, the Bush administration found little domestic support for "Gulf-style" actions to remove the objectionable regime. Additionally, the Haitian crisis produced a flood of refugees to the United States, which reinforced the public sentiment that we should stay out of Haiti's political upheaval.

The motivations of and possibilities for American multilateral leadership based on liberal democratic internationalism were being overtaken by domestic politics. George Bush, "unbeatable" in the spring of 1991, found voters increasingly preoccupied with domestic affairs. An apparent recession, coupled with a large budget deficit, refocused Americans away from Bush's successes in foreign policy. There was also a desire to enjoy the fruits of victory in the cold war. Many sought less commitment to world leadership and a reemphasis on solving problems at home. The historically recurrent theme of *isolationism* experienced a revival in the American political mood. In such a setting new international initiatives, undertaken unilaterally or as part of a United Nations' operation, seemed counterproductive. The popular pendulum was swinging toward making hardheaded calculations about the value of activist UN policies to U.S. national interests.

Interestingly, Bush's electoral defeat halted any immediate slide into a *realist* foreign policy. While Bill Clinton had succeeded in winning the White House by focusing on domestic issues and by criticizing elements of Bush's policies overseas, the election had the consequence of putting another *multilateralist* in office. Educated at Georgetown University's School of Foreign Service in the 1960s, Bill Clinton was an internationalist with a personal affinity for the United Nations and other international organizations. During the Vietnam War he had been a "dove" on the issue of American involvement in Southeast Asia. But his opposition was not nativist. Rather, the future president shared the view of the McGovern wing of the Democratic Party that the United States was caught in an immoral war and was overextended internationally. As governor of Arkansas, while the focus of his attention was on domestic policy, Clinton remained committed to the credo of American leadership in world affairs.

A self-styled "pragmatic Wilsonian," President Clinton picked up in January 1993 where his predecessor had left off. He did so, however, as American public opinion steadily shifted against an expansive role for the United Nations and against what it perceived as excessive involvement by the United States in UN peacekeeping around the world. The new president faced a dilemma inherent in the formation of a democracy's foreign policy: to maintain a consistent set of policies from administration to administration and to pursue his own international objectives, while responding to the changing mood of the electorate.

It may be that during its early days in office the Clinton administration did not appreciate how deep the animosity toward the United Nations ran. The White House, if anything, proceeded to highlight the potential of an active United Nations on the world stage. The president argued, "The U.S. must continue to play its unique role of leadership in the world. But now we can express that leadership through multilateral means such as the United Nations, which spread the costs and [embody] the unified will of the international community."[56] His

---

[56] President's Radio Address, June 12, 1993, *PPP, 1993*, I, 840.

new UN ambassador, Madeleine Albright, promised *assertive multilateralism*, suggesting that when circumstances arose which threaten international peace, it would be in Americans' interest to proceed in partnership with the United Nations. The White House saw the institution as a major venue and instrument for the orchestration of post–cold war foreign policy.

The administration made a strong commitment to UN peacekeeping efforts, endorsing many of the proposals for state-building and preventive diplomacy outlined in Boutros-Ghali's *Agenda for Peace*. In June 1993 President Clinton ordered retaliatory strikes against General Mohamed Farah Aideed's headquarters in Somalia in retaliation for an attack on Pakistani peacekeepers. The following month he committed 350 military personnel to the UNPROFOR contingent in Macedonia, placing them under a UN commander. That action generated strong opposition from Republicans in Congress. The president's decision to allow American soldiers to serve under a non-American officer seemed to violate traditions dating from World War I. While it was "unlikely" that the president would accept UN command in large-scale operations, Clinton indicated that it was in the United States' interest to participate in low-risk efforts like those in Macedonia, which were meant to keep conflict from spreading to neighboring areas. Not to do so might mean that a larger U.S. military commitment would be necessary in the future.

In his first address to the General Assembly, Clinton lauded the organization for its seventeen peacekeeping operations then under way on four continents and involving 80,000 personnel. He urged the creation of a peacekeeping headquarters and promised assistance in the development of its logistics, communications, and intelligence capabilities.[57] On the basis of the president's statements and actions, UN officials felt confident that the new administration would continue to finance current peacekeeping efforts at the rate of 31 percent of total costs, and that Clinton would seek congressional approval for the payment of the United States' arrears to the organization.

The continuing emphasis on the United Nations reflected Clinton's general preference for the idealist course, which had dominated White House thinking since President Carter occupied the Oval Office. On a

---

[57] "Confronting the Challenges of a Broader World," Address to the UN General Assembly, September 27, 1993, *US Department of State Dispatch*, Vol. 4, No. 39, 9/27/93, 650.

broad range of foreign policy issues the president demonstrated his desire to see the Wilsonian order we described early in this text achieved in international relations. In particular, he gave special attention to economic relations in an increasingly interdependent capitalist world. Accepting the collapse of the communist economic system and the concomitant liberalization of planned economies around the world as evidence of the universalization of the American marketplace, the Clinton administration strongly encouraged the expansion of free-trade zones and international trading institutions such as the General Agreement on Tariffs and Trade (GATT). While previous Republican administrations launched the effort to develop a North American free-trade area, President Clinton achieved congressional endorsement for NAFTA and supported expanding it to include Chile and other states of Latin America. He also encouraged the reform of the old Bretton Woods trading system, established in the last days of World War II, culminating in the creation of the World Trade Organization (WTO).

Wilsonian presidents believe not only in international organizations and peaceful commerce as essential ingredients of a lawful and just world, but also in the universality of democracy. In 1913 Woodrow Wilson asserted, "We hold...that just government rests always upon the consent of the governed, and that there can be no freedom without order based upon law and upon public conscience and approval."[58] Ronald Reagan had made democratic reforms in dictatorial regimes the cornerstone of his *unilateral* moralism. President Clinton reiterated the need for democratization in the post–cold war era. He told the United Nations in his speech of September 1993 that "our dream is of a day when the opinions and energies of every person in the world will be given full expression in a world of thriving democracies."[59] Clinton also believed that the United States had become the "indispensable" state in the pursuit of democracy around the world. In May 1997, reflecting on the presidency of Franklin Roosevelt, he told an audience gathered at the Library of Congress:

---

[58] Quoted in L. Thomas Galloway, *Recognizing Foreign Governments: The Practice of the United States* (Washington, DC: American Enterprise Institute, 1978), 27.

[59] Clinton, "Confronting the Challenges of a Broader World," 650.

[FDR] would be a little impatient with those among us who, finding America at the pinnacle of its power, influence, and success, and therefore at the pinnacle of the responsibility outlined by President Roosevelt so long ago, would walk away from what are our plain obligations to engage the rest of the world. For, in the course of human events, it has fallen to us, for our benefit, and because it is right, to extend to a waiting world the ideals to which Thomas Jefferson and his friends pledged their lives, their fortunes, and their sacred honor.[60]

"For the sake of its interests and its ideals," the United States intended to promote democratic institutions, free markets, the peaceful settlement of conflict, and collective security arrangements.[61] In the administration's view there were only a few "backlash states" that had decided to remain outside the family of nations and to assault the basic values of the international community. The task was to isolate those governments, to encourage democratization within them, and to seek multilateral strategies to eliminate the offending regimes. At various times the administration identified North Korea, Iraq, Iran, Libya, Cuba, and Haiti as outlaw governments in the new world order. To achieve their overthrow and to deal with conflicts in the third world, Clinton's officials indicated that it might be necessary to expand UN operations and to place U.S. troops under UN command.

That the new administration might look to the United Nations as the natural vehicle for responding to current international challenges was not surprising, given that President Bush, up to his last days in office, had employed the institution quite effectively. Most of the existing foreign policy initiatives on the day of the inauguration were intertwined with UN operations. Iraq was subject to UN monitoring and inspection. In Yugoslavia weapons embargoes had been imposed and UN

---

[60] "Remarks by the President at Library of Congress Gala," May 1, 1997, Office of the Press Secretary, White House.

[61] The administration's overall foreign policy was spelled out by Anthony Lake, Clinton's first national security adviser, in an article in *Foreign Affairs* entitled "Confronting Backlash States" (March/April 1994, Vol. 73, No. 2), 45–55. Two good critiques of Clinton's early policy can be found in Richard N. Haass, "Paradigm Lost," *Foreign Affairs* (January/February 1995), 43–58; and Charles William Maynes, "The Search for Positive Diplomacy," *Current* (November 1996), 11–18.

humanitarian and diplomatic efforts were proceeding. Bush's hope of withdrawing UN-mandated U.S. troops from Somalia by January 20 had not materialized. In the Caribbean the Haitian military junta headed by General Cedras, while under U.S.-sponsored United Nations sanctions, had succeeded in securing its hold. All of these issues were bequeathed to the new president. If he hoped to resolve them, practical necessity required an effective UN policy. Practicality and proclivity found common ground in Bill Clinton's emphasis on an enhanced role for the UN in the world.

Four international problems required immediate policy decisions concerning UN operations and American involvement in the spring of 1993. They were the multifaceted UN role in postwar Iraq, growing conflict in Bosnia, UNISOM efforts in Somalia, and Haiti. Clinton had been one of the few high-profile Democrats to support President Bush's use of force in Desert Storm. The demonization of Saddam Hussein during the conflict had made the continued isolation and punishment of the Baghdad regime following the war politically popular. On several occasions President Clinton used military reprisals to ensure Iraq's compliance with UN monitoring or to punish Hussein for repressive actions against Kurdish or Shiite minorities.

Clinton's commitment to the UN resolutions on Iraq was tested several times by Baghdad. The concentration of Iraqi troops in the southern provinces during the late summer of 1994 led to Security Council Resolution 949, demanding an end to the deployment, and to Clinton's reinforcement of U.S. troops on the Arabian peninsula. Saddam Hussein's use of the military in the northern Kurdish regions on behalf of a favored Kurdish faction in 1996 produced a decision by the United States to expand the no-fly zone in southern Iraq. Clinton's decision by the United States to further restrict Hussein's freedom of military action was taken in spite of growing opposition by the United States' allies to escalating the confrontation. Responding to continued obstruction by the Iraqi government of the UN Special Commission on Iraq (UNSCOM), the president used air assaults and pushed the Security Council to pass additional resolutions demanding that UNSCOM have immediate, unconditional, and unrestricted access to all locations and officials. When UNSCOM's chairman, Rolf Ekeus, continued to report that Hussein's government was limiting the work of the commission and that the regime seemed still to be developing weapons of mass destruction, the

United Nations imposed Resolution 1115, insisting on the notification by Baghdad of the import of dual use items.[62]

The only concession in the hard-line U.S. position came in the agreement to allow the sale of Iraqi oil, with the revenues being used through a UN escrow account to pay war reparations or to provide food and other humanitarian aid to the Iraqi population. This shift in American policy came after considerable pressure from European allies, including permanent members of the Security Council, and from Arab states. A sense of realism in other capitals led to the conclusion that it would be impossible to continue the isolation of Hussein's regime indefinitely and that the sanctions were doing more harm to the people of Iraq than to its government. There was also a strong desire to resume trade relations with Baghdad and to move Iraqi oil onto the world market. In order to maintain Security Council support for U.S. policies in the Gulf, Bill Clinton reluctantly dropped his opposition to the oil sales.

If policy toward Iraq seemed relatively straightforward, in Bosnia the administration found what Secretary of State Warren Christopher called "the problem from hell." President Bush had hoped that the European Union (EU), with its major national capitals less than one hour's flight time from Sarajevo, would lead the collective effort to resolve the crisis. Following the declaration of Bosnian independence in spring 1992, the administration had given its support to UN efforts in conjunction with the EU. The outcome of diplomacy, however, proved disappointing. The UN-EU solution known as the "Vance-Owen plan" called for the dissection of Bosnia into relatively autonomous provinces reflecting ethnic population concentrations. All sides found the proposal largely unworkable. Only the Bosnian government of Alija Izetbegovic was willing to endorse the division, seeing little alternative to the devastation of Muslim territories by Serbs and Croats.

President Clinton urged stronger action against the Serbian government of Slobodan Milosevic and against the Bosnian Serbs led by Radovan Karadzic. He found little encouragement in the United Nations from the major players on the Security Council. Russia, which historically has had close ties to the Christian Serbs, wanted no further military action undertaken. Britain and France also sought a diplomatic

---

[62] For Security Council Resolution 949, see *YUN, 1994*, 459. Security Council Resolution 1115, passed on June 21, 1997, can be found on the United Nations website at *un.org* by linking into Security Council Resolutions.

solution. Yet the escalating bombardment of Muslim communities from surrounding mountain areas gave the United States an opportunity to press for greater UN action.[63] The first achievement was the creation of six Muslim "safe havens" in May 1993. The world community promised peacekeepers to protect these enclaves for Muslim civilians forced out of their villages by Serbian and Croatian attacks. In June the administration introduced a resolution in the Security Council to lift the arms embargo on the Muslim government. It quickly found France, Britain, and Russia opposed, and little came of the effort.

The focal point of the fighting was Sarajevo. As the Bosnian Serbs tightened their encirclement of the city, President Clinton argued for the use of NATO air strikes against Serbian artillery emplacements. He was shifting his attention from UN-based solutions to the military option available in a refocused NATO. By August the president had persuaded NATO to use its air power in Bosnia to protect the safe havens. The order to do so, however, required the assent of all NATO members and of the UN secretary-general, or his representative in Bosnia. In December Boutros-Ghali appointed Yasushi Akashi, a Japanese national, as chief of the UN peacekeeping mission in Bosnia. Akashi refused several requests from NATO to launch air attacks, fearing reprisals against UN peacekeepers.

By 1994 a quarter-million people may have fallen to the war in the Balkans, and more than 2.5 million had been displaced. The United Nations was demonstrating, by its ineffectiveness, the limits of the institution in the new post–cold war world. The "promise" that had appeared evident in the afterglow of the Gulf War was dissipating. While the old veto crisis on the Security Council that had persisted for forty years because of superpower tensions had disappeared, very real national interests among the permanent five and a determined enemy in the hills of the Balkans made the United Nations a less attractive venue for resolving conflicts.

Under unrelenting diplomatic pressure from the United States, NATO, with UN approval, finally used retaliatory strikes against Serb targets. In August 1994 Clinton threatened to lift the arms embargo with the Muslim government if the latest UN peace plan was not accepted by Bosnian Serbs. Directly through the State Department the president

---

[63] Sabrina Petra Ramet, "The Bosnian War and the Diplomacy of Accommodation," *Current History* (November 1994), 383–385.

launched a diplomatic offensive to convince the parties of the United States' determination to use force, sanctions, and increased international actions to end the fighting. The unilateral undertaking culminated in the achievement of the Dayton Accords in November 1995. In these accords, all parties agreed to establish a permanent cease-fire in Bosnia, repatriate refugees, and create a multiethnic state with a tripartite presidency and autonomous ethnic enclaves. Most important, the Accords inserted NATO ground forces in support of UN peacekeeping operations. Clinton committed 20,000 American troops to the multinational force, noting that unlike the UN forces the new contingent would be heavily armed and ready "to respond immediately…with overwhelming force…to any violations"[64] of the peace agreement. Sensitive to criticism that the Accords would ensnare the United States in a Balkan quagmire reminiscent of Vietnam, the president appealed to the American people for continued leadership: "In Bosnia this terrible war has challenged our interests and troubled our souls. Thankfully we can do something about it.…The people of Bosnia, our NATO allies and people around the world are now looking to [us] for leadership. So let us lead. This is our responsibility as Americans."[65]

The attempt to reestablish peace and stability in the Balkans became an American responsibility. While the administration had hopes that multilateral diplomacy would bring about "burden-sharing" in the new era, Bosnia demonstrated the unique position and role of the United States in contemporary international affairs. It also made clear the limitations of UN-sponsored solutions. Over the next two years President Clinton found it necessary to use strong diplomatic pressure on Serbian and Croatian elements in Bosnia to live up to the Dayton conditions. He also came under increasing pressure to capture indicted war criminals and deliver them to the UN war crimes tribunal in The Hague. In August 1997 NATO seized a number of charged individuals and threatened to take action against Karadzic and other senior Bosnian Serb officials. In the process the Western allies became more deeply involved in the internal struggles of the Serbian ethnic enclaves,

---

[64] President's address to the nation, November 27, 1995.

[65] Ibid.

defending leaders supportive of the Dayton formula against Karadzic's loyalists.[66]

As we have attempted to show through this history of American presidents and their involvement with the United Nations, American policy has a pendular quality to it, swinging between the long-felt desire to see an active and effective United Nations right the problems of world affairs, and perceived, often competing, national interests. In the Clinton years, events in Bosnia and Somalia more than anywhere else set the pendulum swinging back from the idealist course inaugurated in the Gulf War and toward a new concern for the dangers the overextension of UN activity could present for American national interests. In Bosnia President Clinton deserted the multilateral course for direct American leadership, hoping that the rest of the world would follow. In large part it did. In Somalia, as we shall see below, after an early effort to support the most expansive UN mission in Africa since the Congolese civil war, the president simply withdrew U.S. troops and participation when the costs rose too high.

President Bush had inserted American peacekeepers in Somalia in December 1992. The expectation had been that U.S. leadership of UNITAF and UNISOM was to be short-term, quickly turned over to UN administration. The formal transfer of leadership came on May 4, 1993. The new Clinton administration, however, had no intention of deserting the UN mission. Instead, it placed 4,000 support troops under the UN commander, the Turkish general Cervik Bir. The United Nations now undertook UNISOM II, an effort at nothing less than the salvation of a "failed" state. Using Security Council Resolution 814—which for the first time in UN history established a peacekeeping operation under the Charter's Chapter VII enforcement articles—Secretary-General Boutros-Ghali set about the rehabilitation of Somali political institutions. No longer a humanitarian outreach mission, UNISOM II became a UN-sponsored "state-building" exercise.

The "enemy" for the United Nations in Somalia quickly became General Mohamed Farah Aideed, one of the primary competitors for power, and "warlord" of the most powerful faction in Mogadishu. Aideed had not opposed initial UN and U.S. intervention, but as the purposes of UNISOM II increasingly shifted toward political goals, his

---

[66] E. Sipkova (ed.), "NATO Troops Prevent Coup in Banja Luka," *RFE/RL Newsline*, Vol. I, No. 100, Part II, August 21, 1997.

forces challenged the peacekeepers. The United Nations ordered his arrest. The president authorized the use of the "quick reaction force" against Aideed's headquarters. Following the deaths of four U.S. peacekeepers in August, Clinton augmented the forces in Somalia and redoubled efforts to capture Aideed.

Events came to a head on October 3, when eighteen U.S. soldiers were trapped in a firefight and killed. Americans were presented on the evening news with pictures of their dead soldiers, one of which was pulled through the streets of Mogadishu, apparently by gleeful supporters of Aideed. The revulsion with American involvement in Somalia was complete.

Real events have often dampened the idealism of presidents. In this case President Clinton decided to withdraw from Somalia. The major criticism from the public was that the senseless deaths had been the product of an overambitious United Nations and of "mission creep." What had begun as a virtuous attempt to save a starving population had become an open-ended commitment to a UN experiment in national reconstruction, with very serious negative consequences for the United States. National interest now called for withdrawal and for a new assessment of UN peacekeeping in the third world.

American involvement in Somalia lasted fifteen months. By its close the administration was far less willing to lend its support to suggested UN operations. The death of the marines in October had challenged the belief in the merits of "idealist peacekeeping." The first victim of the post-Somalia caution in Washington would be the small central African state of Rwanda. The Clinton administration had supported Security Council Resolution 872 (October 1993) creating the UN Assistance Mission for Rwanda (UNAMIR). But when massacres broke out in April 1994, the United States proposed that the Security Council *cut back* the number of peacekeepers in the region out of fear for their safety. As the problem of refugees in surrounding states grew owing to horrendous fighting between Hutus and Tutsis, the United Nations finally authorized the dispatch of 5,500 African troops. The Clinton administration, however, was worried about even the provision of logistical support, which might drag Americans into unintended greater involvement. In the end Washington provided $500 million in relief through the UN High Commissioner for Refugees (UNHCR), and backed a Security Council endorsement of unilateral French action in Rwanda. The latter would provide a model for future actions by Russia in Georgia, the great powers of the so-called "Contact Group" in Bosnia, and the United States in Haiti.

Reporting to the General Assembly in March 1994, Secretary-General Boutros-Ghali wrote, "I am conscious that the optimism which prevailed one year ago has been diminished as a result of the difficulties encountered in the field, especially in Somalia and the former Yugoslavia."[67] The loss of optimism was just as palpable along the Potomac as it was at UN headquarters. On Capitol Hill, in the White House, and at the Pentagon a reassessment of American commitment to UN peacekeeping was under way. Administration officials not only were showing signs of changing policy but also were increasingly critical of Secretary-General Boutros-Ghali. Faced with strong criticism from conservatives in Congress and the public at large, the president decided to limit his earlier stated commitments to the United Nations, to proceed in Bosnia and Haiti for all practical purposes unilaterally, and to consider a change in leadership at the United Nations when the secretary-general's term ended in 1997.

Of the foreign policy problems facing the new administration on inaugural day, 1993, none was as immediate as Haiti. The overthrow of Haiti's first freely elected president, Jean Bertrand Aristide, by military officers in 1991 had challenged the general course of democratization in the Caribbean. As a candidate, Clinton had criticized the Bush White House for its Haitian policies, and for its unwillingness to admit the growing number of Haitian refugees finding their way to U.S. shores. In January, however, the president-elect shifted his position on "boat people" arriving from the island, fearing an overwhelming armada of refugees after his inauguration. Understanding that there would be strong objection to his change in policy, Bill Clinton entered office with a strong incentive to find a solution to the Haitian problem.

The president's first impulse was to turn to the United Nations. The General Assembly had condemned the overthrow of Aristide[68] and called upon members to support OAS efforts to restore him to power. The Bush administration, as noted above, had urged UN action to force the generals from office. Through orchestrated public pressure on the

---

[67] "Improving the Capacity of the United Nations for Peacekeeping: Report of the Secretary-General," A/48/403, S/26450, March 1994. The relevant part of the secretary-general's full report for 1994 is in *YUN, 1994*, 50–55.

[68] GA Resolution 46/7, *YUN, 1991*, 152.

military regime and negotiations through the United Nations the administration achieved the Governor's Island agreement in July 1993. The parties agreed that the generals would relinquish power and Aristide would return to his post in October. As the deadline approached, Cedras and his colleagues balked. On November 11 the American ship *Harlan County,* carrying American peacekeepers, arrived in Port-au-Prince harbor to find organized angry protesters at the docks. Rather than confront the crowd, the ship retreated.

The event had been a public relations fiasco for the president. Clinton concluded that by one means or another the military leaders would have to go, even if that required direct unilateral American intervention. It took the immediate threat of an invasion and the last-minute dispatch of a high-level delegation headed by former president Jimmy Carter, in October 1994, to force the abandonment of government by the military junta. On the fifteenth of that month President Aristide returned to Haiti bolstered by 20,000 American troops and promises of massive U.S. economic aid to spur recovery. The U.S. military presence was soon reinforced with peacekeepers from Canada and other Western Hemisphere nations. This, however, had been an American operation "endorsed" by the United Nations. As with Somalia, the UN had proved to be more a hindrance to White House interests than a help.

President Clinton was on hand in Haiti the following March to witness the formal transfer of military command from U.S. officers to the United Nations.[69] However, U.S. advisers, military personnel, and experts on police training and other facets of government security remained well after the ceremony. The administration found it necessary to pressure the regime several times in subsequent months to deal with political unrest, and to undertake promised reforms. The president's national security adviser, Anthony Lake, had to be sent to Haiti in 1995 to persuade Aristide to honor his pledge to step down at the end of his term. Well into 1997 the Security Council continually reauthorized the Haitian peacekeeping operation because of continuing threats to the fragile democracy. While the efforts over the previous three years had returned the elected government to power, they had not produced a viable working democracy, nor had they ensured improvement in the

---

[69] Pamela Constable, "A Fresh Start for Haiti?" *Current History* (February 1996), 66.

living conditions of the poorest population in the hemisphere. There was a sense that the world community had achieved little at great cost.

*   *   *

Periods of idealism in American foreign policy naturally wane as strategic necessities, public concerns about overcommitment, and new challenges that do not seem to have idealist solutions present themselves. There is a rhythm to American involvement in the world, and it is reflected in the policies and actions of the country's presidents. The moralist course set by Bush and continued by Clinton went into retreat in spring 1994. Particularly as regards UN peacekeeping and state-building, President Clinton departed from his earlier enthusiastic endorsements.

May 5, 1994, marked the moment of policy change. The administration issued *Presidential Decision Directive 25* (PDD-25), significantly curtailing the American commitment to UN peacekeeping operations. The president's statement confirmed that it was no longer U.S. policy "to expand the number of UN peace operations, or U.S. involvement in [them]."[70] Using the language of realism, PDD-25 identified the primary merit of multilateral peacekeeping to be its value as a cost-effective tool for advancing American and collective interests in key regions of the world. It noted that these operations had served important "national interests" in Cambodia, El Salvador, Cyprus, Namibia, and the Golan Heights. The directive counseled, however, that such UN efforts must be placed "in proper perspective among the instruments of U.S. foreign policy."[71]

The president's policy established detailed criteria that must be met before the United States would vote for a new peacekeeping operation or directly participate in one. The operation would have to advance U.S. interests, and there would have to be "an international community of interest for dealing with the problem on a multilateral basis." Additionally, the operation must have clear objectives. For traditional peacekeeping efforts under Chapter VI, the United States would require

---

[70] "Key Elements of the Clinton Administration's Policy on Reforming Multilateral Peace Operations," (U.S. Administration, Presidential Decision Directive, May 1994) in *Documents on Reform of the United Nations*, 125.

[71] Ibid.

a cease-fire in place and the consent of all of the parties. Chapter VII operations were to be undertaken only where there was a "significant" threat to international peace and security and the consequences of inaction were "considered unacceptable." The United States would contribute personnel to any operation only if the risks were considered acceptable, U.S. involvement was necessary for success, *the support of Congress and the public existed or could be developed*, and the command and control functions were acceptable. Only "well-defined" operations used "as a tool to provide finite windows of opportunity to allow combatants to resolve their differences and failed societies to begin to reconstitute themselves"[72] would be supported by the American government.

Testifying before Congress on the merits of PDD-25, UN Ambassador Madeleine Albright indicated that the administration was in the process of "recalibrating [its] expectations" for the United Nations. In some situations the institution had been effective. In those particular cases the principles being advanced had "'Made in America' stamped all over them."[73] However, she acknowledged, serious reservations about the implementation, scope, mission, duration, and cost of many UN operations recently undertaken. Albright's testimony came one day after the Security Council had authorized an enlargement of the Rwanda peacekeeping force. She noted that it was the first case where the president's new policy had been applied, requiring a detailed plan from the secretary-general before deployment.

PDD-25 did more than lay out new, stricter conditions for UN peacekeeping operations. It also proposed a lengthy list of reforms which the president sought in the UN peacekeeping process. He urged the creation of a unified budget for peace operations with an enlarged reserve fund of $500 million. The United States called for a single annual peacekeeping assessment to be overseen by a standing group of professional budget experts. The directive also proposed the expansion and "rationalization" of the UN Department of Peacekeeping Operations (DPKO), including the creation of a "rapidly deployable headquarters team," the maintenance of a database of available forces, and a "modest"

---

[72] Ibid., 126.

[73] "Tensions in United States–United Nations Relations," *Hearing Before the Subcommittee on International Security, International Organizations, and Human Rights*, Committee on Foreign Affairs, U.S. House of Representatives, 103rd Congress, 2nd Session, May 17, 1994.

airlift capability.[74] The United States indicated that it was willing to provide services to a newly overhauled DPKO, but only on a reimbursement basis. The administration offered to design a new command and control system, to assist in developing a "cost-effective" logistics system, to open up U.S. facilities for training programs which were also devised by the United States, and to provide advisory and support personnel to headquarters. In other words Bill Clinton was offering continued American assistance to UN peacekeeping, but at the price of significant structural reform of the UN's peacekeeping apparatus. By the summer of 1994 domestic political dissatisfaction with the United Nations forced the administration to demand reform or face overwhelming opposition to further U.S. contributions to the UN's operations.

President Clinton's reform proposals for DPKO were part of a much larger effort by the administration to achieve broad changes in the United Nations. Beginning with the Reagan administration, political leaders in Washington sought extensive reforms to make the institution more amenable to U.S. interests, more efficient, and less "political." As we have discussed earlier, there was a steady erosion in American public support for the United Nations during the 1970s and 1980s. The loss of an "American majority" in the General Assembly, the growing anti-American rhetoric at the United Nations, and the continuing stalemate in the Security Council left Americans feeling that their huge financial investment was being used to undermine U.S. interests. President Reagan shared these views and, through Ambassador Jeane Kirkpatrick, lodged broad criticisms of the UN.

As we saw in Chapter 5, the Regan administration decided to limit payment of annual assessments until acceptable reforms were enacted, and to endorse the Kassebaum Amendment—which cut U.S. contributions to UN specialized agencies until greater control over them was established by the major contributors and demanded a 15 percent reduction in the UN staff. In 1985 Congress cut the American contribution to the total UN budget from 25 percent to 20 percent. The legislation had the desired effect of forcing a General Assembly resolution, during the 41st Session, giving industrial states greater control over UN budget levels.[75] The Assembly's action, however, did

---

[74] "Key Elements," 129–131.

[75] Resolution 213.

not produce a revision in U.S. policy. As peacekeeping expenses rose, the American government did not respond with additional contributions. George Bush, despite his less antagonistic attitude toward the United Nations and his use of the UN in the Gulf War, did not pay off the United States' arrears.

Driving the American interest in UN reform was the link between money and responsibility. The United States has been the largest contributor to the United Nations throughout its history. Yet, since the 1960s Americans have believed that the money has been wasted, used for questionable projects in ways that damage U.S. interests. As it tried to balance the federal budget, the Clinton administration found it difficult to support increased allocations to the UN. Ambassador Albright told Congress, "I cannot justify to the taxpayers...some of the personnel arrangements, sweetheart pension deals, lack of accountability, duplication of effort, and lack of attention to the bottom line that we so often see around the UN."[76] Albright's consternation was not new; many of her predecessors had felt the same way.

The financial crisis had its chronological origin in the Congolese civil war and the UN's efforts to bring it to a peaceful resolution. In spite of a ruling by the International Court of Justice in 1962 that peacekeeping expenses constituted "expenses" of the UN within the meaning of Article 17, neither France nor the USSR would make good on its arrears. The U.S. effort to limit their voting rights ended in failure, producing only the "Goldberg reservation," which asserted that the United States had the right to cut future funding.

The arrival of Ronald Reagan in the White House in 1981 meant an even more critical approach to financial support of the United Nations. The Republican Party, particularly its conservative wing, criticized the United Nations for "anti-American" policies and for a seeming inability to solve major international problems. The 1984 Heritage Foundation Report (discussed in Chapter 5) concluded that Americans got few benefits from their participation in the UN. It cited corruption, politicization, and mismanagement in the organization.[77] Conservative groups on Capitol Hill and in the administration argued for using

---

[76] "Tensions in United States–United Nations Relations," 6.

[77] For a detailed history of the United States' pressure on the United Nations to make significant reforms, see Yves Beigbeder, *The Internal Management of United Nations Organizations* (New York: St. Martin's, 1997).

America's financial leverage to change the institution and its specialized agencies radically.

Reagan took up the anti-UN theme in 1985. In addition to halting U.S. payments, the administration withdrew from UNESCO, arguing that the agency had diverted from its mission and had become too highly politicized. The administration further noted that 78 percent of the agency's budget was being spent on administrative overhead. This conclusion was based on an audit of UNESCO by the General Accounting Office (GAO) in 1984. The State Department suggested that the United States would return and would pay its back assessments when significant reforms were enacted. In Congress there was pressure on the GAO to go beyond UNESCO and evaluate all UN auditing and budgeting systems.

The loss of U.S. financing led UNESCO to appoint a new director-general, to reduce its activities by nearly one-third, and to shift many of its resources to the field. To ensure future American support, new systems were put in place for staff appointments and merit promotions. None of the reforms persuaded the Reagan or Bush administration to rejoin UNESCO. However, in September 1993 President Clinton told Secretary-General Boutros-Ghali that the United States intended "in principle" to return to the agency because UNESCO had implemented eight of the GAO's twelve recommended reforms.[78] The Republican victory in the 1994 congressional elections kept the administration from making good on its promise. Instead, the UNESCO episode demonstrated the ability of presidential administrations to force change in the UN system. It proved to be a harbinger of ensuing American pressure for wider reform.

There is nothing in the United Nations Charter that allows national governments to review the management of UN agencies. Yet the United Nations' Joint Inspection Unit, created in 1976 as the primary auditing and evaluation arm of the General Assembly, allowed the U.S. government's General Accounting Office to do exactly that in the 1980s. The GAO reviewed its work and concluded that its reports were of poor quality and did little to improve the quality of UN activities.

Faced with American condemnation of the UN administrative and financial systems, Secretary-General Boutros-Ghali launched a serious public relations campaign to demonstrate that the United Nations was

---

[78] Ibid., 82.

making every effort to put its house in order. He understood that nonpayment of the United States' arrears, approaching $1 billion in 1993, could bankrupt the UN. At the very least, it would drastically limit UN peacekeeping operations. In 1992 he appointed a former U.S. attorney-general, Richard Thornburgh, under-secretary-general for administration and management. He gave Thornburgh wide latitude to review the organization and undertake administrative revisions. Thornburgh in turn initiated a request to the Ford Foundation to conduct a study of the United Nations and to make recommendations for its administrative reform. The Ford Foundation study was headed by Paul Volker, a former chairman of the U.S. Federal Reserve; and Shiguro Ogata, the former deputy governor of the Japan Development Bank. We will summarize the Volker and Ogata recommendations below, but first we should note that Boutros-Ghali was also faced with Thornburgh's scathing review of the secretary-general's staff and organization.

Just before his departure from his UN post in March 1993, Thornburgh submitted his recommendations to the secretary-general. He noted the high percentage of "deadwood" among the staff, and he called for streamlining the personnel system.[79] Most important he urged the creation of an inspector general's office, which would root out fraud, waste, and abuse. The inspector general would take over the responsibilities of the Joint Inspection Unit, would have the authority to conduct independent inspections and program evaluations, and would be largely autonomous with regard to the secretary-general's office.

The Volker-Ogata Report reinforced the basic findings of Undersecretary Thornburgh.[80] Focusing largely on the financial aspects of the United Nations operations, the Ford Foundation Committee recommended a unified peacekeeping budget financed by a single annual assessment. It also suggested that peacekeeping be charged against the defense budgets of the member states, with the amount of the assessment being determined by a three-year average of the state's gross domestic product (GDP), instead of the traditional UN practice of using a ten-year average.

---

[79] "Management and Mismanagement at the United Nations," *Hearings Before the Subcommittee on International Security, International Organizations and Human Rights*, Committee on Foreign Affairs. U.S. House of Representatives, 103rd Congress, 1st Session, March 5, 1993.

[80] Beigbeder, *Internal Management*, 102.

The Clinton administration embraced the reforms put forward by Thornburgh and the Ford Foundation. The United States sought "zero real growth" in the budgets of all UN bodies and agencies. In November 1993 the U.S. delegation formally submitted to the General Assembly's Fifth Committee a proposal to create the office of inspector general. The president hoped to nudge the secretary-general toward substantial administrative reform by promising that his administration would try to obtain from Congress the funds to pay accrued debts to the United Nations. The president asserted that reform required breaking up "bureaucratic fiefdoms" and ensuring that the United Nations could do more with less.

Boutros-Ghali responded in the last years of his term by freezing the UN budget and, in 1994, supporting the creation of the Office of Internal Oversight Services, headed by an undersecretary-general. Madeleine Albright called the new agency a "victory for taxpayers around the world." The first director of Internal Oversight Services, Karl Theodor Paschke, was given a five-year term and extensive independence from the secretary-general to conduct investigations and evaluations throughout the United Nations system.

The aggressive push for reform was not a sign that Bill Clinton hoped to scuttle the United Nations or that he had any desire to see the United States withdraw from it. Like President Bush before him, Clinton was a pragmatic idealist who thought the UN to be *more* important in the post–cold war age than ever before. And idealists are reformers by nature. They seek to improve institutions as substitutes for force and national power in the pursuit of a "better" world. Clinton was also a pragmatic politician who appreciated the strong opposition to the new activist course of the UN and to an apparently "bloated" UN bureaucracy funded largely by the United States and headed by an unpopular secretary-general. He once opined that Americans who were critical of the UN had "made it more difficult for the United States to meet its obligations to the United Nations."[81] He hoped to turn that attitude around by effecting significant structural reform.

As an advocate of the new moralism, Clinton found his task significantly more difficult after the congressional elections of 1994. Voters swept a Republican majority into power in both houses of

---

[81] "Remarks by the President in Address to the 51st General Assembly of the United Nations," September 24, 1996, Office of the Press Secretary, White House.

Congress. Conservative Republican congressmen and senators took up leadership positions through the institution including on important committees. Among the most significant for the fortunes of the UN was the elevation of Senator Jesse Helms of North Carolina to the chairmanship of the Senate Foreign Relations Committee. Helms, a longtime critic of the UN, could now block Clinton's efforts to achieve sufficient funding to pay America's debt to the United Nations. In the policy arena Republicans quickly proposed a National Security Revitalization Act and a Peace Powers Act, both of which were meant to limit U.S. involvement in UN peacekeeping. In the latter the senior Republican senators, including senators Dole, Helms, Thurmond, and McCain, proposed that all Pentagon costs be charged to the United Nations and that the administration be required to explain how it would pay for individual peacekeeping operations.[82] In the spring of 1995 there was even a proposed piece of legislation in the House of Representatives to withdraw the United States from the UN. If the president wanted to repay the United Nations, keep it a critical actor in peacekeeping, and, in fact, expand the possibilities for its use on multilateral issues, he would have to convince a skeptical Congress that radical reform of the institution was indeed under way.

* * *

> The time has come for the United States to deliver an ultimatum: Either the United Nations reforms, quickly and dramatically, or the United States will end its participation....I am convinced that without the threat of American withdrawal, nothing will change....The United Nations has neither reformed nor died. The time has come for it to do one or the other.
>
> —*Senator Jesse Helms*
> *Foreign Affairs*

Senator Helms threw down the gauntlet to the administration and the UN leadership in the lead article of *Foreign Affairs* in September

---

[82] Bennis, *Calling the Shots*, 98–101. The National Security Revitalization Act (H.R. 7) passed the House of Representatives on February 16, 1995. The Peace Powers Act (S.5) was introduced in the Senate as a substitute for the long-standing War Powers Act.

1996.[83] He called the UN a "power-hungry and dysfunctional organization" that was becoming a quasi-sovereign entity in violation of its Charter. He rehearsed all of the woes critics had cited about the UN in previous years and called for a 50 percent cut in its "bloated" bureaucracy. He accused the United Nations of meddling inappropriately in matters rightly left to national governments, and of undertaking peacekeeping operations that it was incapable of handling.

The senator saved his harshest criticism for the secretary-general, writing, "Reform must begin by replacing Boutros Boutros-Ghali."[84] Helms charged that the secretary-general had stubbornly resisted reform "that gets down to the fundamentals." He accused him of protecting the bureaucrats, of seeking the creation of a UN army, and of trying to impose a tax worldwide to support the UN's far-flung activities. The senator particularly noted the "waste" of funds, largely coming from the U.S. Treasury, on worldwide conferences such as the Conference on Women in Beijing in 1995. Helms made it clear that the departure of Boutros-Ghali and the election of a reformer acceptable to the senator would be the cost of continued congressional support of the United Nations.

Unsuspectingly, Secretary-General Boutros-Ghali had made himself an easy target for Helms. Only five months earlier, in the same journal, he had made the case for an active secretary-general and an increasingly active United Nations in the new era.[85] He argued that it was his "moral responsibility" to bring "orphan conflicts" to the attention of the world, and to push for international action to resolve them. He took pride in the international conferences Helms would later condemn: Women (Beijing, 1995); Housing (Istanbul, 1996); The Earth Summit (Rio de Janeiro, 1992); Population (Cairo, 1994). He contended that the most serious problem facing the United Nations was not reform but a need for "financial resources" to accomplish its tasks. He did indeed suggest finding new sources of revenue through some type of fee or tax.

Boutros-Ghali also took note of the criticism that had been directed at him, complaining, "As Secretary-General I have unfortunately had to

---

[83] Jesse Helms, "Saving the U.N.: A Challenge to the Next Secretary-General," *Foreign Affairs* (September/October 1996), 2–7.

[84] Ibid., 5.

[85] Boutros Boutros-Ghali, "Global Leadership After the Cold War," *Foreign Affairs* (March/April 1996), 86–98.

endure [being used as a scapegoat] on occasion." In a barely veiled attack on American efforts to force him to carry out reforms, he concluded his essay with the assertion that the secretary-general "must never be seen as acting out of fear of, or in an attempt to curry favor with, one state or a group of states."[86] Boutros-Ghali's article was a political miscalculation, providing sufficient substance to sustain the criticisms heard on Capitol Hill. It became clear that the Clinton administration would have to veto his reelection as part of the effort to maintain support for the United Nations.

In the face of strong support for the secretary-general by its closest allies, the United States refused to consider another term for Boutros-Ghali. Madeleine Albright made the administration's case that he was not sufficiently committed to reform and could not command the confidence of the administration. Although many delegations and the secretary-general himself confidently hoped that President Clinton would change his mind after the 1996 elections, the administration vetoed his renomination when it was put before the Security Council. In the end Helms and Clinton got their way. As we noted on the opening page of the Introduction, January 1997 witnessed the election of Kofi Annan of Ghana as the new secretary-general. He was the choice of the administration and congressional leaders. American-educated, Annan seemed energetically committed to the kind of administrative reforms sought by Washington. It was symbolic, indeed, of the power of the United States, and of its president, in the United Nations that Secretary-General Annan's first visit to a head of state was his journey in January to the White House to meet with President Clinton.

Beyond the symbolism, Secretary-General Annan promised the president and the Congress a blueprint for reform in the near future. True to his commitment, on July 16, 1997, he announced the most sweeping reforms of the UN administrative and financial system in the institution's history.[87] His plan was nothing less than a capitulation to American demands for change. Never before had a single state had such

---

[86] Ibid., 98.

[87] Kofi Annan, "Renewing the United Nations: A Programme for Reform," UN Document A/51/950, July 16, 1997. All of the secretary-general's reform proposals, including this one of July 16, 1997, may be found on the UN Web site, at *un.org.reform*.

a dramatic influence on the specific internal policies of the United Nations.

Annan recommended establishing the position of deputy secretary-general; the deputy and a newly created Senior Management Group would serve as a cabinet of advisers for the secretary-general. They would assist in the "streamlining" of the United Nations. Annan promised that they would preside over a no-growth budget, which nonetheless would provide sufficient funds for the United Nations to carry out an increased number of activities. This would be accomplished by eliminating 1,000 posts, a 25 percent cut in personnel from a decade earlier. Administrative costs would be slashed 33 percent. Even the use paper was predicted to be cut by one-third.

The proposed administrative restructuring was wide-ranging. Twelve divisions of the Secretariat were to be consolidated into five. A new Strategic Planning Unit was created. The report called for the "decentralization of decision-making at the country level and consolidation of the United Nations presence under 'one flag.'"[88] All human resource policies were to be "overhauled" to ensure that all staff members were qualified for their jobs.

Driving the decision to launch these major reforms was a need for money. The near-bankruptcy of the UN brought on by countries' refusal to pay their assessments meant that the secretary-general had to carry out sufficient financial reforms to convince the United States, which owed nearly $1.2 billion—half of the total arrears to the United Nations—and other states that contributions would be used appropriately. The report called for the creation of a Revolving Credit Fund of $1 billion to ensure solvency. In addition, Annan proposed that the General Assembly adopt a new system of budgeting—a shift from input accounting to "results-based budgeting." The secretary-general asserted that detailed accountability would be required of every subdivision in the United Nations, including the specialized agencies. Very importantly, he proposed that UN initiatives carry "sunset provisions" to guarantee that bodies no longer needed would be disbanded. The Clinton administration's announcement, just weeks before, that the United States was withdrawing from UNIDO because it no longer served a useful purpose may have been a factor in Annan's proposal.

---

[88] Ibid.

Annan's "Programme for Reform" also outlined an ambitious revision of long-standing UN policies and strategies. It recommended making significant changes in peacekeeping operations and strengthening the United Nations' capacity for postconflict peace-building. It contemplated creating a High Readiness Brigade in order to establish a credible UN presence at an early stage of any conflict. In support of this, the secretary-general announced that the United Nations had been negotiating with several member states concerning troops that could be deployed quickly. He recommended that the Security Council draft a model Status of Forces Agreement (SOFA) to be used when a peacekeeping operation was contemplated. Finally, the secretary-general acknowledged that "postconflict peace-building" had proved to be the most problematic of the UN's undertakings. Somalia may well have been on his mind. He recommended that the Secretariat's Department of Political Affairs take responsibility for coordinating these efforts.

Many pressures played a role in the new secretary-general's decision to propose unprecedented change in the operation of the United Nations. Significant among them was the unwillingness of the American Congress to pay its bill. President Clinton's willingness to bar a second term for Boutros-Ghali and his seeming agreement with leaders on Capitol Hill that the United Nations had to change settled the matter. While Annan probably did not believe that it was a "Helmsian" choice between "reforming" or "dying," he clearly understood that American expectations would have to be met if the United Nations was to receive the funds needed to carry out its tasks. With his report in July the secretary-general took a big step down the road of reform proposed by the United States.

*   *   *

Certainly much of President Clinton's commitment to UN reform can be explained by the political pressures of American public opinion and of a conservative Republican Congress. The need to make an accommodation with Senator Helms and the Foreign Relations Committee on all aspects of U.S. foreign policy that meant the administration would have to reach a *modus vivendi* with Helms concerning the United Nations. Particularly if the administration wished to secure funding to cover the United States' arrears, Congress would have to be convinced that the president was serious about pressing reform. That being said, it must be remembered that Clinton had publicly argued for reform well before the 1994 Republican landslide. Precisely because he was committed to enhancing the UN's role as a multilateral forum for the resolution of post–cold war disputes and as a mechanism for "burden-sharing" in the process of peacekeeping, it was essential to make the United Nations more effective in these tasks.

As we review the record of Clinton's efforts at reform, it becomes clear that they spoke to four essential concerns: financial accountability; administrative change in the UN Secretariat; an enhancement, albeit within strict guidelines, of the UN's peacekeeping capabilities; and structural change in the organization's institutions. The first three of these have been detailed already and can be explained by the demands of domestic politics and a turn toward realism in American policy. The last reflected the president's own continuing commitment to the idealist purposes of the United Nations and his vision of how America might still pursue multilateral solutions to the world's problems.

The end of the confrontation between the United States and the Soviet Union necessarily altered established relationships in the United Nations. The tension between the two powers had forced primary decision-making in the United Nations to move from the Security Council to other organs, particularly the General Assembly. The new cooperation between the USSR, later the Russian Federation, and the United States gave a rebirth to the Security Council. The first sign of the Council's restored vitality came during the Iran-Iraq War, when the United States and the USSR joined in Resolution 598, insisting on a cease-fire and threatening penalties for either combatant if it did not accept the terms of the Resolution. The Gulf crisis further refocused attention on the Security Council and particularly on the five permanent members. President Bush worked assiduously to maintain consensus among the major powers in support of the Chapter VII resolutions passed during the war. In his last two years in office, the Security Council met 182 times, with an additional 188 "informal" consultations of the whole.[89] A "Special Consultation Room" had to be established at UN Headquarters, where the permanent members could conduct "formal informals," and "informal informals" on a regular basis.

---

[89] James O. C. Jonah, "Differing State Perspectives on the United Nations in the Post–Cold War World," *Academic Council on the United Nations System*, *Reports and Papers*, 1993, No. 4, 9.

President Clinton continued this effort at consensus among the great powers and the use of the Security Council, not only on matters related to the Gulf but also on peacekeeping, humanitarian assistance, and preventive diplomacy. Of special importance to him was the maintenance of a record begun during the Gulf War—that no permanent member had vetoed a resolution in the new era. In some cases one of the Five had abstained from voting, but none had rejected a formal proposal. Ironically, it would be the United States that would be the first to break ranks. In the spring of 1997 the administration vetoed a Security Council resolution condemning the construction of an Israeli settlement at Har Homa. The president, however, went to great lengths to explain this veto, arguing that the insertion of the United Nations into the issue could jeopardize the ongoing peace negotiations between the Israelis and the Palestinians.

Clinton believed that a harmonious Security Council, in addition to taking joint action in a crisis, could provide "legitimacy" if the United States, or another major power, or a group of states sought to impose peace in a conflict. This essentially had been the role of the United Nations in the American-led invasion of Somalia. In Bosnia, UN authority had made NATO air attacks possible. The president also sought authorization from the Security Council for his actions in Haiti. This legitimization, however, went beyond U.S. peacekeeping actions. In Rwanda, France was authorized to dispatch troops to deal with the political and human crisis. The Clinton White House also endorsed the use of Russian peacekeepers in the conflict between Georgia and Abkhazia in the Caucasus. When the Russians seemed unable to reach an acceptable peace between the parties, the president called for a resumption of talks under the aegis of the UN's "Friends of Georgia" group, a working committee made of several Security Council members.

The president also encouraged the expansion of the Security Council with the addition of new permanent members. The administration supported expanding the five to seven by adding Germany and Japan to the elite group. Such a reform would be the most dramatic revision of the Charter since the founding of the United Nations in 1945. The Security Council was expanded during the Johnson Administration from its original membership to include ten nonpermanent members, but Clinton's proposal would for the first time admit to permanent membership status states that were not among the major allies at the end of World War II. In 1997 the president launched a broad diplomatic campaign to enlist cosponsoring governments for the proposal. The State Department sought support from several east European and Asian nations in particular. The president personally raised the matter in June at the Denver Summit of the Eight, the successor to the old G-7 summits.

Of course, the proposal to enlarge the permanent membership opened a full debate within the United Nations about the role of the veto in the Security Council. The addition of two new states with that prerogative could stymie effective action in a crisis. Many governments feared that it would also enhance the power of the major nations at the expense of the less powerful members. Counterproposals emerged to limit the veto, and to consider the addition of still other governments on a permanent basis. India, Brazil, and other major regional powers campaigned for inclusion.

Shortly after Clinton's second inaugural, the president's national security adviser, Sandy Berger, outlined the administration's foreign policy agenda in a speech at the Center for Strategic and International Studies: "We are embarked on a period of construction, based on new realities but enduring values and interests....Our challenge is to build up new institutions and understandings, and adapt old ones, that strengthen our security and prosperity for the next fifty years and beyond."[90] The United Nations clearly was one of the "old" institutions the president hoped to adapt to the new needs of the international arena. The new needs were not solely those of peace, war, and conflict resolution but also included "transnational" issues such as terrorism, global environmental degradation, drug trafficking, disarmament and arms control, infectious diseases, nuclear smuggling, and even cloning and organized crime.[91] Going well beyond seeking reform simply to meet the objections of a Republican Congress and a skeptical public, President Clinton hoped that changes in the UN system, its administration and financing, and its policy-making process would make it possible for the United States to work more closely with states in the United Nations setting to solve broader "global" problems. It was in

---

[90] "A Foreign Policy Agenda for the Second Term," remarks by Samuel R. Berger, Assistant to the President for National Security Affairs, Center for Strategic and International Studies, Washington, DC, March 27, 1997. The Office of the Press Secretary, White House.

[91] See President's Remarks to the Opening Session of the Denver Summit of the Eight, June 21, 1997, Office of the Press Secretary, White House.

that spirit that the president took great pride in affixing the first head of state's signature to the Comprehensive Test Ban Treaty negotiated at the UN Conference on Disarmament, decided that the United States would join the "Ottawa Process" in September 1997 to bring about a UN ban on antipersonnel land mines, and directed that the United States participate in the negotiations under UN auspices of a World Climate Treaty.

George Bush, following his service as U.S. ambassador to the United Nations, as we have described, strongly criticized the organization for failing to keep the peace or resolve important international conflicts. However, he lauded the UN for the ancillary social and humanitarian tasks it had taken on. After the Gulf War, Bush's new moralism suggested that those secondary areas of UN activity could be enlarged and given new importance. Humanitarian interventions, for example, became a major tenet of the president's new world order. We only have to remember Somalia. Bill Clinton, in spite of modifications in the new moralism to satisfy political demands at home, continued to seek new ways to utilize the United Nations in the service of ameliorating human suffering and solving "human," as opposed to "state," problems. Different observers gave this phenomenon different names. Walter McDougall called it global "meliorism,"[92] which he defined as the projection of American values into the effort to get at the root causes of aggression: poverty, ignorance, oppression, and despair. With Clinton's presidency, in McDougall's view, meliorism in American policy reached its zenith. Michael Mandelbaum called it a "social work" foreign policy.[93] What it reflected was a president willing to continue the idealist commitment to remaking the world, and to expand the American vision of the United Nations as an instrument for that remaking.

---

[92] Walter McDougall, "Back to Bedrock," *Foreign Affairs* (March/April 1997), 140.

[93] Michael Mandelbaum, "Foreign Policy as Social Work," *Foreign Affairs* (January/February 1996), 16–32.

Conclusion

The preservation of a democratic civilization requires the wisdom of the serpent and the harmlessness of the dove. The children of light must be armed with the wisdom of the children of darkness but remain free from their malice. They must know the power of self-interest in human society without giving it moral justification. They must have this wisdom in order that they may beguile, deflect, harness and restrain self-interest, individual and collective, for the sake of the community.

—Reinhold Niebuhr
The Children of Light and the Children of Darkness, 1944

The foregoing pages accent the undeniable role played by the United States and its president in international affairs. For perhaps too long it has been fashionable in academic circles and in some diplomatic circles, as well, to hold that the United States has been in decline from the moment of its zenith of power—maybe in 1945, maybe with JFK's ringing inaugural in 1961.[1] No doubt things at home and in the world have changed markedly over the half century since the period immediately after World War II and the founding of the United Nations. But, given the totality of world events on view at the end of the twentieth century, it would seem that, with starts and stops along the way, the United States at the millennium continues to be in an ascending pattern.

At this moment the United Nations is an aging half century old, bulging with 185 members; and the United States is big and strong and internationally active. As we have suggested in these pages, we believe that we can find what we called in our introduction a persistent, and often tense, warp and woof in America's relationship with the United Nations. On the one hand has been the warp, a penchant for cool "realism" as evidenced by, for example, Henry Kissinger. On the other hand, there is the woof, a kind of sentimental "idealism" associated with Woodrow Wilson and his followers. We use the analogy of warp and woof because these predilections—realism and idealism—clearly have

---

[1] See Donald W. White, *The American Century from Beginning to End* (New Haven, Conn.: Yale University Press, 1996).

intersected in our history and have affected our views about and policies toward the United Nations.

Reinhold Niebuhr, the eminent American theologian, found both dispositions, in isolation, seriously wanting. In 1944, as the Second World War came to a tumultuous close and plans concluded for a new world organization, he issued an ominous demur. Using the terms "children of light" (rather like idealists) and "children of darkness" (those types that realists find everywhere—indeed, some realists could be called "children of darkness"), he urged us to remember that "the children of light are foolish not merely because they underestimate the power of self-interest among the children of darkness. They underestimate this power among themselves." He called the children of light "sentimental" and "blind." They had "robbed bourgeois theory of real wisdom." He was equally dismissive of both the optimism of Thomas Paine and the optimism of Karl Marx. In fact, he insisted, "The actual behavior of...nations is cynical...[while] liberal civilization is sentimental."[2] Henry Kissinger could not agree more.

Niebuhr exhorted us to keep in mind that humans and, importantly, nations have a will to power, a desire for glory, and a need for security. These wills, desires, and needs can succumb to darkly disruptive behaviors, at home and in the world. It would appear that Niebuhr, learning from the crises of the 1930s and 1940s, well anticipated the various troubling international challenges of the late 1990s.

Yet he did not yield to a cynical pessimism. He saw the values and aims of America's optimistic creed as difficult of achievement but worthy of pursuit. To combine elements of realism and idealism in a paraphrase of Niebuhr's hope as articulated at the head of this concluding chapter, we might find him agreeing that "we must be clear-eyed and alert to real things as we seek to make living in the world community just a bit better."

If the American founders of the United Nations had hoped that the new organization would make it easy to improve the world, they were quickly disabused of their cheerfulness. The Israeli diplomat Abba Eban has written that the United Nations was born "amid such euphoria that a

---

[2]   Reinhold Niebuhr, *The Children of Light and the Children of Darkness* (New York: Scribner, 1944); see especially 10–22 and 31–38, which contain the quoted passages.

fall from grace was inevitable."[3] As we have seen, the onset of cold war changed the expected milieu from worldwide cooperation to long-term antagonism, and even the eventual end of the cold war did not bring lasting relief. As the century prepared to turn, critics could point to myriad challenges, particularly in the areas of war and peace, that the United Nations seemed either unable or ill-equipped to manage. From chaos in the Congo and elsewhere in Africa to the former Yugoslavia to Afghanistan to a defiant Iraq, crises multiplied while, according to Edward Luck of the Center for the Study of International Organizations, the United Nations seemed plagued by "a real sense of malaise and lack of direction."[4] Defenders of the United Nations could always point to success stories. Every year UN agencies cared for more than 22 million refugees and displaced persons and delivered some 3 million tons of food to the hungry. The World Health Organization and the UN Center for Human Rights continued to act with vitality, and the new Secretary-General, Kofi Annan, had brought greater cooperation among the varied agencies of the organization, had linked UN and private humanitarian aid programs, and had begun carrying out a serious and broad-based reform of the United Nations; meantime, the media tycoon Ted Turner had doled out the first $55 million of his ten-year, $1 billion gift to the organization.[5]

Still, it would be difficult to imagine at century's end a president of the United States, or a serious presidential candidate, publicly proclaiming that the United Nations was the hope of the world. This is not to say, however, that American presidents, particularly recent presidents, have not rethought the relationship between the nation and the UN. This is due in part to the compelling process of history, in part to the recognizable and realistic limitations of the United Nations. That is, institutions like the United Nations, during the course of their history, have an impact on our beliefs and concepts, and thus on the course of ongoing American policies. And, in this regard, we must keep in mind certain misconceptions about the United Nations and the United States' relationship with it. As we have said much earlier, the United Nations is

---

[3] Abba Eban, "The U.N. Idea Revisited," *Foreign Affairs* (September/October), 1995, 39.

[4] Quoted in Craig Turner, "Challenges Reveal U.N.'s Shrinking Clout," *Los Angeles Times* (November 23, 1998), A11.

[5] Ibid.

a "confederation," not a unitary or federally organized government. That is, it is what its members make of it. As John Stoessenger explained some years ago, the United Nations can act only by way of consensus, not majoritarianism. The United Nations works with and through professional diplomats, within an environment of limits, fallible human nature, and a system of loyalties built around the traditional nation-state. Yet, since we continue to expect that the organization can take on more responsibilities, it tends to become a scapegoat for setbacks and embarrassments that really are setbacks and embarrassments for the member nations. To carry the point further, the United Nations cannot fulfill "utopian notions" of world peace and order because, as Abba Eban has reminded us, it is an "international organization...a *mechanism*, not a policy or principle."[6]

This may well have been FDR's understanding of the United Nations. Brian Urquhart has argued that "Roosevelt's concept of a world organization was not idealistic. It was a pragmatic system based on the primacy of the strong."[7] If this is so, then the durability of the United Nations rests in part on its practicality. Urquhart goes on to note that the UN Charter "turned out to be a surprisingly practical document," providing for a number of ways that the United Nations could serve in emergencies as a forum of last resort, a face-saver, and a scapegoat, all in addition to being the arena for resolution of difficult issues.[8] The pages of this book often illustrate Urquhart's thesis. Moreover, if the postmodernist academics are right that reality is discursively constructed, then the reality about the UN-U.S. relationship has, over a half century, consistently undergone reconstruction. This is in no small part due to the twin roles of presidential speech and action and the intersection of traditional American idealism and realism.

*   *   *

---

[6]   Eban, "The U.N. Idea Revisited," 40. Eban goes on to say, "It is easier to diagnose the world's problems than to find a solution, and easier to formulate solutions than to get the public to accept them."

[7]   Brian Urquhart, "Looking for the Sheriff," *New York Review of Books* (July 16, 1998), 48.

[8]   Ibid., 49.

Jeane Kirkpatrick came to the post of U.S. ambassador to the United Nations in 1981 as a hardened realist, seeing the UN as an antagonist to which the United States, in the tradition of Daniel Patrick Moynihan, should respond with confrontation. But after a year and a half on the job, Kirkpatrick experienced a gradual, interesting transformation in her thinking about U.S.-UN relations. She told the conservative Heritage Foundation that her analysis had undergone "significant evolution." In two speeches—one in January 1982 and another in June 1982—she revealed this evolution and a ripening appreciation of the United Nations and of America's possible role in the organization.[9] Her more mature approach, sober and practical, seemed responsive to the evolution of the United Nations. It may also have been satisfying to Niebuhr, and instructive for those who seek in the United States' approach to the United Nations a complementary merging of idealism and realism.

First, in answer to the urgings that the United States leave the United Nations—urgings rife in the early Reagan years—she responded with a resounding negative. The United Nations, she argued, was important. Moreover, "The relationship between the United Nations and the outside world receives less attention...than it deserves." The organization is not what America's founders thought it would be, and we must accept and deal with that. Thus, "only greater *realism* can lead us closer to the *ideals* that inspired this very human institution" [emphasis added]. The main practical problem was that the United States did not belong to any blocs. That is, we seemed not to understand how the United Nations actually worked. We tended to pronounce the high ideals and singular aims of our country and at the same time complain at the United Nations while going our own way. We paid no attention to the grievances, aims, and wishes of anyone else, including, critically, the "unrich, unpowerful, and unhappy" nations, to whom we could very reasonably be sympathetic. Our distress at the United Nations was due not to the changed character of the organization, but to our own arrogance and unwillingness to understand the real United Nations. Kirkpatrick had watched how skillfully the British ambassador had dealt with the United Nations

---

[9] Jeane Kirkpatrick, "The Problem of the United Nations," Address before the Foreign Policy Association, New York City, January 26, 1982; and "The U.S. Role in the United Nations," Address before the Heritage Foundation, June 7, 1982, *The Reagan Phenomenon*, 92–105.

during the Falklands crisis. She was amazed. Here was an issue important to the United Kingdom, and London, in responding to the challenge, took the United Nations seriously. Why, Kirkpatrick wondered, could the United States not do similarly? Her answer: because "our long-standing lack of skill in practicing international politics in multilateral arenas" was a defect that had "dogged us all our national life." The basic problem, she insisted, was that we had treated the United Nations as though it were something other than a political arena. In summary, she told the astonished Heritage Foundation that (1) the United Nations is important; (2) we must take it seriously; (3) we must appoint outstanding representatives, and they must stay in their posts longer; (4) we must "cultivate" reliable voting alliances; and (5) we must make clear our own "persistent, coherent national purposes." Above all, we must understand that the United Nations is, in the best sense, a political place.

Kirkpatrick's thoughtful assessment blends nicely with George Bush's memory of the moment the United Nations came to represent new hope for him: "I hope we set positive precedents for future responses to international crises, forging coalitions, properly using the United Nations, and carefully cultivating support at home and abroad for U.S. objectives."[10]

Of course, what Ambassador Kirkpatrick defined as the "basic problem"—Americans treating the United Nations as something other than a political arena—is exactly what contributed to her own evolution in thinking about the institution. The United Nations, in addition to serving as a place where realist diplomacy is played out, is a modern expression of an age-old American creed: a belief that human beings and states can create a new world, a world based on the American principles of democracy, representative government, human rights, the rule of law, and justice, rather than on raw might and force. The United Nations' founding generation of American leaders conceived the institution in Wilsonian moralistic terms, as a rather natural extension to the world of the American ideology writ large.

Seymour Martin Lipset put the matter precisely in his book *American Exceptionalism:* "Moralism, as United States history demonstrates, is as

---

[10] George Bush and Brent Scowcroft, *A World Transformed* (New York: Knopf, 1998), 565.

American as apple pie."[11] The United Nations is part of that moralism and will be, or any successor institution will be, as long as Americans seek a better world through their foreign policy. The custodians of that policy, American presidents, whether realists or idealists, from Roosevelt to Clinton, have demonstrated through their speeches, decisions, and diplomacy a continuing hope that the United Nations might ultimately serve its founders' purpose. The dilemma has been to keep that hope alive while defending America's very real interests. It is a dilemma renewed by the rebirth and reform of the UN in the wake of the cold war.

---

[11] Seymour Martin Lipset, *American Exceptionalism* (New York: Norton, 1996), 176.

Appendix A

SECRETARIES-GENERAL OF THE UN

Trygve Lie	Norway	1946–1952
Dag Hammarskjöld	Sweden	1953–1961
U Thant	Burma	1961–1971
Kurt Waldheim	Austria	1972–1981
Javier Perez de Cuellar	Peru	1982–1991
Boutros Boutros-Ghali	Egypt	1992–1996
Kofi Annan	Ghana	1997–

Appendix B

U.S. AMBASSADORS TO THE UN

Edward R. Stettinius, Jr.	January 1946 to June 1946
Herschel V. Johnson (Acting)	June 1946 to January 1947
Warren R. Austin	January 1947 to January 1953
Henry Cabot Lodge, Jr.	January 1953 to September 1960
James J. Wadsworth	September 1960 to January 1961
Adlai E. Stevenson	January 1961 to July 1965
Arthur J. Goldberg	July 1965 to June 1968
George W. Ball	June 1968 to September 1968
James Russell Wiggins	October 1968 to January 1969
Charles W. Yost	January 1969 to February 1971
George Bush	February 1971 to January 1973
John P. Scali	February 1973 to June 1975
Daniel P. Moynihan	June 1975 to February 1976
William W. Scranton	March 1976 to January 1977
Andrew Young	January 1977 to April 1979
Donald McHenry	April 1979 to January 1981
Jeane J. Kirkpatrick	February 1981 to April 1985
Vernon Walters	May 1985 to January 1989
Thomas R. Pickering	March 1989 to May 1992
Edward J. Perkins	May 1992 to January 1993
Madeleine K. Albright	February 1993 to January 1997
Bill Richardson	January 1997 to September 1998
A. Peter Burleigh (Acting)	September 1998 to February 1998
Richard Holbrooke	Appointed February 1999

Bibliography

Primary Sources

Acheson, Dean. *Present at the Creation: My Years at the State Department.* New York: Norton, 1969.

Annual Review of United Nations Affairs Series, 1949 to the present. Dobbs Ferry, N.Y.: Oceana.

Baker, James A. *The Politics of Diplomacy.* New York: Putnam, 1995.

Beschloss, Michael R. *Taking Charge: The Johnson White House Tapes, 1963–1964.* New York: Simon and Schuster, 1997.

Boyle, Peter G., ed. *The Churchill-Eisenhower Correspondence, 1953–1955.* Chapel Hill: University of North Carolina Press, 1990.

Brzezinski, Zbigniew. *Power and Principle: Memoirs of the National Secuity Adviser, 1977–1981.* New York: Farrar, Straus, Giroux, 1983.

Bullitt, Orville H., ed. *For the President: Personal and Secret.* Boston: Houghton Mifflin, 1972.

Bush, George. *Looking Forward; An Autobiography.* New York: Bantam, 1987.

Bush, George, and Brent Scowcroft. *A World Transformed.* New York: Knopf, 1998.

Carmichael, Donald Scott, ed. *FDR, Columnist: The Uncollected Columns of Franklin D. Roosevelt.* Chicago: Pelegrini and Cudahy, 1947.

Carter, Jimmy. *Keeping Faith: Memoirs of a President.* New York: Bantam, 1982.

Christopher, Warren, et al. *American Hostages in Iran: The Conduct of a Crisis.* New Haven, Conn.: Yale University Press, 1985.

Clement, Lee, ed. *Andrew Young at the United Nations.* Salisbury, NC: Documentary, 1978.

Crocker, Chester A. *High Noon in Southern Africa: Making Peace in a Rough Neighborhood.* New York: Norton, 1992.

Dayan, Moshe. *Breakthrough: A Personal Account of the Egypt-Israel Peace Negotiations.* New York: Knopf, 1981

Disarmament Document Series. United States Arms Control and Disarmament Agency, Washington, D.C.

Eisenhower, Dwight D. *Mandate for Change, 1953–1956.* Garden City, N.Y.: Doubleday, 1963.

———. *Waging Peace, 1956–1961.* New York: Doubleday, 1965.

Everyone's United Nations; A Handbook on the Work of the United Nations. New York: Department of Public Information, The United Nations.

Ferrell, Robert H. *Off the Record: The Private Papers of Harry S Truman.* New York: Harper and Row, 1980.

Ford, Gerald R. *A Time to Heal: The Autobiography of Gerald R. Ford.* New York: Harper and Row, 1979.

Foreign Relations of the United States. Washington, D.C.: Government Printing Office.

Gates, Robert M. *From the Shadows: The Ultimate Insider's Story of Five Presidents and How They Won the Cold War.* New York: Simon and Schuster, 1996.

Gorbachev, Mikhail. *Memoirs.* New York: Doubleday, 1995.

Haig, Alexander M. *Caveat: Realism, Reagan, and Foreign Policy.* New York: Macmillan, 1984.

Hannaford, Peter, ed. *Recollections of Reagan: A Portrait of Ronald Reagan.* New York: Morrow, 1997.

Johnson, Lyndon B. *The Vantage Point: Perspectives of the Presidency, 1963–1969.* New York: Rinehart and Winston, 1971.

Kirkpatrick, Jeane J. *The Reagan Phenomenon—And Other Speeches on Foreign Policy.* Washington, D.C.: American Enterprise Institute, 1983.

Kissinger, Henry. *White House Years.* Boston: Little, Brown, 1979.

———. *Years of Upheaval.* Boston: Little, Brown, 1982.

Kutler, Stanley I., ed. *Abuse of Power: The New Nixon Tapes.* New York: Free Press, 1997.

Labrie, Roger P., ed. *SALT Handbook: Key Documents and Issues, 1972–1979.* Washington, D.C.: Arms Control and Disarmament Agency, 1979.

Lie, Trygve. *In the Cause of Peace.* New York: Macmillan, 1954.

May, Ernest R., and Philip D. Zelikow. *The Kennedy Tapes: Inside the White House During the Cuban Missile Crisis.* Cambridge, Mass.: Belknap, 1997.

Moynihan, Daniel Patrick. *A Dangerous Place.* Boston: Little, Brown, 1978.

New York Times. The End of a Presidency. New York: Bantam, 1974.

Nixon, Richard. *RN: The Memoirs of Richard Nixon.* New York: Grosset and Dunlap, 1978.

North, Oliver, with William Novak. *Under Fire: An American Story.* New York: HarperCollins, 1991.

Powell, Colin. *My American Journey.* New York: Random House, 1995.

Public Papers of the Presidents of the United States. Washington, D.C.: U.S. Government Printing Office, 1940–1998.

Public Papers of the Secretaries-General of the United Nations. 7 vols. New York: Columbia University Press.

Quandt, William B. *Camp David: Peacemaking and Politics.* Washington, D.C: Brookings, 1986.

Reagan, Ronald. *An American Life.* New York: Simon and Schuster, 1990.

Roosevelt, Elliott, ed. *F.D.R.: His Personal Letters, 1928–1945.* New York: Duell, Sloan and Pearce, 1950.

Seymour, Charles, ed. *The Intimate Papers of Colonel House.* IV. London: Ernest Benn, 1928.

Shultz, George P. *Turmoil and Triumph: My Years as Secretary of State.* New York: Scribner, 1993.

Taylor, Paul, et al., eds. *Documents on Reform of the United Nations.* Brookfield, Vt.: Dartmouth, 1997.

Truman, Harry S. *Memoirs.* I, *Year of Decision.* Garden City, N.Y.: Doubleday, 1955.

Urquhart, Brian. *A Life in Peace and War.* New York: Harper and Row, 1987.

Vance, Cyrus. *Hard Choices: Critical Years in America's Foreign Policy.* New York: Simon and Schuster, 1983.

Waldheim, Kurt. *In the Eye of the Storm: A Memoir.* Bethesda, Md.: Adler and Adler, 1986.

Walsh, Lawrence. *Iran-Contra: The Final Report.* New York: Random House, 1994.

Weinberger, Caspar. *Fighting for Peace: Seven Critical Years in the Pentagon.* New York: Warren, 1990.

Yearbook of the United Nations. New York: United Nations, Office of Public Information, 1945–1996.

Speeches, Reports, Documentation, Websites

A Foreign Policy Agenda for the Second Term. Remarks by Samuel R. Berger, Assistant to the President for National Security Affairs. Center for Strategic and International Studies, Washington, D.C., March 27, 1997. Office of the Press Secretary, White House.

Albright, Madeleine K. "Building a Consensus on International Peacekeeping," Statement Before the Senate Foreign Relations Committee, October 20, 1993. *U.S. Department of State Dispatch.* Vol. 4, No. 46, November 15, 1993, 789–792.

———. "Use of Force in a Post–Cold War World." *Department of State Dispatch.* Vol. 4, No. 39, September 27, 1993, 665–668.

Annan, Kofi. *Renewing the United Nations: A Programme for Reform.* UN Document A/51/950, July 16, 1997.

Boutros-Ghali, Boutros. *An Agenda for Peace.* New York: United Nations, 1992.

Burgess, Stephen F. *Operation Restore Hope: Somalia and Frontiers of the New World Order*. Unpublished paper presented at the Hofstra 10th Presidential Conference: "George Bush, Leading in a New World," Hofstra University, April 19, 1997.

Issues Before the General Assembly of the United Nations (A Global Agenda). Edited by John Tessitore and Susan Woolfson annually for the United Nations Association of America, New York.

Management and Mismanagement at the United Nations. Hearings Before the Subcommittee on International Security, International Organizations and Human Rights, Committee on International Relations, U.S. House of Representatives, 103rd Congress, 1st Session, March 5, 1993.

Presidential Statements, Letters, Findings, Directives. Office of the Press Secretary, White House. *publications-admin@pub.pub.whitehouse.gov*

Presidential Inaugural Addresses. Bartleby Library Archive, Columbia University. *www.columbia.edu/acis/bartleby/inaugural/index.html*

Reform at the United Nations. *www.un.org*

Reform of United Nations Peacekeeping Operations: A Mandate for Change. Staff Report, Committee on Foreign Relations, United States Senate. Washington, D.C.: U.S. Government Printing Office, 1993.

Report of the Secretary-General. *Improving the Capacity of the United Nations for Peacekeeping*. A/48/403, S/26450, March 1994.

Secretary-General's Bulletin, "Establishment of the Office of Internal Oversight Services." ST/SGB/273, 7 September 1994.

Tensions in United States–United Nations Relations. Hearing Before the Subcommittee on International Security, International Organizations and Human Rights, Committee on International Relations, U.S. House of Representatives, 103rd Congress, 2nd Session, May 17, 1994.

The United Nations and Disarmament, 1945–1965. New York: United Nations, 1967.

United Nations Databases, Documents, Treaties, Home Page. *www.un.org*

United Nations Reform: A Bibliography. *www.un.org/Depts/dhl/reform.htm*

United States Administration, Presidential Decision Directive. *Policy on Reforming Multilateral Peace Operations*, May 1994.

U.S. Department of State. *United States Policy in the Korean Crisis*. Washington, D.C.: Government Printing Office, 1950.

Secondary Sources

Ambrose, Stephen. *Eisenhower: The President.* New York: Simon and Schuster, 1984.

———. *Nixon: Ruin and Recovery.* 1973–1990. New York: Simon and Schuster, 1991.

———. *Nixon: The Triumph of A Politician, 1962–1972.* New York: Simon and Schuster, 1989.

Anderson, David L. *Trapped by Success.* New York: Columbia University Press, 1991.

Bailey, Stephen D. *The Korean Armistice.* New York: St. Martin, 1992.

Bailey, Sydney D. *Four Arab-Israeli Wars and the Peace Process.* London: Macmillan, 1990.

Barilleaux, Ryan J., and Mary E. Stuckey. *Leadership and the Bush Presidency.* Westport, Conn.: Praeger, 1992.

Beigbeder, Yves. *The Internal Management of United Nations Organizations.* New York: St. Martin's, 1997.

Beker, Avi. *Disarmament Without Order.* Westport, Conn.: Greenwood, 1985.

Bennett, A. Leroy. *International Organizations.* Englewood Cliffs, N.J.: Prentice Hall, 1988.

Bennis, Phyllis. *Calling the Shots: How Washington Dominates Today's UN.* New York: Olive Branch, 1996.

Berger, Carl. *The Korea Knot.* Philadelphia: University of Pennsylvania Press, 1964.

Bernhard, John T. *United Nations Reform: An Analysis.* UCLA unpublished doctoral dissertation, 1950.

Beschloss, Michael R., and Strobe Talbott. *At the Highest Levels.* Boston: Little, Brown, 1993.

Bishop, Jim. *FDR's Last Year, April 1944 to April 1945.* New York: Morrow, 1974.

Bjork, Rebecca S. *The Strategic Defense Initiative.* Albany: SUNY Press, 1992.

Bloomfield, Lincoln P. *The UN and Vietnam.* New York: Carnegie Endowment for International Peace, 1968.

———. *The United Nations and U.S. Foreign Policy.* Boston: Little, Brown, 1967.

Bosch, Adriana. *Reagan: An American Story.* New York: TV Books, 1998.

Bourantonis, Demitris, and Jarrod Weiner. *The United Nations and the New World Order.* New York: St. Martin's, 1995.

Bourne, Peter G. *Jimmy Carter: A Comprehensive Biography from Plains to Postpresidency.* New York: Scribner, 1997.

Boutros-Ghali, Boutros. "Global Leadership After the Cold War." *Foreign Affairs*, March/April 1996, 86–98.

Bowles, Chester. *Promises to Keep*. New York: Harper and Row, 1971.

Boyer, Paul. *By the Bomb's Early Light*. New York: Pantheon, 1985.

Brands, H. W., Jr. *Cold Warriors: Eisenhower's Generation and American Foreign Policy*. New York: Columbia University Press, 1988.

Branyan, Robert L., and Lawrence H. Larsen. *The Eisenhower Administration, 1953–1961: A Documentary History*. New York: Random House, 1971.

Brecher, Michael. *Decisions in Crisis: Israel, 1967 and 1973*. Berkeley: University of California Press, 1980.

Brinkley, Douglas. *The Unifinished Presidency: Jimmy Carter's Journey Beyond the White House*. New York: Viking, 1998.

Brown, Archie. *The Gorbachev Factor*. New York: Oxford University Press, 1996.

Bundy, McGeorge. *Danger and Survival*. New York: Random House, 1988.

Bundy, William. *A Tangeled Web: The Making of Foreign Policy in the Nixon Presidency*. New York: Hill and Wang, 1998.

Campbell, Thomas M. *Masquerade Peace: America's UN Policy, 1944–1945*. Tallahassee: Florida State University Press, 1974.

Cannon, Lou. *President Reagan: The Role of a Lifetime*. New York: Simon and Schuster, 1991.

Chace, James. *Acheson: The Secretary of State who Created the American World*. New York: Simon and Schuster, 1998.

Clarfield, Gerard H., and William M. Wiecek. *Nuclear America*. New York: Harper and Row, 1984.

Cohen, Warren I. *The Cambridge History of American Foreign Relations*. IV. New York: Cambridge University Press, 1993.

Crowley, Monica. *Nixon in Winter*. New York: Random House, 1998.

Davis, Forrest. "Roosevelt World Blueprint." *Saturday Evening Post*, April 10, 1943, 20–21,109–111.

Dockrill, Saki. *Eisenhower's New Look National Security Policy, 1953–1961*. New York: St. Martin's, 1996.

Donovan, Robert J. *Conflict and Crisis: The Presidency of Harry S Truman, 1945–1948*. New York: Norton, 1977.

———. *Tumultuous Years*. New York: Norton, 1982.

Draper, Theodore. *A Very Thin Line: The Iran-Contra Affairs*. New York: Hill and Wang, 1991.

Duffy, Michael, and Dan Goodgame. *Marching in Place: The Status Quo Presidency of George Bush*. New York: Simon and Schuster, 1992.

Eban, Abba. "The U.N. Idea Revisited." *Foreign Affairs*, September/October, 1995, 39–55.

Finger, Seymour Maxwell. *Your Man at the UN*. New York: New York University Press, 1980.

Franck, Thomas. *Nation Against Nation: What Happened to the U.N. Dream and What the U.S. Can Do About It*. New York: Oxford University Press, 1985.

Fukuyama, Francis. *The End of History and the Last Man*. New York: Macmillan, 1992.

Galloway, L. Thomas. *Recognizing Foreign Governments*. Washington, D.C.: American Enterprise Institute, 1978.

Gardner, Lloyd C. *Architects of Illusion*. Chicago: Quadrangle, 1970.

Gardner, Richard N. *In Pursuit of World Order*. New York: Praeger, 1964.

Gati, Toby Trister, ed. *The US, the UN, and the Management of Global Change*. New York: New York University Press, 1983.

Glynn, Patrick. *Closing Pandora's Box*. New York: Basic Books, 1992.

Gordon, Wendell. *The United Nations at the Crossroads of Reform*. Armonk, N.Y.: Sharpe, 1994.

Graubard, Stephen R. *Mr. Bush's War*. New York: Hill and Wang, 1992.

Green, Fitzhugh. *George Bush: An Intimate Portrait*. New York: Hippocrene, 1989.

Gregg, Robert W. *About Face? The United States and the United Nations*. Boulder: Lynne Reinner, 1993.

Gross, Franz B. *The United States and the United Nations*. Norman: University of Oklahoma Press, 1964.

Haas, Ernst B. *The Web of Interdependence*. Englewood Cliffs, N.J.: Prentice Hall, 1970.

———. *Why We Still Need the United Nations: The Collective Management of International Conflict, 1945–1984*. Berkeley: University of California Press, 1986.

Haass. Richard N. "Paradigm Lost," *Foreign Affairs*, January/February 1995, 43–58.

Halperin, David, et al. *Self-Determination in the New World Order*. Washington, D.C.: Carnegie Endowment for International Peace, 1992.

Hamilton, Nigel. *J.F.K.: Reckless Youth*. New York: Random House, 1992.

Harbert, Joseph R., and Seymour Maxwell Finger, eds. *U.S. Policy in International Institutions*. Boulder, Colo.: Westview, 1978.

Harper, John Lamberton. *American Visions of Europe*. Cambridge England: Cambridge University Press, 1994.

Heagerty, Leo E., ed. *Eyes on the President: George Bush—History in Essays and Cartoons*. Occidental, Calif.: Chronos, 1993.

Helms, Jesse. "Saving the U.N.: A Challenge to the Next Secretary-General." *Foreign Affairs*, September/October 1996, 2–7.

Henkin, Louis, ed. *Right v. Might: International Law and the Use of Force.* New York: Council on Foreign Relations, 1991.

Herz, John H. *Political Realism and Political Idealism: A Study in Theories and Realities.* Chicago: University of Chicago Press, 1951.

Herzog, Chaim. *The Arab-Israeli Wars.* New York: Random House, 1982.

Herzstein, Robert Edwin. *Waldheim: The Missing Years.* New York: Paragon House, 1989.

Hilderbrand, Robert C. *Dumbarton Oaks: The Origins of the United Nations and the Search for Postwar Security.* Chapel Hill: University of North Carolina Press, 1990.

Hirsch, John L., and Robert B. Oakley. *Somalia and Operation Hope.* Washington, D.C.: United States Institute of Peace Press, 1995.

Hoff, Joan. *Nixon Reconsidered.* New York: Basic Books, 1994.

Hoopes, Townsend, and Douglas Brinkley. *FDR and the Creation of the U.N.* New Haven: Yale University Press, 1997.

Huntington, Samuel P. *The Clash of Civilizations and the Remaking of World Order.* New York: Simon and Schuster, 1996.

Hybel, Alex Roberto. *Power Over Rationality.* Albany: SUNY Press, 1993.

Ikenberry, John. "The Myth of Post–Cold War Chaos." *Foreign Affairs*, May/June 1996, 79–91.

Iriye, Akira. *The Cambridge History of American Foreign Relations.* III. New York: Cambridge University Press, 1993.

Isaacson, Walter, and Evan Thomas. *The Wise Men: Six Friends and the World They Made.* New York: Simon and Schuster, 1986.

Jentleson, Bruce W. *With Friends Like These: Reagan, Bush, and Saddam, 1982–1990.* New York: Norton, 1994.

Johnson, Haynes. *In the Absence of Power: Governing America.* New York: Viking, 1980.

Johnson, Lyndon B. *A Time for Action.* New York: Atheneum, 1964.

Jonah, James O.C. "Differing State Perspectives on the United Nations in the Post–Cold War World." *Academic Council on the United Nations System, Reports and Papers*, 1993, No. 4, 9.

Kaplan, Robert D. *The Ends of the Earth: A Journey to the Frontiers of Anarchy.* New York: Random House, 1996.

Karnow, Stanley. *Vietnam: A History.* New York: Viking, 1983.

Karns, Margaret P., and Karen A. Mingst, eds. *The United States and Multilateral Institutions: Patterns of Changing Instrumentality and Influence.* Boston: Unwin Hyman, 1990.

Kaufman, Burton I. *The Presidency of James Earl Carter, Jr.* Lawrence: University Press of Kansas, 1993

Kay, David A., ed. *The Changing United Nations: Options for the United States.* New York: Praeger, 1977.

Kearns, Doris. *Lyndon Johnson and the American Dream*. New York: Signet, 1976.

Kennan, George. *American Diplomacy, 1900–1950*. Chicago: University of Chicago Press, 1951.

———. *Memoirs, 1925–1950*. Boston: Little, Brown, 1967.

Kennedy, Paul. *Preparing for the Twenty-First Century*. New York: Random House, 1993.

Kennedy, Robert F. *Thirteen Days*. New York: Norton, 1969.

Kimball, Warren F. *The Juggler: Franklin Roosevelt as Wartime Statesman*. Princeton, N.J.: Princeton University Press, 1991.

King, Nicholas. *George Bush: A Biography*. New York: Dodd, Mead, 1980.

Kirkpatrick, Jeane. "Dictatorships and Double Standards." *Commentary*, November 1979, 34–45.

Kissinger, Henry. *American Foreign Policy*. New York: Norton, 1969.

———. *Diplomacy*. New York: Simon and Schuster, 1994.

———. *A World Restored: Europe after Napoleon*. New York: Grosset and Dunlap, 1964.

LaFeber, Walter. *America, Russia, and the Cold War, 1945–1975*. 3rd ed. New York: Wiley, 1976.

———. *Inevitable Revolutions: The United States in Central America*. 2nd ed. New York: Norton, 1993.

Lall, Arthur. *The UN and the Middle East Crisis, 1967*. New York: Columbia University Press, 1968.

Levin, N. Gordon. *Woodrow Wilson and World Politics; America's Response to War and World Politics:* New York: Oxford University Press, 1968.

Lichenstein, Charles M. *The United Nations: Its Problems and What to Do About Them*. Washington, D.C.: Heritage Foundation, 1986.

Link, Arthur S. *Wilson the Diplomatist: A Look at His Major Foreign Policies*. Baltimore, Md.: Johns Hopkins Press, 1957.

Lipset, Seymour Martin. *American Exceptionalism*. New York: Norton, 1996.

Mandelbaum, Michael. "Foreign Policy as Social Work." *Foreign Affairs*, January/February 1996, 16–32.

May, Ernest R. *The Making of the Monroe Doctrine*. Cambridge, Mass.: Harvard University Press, 1975.

McCullough, David. *Truman*. New York: Simon and Schuster, 1992.

McDougall, Walter A. *Promised Land, Crusader State: The American Encounter with the World Since 1776*. Boston: Houghton Mifflin, 1997.

McLellan, David S. *Dean Acheson: The State Department Years*. New York: Dodd, Mead, 1976.

Meisler, Stanley. *United Nations: The First Fifty Years*. New York: Atlantic Monthly Press, 1995.

Melanson, Richard A., and David Mayers, eds. *Reevaluating Eisenhower: American Foreign Foreign Policy in the 1950s*. Urbana: University of Illinois Press, 1987.

Mervin, David. *George Bush and the Guardianship Presidency*. New York: St. Martin's, 1996.

Mingst, Karen A., and Margaret P. Karns. *The United Nations in the Post–Cold War Era*. Boulder, Colo.: Westview, 1995.

Morgenthau, Hans J. *In Defense of the National Interest*. New York: Knopf, 1951.

———. *A New Foreign Policy for the United States*. New York: Praeger, 1969.

———. *Politics Among Nations*. New York: Praeger, 1967.

Natsios, Andres. *From Massacres to Genocide: The Media, Public Policy and Humanitarian Crises*. Washington, D.C.: Brookings, 1997.

Nevins, Allan, ed. *The Diary of John Quincy Adams*. New York: Scribner, 1951.

Newhouse, John. *Cold Dawn: The Story of SALT*. New York: Holt, Rhinehart, and Winston, 1973.

Niebuhr, Reinhold. *The Children of Light and the Children of Darkness*. New York: Scribner, 1944.

Nixon, Richard. *Beyond Peace*. New York: Random House, 1994.

———. *1999: Victory Without War*. New York: Simon and Schuster, 1988.

Nussbaum, Arthur. *A Concise History of the Law of Nations*. New York: Macmillan, 1954.

Ostrower, Gary B. *The United Nations and the United States*. New York: Twayne, 1998.

Packenham, Robert A. *Liberal America and the Third World*. Princeton, N.J.: Princeton University Press, 1973.

Paige, Glenn D. *The Korean Decision*. New York: Free Press, 1968.

Pines, Burton Yale, ed. *A World Without a U.N.: What Would Happen If the U.N. Shut Down?* Washington, D.C.: Heritage Foundation, 1984.

Plimpton, George. *The X Factor: A Quest for Excellence*. New York: Norton, 1995.

Pruden, Caroline. *Conditional Partners: Eisenhower, the United Nations, and the Search for a Permanent Peace*. Baton Rouge: Louisiana State University Press, 1998.

Rostow, W. W. *Europe After Stalin*. Austin: University of Texas Press, 1982.

———. *Open Skies*. Austin: University of Texas Press, 1982.

Russell, Ruth B. *A History of the United Nations Charter: The Role of the United States, 1940–1945.* Washington, D.C.: Brookings, 1958.

Rustow, Eugene V. *Toward a Managed Peace.* New Haven, Conn.: Yale, 1992.

Schaller, Michael. *Reckoning with Reagan: America and Its President in the 1980s.* New York: Oxford University Press, 1992.

Schild, Georg. *Bretton Woods and Dumbarton Oaks: American Economic and Political Postwar Planning in the Summer of 1944.* New York: St. Martin's, 1995.

Schlesinger, Arthur M., Jr. *The Imperial Presidency.* Boston: Houghton Mifflin, 1973.

———. *A Thousand Days.* Boston: Houghton Mifflin, 1965.

Schroeder, Paul W. *The Transformation of European Politics, 1763–1848.* Oxford: Clarendon, 1994.

Schweizer, Peter. *Victory: The Reagan Administration's Secret Strategy That Hastened the Collapse of the Soviet Union.* New York: Atlantic Monthly Press, 1994.

Sherwood, Robert E. *Roosevelt and Hopkins: An Intimate History.* New York: Harper, 1948.

Smith, Gaddis. *Morality, Reason, and Power: American Diplomacy in the Carter Years.* New York: Hill and Wang, 1986.

Smith, Gerald C. *Disarming Diplomat.* Lanham, Md.: Madison, 1996.

———. *Doubletalk: The Story of the First Strategic Arms Limitation Talks.* Garden City, N.Y.: Doubleday, 1980.

Smith, Jean Edward. *George Bush's War.* New York: Holt, 1992.

Smith, Tony. *America's Mission.* Princeton, N.J.: Princeton University Press, 1994.

Sorensen, Theodore C. *Kennedy.* New York: Harper and Row, 1965.

Stoessinger, John G. *Crusaders and Pragmatists: Movers of Modern American Foreign Policy.* New York: Norton, 1979.

———. *Henry Kissinger: The Anguish of Power.* New York: Norton, 1976.

———. *The United Nations and the Superpowers: China, Russia, and America.* 4th ed. New York: Random House, 1977.

Stueck, William. *The Korean War: An International History.* Princeton, N.J.: Princeton University Press, 1995.

Sulzberger, C. L. *The World and Richard Nixon.* New York: Prentice Hall, 1987.

Szulc, Tad. *The Illusion of Peace: Foreign Policy in the Nixon Years.* New York: Viking, 1978.

Talbott, Strobe. *Endgame: The Inside Story of SALT II.* New York: Harper and Row, 1979.

Thompson, Kenneth W. *Political Realism and the Crisis of World Politics.* Princeton, N.J.: Princeton University Press, 1960.

Thompson, Robert Smith. *The Missiles of October.* New York: Simon and Schuster, 1992.

Toland, John. *In Mortal Combat: Korea, 1950–1953.* New York: Morrow, 1991.

Troester, Rod. *Jimmy Carter as Peacemaker: A Post-Presidential Biography.* Westport, Conn.: Praeger, 1996.

Urquhart, Brian. "Looking for the Sheriff." *New York Review of Books,* July 16, 1998, 48–53.

Wead, Doug. *George Bush: Man of Integrity.* Eugene, Ore.: Harvest House, 1988.

Weeks, William Earle. *John Quincy Adams and American Global Empire.* Lexington: University of Kentucky Press, 1992.

Weigel, George. *Idealism Without Illusions.* Washington, D.C.: Ethics and Public Policy Center, 1994.

White, Donald W. *The American Century: The Rise and Decline of the United States as a World Power.* New Haven, Conn.: Yale University Press, 1996.

Wicker, Tom. *JFK and LBJ.* Baltimore, Md.: Penguin, 1969.

Wolfe, Thomas W. *The Salt Experience.* Cambridge, Mass.: Ballinger, 1979.

Woodward, Bob. *The Commanders.* New York: Simon and Schuster, 1991.

Zubok, Vladislav, and Constantine Pleshakov. *Inside the Kremlin's Cold War: From Stalin to Khrushchev.* Cambridge, Mass.: Harvard University Press, 1996.

Index